CHARTING MEMORY: RECALLING MEDIEVAL SPAIN

HISPANIC ISSUES
VOLUME 21
GARLAND REFERENCE LIBRARY OF THE HUMANITIES
VOLUME 2160

Hispanic Issues

Volume 21	*Charting Memory: Recalling Medieval Spain* Edited by Stacy N. Beckwith
Volume 20	*Culture and the State in Spain: 1550-1850* Edited by Tom Lewis and Francisco J. Sánchez
Volume 19.	*Modernism and its Margins: Reinscribing Cultural Modernity from Spain and Latin America* Edited by Anthony L. Geist and José B. Monleón
Volume 18.	*A Revisionary History of Portuguese Literature* Edited by Miguel Tamen and Helena C. Buescu
Volume 17.	*Cervantes and his Postmodern Constituencies* Edited by Anne Cruz and Carroll B. Johnson
Volume 16.	*Modes of Representation in Spanish Cinema* Edited by Jenaro Talens and Santos Zunzunegui
Volume 15.	*Framing Latin American Cinema: Contemporary Critical Perspectives* Edited by Anne Marie Stock
Volume 14.	*Rhetoric and Politics: Baltasar Gracián and the New World Order* Edited by Nicholas Spadaccini and Jenaro Talens
Volume 13.	*Bodies and Biases: Sexualities in Hispanic Cultures and Literatures* Edited by David W. Foster and Roberto Reis
Volume 12.	*The Picaresque: Tradition and Displacement* Edited by Giancarlo Maiorino
Volume 11.	*Critical Practices in Post-Franco Spain* Edited by Silvia L. López, Jenaro Talens, and Dario Villanueva
Volume 10.	*Latin American Identity and Constructions of Difference* Edited by Amaryll Chanady
Volume 9.	*Amerindian Images and the Legacy of Columbus* Edited by René Jara and Nicholas Spadaccini
Volume 8.	*The Politics of Editing* Edited by Nicholas Spadaccini and Jenaro Talens
Volume 7.	*Culture and Control in Counter-Reformation Spain* Edited by Anne J. Cruz and Mary Elizabeth Perry
Volume 6.	*Cervantes's Exemplary Novels and the Adventure of Writing* Edited by Michael Nerlich and Nicholas Spadaccini
Volume 5.	*Ortega y Gasset and the Question of Modernity* Edited by Patrick H. Dust
Volume 4.	*1492-1992: Re/Discovering Colonial Writing* Edited by René Jara and Nicholas Spadaccini
Volume 3.	*The Crisis of Institutionalized Literature in Spain* Edited by Wlad Godzich and Nicholas Spadaccini
Volume 2.	*Autobiography in Early Modern Spain* Edited by Nicholas Spadaccini and Jenaro Talens
Volume 1.	*The Institutionalization of Literature in Spain* Edited by Wlad Godzich and Nicholas Spadaccini

HISPANIC ISSUES

VOLUME 21

CHARTING MEMORY: RECALLING MEDIEVAL SPAIN

STACY N. BECKWITH

◆

EDITOR

GARLAND PUBLISHING, INC.
A MEMBER OF THE TAYLOR & FRANCIS GROUP
NEW YORK AND LONDON
2000

The editors gratefully acknowledge assistance from the Program for Cultural Cooperation between Spain's Ministry of Culture and United States' Universities and from the College of Liberal Arts and the Department of Spanish and Portuguese at the University of Minnesota.

Published in 2000 by
Garland Publishing Inc.
A Member of the Taylor & Francis Group
19 Union Square West
New York, NY 10003

10 9 8 7 6 5 4 3 2 1

Library of Congress-in-Publication Data is available from the Library of Congress.

Printed on acid-free, 250-year-life paper
Manufactured in the United States of America

Hispanic Issues

In Memory—

Mairla Freidl—Marilyn F. Beckwith (1922-1997)
Who gave me many tools for this project

Isaac Benchimol (?-1982)
Balmes Street Synagogue, Madrid
Who first taught me Hebrew from Spanish

S.N.B.

Transliterations of spoken Arabic terms may vary throughout according to local colloquial forms and author preference. Transliterations of some Arabic names may vary as well.

Contents

◆ Acknowledgments

I wish to thank several colleagues for their encouragement and assistance at various stages of this project. Several stimulating discussions with Nicholas Spadaccini, Louise Mirrer, Jenaro Talens, Antonio Ramos-Gascón, and Vincent Chamberlin helped launch the collection. Jenaro Talens, Eugenia Lacarra, Margalit Matitiyahu, and Hsaïn Ilahiane each put me in touch with one contributor. George K. Zucker's *International Directory for Sephardic and Oriental Jewish Studies* (1990, University of Northern Iowa), was also instrumental in this regard. Above all, I wish to thank all the volume's contributors for their dedication and enthusiasm. They have steadily enriched the collection by drawing from their areas of expertise information and assessments that are complementary and diversifying at the same time. I wish to express my special thanks to Reuven Snir for his orthographic guidance, and to Nicholas Spadaccini for his help and encouragement at every stage of this project. I am also grateful to Louise Mirrer for her valuable early suggestions and for the insights in her Afterword.

◆ Introduction

Al-Andalus/Iberia/Sepharad: Memory among Modern Discourses

Stacy N. Beckwith

In 1964 Madrid was the site of a first international Convention on Arabic and Islamic Studies (Safran 1998, 196, n. 24), and of a first international Symposium on Sephardic [Jewish] Studies. The latter conference was held under the auspices of the Arias Montano Institute,[1] whose mission within the Consejo Superior de Investigaciones Científicas has been to promote scholarly research and inform the public on various aspects of Spain's Jewish past and diaspora. In 1964 the contemporary Spanish Jewish diaspora, or what one historian at the conference termed in Hebrew, *sefarad hagedola*, "Greater Sepharad," (Benardete 1970, 150), came to Madrid in a very nuanced "return" to a strangely "recognizable" ancient/contemporary home. A historian of Algerian Sephardic origin, André Chouraqi, claimed to encapsulate the sentiments of all those who had arrived from Mediterranean, Near Eastern, north European, and American locales, in recounting a colleague's reactions to his first physical tour in a "familiar" Iberia, enroute to the conference from Barcelona. Sounding less like a conference participant than a diplomat investing an international entente with cultural and emotional substance, Chouraqi went on to address Spaniards at large, emphasizing that the sentiments of his travel companion

> . . . have been the sentiment[s] of all of us who, since the fifteenth century, have guarded our Spanish loyalty within us; we have the same feelings [as my colleague] seeing your landscapes and your villages; hearing the bright sounds of the Spanish language; finding something that is ours, something to which we belong and which, in a certain way, belongs to us too. (Chouraqi 1970, 161)

Several elements in this situation and in Chouraqi's eloquence enable a comprehensive introduction to this collection of essays on textual and nontextual Jewish, Arab, and Hispanic modes of recalling medieval Spain. Both in their individual orientation and in the issues they raise comparatively, the chapters in this book argue compellingly for an understanding of the sources, shapes, and influences of Iberian memories that is grounded in ongoing human interaction; that is, in the dynamics of collective assembly, permutation, and/or dissolution.

Providing analogous illustration in their methods of investigation, the authors in this collection each write to augment and/or challenge knowledge within their own research communities: in cultural anthropology, ethnomusicology, literary criticism, architecture, and onomastics. At the same time, they also write to elaborate a wider, interdiscursive picture of how medieval Spain has been remembered from well before the fifteenth century to the present. In so doing, they reveal that there would be no persistence, much less any inernal "previewing" of Iberian homescapes absent a range of constitutive, continuously interacting social foundries. Whether it is the direct, or quite indirect object of reminiscent attention, Spanish soil is not the bedrock of its own feel and image in modern cultural memory. This role is played by collective and interpersonal imaginaries that act on individual ideation, however sui generis this may seem.

All of the chapters in this collection illustrate that it is in the interplay of memories both recent and older, from social contexts proximate to a particular Spain(s) in several senses, or hardly so, that modern connections to medieval Iberia are most productively gauged. Accordingly, the volume is not organized by Arab, Jewish, and Hispanic cultural memories, nor is it divided modally. Instead, the chapters fall roughly into three sections based on one particularly illuminating pattern of how Iberian memories have localized in social, geographic, and modal terms, and in so doing, how they continue to influence the construction of personal and collective identities.

The cognitive social scientist Eviatar Zerubavel is not alone in underscoring that the "modern individual" belongs to several "mnemonic communities" or "social worlds" at one time (1997, 17), prioritizing and activating his/her ties to each domain in response to a range of external and internal cues. The conceptual foundation for this claim is the same one that gave impetus to a heightened focus on collective mentalities on the part of historians in the 1960s, particularly those associated with the Annales school of "historical anthropology" and intellectual history in France (Le Goff 1992, xiii). Members of this association, including at one time or another Marc Bloch, Luien Febvre, and Pierre Nora, were influenced by the thought of an Alastian sociologist, Maurice Halbwachs, and especially by his *The Social Frameworks of Memory*, which was published in

1952 after the author's death in the Buchenwald concentration camp.

Traditional opinion from Plato and Aristotle through to Halbwachs's early mentor Henri Bergson held that the formation of human memories is intrinsic to the individual. Halbwachs was the first to reassign this process to the inner- and inter-workings of multiple social milieux, claiming that, "Individual images of the past are provisional. They are "remembered" only when they are located within conceptual structures that are defined by communities at large" (Hutton 1993, 7). In *The Social Frameworks of Memory*, a brief chapter titled, "The Localization of Memory" serves as one methodological entrée into Halbwachs's elaboration of this thesis in the context of family and religious groups, and social classes. In this early chapter, the sociologist asserts that memories are as mobile and as given to change as are people, "so the memory of the same fact can be placed within many different frameworks." Indeed, this is its optimal route toward recollection by individuals and/or communities, since a group's common interests, perspectives, and slanted reflections, along with its ensuing collective memories, provide contextualization that ensures remembrance (Halbwachs 1992, 51-52).

In Halbwachs's view, societies and individuals actively localize memories within supportive "conceptual frameworks." His phrasing here is significant because these milieux need not consist of people physically present in a given moment or situation of recall. The human elements in Halbwachs's social frameworks of memory may be "conceptual" as long as they can be related to past and/or extant "dwelling places of life," to borrow from the liberal Spanish historian Américo Castro. Indeed, Halbwachs's socially informed approach to collective memory, and Castro's deconstruction of essentialist historiography on Spain, with wider implications for other national histories, complement the chapters in this collection in whole and in part. Halbwachs and Castro's theses underscore the volume's attention to multiple processes of memory localization, cultural expression, and signification as a way of re-angling the focus of research on medieval Spain and her ensuing ethnic histories, all of which have traditionally been studied in isolation from one another.

To this end the volume is organized by the re/location of different remembering communities, in Spain and Portugal in the Middle Ages, or today in Arab/Jewish Morocco, and Jewish Greece from 1492 to the present, or until 1945, and in more distant contemporary locales including Israel/Palestine, other Arab countries, the United States, and Latin American countries.[2] These divisions also correspond to contexts in which Peninsular built and human environments, "dense" accumulations of material and habitual reminders of Spain in diaspora (Casey 1987, 80), and thinning linguistic, but other relevantly catalytic ties, have variously supported Iberian connections and memories.

Within these divisions, which productively overlap in many of the volume's chapters, an effort has been made not to cluster essays relating to Jewish, Arab, or Hispanic traditions or issues. This collection aims at an interdiscursive examination of how various peoples have re/articulated memories relating to medieval Spain in and across physical, temporal, and social locations, with different types and degrees of impact. This multicultural and multiethnic approach differs from the way contemporary scholarship has tended to package its findings on Jewish and Arab practices stemming from medieval Spain in separate "legacy" volumes.

Not surprisingly, the quincentennial in 1992 of the Jewish expulsion from Spain and the Muslim demise in the Peninsula saw the publication of two such collections. In them Jewish and Arab Iberian and diasporic cultural histories are separately and extensively surveyed. In Haim Beinart's *Moreshet Sepharad: The Sephardi Legacy* (1992), and in a more recent collection, *From Iberia to Diaspora: Studies in Sephardic History and Culture* (Stillman and Stillman 1998), no chapters are devoted to Arab matters that are not Arab/Jewish issues. One would almost expect the noted anthologist of modern Arab literatures Salma Khadra Jayyusi to have duplicated this pattern in reverse in *The Legacy of Muslim Spain* (1992). Jayyusi's volume does not perpetuate a Jewish semivacuum in its midst, however. Rather, it includes a chapter by the prominent Hebrew medievalist Raymond Scheindlin on "The Jews in Muslim Spain." This certainly enables a more integrative understanding of Andalusian Muslim experience, and perhaps it is also a gesture to the celebrated *convivencia*, or intercaste coexistence in medieval Iberia.

What all of the chapters in this volume of Hispanic Issues series underscore, is that Iberian, Jewish, and Arab descendants of Spain in the Middle Ages only invoke *convivencia* in association with the most general, hazy, and "collapsed" cultural memories and family histories. This belies the fact that a tripartite examination of medieval *convivencia*, as a nexus of discourses managed through strategies of articulation and tribute for minority protection, along with the dismantling of this system, is particularly revealing. It goes far in explaining how related memories have understandably formed in separate channels, but also in and among more transgressive modern discourses that people equilibrate, hierarchize, and/or curtail from their positions within various social/conceptual frameworks.

The Iberian Sphere Before and During the Early Middle Ages

Taking its cue from Américo Castro's premise that Romans and Visigothic Christians in Iberia before the medieval period were not Spanish in any national sense, this multilateral examination of *convivencia* begins with the first nation that did arrive in the Peninsula while it was in Roman hands. The tenor of Jewish experience in Spain and how it has been remembered by Jews was already set in an early legend that dates Jewish origins in the Peninsula to 586 B.C.E. This year saw the destruction of Judaism's primary religious and national anchor, the first divinely endowed Temple in Jerusalem, by conquering Babylonian armies. Historians agree that the collective Jewish turning point in 586 B.C.E. predates the arrival of any Jews in Iberia (Beinart 1992, 11; Díaz-Mas 1992, 1). Nonetheless, the legend immediately situates their coming efflorescence and demise in the Peninsula within a broader context of minorities living in foreign lands, in the shadow of two national exiles following Rome's similar dismantling of a rebuilt Temple and home territory in Palestine in 70 C.E.

The Hebrew name for Spain, *Sepharad*, also points to collective navigation within a wider universe. The Spanish specialist in Sephardic studies Paloma Díaz-Mas explains that the name first appeared in the biblical Book of Obadiah (Chapter 20) "as one of the places where Jews exiled from Jerusalem lived." At this point the reference was most likely to "Sardis, a city in Asia Minor. But Jewish tradition, especially since the eighth century C.E. tended to identify Sepharad with the western edge of the known world—the Iberian Peninsula" (Díaz-Mas 1992, 7). Sephardim, therefore, were Jews who settled in the Peninula and were living in Visigothic Christian societies by the fourth century. By the seventh century, Catholic intolerance was taking a toll on their economic and even their physical well-being, culminating in the first edict for their baptism or expulsion by King Sisebut in 612. This created the "first *converso* [convert] problem" in Iberia (Díaz-Mas 1992, 2).

The first Muslim invasion of Iberia in 711, then, provided a welcome change for Sephardim since Islamic law protected the life, limb, and freedom of worship of Jews as fellow monotheists and as the people of the Bible, in exchange for taxes and recognition of second-class status. Christians living in Muslim lands were similarly protected and many became Mozarabs, or Christians integrated into Arab lifestyles. Their counterparts were Muslim Mudéjars who were protected in Christian territories. No pretenses have been made about designating the different Arab populations in Islamic Spain a single national entity, much less about including all the neo-Muslims, or Muwallads, they created biologically and culturally, under any such label. Instead, the defense of the Islamic religion from heretical interpretation was the touchstone for distinct Muslim strategies of articulating and substantiating claims to Iberian and wider hegemony.

By contrast, Spanish historical writings have predominantly located the birth of Spain as a nation in Roman and Christian Visigothic contexts and inferred character traits. They have downplayed or distorted the euphemistic Arab intervention in the subsequent growth of this early Spanish nation. In a compendium of essays dedicated posthumously to Américo Castro in 1976, Iberian and Muslim historians Julio Rodríguez-Puértolas and James Monroe, outline and critique a tradition of Spanish essentialist historiography on Spain's digestion of its Islamic past in its process of cohering as a nation. To greater or lesser extents, the philological and historical works of Antonio de Nebrija, Francisco Javier Simonet,

Marcelino Menéndez y Pelayo, Julián Ribera, Miguel Asín Palacios, Claudio Sánchez-Albornoz, Ramón Menéndez Pidal, and José Ortega y Gasset, among others, establish the "vertebral" persistence of Spanish nationhood from a Christian base in antiquity through Islam's tenure in Iberia, eight centuries of territorial "Reconquest," and subsequent emergence in kind (Monroe 1976, 70-71; Rodríguez-Puértolas 1976, 115-18). Such scholarship, Monroe notes, has

> tried to show that every achievement of note made by the Andalusian Muslims [was] the result not of Eastern cultural importations, but of the fact that the Andalusians had been ethnically Spaniards, and . . . therefore . . . superior to mere Orientals. Caught within a nationalist cul-de-sac, . . . Arabists in Spain were able to stress not so much the Islamic and Eastern origin and nature of al-Andalus on the cultural level, but rather its Spanish roots. . . . (70)

Monroe grants that Sánchez Albornoz and Menéndez Pidal were not Arabists, and were working from secondary sources in areas "marginal to their main interests in the Romance field" (71). Nonetheless, the supreme irony lies in the Arab name for Islamic Spain. In 710 the Muslim governor of Tangiers, Ṭāriq ibn Ziyād, acting under higher orders, invaded Iberia. The Peninsula was then divided and named regionally, according to Visigothic tribal differentiation and control. The royal army that Ibn Ziyād defeated in the Muslims' first decisive local battle, on July 19, 711, was that of the Vandals, the southernmost band of IberianVisigoths. The incoming Arabs proceeded to name their new territory *al-Andalus*, in precise reference to these "Vandals," or *al-Wandāl*, in Arabic (Makki 1992, 5). Thus a Visigoth society, integral to the imputed cradle of

Christian Spanish national essence, came to signify this nation's ultimate Other—irreducible in fact, if not in memory: Islamic Spain.

Convivencia at Its Height

Also ensconced in this *différance* conditioning al-Andalus is the fact that the Iberian Christians would not have participated in ending medieval intercaste *convivencia*, nor would they have coalesced and emerged as a modern nation in the fifteenth century, without their historic exposure to Muslim strategies of military and linguistic hegemonic ascendancy and control. In 1492 the humanist philologist Antonio de Nebrija presented to the Catholic Queen Isabella the first grammar of the Castilian language, his *Gramática Castellana*. In doing so he underscored its import with the renowned phrase, "Language is the companion of Empire" (1980, 97). Nebrija, of course, would have been the last to draw this comparison, but the same insight guided the Muslim caliph who ruled al-Andalus at its height in the tenth century, and rhetorically led the whole Islamic Empire, as well.

'Abd al-Raḥmān III, an Andalusian Umayyad ruler, had "come to the throne" in "extremely adverse circumstances" (Makki 1992, 38). The caliphate he created "lasted less than a century" and its "territorial extent [was] limited" compared with that of rival Fatimid and 'Abbasid regimes in North Africa and the "Mashriq, or Eastern Arab lands" (Safran 1998, 182, 186). Nonetheless, as Middle Eastern historian Janina Safran analyzes, "'Abd al-Raḥmān III's assertion of his leadership" not just of his Andalusian subjects, but of all Muslims, presents "a case study in the articulation of claims to caliphal legitimacy in the caliphal age" (182).

In the Iberian context, it also presents a case study of *convivencia* managed through tolerance, but also through rhetorical intervention, as ʻAbd al-Raḥmān III strategically articulated boundaries between the coexistence of religious castes and "polytheism" (Safran 1998, 188), against the background of an earlier racial and cultural debate, begun in the East, about the supremacy of neo-Muslims or Arab Muslims within the Islamic Empire (Monroe 1976, 79). The pulls of *Shuʻubiyya*, or popular (non-Arab) sentiment, and of its opposite, *ʻArabiyya*, also translated into Jewish debates over the use of the Hebrew language for the creation of popular, secular poetry (in metaphorical relation to *Shuʻubiyya*), and its reservation for more elevated, sacred communication (cued by *ʻArabiyya*) (Naveh 1998).

Long before he assumed Umayyad control in al-Andalus, ʻAbd al-Raḥmān III's progenitors, the Syrian Umayyads, were overthrown by the antithetical ʻAbbasids. More receptive to *Shuʻubiyya*, the ʻAbbasids "seem to have taught" the Andalusian Umayyads "a lesson" in the political utility of "appeal[ing] to the neo-Muslim elements of society," in loci and around the Islamic Empire (Monroe 1976, 78). ʻAbd al-Raḥmān III also borrowed rhetorically from the Shi'i Muslim Fatimids, who were dominating much of North Africa and had greater political and territorial ambitions to the East and to the Iberian West. In helping Berber tribes in North Africa defend against the Fatimids, ʻAbd al-Raḥmān III learned of "prophecies of the arrival of the messianic figure of the Mahdi [that] had been circulating among the Shi'i at least since the ninth century" (Safran 1998, 184). This was just the face he needed to put on his own political ambitions in and from al-Andalus, especially since these now rested primarily on his meager recapture of a rebellious (Christian) Mozarab stronghold south of Córdoba.

In Chapter 9 of this volume, Reuven Snir discusses modern Arabic "mask poems," wherein a historical figure from medieval al-Andalus stands metonymically for a contemporary problematic. Identifying the Mozarab fort, Bobastro, as "the base of polytheism and . . . the abode of unbelief [in Islam] and falsehood" (Safran 1998, 187-88), 'Abd al-Raḥmān III represented himself "as a Mahdi-like," messianic figure, as anticipated in popular eschatology (189). The caliph thus employed techniques of rhetorical synthesis and intercontextual masking not only in the gold dinars he resumed minting, and in the religious command he assumed over all Muslims, but also in the high/low, *'arabī/shu'ubī*, and sacred/profane registers of the prime medium for communicating his new title and countenance to the public. This was the *khuṭba*, or regular "Friday sermon in every congregational mosque" (183).

Janina Safran describes the "quality of the way ['Abd al-Raḥmān III] articulated his legitimacy," as "Commander of the Faithful" in and beyond al-Andalus, as "multireferential" (189, 182). It was so in a way that allowed the caliph to keep his actual Iberian realm from degenerating into "a proliferation of factions." These eventually undermined the integrity of Islam in 'Abbasid contexts (192), as they had in Bobastro, which 'Abd al-Raḥmān III had strategically identified as an example of *Shu'ubiyya,* or its echoes, gone too far. In its maturity his caliphate would be characterized differently.

Muslim, Jewish, and Christian *convivencia* in al-Andalus significantly reached its height under the aegis of 'Abd al-Raḥmān III's metarhetorical control with its continued, manifold appeal. The "Umayyad Caliphate enjoy[ed] hegemony over the whole of the Peninsula. As such, Muslim al-Andalus . . . emerged as the greatest and most prosperous power in Europe" (Makki 1992, 37). It was courted by Byzantine and Germanic royalty from "beyond the Pyrennes" (37), and as Libby Garshowitz and I examine in Chapter 3, it enabled not only the efflorescence of Hebrew poetry, but also the inculcation of Sepharad as a Jewish homeland with resemblances to Zion.

At the same time, Hebrew and Romance elements were combining to form the "colloquial *kharjas*" that often concluded Arabic *muwashshaḥāt*. These were poems that cast Arabic themes in syllabic and strophic forms drawn from "Romance folk poetry" (Monroe 1976, 73, 80). Individual, mutlitalented Jews rose to prominence in various Muslim courts and enriched schools of translation, as they would that of Alfonso X in thirteenth century Toledo. Indeed, sidestepping their integral roles in Muslim Spain, the "traditionalistic [Spanish] historians," as Julio Rodríguez-Puértolas points out, "normally . . . [mention Jews] in their histories of Spain on only two occasions: in connection with King Alfonso the Learned and his School of Translators in Toledo, and in connection with their expulsion from Spain in 1492" (1976, 121).

Convivencia Dismantled

Well before the latter renowned date, the downturn of *convivencia* in al-Andalus and then in Christian territories registers in political rhetoric and concomitant attitudes that lose their tolerant nuances, however utilitarian. Castro observes that the term "Christians" came into "collective-political" use at the end of the ninth century, as a way of responding in kind to what the Muslims called themselves:

> Since the Moors possessed a collective name with a political-religious dimension—a fact without parallel in the Occident—their opponents, the peninsular

> Christians, injected a significance into the name of their religion that it did not possess in the rest of Europe. ("Historical *We*" 1977, 324)

This was less the case with the term *español*, which a Swiss philologist, Paul Aebischer, identified in 1948 as Provençal in origin. Referring to the pilgrimages made to the Catholic shrine at Santiago de Compostela from every direction, Aebischer noted that

> . . . if all Europe was by definition Christian, it was meaningless for the pilgrims going to Santiago to distinguish the inhabitants of the Peninsula from themselves by calling them Christians. Thus, for very practical reasons, the Peninsular Christians came to be called *españoles* by visitors from beyond the Pyrennes. (Rodríguez-Puértolas 1976, 120)

The Christians gained momentum in retaking territory from the Muslims in the eleventh century (Monroe 1976, 82). In addition to this, an internal voice became a catalyst for tighter, all-Muslim control in al-Andalus. In the same century a "court secretary" of Basque origin, Ibn García, was not alone in singing the virtues of "Muwallad leaders of native ancestry" in al-Andalus. He composed a "famous *shu'ubī* diatribe against the Arabs," even though the old Muslim/neo-Muslim cultural debate had long since faded (81-82). Ending the era of "petty states" that followed the Umayyad caliphate (Makki 1992, 49), new Almoravid, and then more exclusionary Almohad regimes interpreted Ibn García's discourse "as a potentially dangerous source of division within the Islamic community" (Monroe 1976, 84).

The Almohad Muslims, whose leadership and constituents were paradoxically, substantially Berber (Makki 1992, 68-69), invaded al-Andalus to again unite the faithful against false interpretations of their religion. Notwithstanding their name, *al-mu'aḥḥiddūn*, "the Unifiers," in direct contrast to ''Abd al-Raḥmān III the Almohads "persecuted and expelled" all non-Muslims "from Andalusian soil," and "redefined" Arab culture "narrowly in religious terms" (Makki 1992, 70; Monroe 1976, 84). The displacement of Andalusian Jews into Christian territories initiated Jewish modes of remembering and mourning Sepharad as a lost paradise, while within al-Andalus

> . . . the Romance elements in the *muwashshaḥāt* were disguised or eliminated. The colloquial *kharja* disappeared, and the stress-syllabic Romance meter was often replaced by the classical quantitative meters of Arabic. By the time we reach the [last Muslim] kingdom of Granada, where there were no Mozarabs, and where Romance was no longer spoken, Peninsular Islam had become a fossil of its former self, though it continued to produce literary and artistic works of great beauty. (Monroe 1976, 84)

The same deterioriation is encapsulated in Américo Castro's analysis of the differences in language and message between the inscription on the tomb of the Christian King Ferdinand III in 1252, and on the later tombs of the Catholic "Unifiers," Ferdinand and Isabella. The former epitaph is written ". . . in four languages: Latin, Castilian, Hebrew, and Arabic," and contains "not a trace of the later tolerance" that characterizes the Catholic re/conquerors' inscription. Here, "the only thing worthy of eternal memory is the annihilation of the Jewish and Muslim castes by the Christians" (Rodríguez-Puértolas 1976, 126). More in line with the 1252 epitaph, Arab descriptions of Iberian landscapes and daily life in the tenth and eleventh centuries and then in the fifteenth, also evince inclusion and coevalness.

In a 1952 edition of his compilation of foreign travelers' journeys through Spain, José García Mercadal provides readers with a flow of excerpts wherein one after another voyage is recounted. Included are four sets of impressions of Muslim and Christian regions in Portugal and Spain, as recorded by an Arab geographer, a prince, and two chroniclers. In these accounts features of landscape and architecture are described by these Muslim observers in terms that, while detailed, do not aim to typify or pin down a collective or national essence. A town named Silves is praised for the design of its buildings, its abundant markets, and the linguistic and cultural achievements of its Yemenite inhabitants. At the same time, residents of surrounding villages, many of whom are Christian, are described as being "exceedingly hospitable." They have priests in their midsts who are known for telling "marvelous tales" about the steadfastness of crows that never leave their churches (al-Edrisi quoted in Mercadal, 188).

In other areas of Spain, castles and defense walls are noted for their strategic location and their sturdy construction, while towns in and around Toledo, in addition to the city itself, are praised for their beauty and their thriving marketplaces (al-Edrisi quoted in Mercadal, 192-93). Indeed, when sites of public commerce are mentioned, one has the sense of looking in on a moving, diversified scenario. Later in Mercadal's anthology there is an account of the kingdom of Granada as it appeared in 1465 and 1466. An Egyptian visitor compares the city's demographic makeup and intrinsic grace to that of Damascus. During his stay he also witnesses a figure fleeing "as the crow flies" toward "the lands of the infidels" ('Abd al-Basit quoted in Mercadal, 255, 253).

What stands out in this account is not so much the Egyptian traveler or his hosts' awareness of infidel advance. Rather, it is the coeval sense in which the territories outside Granada and the rival forces are mentioned. One again has the sense of being caught up in events as they develop through time that is shared empirically and conceptually (see Fabian 1983). In stark contrast, where Sephardic Judeo-Spanish also registers such multicultural traffic in its linguistic evolution, Antonio de Nebrija's characterization of Castilian, Hebrew, and Arabic in 1492 effectively stopped time for the latter two languages, casting them as the emanations of biblical or more sinister, underdeveloped vocal registers, respectively.

Voices Charted and Suspended between 1492 and 1614

Between the fifteenth and sixteenth centuries in Spain, a prolific inteligentsia advanced several "political-literary programs" (Mackay 1977, 207) whose impact was typically enhanced through privilege in the Catholic court, a growing print readership (205), and expanding circles of literacy around the country. Whether Catholic, or reformist of Jewish *converso* origin, humanist scholars such as Nebrija and Juan Luis Vives, contributed to the structuring of a particular collective worldview, reaching a wider audience with their works on language than would have been possible prior to the current era of print "readability" (McLuhan 1964, 145). As an ideology, this view of the world was premised on the enabling power of language in human endeavor, and on the capacity of letters to "house" (Vives 1948, 693) not only ideas, but distillations of collective and national character, as well. Reified in this way, different societal traits were seen to correlate with familiar "voices" (Nebrija 1980, 111) of prominent political and religious players on the contemporary map.

Continuing to represent the anti-Christ, Muslims were now absent from Spain except for a substantial *morisco* society, whose members remained in the Peninsula after the fall of Granada in 1492, when they ostensibly converted to Catholicism. The Renaissance humanists included Muslim societies in their conceptual, global mapping schemes since Arabic, unlike the unprecedented glyphs being discovered in the New World, was at least alphabetic and in this way similar to Latin and its derived vernaculars. However, in clear distinction to 'Abd al-Raḥmān III's political-religious rhetoric with its manipulation, but nonsuppression of diverse religious currents and *'Arabiyya/Shu'ubiyya* debates, the fact that Arabic was alphabetic only ensured that Muslims would occupy the next to lowest place in a Christian humanist hierarchy of global civilizations.

In sixteenth-century Europe, according to the French historian, Claude-Gilbert Dubois, language was regarded as "no arbitrary system" (1985, 149). Rather, upheld in its material form, it "played an active role in the meaningful framing of the universe . . . reflecting both the objective relations between a speaking subject and his exterior reality, and the ties that governed human society overall" (Julia Kristeva, quoted in Dubois, 51). In her study of the Peruvian mestizo chronicler, Garcilaso de la Vega the Inca, Hispanist Margarita Zamora introduces the "humanist conception of language as the fundamental mediating element between perception and reality (1988, 23-24). In a different study, Zamora also discusses cartography in the era of Columbus, not as "an independent, autonomous form of geographical discourse," but as a complementary, "hermeneutical practice" devoted to the interpretation of the physical world and its spiritual significance (1993, 103-12).

Midway through his *Gramática Castellana*, commissioned by Queen Isabella in 1492, Nebrija established a series of sound-essence equivalences for certain distinguishing letters of the Castilian alphabet, and by way of setting them apart, for various letters of the Hebrew and Arabic alphabets as well. In his view, and in the later writings of Juan Luis Vives, letters functioned as the "dwelling places" of ideas (Vives 1948, 693). The salient "voices," or sounds of certain letters in different alphabets, represented familiar civilizations ancient and modern, turning texts in the new era of print technology into "repeatable" *mappae mundi.*

Nebrija endowed the Castilian alphabet with certain identifying marks, as guideposts for the native speaker, or for the foreigner coming into contact with Spain as an ascendant power on the world map. Both Nebrija and Luis Vives established the written letter as a "countenance for the voice," following Aristotle's claim that the human voice represents the "thoughts in our souls" (Nebrija 1980, 111). Nebrija moved from the thoughts and souls of individuals to those of whole societies. In the *Gramática Castellana*, he distinguished the Castilian *ll* as "proper to our people," and by contrast, the Hebrew guttural letter *ayin* as the "proper voice of the Jews," since their alphabet alone contained its shape (Nebrija 1980, 112).[3]

As the sociocultural theorist Marshall McLuhan would describe, from here Nebrija instituted the "art of making pictorial statements" about peoples around the globe, "in precise and repeatable form" (1964, 145). Nebrija made language both a "companion of Empire" (97) and a tool for referencing any point in and around one's empire, as well. Print technology, which instituted "repeatability as the core mechanical principle" of the contemporary world (145), further ensured that alphabetic letters would become typefaces of societal character. In this way the human universe began to be "miniaturized" according to Claude-Gilbert Dubois (1985, 86). Inferable differences between peoples narrowed to stereotypes haplessly ushered in by their own forms of scripture.

According to Américo Castro, the notion of a smaller, more centered cosmos was to the liking of Juan Luis Vives, who left Spain in 1509, and continued his scholarship in Bruges, having befriended Erasmus. ("Renaissance in Spain" 1977, 168). In his *Works on Education* of 1520-38, Vives continued to portray language as a purveyor of collective identities. At the same time, he proposed that international understanding could be enhanced by training citizens of different countries in a range of languages, in translation schools that would recall similar medieval institutions but for their absolute privileging of Latin. Nonetheless, despite seeming odds, Vives held that the translatability of Semitic letters would allow one to converse clearly with Jewish or Arab interlocutors since, as he wrote, "To the extent that Nature designed a language for you to be understood in, you will understand apace. The grammar will signal those vices and barbarisms you should avoid" (1948, 576).

Apparently, *morisco* voices in Spain constituted a substantial portion of those barbarisms an "Old Christian" was to circumvent since, as historian Roger Boase observes, "much has been written about the exodus of the Jews in 1492," but there has been little examination of the *morisco* expulsion from Spain a century or so later, including these peoples' "terrorization" by the Spanish Inquisition and by popular/clerical "anti-Semitic theology" (1990, 9). Contrary to the implications of their tombstone, when the Catholic kings took Granada from the Muslims in 1492, they promised its residents that they would be "allowed to preserve their mosques and religious institutions, to retain the use of their language, and to continue to abide by their own customs" (10). These stipulations, preserving some flavor of medieval *convivencia*, were undone within seven years, however. Catholic fanaticism replaced moderation, and mass conversions and the burning of Arabic religious texts resulted in the first *morisco* rebellion of the Alpujarras (1499-1500) (10).

A second Alpujarras rebellion followed in 1568, when "Philip II renewed an edict, which had never been very strictly enforced, making the use of Arabic illegal and prohibiting Islamic religion, dress, and customs" (Boase 1990, 11). The latter had already come under attack since five theologians and "anti-*morisco* polemicists" in particular, "voiced the prejudices of the populace" in imbuing *moriscos* with hereditary guilt for an ingrained heresy against Christianity, the likes of which would never allow them to "expunge the memory of their despised origins" (9, 11).

Significantly, the "art of memory" seems to bifurcate in the Renaissance. From their thorough reexamination of Greek philosophy, humanists such as Nebrija, and the clergy they informed, would have perceived the increasing individualization of remembering as a process, as this secularized in Platonic and Aristotelian thought. Indeed, this would have accorded with the humanists' emphasis on the value of classical knowledge in the self-improvement endeavors of contemporary individuals, as conveyed through classical and modern languages distilled of their medieval "barbarisms" (Rico 1981, 10; Maravall 1981, 22). As the cognitive scientist Edward Casey describes in a phenomenological approach to individual memory, the early Greek

> . . . deification of Mnemosyne, and with her of an entire mythical past, could not survive the emergence of philosophy in its specifically Platonic form in the fifth century B.C.E. For Plato, recollection (anamnesis)

> is less of any particular past—personal or mythical—than of eidetic knowledge previously acquired. The highly personified figure of Mnemosyne disappears; not named in the few myths which are allowed to survive in Platonic dialogues . . . a premise of this dialectic is that the knowledge being sought is already possessed by the individual inquirer, who therefore requires no inspired infusions from a presiding Goddess (Casey 1987, 13-14).

In Renaissance Spain, nonetheless, it is clear that the *moriscos*' individual and collective memories of al-Andalus, and the heresies these reputedly contained, were all socially informed, as well. Indeed, the exclusionary, hegemonic understanding of memory emanating from Plato had its popular countercurrents. In 1966 an English historian of the Renaissance, Frances Yates, published a highly acclaimed study of the training undertaken by medieval and sixteenth-century philosophers, who were alive to the "mystical and magical uses" of memory, to artificially strengthen their own. In the first "scholarly monograph" on the relationship of "history and memory" as intellectual discourse (Meyers 1988, 89), Patrick Hutton has written that Yates

> showed the more panoramic dimensions of Renaissance scholarship—its arcane domains of learning, its false starts and intellectual impasses, its exotic and occult philosophies in what was a vastly more pluralistic cultural milieu than historians had previously imagined. (1993, 11)

In Chapter 7 of this volume, Sultana Wahnón examines the interplay of normative aversion and subversive recollection of exotic and "magical" *converso* Jews in Gabriel García Márquez's Latin American fictional universe. Both the clergy in García Márquez's writing and the Spanish friars who "preached to the *moriscos*" in Spain and then "exploded" against them between 1610 and 1618, tapped "social frameworks of memory" on both the "pure blooded" aristocratic, and the popular levels. In skewed resemblance to the medieval 'Abd al-Raḥmān III, the Spanish friars also consolidated their regime of influence, and enhanced their rhetoric against their *morisco* detractors by manipulating local eschatology (Boase 1990, 9). In one example, Saint Paul was said to have painted a picture of the biblical Ishmael aiming arrows at his half-brother Isaac, a progenitor of the Jews, but more significantly, of the Christians, with clear fratricidal intent (21).

In Chapter 4 in this collection, Beebe Bahrami shows that Moroccan Andalusians still collectively remember that their ancestors were frequently forced to choose between their children and starvation in seventeenth-century Spain. The descendants of Ishmael under the age of ten or five (Boase 1990, 13), were considered innocent enough to be bribed away from their parents enroute to exile. The children were then reindoctrinated in the Christian faith and vocationally trained, though never "above their station," in order to counteract the revenue and manpower drain that Spain experienced with the *moriscos*' mass departure between 1609 and 1614 (12-13). Out of a total Spanish population of seven and a half million, Roger Boase estimates that there were "half a million refugees." Creating a sharper picture, he notes that "in the Kingdom of Valencia, which lost a third of its population, nearly half the villages were still deserted in 1638" (12).

Spain Orientalized

This emptiness is especially striking when considered in connection with the etymology of what is still a building block of Spanish society today; its overall and individual *pueblos*. Writing on Castile, but continually referencing "the other parts of Spain," the Spanish sociologist Horacio Velasco underscores in 1989 that the process of populating is what underpins the Spanish term for its constitutive social frameworks:

> The Castilian language transforms lands when they are inhabited by "pueblos." The act of "populating" designates the occupation of lands by peoples, the transformation of deserts and areas of wilderness into places that are lived in—this is the historical process of the formation of Castile itself. Groups populated and repopulated uninhabited zones and places. These were peoples who came from the Northern border of the Peninsula and from other areas of Europe between the tenth and the fourteenth centuries. All Castilian populations (and those of other parts of Spain), regard themselves as "pueblos" . . . the term . . . has been in use since the first half of the twelfth century . . . to denote . . . people who inhabit a place and "the common folk as opposed to the nobility." (1989, 82)

A *pueblo* may invoke a high/low distinction, but in early medieval Arabic terms, *'arabiyya* characterizes Velasco's entire definition. In his description *pueblo* entered Romance vocabularies in the twelfth century, from sources the sociologist does not examine. The people who "populated and repopulated" individual *pueblos* in Castile and elsewhere came only from the country's northern, most assuredly Christian edge, in Velasco's description, and from beyond this frontier. *Shu'ubiyya* is therefore absent from his representation, since no non- or neo-Christians are mentioned as participating in, or even giving way to the population and repopulation of a vacant countryside. Such ulterior elements do infiltrate intermittently, even in contemporary Spain, but they do so as the most negative of expletives:

> The way to draw the sharpest distinction, that is to say, to cut off relations [between *pueblos*], if desired, is to demonstrate one's perception of an extreme difference, by accusing those of another *pueblo* of being "Jewish" or "Moorish," for example. These are the two ethnic or ethnic-religious entities that . . . furnish a paradigm in Spain for [driving home] a cultural difference that is perceived as absolute. (87)

Velasco goes on to note that, "all of this can be conveyed in a nickname, a folksong, a sentence, a little story, a ballad," or in other forms of popular communication. However, the Jewish/Moorish label "always designates a unique sense of identity, that is, identity as difference. This is because the same signs can indicate identity on the part of [an] 'in-group' and difference on the part of [an] 'out-group' (87). Such rhetoric has been double edged throughout Spain's modern history, however. It has especially helped to orientalize Spain in the minds of foreign observers and travelers who have not envisioned lands empty of Jewish and Muslim *pueblos*. A push-pull dynamic, it seems, attracted British romantics such as Richard Ford and George Borrow to the Peninsula in the nineteenth century. They sought retreat from a world that had become too intellectually and industrially regimented. Spain, and especially her "polymorphic" southern region (Gonzalez Troyano 1984, 11), beckoned as uncharted territory in which to wander and come face to face with characters "of old renown" (Borrow 1923, vi).

From "day-dreaming" in his "boyhood," and reading about Jews, Moors, and Inquisitors in Spanish and other literatures, when George Borrow arrived in Spain on a mission to distribute Anglican Bibles in the Peninsula, he was, like André Chouraqi's Sephardi colleague in Madrid, in 1964, almost innately familiar with his surroundings (Borrow 1923, vi). Nonetheless, Borrow's account of his travels, published in England as *The Bible in Spain*, in 1842, differs substantially from those of the Muslim chroniclers and geographers who described al-Andalus in the tenth through the fifteenth centuries, as partially anthologized by José García Mercadal. Borrow claims to have been uniquely "adrift" in Spain, ". . . the land of wonder and mystery . . . [of] strange secrets and peculiarities . . ." (vi). His book is hardly casual in its structure, however, and the author's writing does not treat any "Hebrews [or] *moriscos*" imagined or encountered, coevally. (Goytisolo 1982, 6).

The Hispanist Alberto Gonzalez Troyano has claimed that in the "romantic voyage" through Spain, "above all the power of reason [was] replaced by the sway of subjectivity" (1984, 15). This is not borne out in the static, deliberately ordered image of the Peninsula that Borrow perpetuates in print. Instead, extending Nebrija's sociolinguistic cartography, the British traveler describes one meeting with a "bearded" Sephardic Moroccan "sage" in precise biblical terms. He describes the Jewish figure as "slow to anger and long-suffering," which means that, like the Old Testament God and select righteous men in the Books of Exodus and Numbers, this person is exactly as the Hebrew reads, and in this way he seems to emanate from a premodern, biblical time.[4]

Borrow disavows any "real life" connection between characters he encounters and scenes he comes upon throughout the Peninsula and the Maghreb. His distribution of Anglican New Testaments does bring him into direct conflict with the Catholic Church, however. Both the missionary and his entourage are repeatedly jailed, but when freed, they purportedly manage to find individual Gypsies, Jews, and some sympathetic Christian Spaniards. By their real or imagined, but nonetheless concretely described presence, these diverse personae all help bring to life vestiges of Spain's "black legend." This particularly surfaces in connection with the small-scale Church interrogations and prison sojourns that Borrow experiences. One incident of arrest, for example, particularly awakens the author's textually and socially informed fascination with an essentialized and time-bound Spanish past:

> The "alguazils" conducted me across the Plaza Mayor to the Carcel de la Corte, or prison of the court, as it is called. While going across the square, I remembered that this was the place where, in "the good old times," the Inquisition of Spain was in the habit of holding its solemn "Autos da fe" . . . I cast my eye to the balcony of the city hall, where at the most solemn of them all, the last of the Austrian line in Spain sat, and after some thirty heretics, of both sexes, had been burnt by fours and by fives, wiped his face, prespiring with heat, and black with smoke, and calmly inquired, "¿No hay más?" (Borrow 1923, 544)

The Spanish novelist and social critic, Juan Goytisolo, identifies such typification as the product of highly processed, rather than incidental rhetoric. He compares Borrow to Joseph Blanco White, an expatriate Sevillian whose writings on Spain were deconstructive and far more diversifying:

> . . . without abandoning his critical sense, Borrow knows how to capture the "charm" in our backwardness, and how to use affectionate irony in examining our primitive and almost tribal customs. The same dual vision makes its precise impact on Blanco White's *Letters from Spain* (1822) . . . Writing for an English public fully curious about things Spanish, Blanco White knows how to compensate his book's extremely violent critique, which stems from his own moral anxiety, with sharp intellectual reflection and fine aesthetic contemplation, the likes of which keep him from falling into the one-sidedness and the schematism indicated [in Borrow's case]. (1982, 27)

At the same time, Paloma Díaz-Mas underscores that many Spaniards' conceptions of Sephardim today are one-sided, since they had no social channels that brought them into direct contact with Jews from the sixteenth through the eighteenth centuries (1992, 151). Where "Arab studies practically vanished from the Peninsula" in the seventeenth century, Monroe notes in 1976 that,

> It can be stated without much exaggeration that ever since 1492 Arabic studies in Spain have been largely in the hands of people who were politically dissatisfied with the main currents and trends in Spanish history. (69)

While these currents have been changing, particularly since 1975, Díaz-Mas adds in 1992 that Spaniards "know almost nothing of the history and sociocultural chracteristics of the Sephardim, and they still identify Judeo-Spanish with fifteenth century Spanish, as if a language could avoid evolution over 500 years" (168).

Rhetoric of Re/connection

Díaz-Mas is very complimentary of a campaign to publicize the qualities and presumed identity dilemma of Jewish "Spaniards without a homeland" that was galvanized by a Spanish senator, Ángel Pulido Fernández, at the turn of this century. As Díaz-Mas writes, "Spain rediscovered the Sephardim in the mid-nineteenth century" (1992, 152), when her troops did encounter Moroccan Sephardic communities during the Spanish African war of 1859-60. Character sketches in less than coeval tones, again differing from those of the medieval Arab chroniclers in al-Andalus, began to flow back to Spain. They reached the foremost realist author Benito Pérez Galdós, and from 1867 through 1905, he incorporated into his novels traces of Sephardim, then a few stereotyped foils to Christian characters, and then a version of liturgical and popular Judeo-Spanish which he elaborated from secondary sources (Chamberlin). Galdós was unable to visit Sephardic families to learn Hiqitiá, or Moroccan Judeo-Spanish directly, unlike Pulido who was catapulted into redemptive action upon hearing a conversation in Rumanian Judeo-Spanish on the decks of a boat as he toured eastern Europe.

He and the Sephardic couple he overheard, who headed a Sephardic community school in Bucharest, became so enthusiastic over their mutual encounter that the Bejaranos'

> . . . love for Spain convinced Pulido that all Sephardim felt similarly linked to Spain, and they considered it their homeland, and that, despite their expulsion, and the persecution they had faced there, they had retained an almost religious veneration for the land of their ancestors. Continued use of the Spanish language after almost five centuries of exile was concrete proof of this veneration. Consequently all Spain (and especially

> the government) should reciprocate such generous and unselfish loyalty by strengthening their contacts with the Sephardim, giving them various kinds of aid, and especially, granting them the Spanish citizenship they so desired. (Díaz-Mas 1992, 154)

On the heels of Spain's final loss of overseas territories in 1898, language would again become the companion of empire, albeit in pursuit of New/Old worlds sighted through a highly generalized collective memory. A small intellectual *movimiento pro-sefardita* took shape around Pulido's publishing and political activities. Neither essentialist nor traditionalist in this social/academic context, as Shmuel Refael discusses in Chapter 5, Ramón Menéndez Pidal was an unprecedented collector and archivist of Judeo-Spanish ballads. Miguel de Unamuno also fed Pulido's enthusiasm for his discovery of a diaspora full of potential ambassadors for Spain's historical depths and linguistic riches. In the "sounds" of Judeo-Spanish (Chouraqi 1970, 161), these two Spanish intellectuals identified a people who they imagined were trying to come home culturally and emotionally, if not physically. As Unamuno wrote to Pulido,

> While the Jews of the Orient conserve their Spanish, praying to their God [but] casting their feelings and anxieties in Spanish, their homeland will be Spain, which was so cruel and unjust towards them. One could say that they only seek in Spanish a strong tether to other children of Israel scattered throughout the East. But this chord will also tie them just as tightly to Spain. In order to bring about this [reconnection to Spain], [these Sephardim] are not trying to resuscitate the sacred Hebrew language which has been dead for centuries; they are just trying to

> conserve some of its vitality. That was their mother tongue while this, our language, is their wedded tongue, and it is written that a wife must detach from her parents . . . (Unamuno quoted in Pulido 1905, 104-5)

Both Unamuno and Pulido were clearly responding to the predominance of Romance elements in the contemporary Judeo-Spanish (or Ladino) that the senator was hearing around the Mediterranean. As the Israeli specialist in Judeo-Spanish linguistics David Bunis describes,

> In quantitative terms, it was the elements of Ibero-Romance origin, most of which probably bore a close resemblance to popular Medieval Castilian, which constituted the major component of the medieval Sephardi language, supplying its basic phonological and grammatical framework and the bulk of its lexicon. Native texts replicating the Hispanic elements do not exist, but if we may judge by the Hispanic elements preserved in the modern everyday vernacular, most of the Hispanic elements employed on an everyday basis by the average medieval Spaniard may have differed little, if at all, from the popular forms used by their average Christian neighbors . . . (1992, 403)

In the end Ángel Pulido's campaign to recall Sephardic attention to Spain via these linguistic channels faded for lack of wide and self-sustaining impact at home and in the Jewish diaspora, alike. An aunt of a prominent Israeli journalist of Turkish Sephardic descent takes some of the uniqueness out of Pulido's reconnaissance trips when she remembers the wives of Spanish ambassadors and local expatriates dropping into their family store in Turkey on a regular basis, just to "hear our brethren's language" (Ziffer 1995, 143).

Pulido and some of his cohorts had planned to bring Balkan and Levantine Judeo-Spanish even closer to home by shoring up and, in thinking reminiscent of Nebrija, purifying its Castilian base (Pulido 1905, 156). French schools for Sephardim already run in North Africa and the Middle East by the French Jewish philanthropic organization established in 1860, the Alliance Israèlite Universelle, would serve as a first, unavoidable means of access. Eventually, Spanish schools would include "Jewish religious education as well as secular courses" (Díaz-Mas 1992, 157). However, besides generating little momentum in Spain, the ambitions of the *movimiento pro-sefardita* were also swallowed up by those of the contemporary Jewish *movimiento pro-sionista*. For a persuasive publication, Pulido's second book, *Españoles sin patria y la raza sefardí* [Spaniards without a homeland: the Sephardic race] (1905), is highly unusual. It details the "complete" change of heart which prominent Zionists of Sephardi origin, such as Max Nordau and members of "Esperanza," a Sephardic fraternity in Vienna, expressed to Pulido, "little more than four years" after he first made their acquaintance (Pulido 1905, 156). Ideas of a contemporary Jewish national home, which gained diplomatic trappings of their own after the first Zionist Congress in Basel, Switzerland, in 1887, may not have been the only catalysts for the turnabout that Pulido perceived and regretted.

At base the senator had little respect for the dynamic, diversified properties of Judeo-Spanish, and hence for those of its speakers. To draw one more, inverse comparison with the Andalusian ʻAbd al-Raḥmān III, in trying to re/build a cultural empire out of relatively few concrete achievements, Ángel Pulido did not craft a rhetoric that was in step with the various *pueblos* he sought to convince. Despite the educational and self-reflexive horizons he opened up in Spain (Díaz-Mas 1992, xi) and the research organizations, such as the Arias Montano Institute, that his work helped to found, again like a latter-day Nebrija, Pulido's vision for Sephardim was also normative and ultimately stultifying. If Sephardim were to conserve their Ladino (choosing it over Hebrew which, though it barely involved them as yet, was undergoing its own secular modernization), then Pulido insisted that they do so "based solely on the adoption of modern Castilian" (Pulido 1905, 156). Hence Judeo-Spanish would cease to become a well-trafficked "dwelling place of life," in Castro's pluralistic and counterhegemonic sense.

Indeed, Pulido's consolidating orientation also has a parallel in the program of the marginal Canaanite movement in Palestine/Israel, whose main period of coordinated activity was in the 1930s through the 1950s. A group of immigrant Jewish writers and intellectuals, including Yonatan Ratosh, Aharon Amir, and Benjamin Tammuz, among others, envisioned a confederation of peoples descended from Semitic and other elements indigenous to the local area. Their completely secular domain was to be united under a flag bearing the Hebrew letter *aleph*, to symbolize the revitalization of various native and Semitic cultures. The problem, of course, was that the *aleph* also signaled that Arab and other specificities would be collapsed and subsumed under a Hebrew polity. By the same token, the "many purposes Castilian could serve" (Pulido 1905, 156), in a Spanish hegemony around the Mediterranean, would have undercut Sephardic actualities/mnemonics in the 1900s.

Modes of Charting Memory

As a historian associated with the Annales school and its exploration of the "history of mentalities" since the 1960s, Jacques Le Goff summarizes that the word *modern* "comes into being in the fifth century, with the collapse of the Roman empire" (1992, 23). In the sixteenth century, as shown by the Renaissance humanists, history is "periodized into ancient, medieval, and modern . . ." (25). "Modern" now "marks rupture with the past" since it becomes "loaded" with novel terms such as "new" and "progress" (27). At the same time, in "ushering in modernity" in his essay "The Painter and Modern Life" (1863), Charles de Baudelaire ". . . pushes the meaning of the word "modern" in the direction of behaviors, customs, [and] settings." This highlights the derivation of "modernity" from "mode" (41).

The preceding historical synthesis has aimed at foregrounding not only the coeval interaction of various Jewish, Arab, Christian and/or Spanish social milieux from before the Middle Ages through the first part of this century, but also the modes of articulation in and by which these milieux were constituted, managed, and/or variously "revived" in different physical and temporal settings. Each of the chapters in this collection also focuses on social behaviors and customs that modulate distinct, but co-extant ties to Iberian pasts, as these are diversely felt and expressed in medieval, twentieth century, and intervening contexts.

The volume opens in Spain in the late 1980s, leading up to the 1992 quincentennial. Judith Cohen examines how a rural Galician *pueblo* reads medieval "memories" into its built environment which contains several authentic Sephardic markers. Attempting to bring these to life for purposes of tourism and conservation generates appropriating patterns of musical and theatrical performance which themselves become "traditional" with astonishing rapidity. Temporal distances between twentieth-century recollections and medieval lifestyles in the Peninsula are caught in an even more "gripping abbreviation" (Halbwachs 1992, 60) in Manuel da Costa Fontes's analysis of contemporary townspeople in Portugal who not only recall the lyrics and cadences of Crypto-Jewish (*converso*) oral prayers and ballads, but continue to harbor some of the suspicions that originally informed them, as well. Libby Garshowitz and I then examine emotions ranging from contentment to foreboding and despair as induced by Jewish downturns in medieval Spain. We discuss the semiotics of medieval Sephardic Hebrew poetry and its synesthetic modes of inculcating Sepharad as a Jewish homeland through continuous intertextual associations with biblical, national territory.

In Chapters 4 through 6 the focus of the volume shifts to two locations that particularly welcomed early waves of Muslim, *morisco*, and Jewish emigrés from Iberia between 1492 and 1611. Beebe Bahrami examines the many inflections of Arab Andalusian identity in Morocco, tracing its construction to the memories and continued practices of *morisco* "Hornacheros" who settled in Rabat in the 1600s. In Tel Aviv, in the 1990s, Sephardi Israelis from Greek Salonika still call each other by Judeo-Spanish nicknames which in some cases have "stuck" to the point of consigning a community member's actual name to oblivion, but never his/her Salonikan-Spanish heritage.

Shmuel Refael contextualizes gendered processes of name-giving among Salonikan Sephardim within a wider field of Judeo-Spanish onomastics. He also maps pre-Holocaust Salonika through the humor that prompted the names and nicknames of its many synagogues and Ladino newspapers. These refer not only to precise locations in Spain, but to everyday medieval/contemporary realia and character traits, as well. Hsaïn Ilahiane similarly reconnects residential balconies in the Jewish quarters of Moroccan cities to Sephardic Andalusian models and sources, reading the history of the Islamic City "against the grain," and stressing the persistence of such architectural features as an expression of Iberian cultural memory.

The collection takes a wider turn in its final section, beginning with Sultana Wahnón's analysis of the built and soft features of Latin American non/remembrance of the Sephardic *conversos* and their travails in New Spain, as Gabriel García Márquez's broaches in *One Hundred Years of Solitude*. Dwight Reynolds then charts the history and continued growth and diversification of popular Arab Andalusian music from Manama, Bahrain, to Los Angeles. Emotional ties to a shared Iberian past are also the keynotes that sound in Reuven Snir's study of al-Andalus, as recalled in both the content and stylistics of Arab poetry from the medieval period through the 1990s. Federico García Lorca is particularly invested with medieval/modern connectivity, and revered by contemporary poets who have broad cultural, as well as specific national appeal.

Sephardim in Indianapolis today do not have such an icon and direct link to Spain, and indeed the waning of social mnemonic frameworks among older Balkan Sephardic immigrants in the United States may ensure little more than the persistence of general recollections of an Iberian "golden age." Nonetheless, Jack Glazier's study underscores that it is in communities constructed by families, synagogues, language, and folklore, that collective memories of recent and remote Sephardic pasts have crystallized. As a whole, this volume examines a range of textual and nontextual praxes related to various Jewish, Arab, and Hispanic memories of medieval Spain. It localizes these memories in social frameworks that have formed and re/grouped interdiscursively, such that they do recall *convivencia* in al-Andalus/Iberia/Sepharad as a relevant starting place.

Notes

1. The Arias Montano Institute has recently been renamed the Institute of Philosophy within the Consejo Superior de Investigaciones Científicas. However, in this Introduction and in Chapter 6, the Arias Montano title is used.

2. This list of locales is by no means exhaustive.

3. In keeping with his linguistic hierarchization of civilizations, Nebrija claims that Hebrew "alone" has the letter *ayin*, excluding its presence and similar functions in Arabic as well.

4. See Exodus 34:6 and Numbers 14:18, for example: *'Erech apayim v'rav ḥesed.*

Works Cited

Beinart, Haim, ed. *Moreshet Sepharad: The Sephardi Legacy*. 2 vols. Jerusalem: The Magnes Press of the Hebrew University of Jerusalem, 1992.

_____. *The Expulsion of the Jews from Spain*. Jerusalem: The Magnes Press of the Hebrew University of Jerusalem, 1996 (Hebrew).

Benardete, Mair J. "Las comunidades sefarditas en Nueva York. Promesas de futuro." In Iacob M. Hassán, ed., *Proceedings of the First Symposium on Sephardic Studies* (Madrid, 1964), 149-54. Madrid: Arias Montano Institute, 1970.

Boase, Roger. "The Morisco Expulsion and Diaspora: An Example of Racial and Religious Intolerance." In David Hook and Barry Taylor eds., *Cultures in Contact in Medieval Spain: Historical and Literary Essays Presented to L. P. Harvey*, 9-28. King's College London Medieval Studies III. Exeter: n.p., 1990.

Borrow, George. *The Bible in Spain, or The Journeys, Adventures and Imprisonments of an Englishman in an Attempt to Circulate the Scriptures in the Peninsula.* (1842). London: John Murray, 1923.

Bunis, David. "The Language of the Sephardim: A Historical Overview." In Haim Beinart, ed., *Moreshet Sepharad: The Sephardi Legacy*, 2. 399-422. Jerusalem: The Magnes Press of the Hebrew University of Jerusalem, 1992.

Casey, Edward S. *Remembering: A Phenomenological Study*. Bloomington: Indiana UP, 1987.

Castro, Américo. "The Historical *We*." In Stephen Gilman, Edmund L.King, and Roy Pearce, eds., *An Idea of History: Selected Essays of Américo Castro*, 313-34. Columbus: Ohio State UP, 1977.

_____. "The Problem of the Renaissance in Spain." In Stephen Gilman, Edmund L.King, and Roy Pearce, eds., *An Idea of History: Selected Essays of Américo Castro*, 168-78. Columbus: Ohio State UP, 1977.

Chamberlin, Vincent A. "Recalling the Sephardic Past in the Novels and *Episodios Nacionales* of Pérez Galdós." Typescript received from Vincent Chamberlin.

Chouraqi, André. "L'État Actuel du Judaisme Nord-Africain en Afrique du Nord, en France et en Israel." In Iacob M. Hassán, ed., *Proceedings of the First Symposium on Sephardic Studies* (Madrid, 1964), 161-72. Madrid: Arias Montano Institute, 1970.

Coser, Lewis A. *Introduction: Maurice Halbwachs 1877-1945*. In Maurice Halbwachs, *On Collective Memory*. Ed. and trans. Lewis A. Coser. Chicago: U of Chicago P, 1992.

Díaz-Mas, Paloma. *Sephardim: The Jews from Spain*. Trans. George K. Zucker. Chicago: U of Chicago P, 1992.

_____. "Judíos y conversos en la literatura española contemporanea." In Yedida K. Stillman and Norman Stillman, eds., *From Iberia to Diaspora: Studies in Sephardic History and Culture*, 346-61. Leiden: E.J. Brill, 1998.

Dubois, Claude-Gilbert. *L'imaginaire de la Renaissance*. Paris: Presses Universités de France, 1985.

Fabian, Johannes. *Time and the Other: How Anthropology Makes Its Object*. New York: Columbia UP, 1983.

Gonzalez Troyano, Alberto. "Los viajeros románticos y la seducción polimórfica de Andalucia." In Alberto Gonzalez Troyano, ed., *La imagen de Andalucia en los viajeros románticos y homenaje a Gerald Brenan*. 11-20. Malaga: Diputación Provincial, 1984.

Goytisolo, Juan. "Presentación crítica de J.M. Blanco White." In Juan Goytisolo, ed., *Obra Inglesa de Blanco White*, 3-98. Barcelona: Editorial Seix Barral, 1982.

Halbwachs, Maurice. *The Social Frameworks of Memory* (1952). Reprinted in Maurice Halbwachs, *On Collective Memory* 37-167, Lewis A. Coser ed. and trans. Chicago: U of Chicago P, 1992.

Hutton, Patrick H. *History as an Art of Memory*. Hanover and London: UP of New England, 1993.

Jayyusi, Salma Khadra, ed. *The Legacy of Muslim Spain*. Leiden: E.J. Brill, 1992.

Le Goff, Jacques. *Memory and History*. Trans. Steven Randall and Elizabeth Claman. New York: Columbia UP, 1992.

Mackay, Angus. *Spain in the Middle Ages: From Frontier to Empire, 1000-1500*. New York: St. Martin's Press, 1977.

Makki, Maḥmud. "The Political History of al-Andalus (92/711-897/1492)" in Salma Khadra Jayussi, ed., *The Legacy of Muslim Spain*, 3-87. Leiden: E.J. Brill, 1992.

Maravall, José Antonio. "El pre-renacimiento del siglo XV." In Victor García de la Concha, ed., *Nebrija y la introducción del Renacentismo en España*, 17-36. Salamanca: Diputación Provincial, 1981.

McLuhan, Marshall. *Understanding Media: The Extensions of Man*. New York: Signet, 1964.

Mercadal, José García. *Viajes de extranjeros por España y Portugal: Desde los tiempos mas remotos hasta fines del siglo XVI*. Madrid: Aguilar, 1952.

Meyers, David N. "Between Diaspora and Zion: History, Memory and the Jerusalem Scholars." In David N. Meyers and David B. Ruderman, eds., *The Jewish Past Revisited: Reflections on Modern Jewish Historians*, 88-103. New Haven: Yale UP, 1988.

Monroe, James T. "The Hispanic-Arabic World." In José Rubia Barcia, ed., *Américo Castro and the Meaning of Spanish Civilization*, 69-90. Berkeley: U of California P, 1976.

Naveh, Sharon. "Hebrew as the Holy Tongue: The Hebrew Poets of Medieval Spain and Jewish Tradition on Language." Master's thesis, Villanova University, November 1998.

Nebrija, Antonio de. *Gramática de la lengua castellana* (1492). Ed. Antonio Quillis. Madrid: Editoria Nacional, 1980.

Pulido, Ángel Fernandez. *Españoles sin patria y la raza sefardí.* Madrid: Librería de Fernando Fe, 1905.

Rico, Francisco. "Lección y herencia de Elio Antonio Nebrija, 1481-1981." In *Nebrija y la introducción del Renacentismo en España*, 9-14. Ed. Victor García de la Concha. Salamanca: Diputación Provincial, 1981.

Rodríguez-Puértolas, Julio. "A Comprehensive View of Medieval Spain." In José Rubia Barcia, ed., *Américo Castro and the Meaning of Spanish Civilization*, 113-34. Berkeley: U of California P, 1976.

Safran, Janina. "The Command of the Faithful in Al-Andalus: A Study in the Articulation of Caliphal Legitimacy." In *Internaitonal Journal of Middle East Studies*, 30, no. 2 (May 1998): 183-98.

Scheindlin, Raymond P. "The Jews in Muslim Spain." In Salma Khadra Jayussi, ed., *The Legacy of Muslim Spain*, 188-200. Leiden: E.J. Brill, 1992.

Stillman, Yedida K., and Norman Stillman, eds. *From Iberia to Diaspora: Studies in Sephardic History and Culture*. Leiden: E.J. Brill, 1998.

Velasco, Horacio. "Signos y sentidos de la identidad de los pueblos castellanos: el concepto de pueblo y la identidad." In Richard Herr and John H.R. Polt, eds., *Iberian Identity: Essays on the Nature of Identity in Portugal and Spain*, 81-97. Berkeley: U of California P, 1989.

Vives, Juan Luis. "De las disciplinas." In M. Aguilar, ed. Lorenzo Biber, trans., "Obras de educación," Book 3 of *Obras Completas de Juan Luis Vives*, 573-87. Madrid: Real Academia Española, 1948.

Yates, Frances. *The Art of Memory*. Chicago: U of Chicago P, 1966. Reprinted 1984.

Zamora, Margarita. *Language, Authority and Indigenous History in the Comentarios Reales de los Incas*. Cambridge: Cambridge UP, 1988.

_____. "In the Margins of Columbus," and "Voyage to Paradise." In *Reading Columbus*. 63-94; 95-139. Berkeley: U of California P, 1993.

Zerubavel, Eviatar. *Social Mindscapes*. Cambridge: Harvard UP, 1997.

Ziffer, Benny. *La Marche Turque*. Tel Aviv: Am Oved, 1995 (Hebrew).

◆ Chapter 1

"We've *Always* Sung It That Way": Re/Appropriation of Medieval Spanish Jewish Culture in a Galician Town

Judith R. Cohen

"You know, if you want to see the *real* Jews, the real ones from the Inquisition, they're right near here, in Ribadavia." I was told this several times during research in Spain and Portugal, in 1995-97: in a tiny mountain hamlet in Galicia; on the midnight train out of Vigo; at a Jewish New Year dinner in a private home in Madrid. None of these people knew of my personal and professional involvement with Ribadavia, a small town in Galicia; rather, the remarks were spontaneous reactions to my explanation of my presence in that part of the Peninsula: research on the musical ethnography of Crypto-Jewish regions of the Spanish-Portuguese border areas.[1]

The most obvious question arising from this encounter is: "Well, *are* there 'real' Jews in Ribadavia?" Is this really an exotic, out-of-the-way remnant of circa-Expulsion Peninsular Jewish life? If not—then what is it? In order to answer this question, several levels of investigation are involved. On an immediate level, there is the town's annual

Festa da Istoria, the event which has highlighted the historical Jewish presence in Ribadavia, while helping turn it into a complex mixture of history, memory, image-making, fantasy, and tourism. The *Festa* in turn must be situated within the context of the Spanish Quincentennial of 1992, marking both Columbus's voyage and the expulsion of the Jews from Spain. This year and its related and generated activities, are tied to a Spanish preoccupation with repossessing their pre-Expulsion past, sometimes adjusting their memories of it in the process. This in turn leads to the examination of such issues as cultural appropriation, insider-outsider status, folklorization, and the anthropological study of tourism.

Reclaiming the Past and Its Memories: Ribadavia and Its *Festa da Istoria*

The main focus of this essay is the annual *Festa da Istoria*, which takes place in Ribadavia (Orense Province), a small inland town of some three thousand residents, not far from the Portuguese border, on the Avia River which gave it its name. I have commented elsewhere on certain aspects of the *Festa da Istoria* and particularly on its appropriation of Moroccan and eastern Mediterranean Judeo-Spanish songs as part of local repertoire (Cohen 1996). Here I will update the discussion of the use of music and folklore in the *Festa da Istoria*, and briefly relate it to some other events in Spain and Portugal, in an attempt to examine how memory and recall work together with invention and reinvention to rework an image of medieval Spain. The data presented below were obtained largely through ethnographic participant observation: my roles in Ribadavia have included musical performer, consultant, academic researcher, workshop leader, and friend, from late 1993 through to the present. These simultaneous, overlapping roles have provided a multifaceted perspective. As well, during the same period, my ongoing research projects in Judeo-Spanish music, and in musical traditions of historically Crypto-Jewish areas along the Spanish/Portuguese border, have enabled me to view Ribadavia and its *Festa* within a broader context.

After Franco's death and the end of the Spanish dictatorship, Spain became preoccupied with presenting itself as an open, modern country and culture. An ongoing problem has been the persistence of the *"España Negra"* image, and one of the "blackest" aspects of Spanish history is, not surprisingly, the Catholic Inquisition, accompanied by the expulsion of the Jews, and, later, the Muslims. One way to make the history of the Jewish presence in Spain seem less *negra* has been to promote the concept of *convivencia*, a rather rosy vision of the three monotheistic religions convivially sharing the Peninsula. One way to awaken and then reinforce or even "correct" memories of this supposedly convivial tricultural past is to offer concrete remnants of it in the form of "authenticated" *barrios judíos,* "Jewish quarters," in cities, towns, and villages all over the country. As 1992, the quincentennial of the main expulsion date (in Portugal, the expulsion/mass forced conversion date was 1497) approached, and after Spain established diplomatic relations with Israel in 1986, a plethora of activities began, many of which, in 1998, are still going on, or have paved the way for new ones. These have included academic conferences and publications, festivals, recordings, broadcasts, tourist office brochures, and tours of "Jewish Spain."

Memory, Tourism, and the Social Scientists

Before going on to the details of the *Festa* and its role, let us take a brief look at recent developments in scholarly approaches to tourism's impact on both traditional arts and perceptions of authenticity and of history; many of these studies were inspired by British historian Eric Hobsbawm's seminal collection *The Invention of Tradition*—or by the title itself. In the past couple of decades, scholarly interest in tourism has gathered considerable momentum: as Davydd Greenwood puts it, ". . . now, like the tourists themselves, social researchers are flocking to tourist centers" (quoted in Bendix 1989, 133). One scholarly trend exemplifies the past two decades' aversion to any anthropological statement which resembles a value judgment: changes, even outright inventions are not negative, they are transformations, or new cultural expressions. A different approach, much less apparent in anthropology and its related disciplines, deplores anything identifiable as a falsification of known facts, refusing it any new creative status. Thus, harnessing and reshaping memory may be seen in neutral, implicitly positive, terms by one group of scholars, and as reprehensible by another.

Folklorist Barbara Kirshenblatt-Gimblett is one of the scholars who discusses the problem of appropriating and marketing the past in fairly neutral terms. Using the term "transvaluation," she defines "heritage" as "a mode of cultural production in the present that has recourse to the past" (1995, 369). Jules-Rosette found (quoted in Bendix 1989, 133) that artisans involved in producing tourist arts developed their own aesthetic within this new "genre" and in fact "eventually appropriated an externally imposed notion of authenticity." For Martí, a "folklorized version" of a given song, dance, ritual, or fiesta is a "faithful and authentic manifestation of its real sociocultural context" (quoted in Bendix 1989, 226). "Staged authenticity" may not be a travesty, for "folklorists have also begun to deconstruct the scholarly; the concept of tradition . . . what was previously categorized as 'impure' and 'anomalous' can suddenly belong to the realm of expressive culture" (132), or be related to "working in the present" (see essays in Fox 1991). Ironically, the very scholars who spurn nineteenth-century romanticism seem to have developed a late-twentieth-century version of it in their "I'm-okay-you're-okay" vision.

Ethnomusicology, while it often reflects this "nonjudgmental" approach, at other times may be less romantically oriented. Ethnomusicologists Malm and Wallis (1988) express some ambivalence: on the one hand "commercial revitalization" generated by tourism may have positive results for them; on the other, traditional music and dance are altered and repackaged for tourists who "seem to want what they believe is authentic traditional culture," leading to the threat of increasing "cultural domination and exploitation" (187).

Ethnomusicologist René Lysloff takes Malm and Willis's almost cautious reservations further, speaking of "plunderphonics" in the following manner: "history itself is the object of economic exploitation and expansion, offering a virtually limitless supply of natural and cultural resources while also providing an abundance of cheap industrial labor as well as a vast market for inexpensive and disposable manufactured goods. In a nutshell, the past becomes the future's third world" (Lysloff 1997, 206). This reflection provides a thought-provoking gloss on the studied neutrality of Kirshenblatt-Gimblett's reflection that "the attribution of pastness creates a distance that can be travelled" (1995, 370), or James Clifford's extended and perhaps rather forced use of travel as an academic metaphor (1997).

Meanwhile, another form of travel has become available, in the form of electronic home pages and discussion lists—in a way, virtual pilgrim routes. Conferences and festivals are held in (and about) the renovated old Jewish quarters, and ever-increasing numbers of tourist buses pull up in predictable spots in both Spain and Portugal. All these voices—the scholarly and the popular, the magic and the academic or materialistic-skeptic, those of the historian and of the tourist brochure writer, can no longer be treated exclusively. For better or for worse, this new phenomenon of tourism and scholarship as fellow travelers through cyberspace, shaping collective memory along the way, is likely to grow dramatically in the near future, and it is becoming impractical to consider either aspect without the other.

Discovering and Refurbishing Sephardic Remnants

The development of the idea of touring the Iberian Jewish past exemplifies Dean MacCannell's classic study of tourism and anthropology, partcularly in MacCannell's notions of sight sacralization, ritualization of attitude front/back areas, and the semiotics of tourism (1976, 42 ff). While many Iberian cities, towns, and villages can be shown to have had at least some level of historical Jewish presence, eight Spanish towns were selected in the mid-1990s to form in conjunction the *Caminos de Sefarad*, "Routes of Sepharad": Cáceres, Córdoba, Girona, Hervás, Ribadavia, Segovia, Toledo, and Tudela. Each of these, as well as several other places, such as Tomar and Castelo de

Vide in Portugal, can boast the remnants of former Jewish or *converso* neighborhoods (old Jewish quarters). In many cases synagogues and old Jewish quarters have been named or identified (sacralized), then restored, framed, and/or enshrined, and given semiotic markers following a process described by MacCannell. Such semiotic markers might include decorative wall plaques, usually along the lines of *Barrio Judío Medieval*, "Medieval Jewish neighborhood," and other indicators of tourist itineraries. Here the concept of tourist as not only traveler, but also as pilgrim comes into play: the very use of the word "*camino*" recalls not only pilgrimage in general but, more specifically, the famous *Camino de Santiago*, the road to the pilgrimage site of Saint James of Compostela, little more an hour's drive from Ribadavia.

While many identifications of "sacralized sites" are accurate, such as the famous Samuel Lévi synagogue, now the Jewish Museum of Toledo, others may be partly conjecture, or else they may not coincide totally with historical documentation. Hervás boasts a well-indicated and satisfyingly picturesque *barrio judío*, whose inhabitants are always ready to oblige awestruck tourist/pilgrims with tidbits of collective "memory," while the entrance to the town is dominated by a huge billboard advertisement for the *Hotel Sinagoga*. But no consensus seems to have been reached on which of the buildings confidently and even officially promoted as the "medieval synagogue" actually was this sanctuary—if, indeed, it is any of them. In fact here in tourist-friendly Hervás, it seems that there *was* no actual *barrio*, either in documents or in oral tradition: Jews did live there, but not in a "Jewish quarter" (Cohen interviews in Hervás August 19, 1996,

July 17-18, 1998; Marciano de Hervás 1997 "Los judíos," 11).

Historian Marciano de Hervás has no patience with the "it's a hybrid new expressive culture" viewpoint. His detailed and carefully documented analysis of "apocryphal legends about the Jews of Hervás" (1997) is replete with such unequivocable terms as "pseudomythology" (178), "pseudohistorical stories" (182), "falsifications" and "deformations" (202) which have become "the most dangerous enemies of the history of a town . . ." (202). One of the most fascinating aspects of the Hervás situation is the interplay of popular memory with its manipulation by institutional publications and proclamations. In one of Hervas's tourist booklets, Miguel Gómez Andrea voices an objection to "materialist excepticysts," articulating a wistful preference for "the magical side of life," ("Algunos misterios hervansenses," *Ferias*, Ayuntmiento de Hervás). This "magic side" of life reaches what may be its nadir in the tourist office's comic book (Roa and Gómez Andrea 1996). In this popular sales item, superficially presented historical elements are interspersed with scenes in which a middle-aged Sephardic woman explores her Iberian roots with her son (who does the driving), and every few pages has sudden dizzying, mystical visions of her own ancestors' past in Hervás.

Not too far from Hervás, almost at the Portuguese border, is Valencia de Alcántara, where the local historian, Señor Bejarano, commented to me that the Jews of the town did not have a separate neighbourhood; the *Barrio Gótico/Judío*, he quipped, "is neither *barrio* nor Gothic nor Jewish, just as Santillana del Mar is neither saintly nor flat nor of the sea!"[2] Historians, archaeologists, and tourist brochure writers have developed a veritable obsession with hunting down and counting up symbols such as crosses on doorways placed to ward off the Inquisition, or seven-branched figures representing the Jewish menorah: objects become "sacralized" and sites highlighted. These signs and sites serve several functions: emphasizing their presence fortifies the reconstructed memory of Spain's Jewish past. The fact that the engravings may be found on actual houses rather than relegated to museums gives the tourist/pilgrim the impression of having penetrated what MacCannell terms "back" areas (1976 92, 101), or those spaces reserved for the discerning traveler who does not what to be seen as part of tourist "rabble." Retiring for a round of drinks in Ribadavia's *Bar O Xudeu* (Bar of the Jew), fulfills a similar back-area function, though from the opposite perspective of carnivalesque desacralization.

Identification of formerly Jewish or *converso* areas, then, has often been a combination of scholarship and popular culture: historical and archeological research, local oral tradition, and at times tourism strategies, personal interpretations, or even wishful thinking. Scholars have been asked to contribute short, accessible pieces for inclusion in tourist brochures or recording jacket notes, or to speak at Sephardic festivals whose popular aspect is very different from the atmosphere of an academic conference. The lay person also receives information from nonscholarly sources, such as tourist offices, television shows, films, newspaper articles, electronic websites, and so forth. Add local oral traditions, and sprinkle liberally with romantic notions of a medieval past and miraculous survivals, and what seems to appear is a re-remembered medieval Jewish Iberia which is acquiring its own traditional status.

Ribadavia and Its *Festa da Istoria*

In the late Middle Ages, Ribadavia's Jewish population was estimated by the chronicler Froissart to stand at fifteen hundred (1871, 2:11), a figure which historians usually find exaggerated. Whatever their numbers, the medieval Ribadavia Jews played a prominent role in the unsuccessful defense of the town against the duke of Lancaster in 1386, in retaliation for which their homes were sacked by the English (see Meruéndano 1981; Onega 1981; Atienza 1986). After the expulsion of a percentage of the Jews from Portugal, Portuguese Jews took refuge in and near Ribadavia, and over the next century established and maintained contacts with Jewish communities in southern France, in Amsterdam, and in Venice (Estévez 1993, 54-55).The Inquisition arrived relatively late in Ribadavia, and it is thought that many Jews remained as *conversos* there and/or nearby, so that there may well be a high proportion of their descendants in the town and surrounding areas. This, of course, is the case in much of the Iberian Peninsula; in fact, there seems to be almost as much effort put into recuperating its Jewish past as there formerly was to eradicating what was its Jewish present.

Today, though there are no Jews in Ribadavia (when I first visited in 1994 there were two households, neither one of Spanish descent, and both recent arrivals), the town is an integral part of the Spanish *Caminos de Sefarad,* along with several others, and has been receiving increasing attention from tourists. It has played host to conferences and festivals on Sephardic themes, and a large conference on old Jewish quarters in 1997. Meanwhile, its own old Jewish quarter has been declared a cultural monument. The former synagogue and the *mikveh* (ritual bath) are currently privately owned; in fact, the latter is now part of the floor of a popular bar (residents advise ordering a drink and staying awhile before looking around to identify the water pipes, so as not to antagonize the owner, who needs to keep his business viable). Among its residents, Ribadavia's *barrio judío* is part of local memory, as it has always been recognized in oral tradition, and referred to with pride and affection: "my family has *always* lived here." These memories have now been formalized, and the old Jewish quarter sacralized, with its marker at the entrance off the plaza.

Now, a decade since the old Jewish quarter was so marked, its resident women have added recently acquired Judeo-Spanish songs to their "memories," so that the latter have veritably become a hybrid of memory and construct. These songs are of relatively recent composition, and the women have learned them only over the past few years, mostly from recordings. It is common in traditional cultures for a song to acquire "generations" status after only one or two generations have sung it; in Ribadavia this elevation from acquisition to remembered tradition seems to have been accelerated by the ongoing pressure to generate ever more collective "memories" of a Sephardic past, even if the songs themselves are a few centuries younger than the actual "remembered" period.

The origins of the *Festa da Istoria* are linked to Ribadavia's *conversos*, and go back to the late sixteenth and early seventeenth centuries, through the mid-nineteenth. The *Istoria* was a street performance of a play, often by a *converso* author, with Old Testament themes and characters. Various plays were associated with the festival, including *La Prudente Abigail* and other works by the seventeenth-century *converso* poet Antonio Enriquez Gómez. In 1986 a group of residents concerned about the survival of the Jewish quarter came up with the idea of reviving the *Festa da Istoria* and adapting it to appeal to a broad public.[3] José-Ramón Aparicio, one of the group, prepared a new dramatic work for the festival: *El malsín*. The early September date was retained, and, more importantly, the historic location in the old Jewish quarter. In 1989 the group formed the Centro de Estudis Medievais, and have continued their activities under that name. The reconfiguration of the old *Festa da Istoria*, combining history, education, reinforcement of local identity, fund-raising, and entertainment, is hardly an isolated phenomenon in Spain. Catalan ethnomusicologist Josep Martí describes the 1975 revival/re-creation of an extinct festival, in Mallorca, at the other end of the Peninsula from Galicia. This, like the *Festa da Istoria* in Ribadavia, has now become "traditional": "out of the ashes rose a new festival, or in better terms, an 'ancient festival was invented'" (1996,139). In fact the Ribadavia *Festa da Istoria* itself now has several clones or semiclones scattered both around the area and further afield (Cohen, communication with R. Aparicio, March 9, 1998).

As of 1998, the *Festa da Istoria* has been held in its revived and adapted form for a decade, with a Sephardic mock-wedding included from 1993 on. The *Festa da Istoria* attracted ten thousand visitors in 1993, and an estimated thirty to thirty-five thousand in 1997—this in a town of only three thousand. As it became an important tourist attraction, Ribadavia's Town Hall took over most of its management and organization from the original organizers, appointing a *coordinadora* (organizing committee). According to some original Centro de Estudis Medievais members, this new committee has neglected aspects of the Jewish components of the *Festa da Istoria*, while emphasizing the commercial aspects of the medieval components overall. At the same time, the *convivencia* myth has been emphasized, as was pointed out to me recently by José-Ramón Aparicio (Cohen, communication March 10, 1998). While at the local level this shift toward commodification led to some tension between the *coordinadora* and the original Centro de Estudis Medievais, in more neutral terms, it reflects the "value-added" nature of the heritage industry as discussed by Barabara Kirshenblatt-Gimblett: adding value to "existing assets that have either ceased to be viable . . . or never were economically productive" (1995, 370).

At first glance, particularly with the emphasis on tourist-aimed "medievalism," the *Festa da Istoria* could be any self-styled medieval or renaissance fair in some modern urban center. Physically, unlike the situation in North American towns, the medieval aspect need not be re-created since it already exists. In the early years of the *Festa da Istoria*, many artisans in the street markets were actually practising their own crafts and skills rather than re-creating them, and the mounted "knights" in the mock tournament were not imports from the Society for Creative Anachronism, but almost all local village men, which recalls Bendix's "strategic use of local symbols . . . cows and goats, herdsmen in costume" (1989, 138). A common strategy of creating "back areas" for tourists is making a "fetish of the work of others" (MacCannell 1976, 6), and some craftspeople have adapted their work for public display at the festival. Local baker Herminia's traditional six-pointed pastries have become a symbol of Ribadavia's Jewish past; correspondingly, her bakery has become an official "sight" and sports a new "marker": a medieval-style sign and matching paper bags, advertising "*Doce Artesanal, Especialidade en Doces Hebreos*," "Creative Confectioners,

Specializing in Hebrew Pastries." One might wonder just what constitutes a "Hebrew pastry," but meanwhile Herminia is assiduously collecting recipes from around the Sephardic diaspora to reconstruct a culinary past, whose authenticity visitors seldom question past the first happy bite.

The day's program, as I saw it in 1996, had been more or less set for a few years. It opened with a midmorning parade followed by electronically amplified announcements in the main square, temporarily sacralized by restoring its social gathering function, as distinct from its usual function as a parking lot. Rodriguez describes a similar plaza transformation at a New Mexican event, "during [a] fiesta the plaza becomes the transformed site of multiple social, symbolic, and political inversions . . ." (1998, 45). In Ribadavia visitors lined up to purchase the special currency used for the *Festa da Istoria*, the old maravedí; the exchange goes toward covering costs. Scheduled activities included children dressed and moving about as giant chess pieces; a pseudomedieval women's dance, a few concerts of baroque or Sephardic or local traditional music (seldom, if ever, music which actually corresponded to the medieval period suggested by the event), a late night, quite expensive "medieval dinner," and an evening theater production, often of the *Malsín*.

An innovation in 1996 lay in refusing admission to the grounds of the local castle ruins, normally an open, public space, to anyone not in "medieval" garb: the sign reads, "*só xente vestida de época*," "visitors in periodic garb only"—an example of MacCannell's "sight . . . dominated by some *action* that occurred in the past" (1976, 127). This new regulation, whose enforcement required extra personnel, may have been inspired by the increased presence of television and newspaper cameras, and encouraged by the costume rental stores set up for the event. Food, wine, and crafts booths ran all day throughout the narrow streets of the *barrio judío*, though the crafts have become progressively less "medieval" every year. In 1996 there was an attempt to ban street musicians: young Galician bagpipers playing traditional dance tunes to African and Middle Eastern drums, and *Festa* visitors dancing in festive spontaneity, were ordered to stop, as they were not part of the program! This may have seemed ironic for a supposedly "medieval" street festival, but in fact, it typified the frequent tension in festivals between carnival-type subversion/inversion and institutional insistence on control.

Jewish Elements in the *Festa da Istoria*

The two main "Jewish" aspects of the program are the "Sephardic wedding" performance and a 1996 innovation, an actual Friday night Sabbath service. The *coordinadora* has opened an "official" souvenir store in the old Jewish quarter, with the laconically Jewish name "Menorah." Octopus and sausage stands are nothing unusual for the area, but along with the pork sausages and ham sandwiches, they are totally contrary to the Jewish dietary laws. The ubiquity of these meats aside, displaying them under bright banners sporting the Magen David, the Star of David, seemed incongruous at best. However, no one I spoke to found the use of these markers even ironic, let alone inappropriate or sacriligious/desacralizing. This showed a curious lapse of concern, considering that the absence of these foods in a *converso* household often served to betray it to the Inquisition. Outside the *Festa* itself, but also organized by the Centro de Estudis Medievais, and held around the same time, were two other activities: a 1991 academic conference (see Barros 1994), and a 1994 conference and festival of Sephardic music entitled, "Sons de Matria." Similar events are being planned for the future.

The "Sephardic Wedding" and Tradition

The *Voda Sefardi*, the "Sephardic wedding," has been a main feature of the *Festa da Istoria*, since its inception. As the *Festa da Istoria* is held on a Saturday, this means the mock wedding is as well, contravening Jewish practice since weddings cannot be held on the Sabbath. Interestingly, it was not the Centro de Estudis Medievais, but a group of women from the Jewish quarter itself who in 1992 came up with the idea of staging a Sephardic wedding as part of the *Festa da Istoria*. These women began their own research, initially on period costumes. As performed, the *Voda*, "wedding," includes a pastiche of musical and ceremonial elements from post-Expulsion Moroccan and Ottoman Sephardic cultures, strung together with at least as much creativity as authenticity. The representation of the actual wedding ceremony originally took place in an outdoor "synagogue" specially erected for the event, but in 1996 moved to the Madalena, a church in the old Jewish quarter.

This site was first desacralized as Christian, its customary decorations and functional objects removed, and was then resacralized for both the mock wedding and the Friday night service to welcome in the Jewish Sabbath. A *ketubbá*, "wedding contract," calligraphed by a local artist is read out. The ritual readings in Hebrew are carried out by a Ribadavian who is an ex-priest, now married and a father. When the original association was in charge of the event, as

I saw in the video of the 1993 *Festa da Istoria,* the mock wedding was allotted much more time, and included the "couple's" being led to a specially prepared bed, as well as more songs and dancing in the streets. As I saw and filmed it in 1996, with the responsibility mostly taken over by the *coordinadora*, the "wedding" lasted much less time. There was no dancing, only a few songs were performed, and much of the musical style which had been developed in the first couple of years had eroded away—ironically encapsulating the gradual, inexorable demise of "real" traditional weddings.

It would take too long to describe, much less analyze, every change, inaccuracy, or omission of the staged wedding, though it is irresistible to mention such immortal scenes in the 1993 video as the bride in her elaborate, if historically irrelevant, Moroccan wedding garb calmly smoking a cigarette, and then, contrary to Orthodox Jewish custom, dancing with the "rabbi"! As an ethnomusicologist, my attention was first drawn to the selection and performance style of the song repertoire. It is important to realize that no traditional Judeo-Spanish tunes that we know of have survived from the Middle Ages, either for the Sephardic or other Iberian communities. Folk songs melodies were not generally written down until much later, and, while some early texts have survived, their melodies have changed, new or local melodies have been adopted, and new songs have been composed; so an "authentic" pre-Expulsion musical re-creation is not a possibility.[4]

Though Judeo-Spanish songs do not constitute part of the early music corpus, the myth of their medieval origins has persisted, and they have often been given an early music interpretation permeated with cavalier anachronisms, not only at the *Festa da Istoria* but in recordings from many different countries over the past two decades.[5] For the first of the staged weddings, in 1993, the organizers gathered whatever recordings of Judeo-Spanish songs were available to them, from both the Moroccan and eastern Mediterranean Sephardic traditions, in a range of traditional and more modern styles. By sheer coincidence, as the selections were made before we had met, these recordings included one by my own Sephardic performance group.[6] There were also non-Sephardic songs, including a local, relatively recent composition entitled "Let the Jews Go By!" [*A los judíos dejad pasar*], referring to the inhabitants of the Jewish quarter.

José-Ramón Aparicio coordinated the singing. Rather than impose his choice on the singers, he invited them to listen to the recordings together and make their own selections. This ended up as a mixture of older-style traditional songs and more modern items; the unifying factor in the selection of the repertoire was the songs' appeal to the singers, and the likelihood of their being sung with conviction. Most of the singers' favorite item was not one of the older traditional songs, but the early-twentieth-century Turkish Sephardic hit "I'd Give My Life For *Rakí*."[7] In 1995 I taught the singers a few traditional wedding songs, basing my selection on my observation of what had appealed to them earlier.[8] While I was there, a group of mandolin players was also working on a selection of songs by Bosnian-Sephardic-American Flory Jagoda, who had performed in Ribadavia's 1994 Sephardic Festival, and had subsequently sent the organizers a song she composed about her experience there. In 1996 the songs featured in the *Festa* were mostly songs composed and/or introduced by Mrs. Jagoda—that is, songs that no one could possibly mistake for being of "medieval" origin, and a similar emphasis was planned for 1997.

Changes to the Songs: Appropriation or Reclaiming?

Aparicio had tried to avoid or at least modify the occidental choir sound which many of the women had acquired from years of singing in a choral group. However, as the women worked entirely aurally/orally, and were used to singing both choir music and the local repertoire, they made unconscious changes to the *Festa* songs as they learned them, and integrated them into their own repertoire of local folk songs. These, however, were rather different from the type of typical changes discussed by Martí, which mostly relate to simplification and occidentalization (1996, 75-76). Some, such as altering Judeo-Spanish to standard Castilian pronunciation, minor rhythmic adjustments, or occasional harmonizing in thirds, are easily explained by local practice. I was especially intrigued, however, by melodic changes the women made in two songs; Aparicio had in fact detected one of them, and tried to correct it, but explained that the guitarist kept playing it "their" way, while the women went back and forth between the two versions. This suggested to me that in their "emic" perception there was no difference between the two pitches.[9]

In 1995 the women I interviewed about these changes did not initially perceive "their" version as any different from the original. I sang the song with them several times, all of us stopping on and holding the altered notes: only then did they agree that their version was different, and suggested it was a "bad habit." I suggested that it was simply different, and asked whether they wanted to change it to the original version. The women replied simply, "We've *always* sung it that way." ("Always"??) This matter-of-fact remark astonished me, for it suggested that not only had they integrated Sephardic songs into their repertoire five hundred years after Sephardic Jews had officially ceased to live there, and not only did they feel comfortable enough to make changes in these songs, but they had even appropriated them as part of their own oral tradition, part of their own memories, knowing perfectly well that they had been introduced from outside only a year earlier! This raises quite a different set of issues from the "plunderphonics" which is preoccupying many ethnomusicologists today (see Lysloff 1997), since the "plundering,"or "appropriating" which has been wreaking havoc on the intellectual ethics of ethnomusicology can be seen in this case as possibly coming from actual descendants of the original group.

Sons de Matria: Ribadavia's Sephardic Festival

Another Ribadavia event with a large, in fact predominantly, musical component, was the 1994 Sephardic festival. This took place only a couple of weeks before that year's *Festa da Istoria*, and complemented the interest in Sephardic culture sparked by the Jewish wedding enactment, and by a very successful academic conference the committee had organized in 1991. The festival, called "Sons de Matria" (all the performers were women), also included academic talks by specialists on various aspects of Judeo-Spanish culture; a more informal version of the 1991 conference. Since the performances and lectures were held in the same time frame, performers, speakers, and townspeople spent their evenings together after the presentations, talking and singing in bars or cafés into the early morning hours while the open-air bar in the main square continually played performers' tapes. In this way, not only were Judeo-Spanish songs further integrated into the local repertoire, but the staged wedding, the *Festa da Istoria*, and the new festival's concerts and lectures reinforced each other, contributing to a general awareness of Sephardic culture. By 1997 many of the songs from both events still remained in the local repertoire, and, as mentioned above, those by Flory Jagoda formed a central part of the formal concerts of the *Festa da Istoria.*

The Friday Night Sabbath (*Shabbat*) at the *Festa da Istoria*: Performance or Service?

In 1996 the small (under fifty) Jewish community of Porto, some three hours southwest of Ribadavia in Portugal, decided to hold a Friday night Sabbath service in Ribadavia's old Jewish quarter the night before the *Festa da Istoria* opened. The "Sephardic wedding" at the *Festa da Istoria* had always been presented as a performance, never as a "real" wedding, so it was difficult to explain to a public with little or no knowledge of Jewish tradition that this was *not* a performance of some imagined historical vestige.

Porto was home to Arturo de Barros Basto, the charismatic figure who dedicated most of his life to his grandiose project of "redeeming" the Portuguese Crypto-Jews in the first half of this century. The community today is very small, but cohesive and active; it includes Jews from outside Portugal with no connection to Crypto-Judaism, as well as descendants of the latter, now converted to formal Judaism. So, as the Sabbath service was their own idea, rather than a program event conceived for the occasion, as was the Ribadavia wedding, it could be seen as an "insider" reappropriation rather than an outsider "appropriation"—

though, in a rather ironic inversion, it is an "outsider" to the new tradition of the actual *Festa.*

There was no rabbi officiating at this Friday night service. While a rabbi's presence is not required for a service to be held, for an Orthodox service (and Sephardim are, at least in principle, Orthodox), there must be a *minyan*, or quorum, of ten male adults. I counted only nine among the officiants; if there were more, they were from the public—or the "congregation." No clapping, of course, was permitted, but some did take place, again owing to the confusion of service and performance. No photographs or videos could be taken during the actual service; this was, as far as I could see, observed. The service was held in Ribadavia's former church, the Madalena, also typically used for the *Festa*'s staged wedding. This seemed incongruous to some, but most felt that since it no longer has any Christian worhip function or ritual objects, it has become just another building, perhaps even an ironic reversal of the many synagogues transformed into churches after the Expulsion. One might even see it as a resacralization through desacralization. At the conclusion of the service, the (non-Jewish) members of the local singing group appeared with guitars, unaware that observant Orthodox Jews, including Sephardim, do not use instruments on the Sabbath and certainly not in the synagogue. They sang a variety of well-known Judeo-Spanish and Hebrew songs of relatively recent vintage, further blurring the boundaries between worship service and performance, particularly for the public. The entire service was over before sundown, whereas to welcome in the Sabbath it should have ended after sundown, when Sabbath (and any Jewish holiday) officially begins.

The Porto group considered it a true service, but how were the tourists to know this? A good deal of discussion took place about whether an actual religious event should be included in what was a liberally interpreted, commercially presented historical recreation. Indeed, for most of the attendees, the service was just another part of the "show." While journalists and television crews were cooperative about not filming it, many members of the "audience" (which, of course, should have been a congregation) automatically applauded, though they had been asked not to. The initiative for the service came from the group itself; that is, it was insider-initiated, but no rabbi was present—would a Sephardic rabbi have agreed to the event? It might be argued that in some ways it was no more "authentic" than the staged wedding. This raises questions about what defines a ritual as "authentic," and who can make or legitimize changes to it. Whatever one's opinion, as of early August 1997, the Porto group had already reserved nearby hotel rooms for a larger delegation, to hold a similar service for the 1997 *Festa da Istoria.*

Selective Searching for "Authenticity"

My own role in the 1994 "Sons de Matria" festival, besides performing, included ensuring that all the performers chosen were either Sephardic themselves or had worked closely with traditional Sephardic singers. This, however, was a one-time occasion; the annual staged wedding is not actually monitored for inaccuracies, historical or ethnographic. In 1995 I asked Aparicio whether the substantial Jewish community in Madrid had been involved in planning the wedding, or had attended and/or reacted to its performance. He explained that, while he felt the planning committee were on fairly solid historical ground concerning the origins and general plan of the *Festa da Istoria* itself, he had in fact been concerned about the representation of the wedding ceremony. Besides reading what materials were available, he had tried to consult the Madrid community, but with limited success. (It should be noted that Madrid is at least six hours' drive from Ribadavia, and that the committee members all had day jobs unrelated to the *Festa*; this, together with a budget that was limited at best, made ongoing consultation difficult.)

Originally, some members of the Madrid Jewish community had planned to attend the festival. The fact that it was held on a Saturday, the Jewish Sabbath, made this impossible on a community level, however, and in fact generated some negative feeling. Several Argentinian Jews, who tend to be more loosely associated with the Jewish community, did attend and they reacted enthusiastically. Later the organizers were able to show the video to some members of the Madrid community, and they commented that the younger adults, in particular, liked it.

In July 1995 I discussed the *Festa da Istoria* and staged wedding with the rabbi in Madrid, and a couple of older community members. I was able to screen it together with only one member, however, who was known for her expertise in traditional weddings. There was general agreement, including from the rabbi, that, so long as the wedding was put together and performed with respect, there was no objection to the "staged authenticity" (MacCannell 1976, chap. 5) of non-Jews staging a Sephardic wedding. The wedding expert pointed out several errors, from the bride casually smoking in the street, to men and women—including the "rabbi"—dancing together. Several Sephardim, mostly scholars, present at a Judeo-Spanish conference in England viewed it with me; they caught all the errors immediately, but mostly laughed good-humoredly about them. However, these viewers were "insiders" and know what was and wasn't "authentic" in the presentation: for them it corresponded or didn't correspond to their own memories. For most of the public attending the *Festa da Istoria*, they were witnessing a reenactment of memory: "the lie contained in the touristic experience presents itself as a truthful revelation" (102).

How "authentic" or accurate can the *Festa* be, altogether? As the original event, the "*Istoria*," spanned three centuries, it is not obvious which moment would be the "accurate" one to represent. The wedding presents several choices as well: one could omit it altogether; or try to reenact a pre-Expulsion wedding, with more historical accuracy but less music and joie de vivre. One might choose, for example, nineteenth century Salonica, early twentieth century Tangier, some vague ethnographic present—or perhaps an example as specific as the 1992 wedding ceremony I saw in Istanbul with the bride's white European dress and prerecorded music. As for the inaccuracies in the *Festa* wedding's performance aspect, one wonders whether they were any worse than the inaccuracies in the actual Sabbath service, which was *not* intended as a performance. Martí emphasizes that folklorismus has its "own internal dynamic," its own "*nuevo ámbito cultural*," "new cultural environment," which is not part of the world of tradition (1996, 187). However, does this justify the dissemination, conscious or not, of misunderstandings about a culture in the very process of trying to heighten awareness of it?

Whose Tradition Is It, Anyway? Insiders, Outsiders, Rights, and Responsibilities

It is tempting to analyze the Ribadavia events in the context of Spain's interest in Sephardic culture and, more recently, *converso* survivals, especially over the past decade. The para-1992 years saw a dizzying array of festivals, conferences, recordings, and publications related to Judeo-Spanish history and culture. One might see the Ribadavia events as just another few in the series; however, the organizers say clearly that their event was conceived independently and that, in fact, the 1992 events were not particularly noted in Galicia, certainly not in their corner of it.

For me the main difference was not whether the Ribadavia event was conceived independently of *Sefarad 1992*, but rather the feeling of connectedness to Sephardic culture which was evident in the residents. This had already existed to some extent before the *Festa da Istoria*'s revival, and was clearly reinforced by it, and especially by the staged wedding. In fact, the committee members included more than one who had been wondering about Jewish descent in their own families and felt a personal interest in researching the *Festa*'s origins for that reason. Authentic details or not, Ribadavians clearly felt that in many ways Sephardic culture *was* their own.

Kirshenblatt-Gimblett postulates, as a main feature of heritage industry, the "foreignness of the tradition to the presentation context" (1995, 374). In this case, the "foreignness" is only partial, though it is increasing: the Ribadavians are still, to some extent, re-creating and reenacting their own past, in their own streets and castle grounds—one might argue that they are reenacting themselves. But can "reenacting their own past" be extended to their representation of an anachronistically staged Sephardic wedding? The Ribadavia group is, of course, not the first to stage a similar event nor, indeed, to videotape it, though they did arrive at the idea independently. The special interest of the Ribadavia event lies in its conception and execution entirely by non-Jews and nonprofessionals, and its location in a historic pre-Expulsion Jewish quarter whose inhabitants are the main actors in the event. In fact, there is the poignant possibility, even likelihood, that some of them are probably themselves descendants of *conversos*. Bendix reports (1989, 135) that not only "locals" but also "professionals not involved with tourism" felt that their event in Interlaken "did represent authentic cowherders' culture, and that furthermore it was possible to stage, perform and parade this culture." The same could be said of the *Festa*, substituting "authentic medieval Spanish Jews," or at least *conversos*, for "cowherders."

This situation raised questions for me as an ethnomusicologist, beyond trying to understand why the singing women changed some notes in a wedding song. In that same element of the staged wedding, the fact that boundaries between organizers and the public, actors and audience were dissolved for the event, making it an effective learning and human experience, was itself the catalyst for my concern about cultural appropriation. Where a straightforward conference is concerned, the answers are a little easier. But in performance, however laudable the motives, is it ever justifiable to perform aspects of a culture not one's own, particularly aspects concerned with ritual and ceremony, and if so, under what circumstances? How justified, if at all, is it to make changes in the traditions represented; indeed, to what degree is accuracy possible?

Returning to Martí, yes, the folklorized form has its own essential validity, being "absolutely faithful to the sociocultural system from which it has emerged" (1996, 191), even possessing a "semantic and functional coherence in its human context" (192). It can be read as its own "cultural text," just as Lysloff argues for studio recordings of "authentic" field tapes (1997, 210). Kirshenblatt-Gimblett suggests that "heritage is not lost and found, stolen and reclaimed" (1995, 369). Yet perhaps these attractively open-minded approaches need not apply to *all* aspects of heritage, including religion and ritual. The staged wedding of the *Festa da Istoria* may indeed be, like Lysloff's recordings, a new "cultural text," or it may be, as de Hervás sees the reshaping of Hervás's Jewish past, a reprehensible and indeed dangerous falsification. Moving from theoretical to concrete terms, one village woman told Aparicio and myself that one could tell the Ribadavians were "real Jews" because their festival "made so much money" (Cohen, fieldwork tape, Lueda, Orense, July 8, 1997). While the *Festa* may promote positive attitudes of a multicultural past, in this case it ended up working with popular memory reinforcing the very kind of negative stereotype which was a factor in the expulsion of the Jews in the first place!

Inevitably, questions of appropriation bring us to questions about boundaries and identity, about who is the insider, who the outsider, and who is qualified to authenticate these activities, if indeed they can or should be "authenticated." The answers are seldom easy. In Spain in general, and in this remote corner of Spain in particular, where so many people may be descendants of *conversos*, such questions are even more difficult to answer. How much is appropriation and how much reappropriation? When I posed this question at a Spanish ethnomusicology conference in 1996, there was considerable resistance to the idea of appropriation in this context. I came away still wondering whether singing an early-twentieth-century Judeo-Spanish song while roaming the old Jewish quarter in modern versions of medieval garb was simply a commodified anachronism, no matter how laudable the original motive. I wondered whether it was merely part of the para-1992 Spanish enthusiasm for Sephardic culture or the ever-increasing interest in *converso* survivals. Perhaps it is an illustration of the past as part of the heritage industry's "value-added" approach: as Kirshenblatt-Gimblett puts it, this value-added past "transports tourists from a now that signifies hereness to a past that signifies thereness . . . ," part of the "collaborative hallucination" (1995, 375) or the "tourist surreal" (371).

The 1996 addition of the Friday night service, not surprisingly, reinforced the misconception that the *Festa da Istoria* is a long-standing survival of remembered Jewish tradition. Shortly afterward, I spent Jewish New Year in Madrid, and was invited to have lunch at the home of one of the families. Another guest, also Jewish, who knew nothing about my connection to Ribadavia, enthusiastically described her visit to the *Festa da Istoria*, commenting that it was "miraculous" that this "authentic medieval Jewish tradition" had been preserved. It was a theme I was to hear increasingly over the year and one which, again, the tourist propaganda does little to correct. Late in 1994 some original committee members were invited to celebrate the Jewish holiday of Hanukkah with the Porto community. The Ribadavia contingent sang some of the songs which they had learned from recordings for the mock wedding, and though they explained where they had learned the repertoire, the Porto community itself, including a non-

Jewish historian, remained convinced that these songs were "authentic Crypto-Jewish survivals." In 1996 a highly educated Jewish man I interviewed in Lisbon kept insisting that the *Festa da Istoria* "must" be a "veritably Jewish" event and was extremely disappointed when I explained what its origins are. It is as if people are eager to acquire new memories or perhaps reshape the ones they have.

For Aparicio in Ribadavia and his colleagues, the outsider component is indeed present in the Jewish aspects of the *Festa da Istoria* program, but on the other hand, the real outsiders are not the Ribadavians still living a partly traditional life reflected in aspects of the *Festa*, but rather the people brought in from outside to organize it now that it has become "big business." Ribadavians are living "*a caballo entre dos mundos*," "straddling two worlds," as Aparicio puts it: between the traditional and the contemporary, the semirural, and the semiurban. For them, he feels, the outsider component of their rendition of the *Festa* has its own traditional aspect: it is the Ribadavians' vehicle for enabling their traditional "lucid spirit." The latter involves coming to know other people through play and joie de vivre, "*alegría*." This approaches Kirshenblatt-Gimblett's conclusion that it is not a "vivid museum experience" which is "at stake," but that performance is indispensable: "nothing is more multi-sensory than the lifeworld itself, particularly in its most intense, which is to say, its performative modes" (1995, 378-79); the "interface" which creates the "illusion of ethnographic reality" consists of "cultural forms in their own right and powerful engines of meaning" (375).

Lysloff remarks accurately that the ethnomusicologist is "caught in a web of conflicting notions of aesthetics, ethnographic truth, acoustical reality, cultural legitimacy, and specific intellectual interests" (1997, 210). He does not include ethical dilemmas in this already daunting list, but it is another element to be considered. With respect to reimaging Iberia's Jewish past, one should remember that, particularly in areas of Portugal, there is not only a Jewish past, but a Jewish or Crypto-Jewish present as well. The ethics of tourism and, indeed, scholarship, should not be the same for human beings as they are for buildings and streets with a documented, reconstructed, or even imagined past. If, as he suggests, the past is indeed the future's "third world" (206), care must be taken not to consign those who are descended directly from this past back to it.

Meanwhile, for Sephardic Jews watching a video of a representation of their tradition performed inaccurately by outsiders on the Jewish Sabbath, the question must still remain: even if the motivation is all positive, is this representation justified by the actors' sincere conviction that what they are doing is reclaiming a past cruelly taken from them—while educating the public about it? And, after all, historians' interpretations of the past differ widely—witness the deeply differing presentations of the Inquisition and the existence of Crypto-Jews by scholars in the past decade alone, let alone those of the past centuries! All things considered then, which is the truth, and whose representation—or misrepresentation—of the past will most inform the present and the future?

Notes

1. I would like to acknowledge the Office of Research Administration of York University, Toronto, for the research grants which enabled me to carry out fieldwork for this project, York's Music Department for its continuing support; the invaluable expertise and insights of my research assistant José-Ramón Aparicio, of Galicia; and the help with videotaping and photography of my daughter, Tamar Cohen Adams.

A record of my fieldwork relating to this essay and to my wider research is as follows. All of my personal interviews took place in Sephardic and Crypto-Jewish communities and regions in Spain and Portugal between 1991 and 1998, with the assistance of José-Ramón Aparicio. Where no specific dates are noted the conversations were ongoing over several days. Some discussants prefer not to have their names cited when their remarks are quoted or summarized.

Interview in Hervás, Spain, August 19, 1995; with members of the musical performance ensemble "Retama" in Hervás, August 1996, July 1998. Interviews with José-Ramón Aparicio in Ribadavia, Spain, August 10-21, 1994, July 1995, August 1996. Electronic correspondence with José-Ramón Aparicio 1996-1998. Interviews in Vigo, Spain, July 1997, July 25-27, 1998, August 25-30, 1998. Interviews with Centro de Estudis Medievais members, Ribadavia, Spain, August 10-21, 1994, August 28-30, 1996, August 1998; with Ribadavia choir members, July 1995, August 25-31, 1995, August 28-30, 1996, August 1998. Interviews with Ribadavia *Coordinadora da Festa* (*Festa da Istoria* Steering Committee) July 6, 1998, August 25-26, 1998. Interview with F. Bejarano, Valencia de Alcántara, Spain, August 9, 1997; with members of the Oporto Jewish Community, particularly Carlos Prazeres, Porto, Portugal, March 1996, November 1996, April 1998; with Miriam Azancot, Porto, Portugal, may 1997, September 3, 1998; with an anonymous member of the Lisbon Jewish Community, Lisbon, Portugal, December 1996, May 1997, May 1998.

2. Conversation with Señor F. Bejarano, Valencia de Alcántara, August 9, 1997.

3. This series of events is strongly reminiscent of one described by Martí for the festival of Santa Catalina in Porreres, Mallorca: a group of concerned residents recovering and reinventing a lost tradition, researching into past aspects of the festival, and modifying and adding new elements; a source of income for the municipality (1996, 130-42), as well as, to varying degrees of resemblance, other events in Spain and Portugal too numerous to list here.

4. In a recent paper I experimented with setting medieval Hispano-Jewish poetry, some appropriate for weddings, to contemporaneous music which fit the structure of the texts. ("The Ethnomusicologist as Applied Contrafactotum," in preparation for the Acts of the World Union for Jewish Studies Congress, Jerusalem, August 1997).

5. See Judith R. Cohen, "Sonography of Judeo-Spanish Song," *Jewish Folklore and Ethnology Review*, no.15 (1993) and update in no.17 (1995).

6. *Gerineldo*, a Moroccan Judeo-Spanish ensemble founded and directed by my colleague and friend Dr. Oro Anahory-Librowicz, based in Montreal, had only recently begun to distribute recordings in Spain. The other recordings used were those of Gloria Levy, a rerelease on CD of her 1958 Folkways LP; and of Flory Jagoda (Bosnia/USA, 1980s).

7. Eau-de-vie from grapes, popular in the Middle East.

8. In 1995, as part of a minicourse I was teaching on Balkan dance and Balkan and Sephardic singing in Ribadavia, I introduced "Poco le das mi

consuegra," "Oy que buena," "Estas casas tan hermosas" (the latter two with Turkish 9/8 rhythms), and from the Moroccan repertoire, "Raquel lastimosa"; I also worked on correcting "Ansí se me arrimó" and at least pronunciation for "Ya salió de la mar." The biggest success was "Poco le das" sung in dialogue form, where the singers really entered into the spirit of the rival mothers-in-law; the experience of singing while playing the 9/8 karsilama rhythm was also appreciated. None of these, of course, hearkens back to pre- or para-Expulsion times.

9. The change was from a major to a minor third, and is discussed more thoroughly in Cohen 1996. In ethnomusicology, an early adaptation of Kenneth Pike's 1947 coinage of "emic" and "etic" from "phonemic" and "phonetic" was presented by Vida Chenoweth (1972, 50-58). Though one may be cautioned not to "confuse emics with native discourse" (Alvarez-Pereyre and Arom 1983, 12) it is precisely in this popularized, very convenient sense that I am in fact using it: that is, the singers themselves may not consciously distinguish between two intervals as meaningfully different.

Works Cited

Alvarez-Pereyre, Frank, and Simha Arom. "Ethnomusicology and the Emic/Etic Issue," *The World of Music*, no. 35/1 (1983): 7-33.

Atienza, Juan. "Ribadavia: un modelo remoto de integración," *Raíces*, no. 2 (1986): 42-44.

Barros, Carlos. "El otro admitido, la tolerancia hacia los judíos en la edad media Gallega." In *Xudeus e conversos na historia*, 1:85-115. Diputación de Orense, 1994.

Bendix, Regina. "Tourism and Cultural Displays." *Journal of American Folklore*, no. 102/404 (1989): 131-46.

Centro de Estudis Medievais. *Festa da Istoria: Voda Xudea*. Ribadavia, 1993 (booklet and video), program booklets 1995, 1996.

Chenoweth, Vida. *Melodic Perception and Analysis: A Manual on Ethnic Melody*. Papua New Guinea: Summer Institute of Lingusitics, 1972.

Clifford, James. *Routes: Travel and Translation in the late Twentieth Century*. Cambridge: Harvard UP, 1997.

Cohen, Judith R. "Pero la voz es muy educada: Reactions to Evolving Styles in Judeo-Spanish Song Performances." In Winifred Busse and Marie-Christine *Varol eds.*, Sephardica: Hommages à Haim Vidal Sepipha. *Berlin: Peter Lang,* 1996. 65-82.

_____. Fieldwork in Sephardic and Cryptio-Jewish communities and regions in Spain and Portugal between 1991 and 1998, assisted by José-Ramón Aparicio.

_____. Personal interviews August 19 1996, July 17-18, 1998, with residents of Hervás, Spain.

Estévez-Pérez, José Ramón. "Los Judaizantes de Ribadavia." *Nuevo amanecer sefardi* (Uruguay), no. 10 (April 1993): 53-60.

Fox , Richard G., ed. *Recapturing Anthropology.* Santa Fe: School of American Research, 1991.

Froissart, Jean de. *Oeuvres de Froissart: Chroniques.* Vol. 2. 1386. Brussels: V. Deveaux, 1871.

Hervás, Marciano de. "Los judíos de Hervás," Hervás: Artesanía "El Lagar," 1997.

_____. "La invención de la tradición: leyendas apócrifas sobre los judíos de Hervás." *Revista de dialectología y tradiciones populares.* No. 21 (May, 1997): 177-203.

Kirshenblatt-Gimblett, Barbara. "Theorizing Heritage." *Ethnomusicology,* no. 39/3 (1995): 367-80.

Lysloff, René T.A., "Mozart in Mirrorshades: Ethnomusicology, Technology and the Politics of Representation." *Ethnomusicology,* no. 41/2 (1997) 206-19.

MacCannell, Dean. *The Tourist, a New Theory of the Leisure Class,* New York: Schocken, 1976.

Malm, Krister, and Roger Wallis. "What's Good for Business . . . : Some Changes in Traditional Music Generated by Tourism." In Olive Lewin et al. eds., *Come Mek Me Hol' Yu Han': the Impact of Tourism on Traditional Music.* 175-88. Kingston: Jamaica Memory Bank, 1988.

Martí, Josep. *El folklorismo: uso y abuso de la tradición,* Barcelona: Ronsel, 1996.

Meruéndano L. *Los judíos de Ribadavia.* 1915. Facsimile ed. Alvarellos: Lugo, 1981.

Onega, José-Ramón. *Los judíos en el reino de Galicia.* Madrid: Editorial Nacional, 1981.

Portuguese Government Tourism Information Department. *The Jews in Portugal.* Lisbon, n.d. (ca. 1996)

Roa Cilla, Antonio, and Miguel Gómez Andrea. *Hervás, imagenes de su historia.* Cáceres: Diputación de Cáceres, 1996.

Rodriguez, Sylvia, "Fiesta Time and Plaza Space: Resistance and Accomodation in a Tourist Town." *Journal of American Folklore,* no. 439 (March 1998): 39-56.

Portuguese Government Tourism Information Department, *The Jews in Portugal,* Lisbon, n.d. (ca.1996).

◆ Chapter 2

Crypto-Jewish Ballads and Prayers in the Portuguese Oral Tradition[1]

Manuel da Costa Fontes

Crypto-Judaism was born in Spain in 1391 when the pogroms that began in Seville spread to other cities, and thousands of Jews had to accept Christianity from one moment to the next in order to save their lives with little or no knowledge of their new faith (Caro Baroja 1986, 1:115-16; Domínguez Ortiz 1992, 11-13). Although they had to behave publicly as Christian, most continued to practice Judaism in secret. In 1480, when the Inquisition was implemented in Spain, many of their descendants, fearing for their lives, decided to leave their homes. Some settled in Portugal and other countries (Caro Baroja 1986, 1:158). In 1492, partly because of allegations that the very presence of Jews caused many of their converted relatives to betray Christianity, that is, to practice Crypto-Judaism, the Catholic monarchs decided to expel all the Jews from Spain.[2] About thirty thousand sought refuge in Portugal, whose king, John II, allowed them to come in for a period of eight months, on payment of a head poll. Most of them stayed, doubling the number of Jews in the country to sixty thousand (Tavares 1982, 74, 253-56).[3]

Manuel I, who succeeded John II in 1495 because of the accidental death of his son and heir, Prince Afonso, in 1491, decided that he also wanted to marry the prince's widow, Isabel, daughter of the Catholic Kings. Referring to the relapsed converts from Spain in Portugal, the princess replied that she did not want to live in a country where there were so many "heretics," but perhaps she meant non-Christians as well. Whatever the case, in December 1496, King Manuel responded by proclaiming an edict according to which everyone who refused to accept Christianity had to leave the country in ten months, that is, by October 1497 (Herculano 1982, 1:70-71).

Manuel did not really wish to lose such a productive sector of the population, however. When it became obvious that many people were getting ready for exile, he had all the Jewish children below fourteen years of age taken from their parents and placed with Catholic families in order to be raised as Christians. To make the departure of the Jews even more difficult, the three ports originally designated for embarkation were reduced to only one, Lisbon. Even so, about one-third of the Jews in the country—more than twenty thousand people—still gathered in the Rossio in order to board the waiting vessels. Manuel ordered them baptized, and only eight individuals had the strength to resist (Herculano 1982, 1:74-77). It is not clear how the other Jews in the country were converted, but, afterward, the whole country was officially Christian. Thus, the Portuguese expulsion of 1497 constitutes a red herring. It never took place.

Obviously, the population was far from being completely Christian, as claimed, and the number of Crypto-Jews in the country increased tremendously. It does not make any sense to think that all of these people could accept the new faith that had been imposed upon them in such a manner, becoming sincere "New Christians" from one moment to the next. Their contemporaries refused to believe it. Even though these converts had to go to church, baptize their children, and behave publicly as Christians, they continued to be regarded as Jews, which they probably were (Tavares 1987, 51).

Manuel did what he could in order to protect them, hoping that, in time, they would be completely assimilated, becoming as Christian as the rest of the population. He forbade inquiries into their religious beliefs until 1534 (Manuel himself died in 1521), and refused to allow the implantation of the Inquisition in Portugal. When two thousand converts were killed in the Lisbon pogrom of 1506, he punished those responsible severely, so as to prevent such pogroms from happening again in the future (Herculano 1982, 1:77-91). In appreciation for his efforts on their behalf, New Christians in exile referred to Manuel in their writings as *rei santo*, and *rei dos judeus*—"holy king" and "king of the Jews" (Kayserling 1971, 132).

Because Manuel had forbidden inquiries into the religious beliefs of the New Christians until 1534, the Portuguese Inquisition was not approved by Rome until fifteen years after his death, in 1536, beginning to function four years later, in 1540, when the first auto-da-fé was held. The Inquisition was to last another two hundred years, until the 1740s, when the marquis of Pombal practically forced it to cease its activities (Azevedo 1989, 346-58; Saraiva 1985, 202-9), but it was not formally abolished until April 5, 1821. During nearly two and a half centuries of existence, the Portuguese Inquisition had 31,349 victims, 1,175 of whom were burned at the stake. These figures include people accused of witchcraft, sodomy, and bigamy, but most were accused of Judaizing (Mendonça and Moreira 1980, 145-279).

Although King Manuel wanted them to stay in Portugal, beginning in his reign some New Christians, converts, or *marranos*, as they were called, managed to escape to countries where they could live openly as Jews, founding communities in Bordeaux, Amsterdam, Hamburg, London, various Italian cities, and elsewhere (Azevedo 1989, 357-430). A good number joined the Spanish communities formed after the expulsion of 1492; both in its Western (North Africa) and Eastern (Balkan) forms, the Judeo-Spanish language has a Portuguese substratum, which, as far as I know, has not yet been systematically studied.

The exodus increased when the crowns of Portugal and Spain were brought together in 1580 by Philip II. The union lasted until 1640. Many Portuguese New Christians used the opportunity to move to Spain and its American colonies, partly because, having realized its aims, the Spanish Inquisition had almost ceased to function. Spaniards soon realized that many of the Portuguese were Crypto-Jews. The Spanish Inquisition resumed its activities, and the word "Portuguese" became practically synonymous with "Jew," both in Spain and the Americas (Domínguez Ortiz 1992, 78, 80, 85-90, 95).

Many Crypto-Jews still remained in Portugal, however. Because of inquisitorial persecution, the pressures of the Old Christian environment, and assimilation, their number continued to dwindle with the passing of the years, but, nevertheless, there still exist Crypto-Jewish communities in villages and cities of the district of Bragança (Trás-os-Montes) such as Bragança, Rebordelo, Chacim, Campo de Víboras, Vilarinho dos Galegos, Vimioso, Argozelo, Carção, Felgueiras, Fornos, Lagoaça, and Freixo de Espada-à-Cinta.

There are some communities in the two Beira provinces as well—Pinhel, Covilhã, Guarda, Belmonte, Fundão, and Penamacor. Note that these communities are concentrated in northeastern Portugal, near the border. This suggests that many Crypto-Jews descend from those Spanish refugees who, in 1492, decided to settle as soon as they arrived in Portugal.

Being officially Christian, Crypto-Jews had to practice their religion secretly, so as not to fall into the hands of the Inquisition. What they did was constantly scrutinized by their neighbors, including their eating habits. In time this secrecy became an integral part of their faith. As far as they are concerned, a true Jew must never say that he is one, even though, in the villages where they live, people have long memories, and know perfectly well who they are. A similar phenomenon has occurred with the Crypto-Catholics of Japan. In their opinion, a true Catholic must never identify himself as such ("Japan's" 1982, 71).

Artur Carlos de Barros Basto was an army captain of *marrano* stock. Beginning in 1922 he tried to revive Judaism, albeit unsuccessfully. He founded a synagogue in Oporto, as well as a magazine, *Ha-Lapid* [The torch], in order to propagate the movement (Canelo 1996, 59-154). In 1961 he estimated that there were still four to five thousand Crypto-Jews in the country (Friedenberg 1961, 90). At the end of the 1980s and early 1990s, about sixty persons from Belmonte decided to adhere publicly to Judaism, founding a synagogue, but, even in this town, many of their coreligionists chose to adhere to the rule of secrecy, remaining Crypto-Jews (Shapiro 1991; see also Garcia 1993, 120).

These Crypto-Jews have special festivities and a liturgy of their own. They celebrate the Sabbath by preparing their food the day before. This remains in accordance with Jewish religious law which forbids the lighting of fires on the Sabbath. In a slightly different manner than openly practicing Jews, however, these Crypto-Jews do not light customary candles on Friday nights, before the onset of the twenty-four-hour Sabbath period. Instead, on Fridays at sundown they prepare a special lamp, made with a wick of virgin linen and olive oil, which, when lit, is placed in a clay pot, so that neighbors cannot see it. This custom seems to go back to the days of the Inquisition (Schwarz 1925, 30).

Two important festivities are Yom Kippur and Passover. Yom Kippur is known as *Dia de Kipur*, *Dia Puro*, or *Dia do Perdão*, but, rather than celebrating it on the tenth day of the moon (Hebrew month) of Tishri, which generally coincides with September, they observe it the day after. This delay seems to have begun as an effort to elude the vigilance of the Inquisition. There is a rigorous fast, and people gather in each others' homes in order to pray. The prayers are divided into five sessions, with a break of about one hour between sessions (Schwarz 1925, 31).

Passover begins on the fourteenth day of the Jewish month of Nisan, which usually falls in April, around the time of the corresponding Christian Easter. The Crypto-Jews eat a previously prepared unleavened bread, gathering for a special meal, but, unlike mainstream Jews, who have the tradition of the Passover lamb, they abstain completely from meat. The community also used to go to a nearby river or stream, and people would strike the water with olive branches in remembrance of the parting of the Red Sea, while reciting "A Passagem do Mar Vermelho" (Spanish: "El paso del Mar Rojo"), a ballad that they and the Eastern Sephardim are the only ones to preserve (Schwarz 1925, 32-35).

In addition to "A Passagem do Mar Vermelho," the liturgy of the Crypto-Jews includes five biblical ballads (see Ferré 1987) to which I will return later. For the most part, their liturgy consists of prayers. These materials began to be collected and published by Samuel Schwarz, a Polish mine engineer who had settled in Portugal in 1915 (see Schwarz 1925), and his example was soon followed by others.[4]

In July 1980 my wife and I also recorded fourteen variants of eleven prayers from two informants, in Rebordelo (Vinhais), while conducting fieldwork in order to put together a ballad collection for the district of Bragança (TM). We tried to find other informants, but could not. The tradition of secrecy is still extremely strong, and one of our informants, the ninety-year-old Deolinda Mota, who, in her own words, still followed "the old law" in spite of attending church services, did not want any of her neighbors to realize that she knew those special prayers. There is no doubt that she feared the discrimination that never ceased to exist in those villages.

Although the Jewish historian Cecil Roth, who studied the liturgy of the Crypto-Jews as represented in inquisitorial trials, referred to its dearth, pointing out, and rightly so, that the prayers were extremely difficult to transmit because of the danger involved (1960, 177), the truth of the matter is that their descendants preserve a good number of prayers. They are transmitted orally, but have also been brought together in some family manuscripts. Our first informant, the sixty-year-old Francisco dos Santos Gaspar, learned the three prayers that he recorded from his father. Deolinda Mota learned hers not from her parents, but from an aunt who followed "the Old" (Judaism) rather than "the New Law" (Christianity). Later I discovered that

Mr. Gaspar had a brother who kept a prayer manuscript that had belonged to their father (Paulo, *Os Judeus*, 117). Unfortunately, I was unable to see it, but the investigators who saw similar prayer manuscripts agree that they date from the eighteenth century (Schwarz 1925, 17; Basto 1928; also Paulo, *Os Judeus*, 1985 117). This suggests that people did not dare to put the prayers in writing until the Inquisition ceased its activities against them thanks to the measures of Pombal in the 1740s, but the subject still needs further study.[5]

There are prayers for practically every occasion—morning prayers, noon prayers, evening prayers, prayers to be said while washing in the morning, picking fruit, killing animals, prayers for fasts, to knead the bread for Passover, to purify women after giving birth, for illnesses, for the dead, and while visiting cemeteries; prayers to be said when leaving the house, for protection from danger and for one's children, and for travel; and prayers for special occasions such as a new moon and Passover. The songs to praise God, of which there is a good number, are based especially on biblical Psalms. There is even a prayer to confess one's sins directly to God (see Fontes 1990-93, 79-82).

The New Christians who continued to practice their faith after the forced conversion of 1497 were still familiar with classical Judaism, but that was no longer the case with their descendants. The difficult circumstances in which they lived, trying constantly to prevent suspicions and anonymous denunciations, led to increasing isolation from each other and to a gradual dilution of classical Jewish liturgy. The situation worsened with the inception of the Inquisition in 1540, for books in Hebrew were forbidden, and the possession of books or manuscripts in the vernacular was extremely dangerous. Since anyone caught with such materials would be automatically condemned for

Judaizing, the only solution was to rely on memory, transmitting the prayers that were still remembered orally, from generation to generation.

The problem was aggravated by assimilation and mixed marriages. While some members of a family continued to practice Crypto-Judaism, others did not, and there were cases in which relatives denounced each other. Given these conditions, the liturgy of the Crypto-Jews became further and further removed from classical Judaism. Even the Hebrew "Shema," a declaration of faith whose importance corresponds to that of the Christian Creed, disappeared.[6] Although it is possible to trace one or two ballads to pre-Expulsion days, in time the Crypto-Jews ended up creating what amounts to a new liturgy of their own. Many of the prayers seem to be exclusively theirs, for they cannot be documented elsewhere, but the Crypto-Jews also used Psalms taken directly from the Old Testament and official Christian prayers such as the Lord's Prayer, which is addressed exclusively to God the Father, without any references to God the Son and the Holy Ghost. In addition they adapted paraliturgical Christian prayers, that is, those folk prayers that mothers and grandmothers still often teach to their children and grandchildren. The influence of the surrounding Christian environment was such that figures from the Old Testament such as Moses, Esther, and Tobias came to be revered as saints (Paulo 1971, 80-81; Schwarz 1925, 28). Notwithstanding this syncretism, however, the Crypto-Jews remained uncompromising in their monotheism, and some of the prayers were adapted in such a manner that they seem to constitute a reaction against the Christianity which they were forced to observe publicly.

Before these prayers began to be written down, apparently during the eighteenth century, their transmission was strictly oral. Thus, to a large extent, Crypto-Judaism can be said to depend on memory, a memory that, besides allowing the Crypto-Jews to keep their faith, also enabled them to preserve their identity.

The prayers can be organized in several ways, both synchronically and diachronically. For now I have divided them into five main groups, according to their origins, even though some prayers fall into more than one category: (1) Modern prayers which, being variants of prayers found in inquisitorial trials from the sixteenth, seventeenth, and eighteenth centuries, testify to the continuity of the Crypto-Jewish tradition; (2) prayers derived from the Psalms and other parts of the Old Testament; (3) prayers which were adapted from the folk or paraliturgical Christian tradition; (4) prayers taken from the official Christian tradition; (5) exclusively Crypto-Jewish prayers whose origins I have not yet been able to determine. In the pages that follow, I will discuss the first three categories and will survey the six ballads that also form part of the liturgy of the Crypto-Jews.

The prayers were first documented in inquisitorial trials, both in Portugal and Spain, because the inquisitors took great care to document the cases against each person in great detail, writing down anonymous denunciations, witness depositions, interrogations, confessions extracted through torture, as well as the prayers of their victims.[7] The following prayer, written down by the Coimbra Inquisition in 1583 and 1584, was repeated to the Lisbon Inquisition by the twenty-year-old Brites Henriques sometime after being jailed in January 1674, together with her father, the merchant António Rodrigues Mogadouro, three brothers, and two sisters. The same prayer was extracted again in 1701 by the Coimbra Inquisition from António de Sá

Carrança, a weaver from Bragança. The prayer in question still exists in the modern tradition:

1584

Alto *Dios* de Abraham,
grande Senhor de Israel,
tu que ouviste a Samuel,
ouve minha oração.

Senhor que te aposentaste

nesas mui grandes alturas,
ouve a mim, pecador,
que te chamo das baixuras. . . .

(Mea 1985, 160)

[High God of Abraham,
great Lord of Israel,
you who heard Samuel,
hear my prayer.
Lord who presented yourself

in those very great heights,
hear me, a sinner,
who calls you from these
depths.]

1674

Alto Deus de Abrahão,
forte Deus de Israel,
tu que ouviste a Daniel,
ouve, Senhor, minha
oração.
Tu, Senhor, que te
aprezentaste
em tão altas alturas,
ouve a *my*, peccadora,
que te chamo das
baixuras. . . .

(Schwarz 1925, 101)

[High God of Abraham,
strong God of Israel,
you who heard Daniel,
hear, Lord, my prayer,
you, Lord, who presented
yourself
in such great heights,
hear me, a sinner,
who calls you from these
depths.]

1701

Ó alto Deus de Abrhão,
ó forte Deus de Israel,
tu que ouviste a Daniel,
ouve-me a mim e a todas
as minhas coisas.

(Freitas 1952, 22)

Modern Version

Grande Deus de Israel,
grande forte de Abrhão,
já que ouviste a Daniel,
ouve a minha oração.

(Paulo, *Os Judeus*, 1985, 105)

[O great God of Abraham,
O strong God of Israel,
you who heard Daniel,
hear me and all of my things.]

[Great God of Israel,
great fortress of Abraham,
since you heard Daniel,
hear my prayer as well.]

This prayer, which does not exist among Old Christians, can be documented in the sixteenth, seventeenth, eighteenth, and twentieth centuries, constituting, therefore, a good example of the continuity of the Crypto-Jewish tradition. The 1584 version, from Coimbra, *refers* to God with the Spanish *Diós* instead of the Portuguese *Deus*. There are other such cases in old Crypto-Jewish prayers. For example, the prayers of Brites Henriques, who was twenty years old when jailed by the Lisbon Inquisition, include numerous Castilianisms (Schwarz 1925, 95-105). This suggests that some of the prayers were originally Spanish, having been transmitted by refugees who arrived in 1492 to their descendants, and that the translation took place very slowly. As Caro Baroja observed, many of the émigrés never learned how to speak Portuguese well, and this at times affected the language of their descendants (1986, 1: 211-12). Thus, the Castilian terms found in some of those early prayers probably constitute a memory of their origin.

At one time the prayer under scrutiny also belonged to the biblical category. A variant from 1583, also documented by the Coimbra Inquisition, incorporates passages from Psalm 121 (*Biblia Sagrada* 804-5), but since the modern tradition preserves only the beginning of the prayer, it is no longer related to that Psalm.

1583

Ó grande de Abrahão,
ó grande d'Israel,
tu que ouviste a Daniel
ouve minha oração.
Tu que nas alturas te poseste,
ouve a mym cheo de pecados
e de maldades,
que te chamo das baixuras.
Ergo meus olhos aos montes
e do céu me venha ajuda
de ti, Senhor,
que fizeste o ceo e a terra.
Tira me de tanta guerra
poys que somos do teu ver.
Povo que arrevelle e
adormece.
Abaste que sou filho de
homem
e de molher,
que pequei diante de Ti.
Ha piedade de mym
e de todo o filho d'Israel.
Amen.
(Mea 1985, 160-61, n. 24)

[O great one of Abraham,
O great one of Israel,
you who heard Daniel,
please hear my prayer.
You, who placed yourself
in the heights,
hear me, for I am full
of sins

Psalm 121

Levanto meus olhos
para as montanas;[1]
donde me virá o auxílio?
O meu auxílio vem do
Senhor,[2]
criador do céu e da terra.
Não deixará que os teus
pés vacilem![3]
Não dorme quem te
guarda!
Não dorme, de facto,
nem dormita[4]
quem guarda Israel.

O Senhor é o teu guarda,[5]
Ele é a tua sombra,
colocado à tua direita. . . .

and evil,
and I call you from
these depths.
I raise my eyes to the
mountains.
May help come to me
from heaven,
from you, Lord,

who created heaven and
earth.
Take me from so much
trouble,
we agree with you
[follow your law].
People wake up and fall
asleep.
Let it suffice that I am
the son of man
and woman,

and I have sinned before you.
Have pity on me

and all the children of Israel.
Amen.]

[[1]I lift my eyes toward the
mountains
whence shall help come to
me?
[2]My help is from the
Lord,
who made heaven and
earth.
[3]*May he not suffer your
foot to slip*;
*may he slumber not who
guards you,*
[4]*indeed he neither
slumbers nor sleeps,
the guardian of Israel.*

[5]*The Lord is your
guardian;
the Lord is your shade;
he is beside you at your
right hand* . . .]

The somewhat cryptic verse 15, “Povo que arrevelle e adormece,”[8] suggests that the prayer had been orally transmitted for some time, becoming somewhat unintelligible in the process. This verse is no doubt related to verse 4 of the Psalm, which says that the one who guards Israel neither slumbers nor sleeps. Also note that, like the remainder of the prayer, Psalm 121 concludes by asking for the protection of the Lord, who is also the guardian of Israel.

Other prayers derive from the narrative parts of the Old Testament. A good example is a prayer that our ninety-year-old informant Deolinda Mota used to say for her children as they left the house, asking God to guide them as he had the three boys who were not harmed by fire or bullets (obviously a modern addition), and to deliver them from every danger, including the Inquisition:

O Senhor vos encamine.	[May the Lord guide you.
Encaminhai-os, o Senhor,	Please guide them, Lord,
pelos vossos santos caminhos.	in your holy ways.
E assim como vós encaminhásteis	As you guided
os teus meninos (?) varões	the three [your] boys,
que não (?) les chegou o fogo,	so that neither fire
nem balas,	nor bullets touched them,
que ficavam feitas em carvões,	for they were turned into carbon,
livrai-os, o Senhor,	please deliver them, O Lord,
d'inquisições,	from Inquisitions,
de coisas insensíveis,	things that cannot be seen,
de todos os perigos maus	from all the evil dangers
que le puderem acontecer.	that can befall them.
O Senhor nos retire deles.	May the Lord deliver us from them.
Adonai, amém.	Adonai, (*My Lord*— Hebrew) amen.]

The other two versions of this prayer that I found differ somewhat from Mrs. Mota's, which I had difficulty in transcribing, because she spoke very quickly. Where she seems to say "os teus meninos" (5), the others say "os três meninos," and, instead of saying that they were not harmed by fire, they state that the Lord delivered them "de prisões e de grelhas e de coisas sensíveis" (Basto 1928, 8; Paulo, *Os Judeus*, 1985, 106). These "grelhas" are no doubt an old torture instrument used by the Inquisition.

The miracle of the children who remained unharmed in the middle of the fire derives from the Book of Daniel. When Nebuchadnezzar, King of Babylon, conquered Jerusalem, he had some young noblemen from Israel brought to serve him. This included Daniel, Anania, Misaḥ, and Azaria. The names of the last three were changed to Sidraḥ, Misaḥ, and Abdenago (Dan. 1:2-7). Happy with Daniel because he was the only one who could decipher a dream he had, Nebuchadnezzar made him governor of the province of Babylon, and, at his request, he made the other three young men administrators of the province. Sometime later, Nebuchadnezzar had a great golden statue made, and ordered everyone to fall down and worship it. Sidraḥ, Misaḥ, and Abdenago were denounced for refusing to do so. Nebuchadnezzar called them to his presence, threatening to throw them into a fiery furnace, but the boys persisted. The king then "ordered the furnace to be heated seven times more than usual" (3:19). The flames devoured the men who threw the boys into the furnace, but the three young men "walked in the flames, singing to God and blessing the Lord" (3:24).

Like the Crypto-Jews, the three boys lived in exile and had to worship a God in whom they did not believe under the threat of death. The furnace in which they were thrown coincides with the bonfires of the Inquisition. Because of these parallels, the Crypto-Jews used the biblical story for their prayer, adding references to the Inquisition and to the irons used during torment.

Since Mrs. Mota insisted on being interviewed alone, by my wife—I had to wait outside—I first heard the prayer on tape, with great emotion, as we were driving away from Rebordelo. In 1980 Mrs. Mota prayed to God to protect her children from the Inquisition as if time had stood still, and the Inquisition had not been abolished 169 years before. Clearly, the fear provoked by that horrible institution was such that memory of it continues to linger among the Crypto-Jews, long after it ceased to exist.

The prayers in the third category are those adapted from the paraliturgical Christian tradition, which includes morning and evening prayers, prayers for leaving the house and entering church, protective spells, and incantations. Some of them probably go back to pagan, pre-Christian times. When they adapt these prayers, the Crypto-Jews remove all the references to Jesus, the Blessed Mother, the Holy Trinity, and the saints. One good example is the prayer that many Crypto-Jews say upon entering church, whose rites they pretend to observe for the sake of appearances:

Nesta casa entro, não adoro nem o pau nem a pedra, só a Deus, que em tudo governa.	[I enter this house, I worship neither wood nor stone, only God, who governs everything.]

(Schwarz 1925, 79)

The wood and the stone are the statues of Jesus, the Blessed Mother, and the saints in which the Crypto-Jews refuse to believe. They only accept the God "que em tudo governa," that is, God the Father, as in the Old Testament. With this prayer the Crypto-Jews reaffirm their faith. Although they see themselves forced to go to church, just like their ancestors did back in 1497, they do not believe in anything that takes place there.

Originally, this prayer, which has been considered exclusively Crypto-Jewish until now, was probably a reaction against a paraliturgical Christian prayer used upon entering church. The first example is from the Azores (Guadalupe, island of Graciosa); the second one is from Gulpilhares (Vila Nova de Gaia). As can be readily observed, the Crypto-Jews adapted the beginning of the Christian prayer, suppressing the references to Jesus and the Holy Sacrament:

1

Pela igreja de Deus vou entrando,
a *Jesus* vou adorando.
A minha alma vai doente
de pecar tão feramente.

O Santíssimo Sacramento,
o manjar de toda a doçura;
todos os anjinhos no céu
estão cantando aleluia . . .
(Fontes 1979, No. 572)

2

Pela casa de Deus entro,
por ela quero entrar.
Pecados, ficai aqui,
que eu vou ver a *Jesus Cristo*,
que há muito que o não vi.
(Valle 1964, 143)

1

[I enter God's church,
I worship *Jesus*.
My soul is ill
from sinning so fiercely.

Holy Sacrament,
nourishment of great sweetness,
all the angels in heaven
are singing alleluia.]

2

[I enter God's house,
I wish to enter.
Sins, you stay outside,
for I am going to see *Jesus*,
whom I have not seen for a long time.]

Another example of the methods used in the adaptation of Christian prayers can be seen by comparing a popular Crypto-Jewish morning prayer with its Christian counterpart. The version that follows was recited by Mrs. Mota:

Senhor, deitar-me quero, minha i-alma vos entrego. S'eu dormir, alumiai-me e s'eu morrer, acompanhai-me. . . .[9]	[Lord, I want to sleep, my soul I confide in you. If I sleep, enlighten me, and if I die, be with me.]

Since the versions of the corresponding Christian prayer differ considerably from each other, I have given two examples below:

1

Jesus, deitar-me quero,
corpo e alma vos entrego.
S'a morte me vier buscar,

qu'eu por vós não possa
bradar,
Jesus na minha boca,

Jesus no meu peito,
Jesus na cama
onde m'eu deito.
Jesus, Jesus, Jesus.
Ó *Virgem* pura,

que sempre fostes pura,
quem todo o mundo remistes,
peço que me remides também,
qu'eu sou um grande pecador.
(Fontes 1980, No. 272)

2

Senhor, eu dormir quero,
a minha alma vos entrego.
S'eu mal dormir, acordai-
me,
s'eu morrer, alumiai-me

co'as três candiinhas
bentas
da *Santíssima Trindade.*
Creio em Deus Pai,
Deus Filho,
Deus Espírito Santo,
por todos os séculos dos
séculos.
Amén.
(Fontes 1980, No. 276)

1

[*Jesus*, I want to go to sleep,
body and soul I confide
in you.
If death comes for me
and I cannot cry out for you,
Jesus on my lips,
Jesus in my heart,
Jesus in the bed
where I lie.
Jesus, Jesus, Jesus.
O pure *Virgin*,
you were always pure,
you redeemed the whole world;
pray redeem me also,
for I am a great sinner.]

2

[Lord, I want to sleep,
my soul I confide in you.
If I sleep poorly, awaken
me,
if I die, light my way
with the three blessed
little candles
of the *Holy Trinity*.
I believe in *God the
Father*,
God the Son,
God the Holy Ghost
forever and ever. Amen.]

As we can see, the Crypto-Jews retain the beginning of the Christian prayer, but discard the rest, thus eliminating the references to Jesus, the Blessed Mother, the Holy Trinity, God the Son, and the Holy Spirit.

So far we have examined three types of prayers: (1) prayers documented in old inquisitorial trials; (2) prayers derived from the Bible; and (3) prayers adapted from the paraliturgical Christian tradition. The fourth category, we recall, consists of adapted official Christian prayers. It includes a versified version of the Lord's Prayer, which is addressed only to God the Father (Schwarz 1925, 79-82; Cruz 1995, No. 233), a morning prayer which, though paraliturgical today, used to appear in old missals (Fontes 1990-93, 90-92), and there is one confession which seems to echo a similar prayer said by Catholics just before they confess their sins to a priest (see Fontes 1990-93, 79-82, and Schwarz 1925, 70-71). The Crypto-Jews, of course, address theirs directly to God. Christians often conclude the Lord's Prayer with the "Gloria Patri et Filio et Spirito Sanctum," which reaffirms their trinitarianism; being strictly monotheistic, the Crypto-Jews refuse to believe that God the Father, the Son, and the Holy Ghost are one, and omit the "Gloria Patri."

This syncretism with the surrounding Christian tradition took place in time, as the Crypto-Jews lost memory of the classical Jewish tradition. The impoverishment of their liturgy is what caused them to adapt Christian materials. Obviously, this would not have happened if they had been allowed to live freely as Jews.

The prayers in the fifth category are exclusively Crypto-Jewish, including those said before slaying animals, fasts, to knead the bread for Passover, to purify women after giving birth, and so on. So far, I have been unable to determine their origins, but a comparison with the Sephardic tradition may yield some parallels.

The Crypto-Jewish liturgy also includes six biblical ballads. In general terms, ballads are easier to remember than prayers, because they always tell a story, and, unlike prayers, whose verse is highly irregular and varies from prayer to prayer, they usually have a regular form, consisting of seven-syllable verses (octosyllabic by Spanish count) with assonant rhyme in the even-numbered lines. Nevertheless, the deterioration exhibited by these six ballads, which are exclusively Crypto-Jewish in Portugal, shows that they were poorly remembered, being adapted to the strophic quatrains that came to prevail as the more modern narratives collectively designated as *literatura de cordel* became popular. Even the two poems with counterparts in other traditions, "O Sacrifício de Isaac"

(Spain, Morocco) and "A Passagem do Mar Vermelho" (Eastern Sephardim), retain only part of the old assonance. This indicates that, like the prayers, the ballads were transmitted with difficulty, in the greatest secrecy. If that had not been the case, they would never have deteriorated to such a point. After all, the surrounding Christian ballad tradition, which is extremely rich, was not affected by the same phenomenon.

Surprisingly, one of the ballads, "No Céu Está um Castelo" (RPI, E11), adapts the portion of the Christian Christmas ballad "Noite de Natal" (*í-a* RPI, U1), which, in its turn, adapts the Carolingian "Rosaflorida y Montesinos" (CMP, B20; RPI, B6). The portion of the Portuguese ballad that corresponds to the latter may constitute a contamination with a separate, originally independent version of that ballad "a lo divino" but this needs to be studied in detail elsewhere. For now, in order to give a better idea of the contents of the Christian ballad, I will summarize one of the contaminated versions. During Christmas night, the Virgin Mary and Saint Joseph journey toward Bethlehem, when everyone is already sleeping. Since the doorman refuses to let them in, Saint Joseph leaves to search for fire. When he returns, Mary has already given birth to Jesus. An angel visits and salutes her with the Ave Maria, returns to heaven, and informs the Eternal Father that she is in a stable. A convent of chiseled stone is built for her. Saint John pulls up the stone, Saint Peter cuts it, and there are three thousand angels between the battlements:

Pela noite de Natal,   noite de tanta alegria,
caminhando vai José,   caminhando vai Maria, 2
ambos os dois p'ra Belém,   mais de noite que de dia;
e chegaram a Belém,   já toda a gente dormia. 4
—Porteiro, abri a porta,   porteiro da portaria.
A porta não quis abrir   a gente que não conhecia. 6
—Dilatem-se aí, senhores,   até que rompa o dia;
comam dessa erva verde,   bebam nessa água fria. 8
São José foi pelo lume,   que ele temor lhe fazia.
Quando José veio co'o lume,   já a Virgem 'stava parida. 10
. . . .
E veio um anjo do céu,   rezando uma ave-maria. 18
Perguntou o Padre Eterno: —Como fica lá a parida?
—A parida ficou boa,   num serja recolhida. 20
—Uma serja não é nada   para o que ela merecia.
Lá mandaram fazer um mosteiro   todo de pedra ladrilha: 22
São João a arreguingá-la,   São Pedro a retorná-la.
Antre almenda e almenda   três mil anjos aí estavam. 23
(VRP, No. 769)

20*b*, 21*a* serja: *Read* "estrebaria"; 22*a* arrenguingá-la: *Read* "arrancá-la"; 22*b* retorná-la: *Read* "picá-la"; 23*a* almenda: probably from the Spanish, "almena," Portuguese, "ameia."

[Christmas night, night of so much joy, Joseph walks, Mary walks, both to Bethlehem, more at night than day. They arrived in Bethlehem, everyone slept. "Doorman, open the door, doorman of the entrance gate." He refused to open to people he did not know. "Stay there, Ma'am and Sir, until daylight breaks, eat that green grass, drink that cold water." Saint Joseph left to fetch fire, for he was afraid of him. When he returned with the fire, the Virgin had already given birth. [. . .] An angel came from heaven, saying an Ave Maria. The Eternal Father asked: "How is the one in childbed doing?" "The woman in childbed is well, she is sheltered in a stable." "A stable is very humble, she deserves much more." A convent was ordered built, all of chiseled stone. Saint John pulled out the stone, Saint Peter cut it. Between the battlements there were three thousand angels.]

As the following comparison demonstrates, the concluding verses of this ballad constitute a religious contrafact of "Rosaflorida y Montesinos":

Noite de Natal		*Rosaflorida y Montesinos*
*Lá no céu há um castilho		En Castilla está un castillo,
pintado à maravilha;		que se llama Rocafrida;
(VRP, No. 788)		
lá mandaram fazer um mosteiro	3	al castillo llaman Roca,
todo de pedra ladrilha.		y a la fonte llaman Frida.
(VRP, No. 769)		
O ferrolho era d'ouro,		El pie tenía de oro,
a armela de prata fina;		y almenas de plata fina;
entre o ferrolho e a armela	4	entre almena y almena
doze mil anjos havia.		está una piedra zafira
(VRP, No. 771)		
		tanto relumbra de noche
		como el sol a mediodía.
Lá no meio do castilho		Dentro estaba una doncella
está uma rosa florida,		que la llaman Rosaflorida.
e no meio dessa rosa	6	(*Primav.* 179.1-6)
está a Virgem Maria.		
(VRP, No. 788)		
[There is a castle in heaven,		[In Castile there is a castle,
it is wondrously painted;		which is called Rocafrida.
there they had a convent		the castle is known as

built,
all of chiseled stone.

The bolt was of gold,
the catch of fine silver;

between the bolt and the catch
there were twelve thousand angels.

In the middle of the castle
there is a blooming rose;
in the middle of the rose
is the Virgin Mary.]

Roca,
the fountain is known as Frida.
The foundation is of gold,
the battlements of fine silver;
between battlement and battlement
there is a fine sapphire

that shines at night
like the sun at midday.
Inside there is a maiden,
they call her Rosaflorida.]

In its turn, the Crypto-Jewish poem adapts the Christmas ballad as follows:

Noite de Natal

Lá no céu há um castilho
pintado à maravilha.
(VRP, No. 788)
São Pedro apanhava a pedra, 2
São João a comparia.
Entre o ferrolho e a armela

doze mil anjos havia.
(TM, No. 969)
Desceram nos anjos do céu 4
cantando a avé-maria:

—Avé-Maria de graça,
de graça avé-maría.
(TM, No. 949)

No Céu Está um Castelo

No céu está um castelo
lavrado de mil maravilhas;

Jacob apanhava a pedra, 2
Abraão a componia.
Entre as árvores e o castelo
doze mil anjos havia,

dando graças e louvores, 4
e o Senhor ainda mais queria.
Glórias ao Senhor no céu,
paz entre nós na terra

para sempre, sem fim. 6
Amén, Senhor. Ao céu vá.
(Machado 1952, 28)

[There is a castle in heaven,	[There is a castle in heaven
it is wondrously painted.	chiseled with a thousand wonders;
Saint Peter fetched the stone,	Jacob fetched the stone,
Saint John would cut it.	Abraham would cut it.
Between the bolt and the catch	Between the trees and the castle
there were twelve thousand angels.	there were twelve thousand angels
The angels descended from heaven	giving thanks and praise,
singing the Ave Maria:	and the Lord wanted even more.
"Hail, Mary, full of grace,	Glory to God in heaven,
full of grace; hail, Mary."]	peace among us on earth,
	forever and ever.
	Amen. May it go to heaven.]

In some Christian versions, a castle is built instead of a monastery, at times in heaven. Saint Peter brings the stone, Saint John works as mason, and there are one thousand angels between the bolt and the catch. Then more angels come down from heaven, singing the Ave Maria.

The Crypto-Jewish adaptation exchanges two figures of the Old Testament, Jacob and Abraham, for Saint Peter and Saint John, and, rather than singing the Ave Maria, the twelve thousand angels sing the praises of the Lord, who wants even more praise. Verses 5 through 6 adapt the Christian "Gloria Patri," which says "Glória ao Pai, e ao Filho, e ao Espírito Santo, para todos os séculos dos séculos e para sempre, sem fim. Amén," by eliminating the references to the Son and the Holy Spirit.

The second Crypto-Jewish ballad, "O Sacrifício de Isaac" (CMP, E5; RPI, E2), derives from a Spanish poem first published ca. 1535 (Catalán 1970, 64 nm. 20-21) and reprinted in 1550 (Rodríguez-Moñino 1970, 292-93). This poem, which is still sung among the Sephardim and in Spain, is exclusively Crypto-Jewish in Portugal. The early version begins as follows:

Si se partiera Abraam, patriarca muy honrrado,
partiera se para el monte, donde Dios le hauia mandado
sacrificar su propio hijo, que Ysaac era llamado;
toma el niño por la mano obediente a su mandado.
(Catalán 1970, 65)[10]

[Abraham left, he was an honored patriarch, he left to the mountain where God had commanded him to sacrifice his own son whose name was Isaac; he takes the boy by the hand, obedient to his command.]

Of the modern versions, the Sephardic renditions are the most faithful to the early tradition, even though they expand it with new motifs, such as the assertion that the sacrifice of Isaac is the Lord's tenth trial of Abraham (1-3). These versions also change parts of the early ballad from indirect to direct discourse. For example, God now addresses Abraham directly (4-5):

*Al Dio del cielo Abraham, al Dio del cielo Ishaac horrado.
A nuestro padre Abraham nueve veces le ha probado,
para cumplirle las diez fuerte cosa le ha mandado:
—Dame al tu hijo, Abraham, a tu hijo Ishaac horrado,
lo pondré por sacrificio en el monte aseñalado.—
De alma y de coraçón el sí le había otorgado. . . .
(Catalán 1970, 70)

[To the God in heaven, Abraham, to the God in heaven, worthy Isaac. Our father Abraham, [God] has tested him nine times, and to test him a tenth time He commanded a dire thing to him: "Give me your son, Abraham, give me worthy Isaac, for I want him as a sacrifice in the appointed mountain." With his soul and heart he had given his consent.]

The modern Spanish ballad deviates considerably from the early version and its Sephardic congener. Isaac is portrayed as a well-dressed, spoiled only son (1-3), and Abraham hears the Lord's command to slay him while having an afternoon snack (4-5):

Un hijo tenía Abrán,   un hijo sólo tenía,
le traía bien vestido,   le traía bien calzado,
de los regalos del mundo   le traía regalado.
Estando un día por la tarde   de reposo merendando,
oyó una voz que decía   estas palabras hablando:
—Este tu hijo, Abrán,   ha de morir degollado.
—El rey del cielo lo manda,   que se cumpla su mandado.—
(Catalán 1970, 56)

[Abrán had a son, he had an only son. He kept him well dressed, with good shoes to wear, and he also gave him plenty of the pleasures of the world. One day in the afternoon as he rested and snacked, he heard a voice that said and spoke these words: "That son of yours, Abrán, has to die beheaded." "Since the King of Heaven so commands it, may His will be done."]

As Barugel brilliantly demonstrated, the sixteenth-century version includes details that, although absent from the biblical narrative (Gen. 2), appear in the Midrash, a compilation that brings together a large corpus of Jewish oral literature. This shows that the ballad was originally composed by a Jew, for Christians were very unlikely to be familiar with the Midrash (Barugel 1990, 35-91). The modern Sephardic, Spanish, and Portuguese versions retain some of the old midrashic motifs, and also add new ones, thus supplementing the early version that happened to be printed.

The Crypto-Jewish ballad preserves some verses in *á-o*, but many are irregular in meter and have lost their rhyme, which indicates that people were beginning to forget it. Moreover, the poem includes three interpolations which I have italicized which show that someone tried to restore and supplement it with the biblical narrative.[11] Because the ballad's form is quite irregular, I did not attempt to edit it in verses of two hemistichs. Better to show how this form relates to the other Crypto-Jewish ballads, I have emphasized the verses that retain the rhyme in *á-o*:

—Pela jura que juraste	*"By the oath that you swore*
ao nosso pai Abraão,	*to our father Abraham,*
mandamentos que fizeste	*commands that you gave*
nos campos de Morião.	*in the fields of Morião."*
Depois das palavras ditas	After these words were said
partiu Abraão pelos montes	Abraham went to the mountains
onde o Senhor o mandava.	where the Lord had sent him.
Mandou aos seus mancebos:	*He commanded his servants:*
—Mancebos, ficai aqui,	*"Servants, remain here,*
que eu e o moço iremos,	*for the boy and I will go*
a vós tornaremos.	*and will return to you."*
Disse Isaac lá no campo:	Isaac said there, in the

—Senhor pai, está aqui o fogo
e a lenha para acender;
mas onde está a vítima?
—Olhai vós, meu filho,
isso não vos dê cuid*ado*,
que manda o Senhor
que sejais sacrific*ado*.
—Se o Senhor manda
e ordena,
cumpra-se o seu santo
mand*ado*;
quem morre pelo Senhor
no céu é coro*ado*.
Peai-me de pés e mãos
para que, na hora da
minha morte,
não faça algum desavis*ado*,
não erga os olhos
contra o Senhor
nem contra vós, meu
pai, ir*ado*.
Tapou Abraão os olhos a seu
filho Isaac
e ergueu a mão para dar
o golpe.
Neste tempo veio um anjo:
—Tate, Abraão,
velho honr*ado*!
Está o Senhor satisfeito
e de ti já está p*ago*.
Manda-te o Senhor
que vás àquela silveirinha,
que está lá um cordeirinho

field:
"Father, here is the fire
and the wood to be burned,
but where is the victim?"
"Look here, my son,
do not worry about that,
for the Lord has
commanded
that you be sacrificed."
"If the Lord so
commands,
may His holy will be
done.
He who dies for the Lord's
sake
is crowned in heaven.
Bind my hands and feet
so that, as I am
about to die,
I do not do something
unseemly
and raise my eyes
against the Lord
or you, father, in
anger."
Abraham covered
the eyes of his son Isaac
and raised his hand
to deliver the blow.
An angel came at this
time:
"Stop, Abraham,
worthy old man.
The Lord is already
satisfied
and happy with you.
The Lord commands you
to go to that little bramble
where there is a little lamb

preso pela barbela,
e dele farás sacrifício
ao Senhor.
Oh, benzer-te, benzerei,
aplicar-te, aplicarei.

Que as tuas sementes
sejam tantas
como o mar de areias,
céu de estrelas,
árvores de folhas,
e sementes por todo
o mundo.
Amén, Senhor.

caught by the bridle.
You will sacrifice it
to the Lord."
O I will bless you, bless
you,
multiply you, multiply
you.
May your seed be
as many
as the sands in the ocean,
stars in the heavens,
leaves on the trees
and seeds in the whole
world.
Amen, Lord.

(Schwarz, pp. 57-58)

Despite its poor condition, this ballad is the only modern one to preserve the verses "quem morre pelo Senhor/ no céu é coroado" (22-23), which correspond to the mid-sixteenth-century "que quien muere por su Dios/en el cielo es coronado" (quoted in Catalán, 65-66, verse 33). This helps to confirm that the Portuguese ballad was transmitted in great isolation, without any contact with the other traditions, and that, despite its strophic interpolations, it must go very far back in time. Moreover, had there been any contact with the neighboring Leonese tradition, then it would probably have been possible to restore the ballad without having to resort to the Bible.

The third and fourth ballads, "Jonas" (RPI, E4) and "Daniel na Cova dos Leões" (RPI, E5), do not have known early antecedents, existing only among the Crypto-Jews of Portugal. Both poems are essentially strophic, but may retain some vestiges of assonance, which I have emphasized in the even-numbered verses, which would have been in rhyme position, and also in the odd-numbered verses, because the predominantly strophic character of these ballads could have caused them to be displaced.

In the first poem, God sends Jonah to preach in Nineveh, but he disobeys. While he is on a sea voyage, there arises a great tempest. Jonah tells the pilots that they must throw him overboard for it to cease. They do this and Jonah is swallowed by a whale, in whose belly he stays for forty hours. He prays, asks God for forgiveness, and the whale vomits him on the shores of Nineveh. Jonah begins preaching, and warns the inhabitants that God will send them a great punishment if they do not repent.

Note that the poem has seven verses with rhyme in *á-a* and four in *á-o*:

Jonas, desobediente
ao que o Senhor o mandou:

fosse pregar à Nívia,
onde Jonas desembarcou.
ndo na sua jornada,
felizmente naveg*ava*,
pensando que o não via
aquele que o conden*ava*.

O vento vai favorável.
Um par de léguas and*adas*
depara-se uma tormenta.
Disse Jonas aos pilotos:

—A tormenta vai armada,
as vidas vão arrisc*adas*:
se quereis que ela passe,

mandai-me deitar ao mar,

pois enquanto aqui for
ela não há-de cessar.

[Jonah disobeyed
what the Lord
commanded:
To preach in Nineveh,
but he landed there.
On his journey
he happily sailed,
thinking he was not seen
by the one who
condemned him.
The wind is favorable.
After a couple of leagues
there comes a storm.
Jonah said to the pilots
(seamen):
"The storm is strong,
lives are at risk:
If you want the storm to
cease
have me thrown into the
sea,
for, while I am here,
it will not quit."

Responderam os pilotos
todos, em grande cuid*ado*:
—Ó homem, estás louco,
vário ou desesper*ado*?
—Não estou louco ou vário
nem tão-pouco desesper*ado*;
tenho ofendido o Senhor,
quero castigar o meu pec*ado*.
A instâncias que fez
ao mar o foram lançar,
mas o Senhor lhe deparou
um barco para o salvar.
Esta estranha embarcação
por Deus foi orden*ada*;
no ventre duma baleia
felizmente naveg*ava*.
Quarenta horas esteve
no ventre dessa baleia,
sempre posto em oração,
pedindo ao Senhor perdão
de todo o seu coração.
Chegou a baleia à Nívia
com vontade de lançar;
abriu a enorme boca,
lançou Jonas no areal.
Ficou muito contente
por nascer segunda vez;
pôs-se a louvar o Senhor
p'lo milagre que lhe fez.
Procurou a alguma gente
que cidade era aquela.
Disseram-lhe que era Nívia.

All the seamen replied
with great anguish:
"Man, are you insane,
delirious, or desperate?"
"I am neither crazy nor delirious,
and I am not desperate;
I have offended the Lord,
I want my sin punished."
At his urging
they threw him into the sea,
but the Lord provided
a ship to save him.
This strange vessel
God determined:
In the womb of a whale
he sailed happily.
Forty hours he was
in that whale's womb,
always in prayer,
begging for the Lord's forgiveness
with all his heart.
The whale arrived in Nineveh
feeling like vomiting;
it opened its great mouth,
vomited Jonah on the beach.
Jonah rejoiced
for being reborn;
he praised the Lord
for the miracle he made.
Jonah asked some people
the name of the town.
They said it was Nineveh.

Entrou a pregar, dizendo:	He began to preach, saying:
—Homens maus e errantes,	"Evil, errant men,
tratai de vos emendar;	try to mend your ways;
tendes o Senhor agravado,	the Lord is angry
porque o tendes ofendido.	because you offended him.
Se não vos emendardes,	If you do not mend your ways
vos dará grande castigo.	He will send a great punishment."
—Se o Senhor tem algum	"If the Lord has some punishment
castigo para nos dar,	to give us,
reparta-o por monte e vale	let him divide it between mountains and valleys,
e por onde não fizer mal.	where it can do no harm."
Tanto mal nos têm feito	People have caused us so much harm
e nos querem fazer;	and want to cause even more;
dai-nos o vosso bem,	give us your goodness
para que na santa paz	so that in holy peace
gozemos a glória. Amén.	we can enjoy glory. Amen.]

(Machado 1952, 33)

In "Daniel na Cova dos Leões," the prophet Habakkuk and his shepherds thank the Lord for the wheat, wine, and cattle that permit them to live in abundance. Habakkuk also laments the misfortune of the people, for some live in captivity in Babylon, while others remain in Jerusalem. He raises his eyes to heaven to beg for God's help. An angel appears at that moment and tells Habakkuk that God has commanded him to take dinner to Daniel, who was thrown into the lions' den six days before by evil men whose hearts are harsher than those of the beasts. The angel will take the prophet there by holding on to one of the hairs on his head;

he will not fall to the ground, for he is protected by the great God of Abraham. They arrive in Babylon. Daniel sets the table and shares the food that God sent with the lions. Having dined, Daniel and Habakkuk thank the Lord. Then Daniel hears a song that prophesies freedom for the children of Israel. The angel returns for Habakkuk, and Daniel remains behind.

Although predominantly strophic, the poem has eleven verses which rhyme either in *ó-e* or *-or*, and nine in *á-o*:

Estando Habacuc profeta
no campo,
ele mais os seus past*ores*,
dando graças ao Senhor
que lhe fazia tantos fav*ores*:
dava-lhe com abundância
trigos, vinhos e g*ados*
para viver com fartura
ele mais os seus cri*ados*.
Também estava lamentando
as penas que o povo
tem,
uns presos em Babilónia,
outros em Jerusalém.
Levantou os olhos ao céu
para pedir ao Senh*or*:
—Queirai-vos lembrar
de nós
pelo vosso divino am*or*.
Lá nessas alturas
viu um grande resplend*or*;
era um anjo do céu,

[The prophet Habakkuk
was in the fields,
he and his shepherds,
thanking the Lord
who gave him such
blessings:
With abundance He gave
him
wheat, wine, and cattle
to live with plenty,
he and his servants.
He was also bemoaning
the suffering of the
people:
Some were captive in
Babylon,
others in Jerusalem.
He raised his eyes to
heaven
in order to ask the Lord:
“Pray remember
us,
for the sake of your divine
love.”
There, in the heights
he saw a great light;
it was an angel from

serafim do Senh*or*.
O anjo disse: —Manda-te o Senhor
que leves o jantar a Daniel,

que há seis dias que o lançaram
no lago dos le*ões*
homens piores que feras,
condenados coraç*ões*.
—Como hei-de ir contigo, Senhor,
se eu não posso andar depressa?
—Eu te levarei pendente
por um cabelo da cabeça,
que não hás-de cair no chão.

Quem levas na tua guarda
é o grande Deus de Abraão.

Chegaram a Babilónia,
lá no lago o achou;
enquanto comeu e falou,
o anjo se retirou.
Daniel, admirado, disse:
—Quem vos trouxe aqui, meu pai?
—Manda-te o Senhor socorrer
o teu miserável est*ado*.
Habacuc, banhado em lágrimas, disse:
—Dá-me os braços, filho am*ado*;
como estás? —Muito bem, meu pai,

heaven,
one of the Lord's seraphs.
The angel said:
"The Lord commands
you to take dinner to Daniel,
who six days ago was thrown
into the lion's den
by men worse than
beasts,
with evil hearts."
"How can I go with you, Sir,
since I cannot walk quickly?"
"I will carry you, hanging
by a hair in your head,
and you will not fall to the ground.
The one who keeps you
is the great God of Abraham."
They arrived in Babylon,
in the den he found him;
while he ate and spoke
the angel disappeared.
Surprised, Daniel said:
"Who brought you here, Father?"
"The Lord has sent help
for your sorry condition."
Bathed in tears,
Habakkuk said:
"Give me your arms,
beloved son;
how are you?" "I
am fine, Father,

melhor do que mereço.
Oh grande Deus de Adonai,
que há seis dias que aqui estou
de leões acompanh*ado*,
do grande Deus poderoso
favorecido e ampar*ado*.
Louvado seja o Senhor
que a vida me tem guard*ado*;
seja para o amar e servir
e para lhe fazer obras
do seu santo, divino
agr*ado*.
Pôs a mesa Daniel
e pelos leões chamou,
para repartir com eles
o que o Senhor lhe mandou.
—Come, filho abenço*ado*,
que isso não está bom;
foi feito por past*ores*.
—Bom é e bom será;
louvado seja o Senh*or*
que tanto nos dá.
Acabaram de jantar,
deram graças ao Senh*or*.
Nisto ouviu Daniel
uma música cantada;
o que a música dizia
Daniel escutava.
Dizia desta maneira:
—Olhai, filhos d'Israel,
que liberdade feliz
o Senhor anunciou!
Pôs-se a contar as semanas,

better than I deserve.
O great God Adonai,
I have been here for six days
together with lions,
by the great, powerful God
favored and sustained.
Blessed be the Lord
who has preserved my life;
may it be to love and serve him
and to perform deeds
pleasant to his holy,
divine will."
Daniel set the table
and called for the lions
in order to divide with them
what the Lord had sent.
"Eat, my blessed son,
it is not very good
because it was cooked by shepherds."
"Good it is, good it will be;
blessed be the Lord
who gives us so much."
They finished eating
and thanked the Lord.
Then Daniel heard
music and song;
to what the music said
he listened.
It said as follows:
"Listen, children of Israel:
Happy liberty
the Lord has announced!"
He began to count the weeks

não as pôde contar;
pôs-se a somar os dias,
não os pôde somar:
os segredos do Senhor
ninguém os pode penetrar.
—Chorai, filhos d'Israel,
chorai o vosso pecado
com todo o vosso coração;
quem com o Senhor
se pegou,
nunca lhe faltou o perdão.

A esse tempo chegou o anjo,
por Habacuc chamou;
com as lágrimas nos olhos
um se foi e o outro
ficou.
Bem-dito seja o Senhor
que a vida nos guardou;

seja para o servirmos,
para o louvarmos,
e para o nunca olvidarmos.
Amén, Senhor.

and was unable to do it;
he began to count the days
and could not add them:
The secrets of the Lord
cannot be comprehended.
"Weep, children of Israel,
weep for your sin
with all your heart;
those who have
sought the Lord
have never lacked
forgiveness."
Then the angel arrived
and called Habakkuk;
with tears in their eyes
one left, the other
stayed.
Blessed be the Lord
who has preserved our
lives;
may it be to serve him,
to praise him,
and never forget him.
Amen, Lord.

(Schwarz 1925, 55-57)

Thanks to the existence of an early version, we know that the original rhyme of "O Sacrifício de Isaac" was in *á-o*, but the Crypto-Jewish ballad only preserves eight verses with that rhyme, the last two of which are quite far apart from the others. Were it not for our knowledge of the early version, the poem could have been easily regarded as being strophic. Since "Jonas" has seven verses in *á-a* and four in *á-o*, it could well have consisted of two assonanted series, which is very common in Pan-Iberian balladry. As we know, because of the archaic paragogic *-e*, in early Spanish ballads verses in *ó-e* often rhymed with verses in *-or*.

"Daniel" has eleven such verses, and no less than nine in *á-o*. Although coincidence must be taken into account, this suggests that both "Jonas" and "Daniel" could have been originally in one or more assonances. In other words, they could be very old, supplementing our knowledge of the early tradition. Although it would seem that only the discovery of early versions could confirm this hypothesis, there still remains another possibility. If, like "O Sacrifício de Isaac," the two ballads included motifs of midrashic origin, then there would be no question of their early origin, but, as far as I know, the two poems have not yet been studied from this perspective.

In the fifth Crypto-Jewish ballad, "A Passagem do Mar Vermelho" (RPI, E8), the people depart from Egypt on the fourteenth day of the first month of the year. They sing in praise of the Lord and ask Moses if he intends to take them to that desert without bread, wine, or shepherds with their sheep (cattle). Moses raises his staff, hits the salty sea, and twelve paths open to let the people pass. They cross the Red Sea safe and sound because the Lord has commanded it, and they go toward the Promised Land. Being very thirsty, they beg for water. The ballad ends with a prayer that asks the Lord to free His people from captivity and from their enemies:

Aos catorze de la luna	[On the fourteenth day of the moon
do primeiro mês do *ano*,	of the first month of the year,
parte o povo do Egipto	the people leave Egypt
com Israel, seu irm*ano*.	together with Israel, their brother.
Cantigas iam cantando,	They sang songs,
ao Senhor iam louv*ando*.	they praised the Lord.
Louvavam o Senhor	They praised the Lord

com todo o seu coração.	with all their hearts.
—Aonde nos trazes, Moisés?	"Where do you bring us, Moses?
A este despovo*ado*	To this barren place
onde não há pão nem vinho	where there is neither bread nor wine,
nem pastor com gan*ado*?	nor a shepherd with cattle?
Pede ao alto Senhor	Ask the great Lord
que nos leve a nossas casas.	to take us to our homes."
Moisés, com vara	Moses, with his staff
alçada,	raised,
bateu no mar salg*ado*;	stroke the salty sea;
abriram-se doze carreiros	twelve passages opened
para passar o seu povo.	for his people to pass.
Passaram a são e s*alvo*	They passed safe and sound
porque o Senhor o	because the Lord so
mandou;	commanded;
passaram o Mar Vermelho	they crossed the Red Sea
para a terra da promissão.	towards the Promised Land.
O povo, aflito de sede,	Suffering with thirst, the people
ao céu clamava por *água.*	prayed to heaven for water.
Adiante vai Moisés	Moses walks ahead
com a sua vara alç*ada*;	with his staff raised;
por mandado do Senhor	by the Lord's command
bateu numa pedra m*ara*	he stroke a Mara (*bitter—Hebrew*) rock
e lançou água cl*ara.*	and clear water came forth.
Bendito seja o Senhor,	Blessed be the Lord,
para sempre engrandecido;	for ever exalted;
de uma pedra lançou á*gua*	from a rock he provided water
para aquele povo tão aflito.	for that suffering people.
Moisés, profeta santo	Moses, holy prophet,

do Senhor amado,
querido
imperador da nação,
destruidor do Egipto,
pede por misericórdia
àquele Deus infinito
que nos dê o seu bem,
nos leve ao seu reino,
nos livre do cativeiro.

Conhecei, irmanos da irmandade,

o Senhor criou
os quatro elementos:
pó, vento, água,
sombra de paredes.
Assim como nos livrou
de tão grandes perigos,
nos livre dos inimigos.

O Senhor nos defenda
de trabalhos e perigos.
Quando formos acometidos,
nós sejamos vencedores
e os inimigos vencidos.

Permita Deus que assim seja
e os anjos digam amén.

Amén, Senhor. Ao céu vá.

(Machado 1952, 39-40)

dear to the Lord,
beloved
emperor of our nation,
destroyer of Egypt,
for mercy's sake ask
the great, infinite Lord
to grant us his goodness,
to take us to his kingdom,
to deliver us from captivity.
Let it be known, brothers of the brotherhood,
the Lord created
the four elements:
Dust, wind, water,
the shade of walls.
As He has delivered us
from such great dangers,
may He also deliver us from our enemies.
May the Lord defend us
from worry and danger.
When we are attacked,
let us conquer
and our enemies be vanquished.
May the Lord so will it
and may the angels say amen.
Amen, Lord. May it [this prayer] rise to heaven.

Note that there are only seven verses in *á-o* and that the rest of the poem is strophic. Although early versions never reached print, there is no doubt that this ballad goes far back in time, perhaps to pre-Expulsion days, because it is also preserved by the Eastern Sephardim. Since the Jewish versions are all in *á-o*, there is no doubt that this constituted the original rhyme of the ballad:

’En katorze de nîsān, ’el primer dí’a del anyyo,
’el puíevlo de Yiśrā'ēl de Ayifto salyyó kantando,
ken kon las masas al ’ombro, ken kon los ižos ’en brasos;
las mužeres kon ’el ’oro, lo ke ’era lo más livyyano.
Aboltaron la kara atrás, por ver lo ke an kaminađo.
Vyeron venir ’a Par^{c}õh, kon ’un pendón korolađo.
—¿Ande mos truśites, Mõšeh, ’a mu’erir ’en despovlađo;
’a mu’erir sin sinbultura ’i ’en la mar ser a’ogado?
—Azed Θefîlāh, gidyyós, ’i yyo aré por ’el mi kavo.
Tanto fu’e sus ’esklamasyyones, al syelo ’izo burako.
Saltó ’una boz del syelo, kon Mõšeh ’uvo avlađo:
—Toma la vara, Mõšeh, toma la vara ’en tu mano.
Parte la mar ’en 12 kalezas, kita ’a los ğidyyós a nađo.
Ande kaminavan ğidyyós, la mar se ’iva aresekađo.
Ande kaminava miçrî, la mar se íiva arenovanđo.
(Armistead and Silverman 1971, 129)

[On the fourteenth day of Nisan, the first day of the year, the people of Israel left Egypt, singing; some carried maces, some held children in their arms; the women carried the gold, which was the lightest of all. They turned their faces to see how much they had walked. They saw Pharaoh coming with a scarlet banner. “Where have you brought us, Moses, to die in this barren place, to die without burial and be drowned in the sea?” “Pray to God, Jews, and I will do my part.” Their outcries were such that they pierced heaven. A voice came from heaven and spoke to Moses: “Take the staff, Moses, take the staff in your hand. Divide the sea into twelve passages, let the Jews swim to safety.” Where the Jews walked the sea became dry. Where an Egyptian walked the sea closed in again.]

Before coming to an end, I would like to propose the existence of a sixth, previously unknown ballad. In the Crypto-Jewish poem, the crossing of the Red Sea concludes with verse 22. The eleven verses that follow (23-33) continue with a different subject:

O povo, aflito de sede,	[Suffering with thirst, the people
ao céu clamava por *água*.	prayed to heaven for water.
Adiante vai Moisés	Moses walks ahead
com a sua vara alç*ada*;	with his staff raised;
por mandado do Senhor	by the Lord's command
bateu numa pedra m*ara*	he stroke a Mara rock
e lançou água cl*ara*.	and clear water came forth.
Bendito seja o Senhor,	Blessed be the Lord,
para sempre engrandecido;	for ever exalted;
de uma pedra lançou *água*	from a rock he provided water
para aquele povo tão aflito.	for that suffering people.]

These verses refer to the biblical episode where, having traveled in the desert for three days without finding water, the Jews arrive at a place called Mara. There was water there, but it was so bitter that they could not drink it. God then told Moses to throw a certain piece of wood into the water, and it became fresh (Exod. 15:22-25). At Raphidim, when the people clammored for water once again, God told Moses to strike a certain rock in Horeb, and water flowed from it (Exod. 17.1-6). By referring to the rock as Mara, the Crypto-Jewish ballad conflates the two episodes, turning them into one. Notice that five of the eleven verses rhyme in *á-a*. This suggests very strongly that they derive from a separate ballad, which now survives only in contamination with another, as often happens in the oral tradition. In fact, the combination of the two episodes constitutes another aspect of the condensation which also characterizes oral transmission. Consequently, what we have here is a new, previously unknown ballad, which I shall entitle "A Pedra Mara."

In sum, the Crypto-Jewish poem just examined constitutes a composite text. It opens with "A Passagem do Mar Vermelho" (verses 1-22), and continues with "A Pedra Mara" (verses 23-33), and with the non-narrative closing verses (34-56). All of these verses consititute a prayer in which Moses is asked to intercede before God for His people, so that He will deliver them once again from captivity and from their enemies. What we have here is an example of syncretism, for the Crypto-Jews have transformed Moses into a saint, and expect him to intercede on their behalf, thus according him the same role as Catholics give to their saints.

To conclude, we have examined three of the five groups or types of prayers into which I have divided the Crypto-Jewish tradition: (1) prayers documented in inquisitorial trials, (2) prayers inspired by the Bible, and (3) prayers adapted from the paraliturgical Christian tradition and de-Christianized in the process. It was not within the scope of this essay to examine prayers of the fourth type: those taken from official Christian tradition, and of the fifth type: those that are exclusively Crypto-Jewish, of undetermined origin.

The modern prayers examined here, with variants in inquisitorial trials, document the continuity of Crypto-Judaism in Portugal from the sixteenth century until modern times, but, as we know, Portuguese Crypto-Judaism goes further back, for it dates from the end of the fifteenth century. The Crypto-Jews also preserve a total of six ballads. Except for "O Sacrifício de Isaac" and "A Passagem do Mar Vermelho," all are exclusively Crypto-Jewish. "No Céu Está um Castelo" adapts and de-Christianizes part of a Christian nativity ballad. "O Sacrifício de Isaac" seems to go far back in time, for it is the only one to preserve two verses matched only in the version published in 1550. "Jonas" and "Daniel na Cova dos Leões" exist only among the Crypto-Jews, but, since the manner in which they combine strophic and assonanted verses does not differ from the other ballads, they are probably very old as well. The previously unnoticed fragment entitled "A Pedra Mara" constitutes a ballad about the thirst suffered by the Jews in the desert during Exodus. The jewel of the Crypto-Jewish ballads, however, is "A Passagem do Mar Vermelho." Although there are no early versions of it, it corresponds to "El paso del Mar Rojo" which is still sung very far away from the Iberian Peninsula, by the Sephardim of Greece and Turkey. It probably goes back to the fifteenth century, thus linking two peoples that, although very far apart from each other, have a common origin, and who, five hundred years ago, formed one rather than two different peoples.

These prayers and ballads, of course, testify to the crucial role played by memory in the preservation of the Crypto-Jewish tradition. Because the Inquisition forbade books in Hebrew and possession of written materials in the vernacular was extremely dangerous, the Crypto-Jews soon lost memory of classical Jewish liturgy, and felt it necessary to form a new one of their own. They created prayers for practically every occasion. Some of those prayers must have been composed by them, for they have not been documented elsewhere, but others were based on the Old Testament or adapted from the surrounding official and paraliturgical Christian tradition. During the sixteenth and seventeenth centuries, the transmission of this liturgy depended completely on memory. The prayers and the ballads were orally transmitted from generation to generation in secrecy, without any written support. Since the few manuscript family prayer books that exist are said to date from the eighteenth century, it was probably after Pombal forced the Inquisition to cease its activities in the 1740s that some Crypto-Jews began to write them down. As a comparison of these relatively modern prayers with their earlier inquisitorial counterparts indicates, many of them had deteriorated considerably. This is also true of the ballads. The only plausible explanation is the caution and secrecy with which they had to be transmitted. When a person makes mistakes or introduces unacceptable changes while singing Christian ballads, listeners correct them immediately, because they also happen to be familiar with the poems. Thus, the community serves as a control, helping to preserve tradition. Because of their lack of freedom, this did not apply to the same extent in the Crypto-Jewish community. Fear caused them to meet infrequently, and much was forgotten. Nevertheless, the Crypto-Jews were able to transmit a considerable body of liturgy orally. For two centuries, their faith depended exclusively on memory, a memory which, besides perpetuating their reaction to the circumstances in which they had to live, also enabled them to preserve a unique, separate identity.

Notes

1. To a great extent, this essay brings together and summarizes findings that I presented in several previous studies (Fontes 1990-93, 1991, "Mais Orações," 1992, "Tres Orações," 1992, 1994, 1997, 1998). A slightly different Spanish version is under consideration for *Ispania: Revista interdisciplinaria sobre las culturas de España.* An asterisk at the beginning of a poem indicates that what follows is a synthetic, factitious version.

2. The edict of expulsion states the following: "Bien sabedes o deuedes saber que . . . nos fuemos ynformados que en nuestros reynos auia algunos malos christianos que judaysauan e apostotauan de nuestra santa fe catolica, de lo qual era mucha cabsa la comunicaçion de los judios con los christianos" [You must know or ought to know that . . . we were informed in our kingdoms there were some bad Christians who judaized and committed apostasy against our holy Catholic faith, and that to a great extent this was caused by the contact between Jews and [New] Christians] (Beinart 1993, 224).

3. These figures are based on tax documents and the head polls that the Spanish refugees had to pay upon crossing the border. For the traditional, highly exaggerated estimates, see Tavares 1982, 270-71, n. 278, and Kayserling 1971, 98, n. 7.

4. Artur de Barros Basto (1927, 1928, 1929, 1934, 1935, 1937, 1938), Samuel Rodrigues (1932), Casimiro de Morais Machado (1952), José Leite de Vasconcellos (1958), Amílcar Paulo (1956, 1959, 1969, 1971, *Os Judeus* 1985 [here the author brings together the prayers and ballads that he collected over the years], "O Ritual" 1985), David Augusto Canelo (1987), and Maria Antonieta Garcia (1993).

5. Regarding the role of Pombal, see Azevedo 1989, 346-58; Saraiva 1985, 202-9.

6. This prayer, however, figures in a Spanish inquisitorial trial (Blázquez Miguel 1988, 67-68; the author does not indicate the date). In 1574 a Hebrew manuscript containing the "Shema" was discovered in Cabeço de Vide, in a wall that had to be torn down in the house of a New Christian (Coelho 1987, 1:201).

7. Some of these prayers were published in Azevedo 1989, 484-86; Schwarz 1925, 95-107 (from the same trial as Azevedo, but more prayers are transcribed); Freitas 1952, 1954; Coelho 1987, 1:199, 201-2, 204, 210-11, 216, 223-24; Mea 1985; Tavares 1987, 96; see now David Gitlitz's splendid book as well, which brings together a great number of Spanish and Portuguese prayers culled from various sources (1996, 443-49).

8. The sentence is grammatically incorrect, and therefore difficult to interpret. "Arrevelle" (from "arrevelar," "to wake up") is in the imperative; "adormece" is in the present indicative. If we correct the first verb to "arrevella," then the sentence means "People who wake up and fall asleep";

if we make the second verb agree with the first—"Povo que arrevelle e adormeça"—then it means "Let people wake up and fall asleep."

9. Other versions: Paulo, *Os Judeus* 1985, 64; Canelo 1987, 159; García 1993, 189. Mrs. Mota recited two other prayers right after, combining them as one (Fontes 1991, 515).

10. I chose to follow Catalán because he edits the ballad, adding punctuation.

11. For a detailed study of this ballad, see Fontes 1994.

Works Cited

Armistead, Samuel G., with the collaboration of Selma Margaretten, Paloma Montero, and Ana Valenciano. Musical transcriptions edited by Israel J. Katz. *El romancero judeo-español en el Archivo Menéndez Pidal (Catálogo-índice de romances y canciones)*. 3 vols. Madrid: CSMP, 1978. (cited in text as CMP).

_____. and Joseph H. Silverman. *The Judeo-Spanish Ballad Chapbooks of Yacob Abraham Yoná*. Folk Literature of the Sephardic Jews. Berkeley and Los Angeles: University of California Press, 1971.

Azevedo, J. Lúcio de. *História dos Cristãos-Novos Portugueses*. 3d ed. Lisbon: Clássica Editora, 1989.

Barugel, Alberto. "The Sacrifice of Isaac." In *Spanish and Sephardic Balladry*. American University Studies, no. 2, Romance Languages and Literatures, no. 116. New York: Peter Lang, 1990.

Basto, Artur Carlos de Barros. "Tradições Cripto-Judaicas." *Ha-Lapid*, no. 2.8 (September-October 1927): 8.

_____. "Tradições Cripto-Judaicas: O Manuscrito de Rebordelo." *Ha-Lapid*, no. 2.10 (April 1928): 4-8.

_____. "Tradições Cripto-Judaicas: O Manuscrito de Perpétua da Costa." *Ha-Lapid*, no. 3.22 (August-September 1929): 6-8.

_____. "Tradições Cripto-Judaicas: Orações dos Maranos [sic] de Vilarinho de Mogadouro." *Ha-Lapid*. no. 9.67 (September 1934): 3-5.

_____. "Tradições Cripto-Judaicas Trasmontanas." *Ha-Lapid*, no. 10.72 (September-October 1935): 2-4.

_____. "Tradições Cripto-Judaicas: Orações dos Cripto-Judeus Transmontanos." *Ha-Lapid*, no. 11.80 (June-July 1937): 7-8.

_____. "Orações dos Cripto-Judeus: Tradições Maranas [sic]." *Ha-Lapid*, no. 13.88 (October 1938):3.

Beinart, Haim. *Los judíos en España*. 2d ed. Madrid: Mapfre, 1993.

Bíblia Sagrada. 4th ed. Lisbon: Difusora Bíblica (Missionários Capuchinhos), 1969.

Blázquez Miguel, Juan. *Inquisición y criptojudaísmo*. Madrid: Kaydeda, 1988.

Canelo, David Augusto. *Os Últimos Criptojudeus em Portugal*. Belmonte: Centro de Cultura Pedro Álvares Cabral, 1987.

_____. *O Resgate dos Marranos Portugueses*. Belmonte: Edição do Autor, 1996.

Caro Baroja, Julio. *Los judíos en la España moderna y contemporánea*. 3 vols. 3d ed. Madrid: Istmo, 1986.

Catalán, Diego. *Por campos del Romancero. Estudios sobre la tradición oral moderna*. Madrid: Gredos, 1970.

CMP. See Armistead et al., 1978.

Coelho, António Borges. *Inquisição de Évora (Dos Primórdios a 1668)*. 2 vols. Lisbon: Caminho, 1987.

Cruz, José Pires da. *Romanceiro Tradicional da Beira Baixa*. Idanha-a-Nova: Câmara Municipal, 1995.

Domínguez Ortiz, Antonio. *Los judeoconversos en la España moderna*. Madrid: Mapfre, 1992.

Ferré, Pedro. "O Romanceiro Entre os Cristãos-Novos Portugueses." *Anais da Real Sociedade Arqueológica Lusitana*, 2.ª Serie, 1 (1987): 145-75.

Fontes, Manuel da Costa. *Romanceiro Português do Canadá*. Preface by Samuel G. Armistead and Joseph H. Silverman. Acta Universitatis Conimbrigensis. Coimbra: Universidade, 1979.

_____. *Romanceiro Português dos Estados Unidos*, 1: *Nova Inglaterra*. Preface by Samuel G. Armistead and Joseph H. Silverman. Acta Universitatis Conimbrigensis. Coimbra: Universidade, 1980.

_____. *Romanceiro da Província de Trás-os-Montes (Distrito de Bragança)*. Collected with the collaboration of Maria João Câmara Fontes. Preface by Samuel G. Armistead, and Joseph H. Silverman. Musical transcriptions by Israel J. Katz. 2 vols. Acta Universitatis Conimbrigensis. Coimbra: Universidade, 1987 (cited in text as TM).

_____. "Four Portuguese Crypto-Jewish Prayers and Their 'Inquisitorial' Counterparts." *Mediterranean Language Review*, no. 6-7 (1990-1993): 67-104. (Special Issue Commemorating the Fifth Centenary of the Expulsion of the Jews from Spain: 1492-1992. In memoriam Henry R. Kahane [1902-1992].)

_____. "Orações Criptojudias na Tradição Oral Portuguesa." *Hispania*, no. 74 (1991): 511-18.

_____. "Mais Orações Criptojudias de Rebordelo." *Revista da Universidade de Coimbra*, no. 37 (1992): 457-69. (Also titled *Homenagem a Luís de Albuquerque*).

_____. "Três Orações Criptojudias de Rebordelo (Vinhais) e os Seus Paralelos Inquisitoriais." In Manuel Viegas Guerreiro, ed., *Literatura Popular Portuguesa: Teoria da Literatura Oral/Tradicional/Popular*, 129-55. Lisbon: Acarte, Fundação Calouste Gulbenkian, 1992.

_____. "Between Oral and Written Transmission: *O Sacrifício de Isaac* in the Portuguese Oral Tradition." *Journal of Folklore Research*, no. 31 (1994): 57-96.

_____. "O *Justo Juiz* Cristão e a Inquisição em Duas Orações Criptojudaicas de Rebordelo." *Hispania*, no. 80 (1997): 1-8.

_____. *O Romanceiro Português e Brasileiro: Índice Temático e Bibliográfico (com uma bibliografia pan-hispânica e resumos de cada romance em inglês)/Portuguese and Brazilian Balladry: A Thematic and Bibliographic Index (with a Pan-Hispanic bibliography and English summaries for each text-type).* Selection of the musical transcriptions and commentary by Israel J. Katz. Pan-European correlation by Samuel G. Armistead. 2 Vols. Madison, Wisconsin: HSMS, 1997 (Cited in text as RPI).

_____. "Duas Novas Orações Criptojudaicas de Rebordelo." In *II Jornada Sergipana de Estudos Medievais. Romanceiro Tradicional*, 69-99. Aracaju, Sergipe: Secretaria de Estado da Cultura, 1998.

Freitas, Eugénio de Andrea da Cunha e. "Tradições Judio-Portuguesas." *Douro-Litoral*, no. 4.5-6 (1952): 17-22.

_____. "Tradições Judio-Portuguesas: Novos Subsídios." *Douro-Litoral*, no. 6.1-2 (1954): 145-49.

Friedenberg, Daniel M. "Las catacumbas judías de Portugal." *Davar*, no. 88 (1961): 81-91.

Garcia, Maria Antonieta. *Os Judeus de Belmonte. Os Caminhos da Memória.* Lisbon: Instituto de Sociologia e Etnologia das Religiões, Universidade Nova, 1993.

Gitlitz, David M. *Secrecy and Deceit: The Religion of the Crypto-Jews.* Philadelphia and Jerusalem: The Jewish Publication Society, 1996.

Herculano, Alexandre. *História da Origem e Estabelecimento da Inquisição em Portugal.* 3 vols. Livros de Bolso Europa América, [Mem Martins]: Publicações Europa-América. 1982.

"Japan's Crypto-Christians." *Time* (January 11, 1982): 71.

Kayserling, Meyer. *História dos Judeus em Portugal.* Trans. Gabriele Borchardt Corrêa da Silva e Anita Novinsky. São Paulo: Livraria Pioneira, 1971.

Machado, Casimiro de Morais. "Subsídios para a História do Mogadouro: Os Marranos de Vilarinho dos Galegos." *Douro Litoral*, no. 5.1 (1952): 17-49.

Mea, Elvira Cunha de Azevedo. "Orações Judaicas na Inquisição Portuguesa: Século XVI." In Yosef Kaplan ed., *Jews and Conversos: Studies in Society and the Inquisition*, 149-78. Jerusalem: World Union of Jewish Studies, and The Magnes Press, the Hebrew University of Jerusalem, 1985.

Mendonça, José Lourenço D. de, and António Joaquim Moreira. (1842-1861). *História dos Principais Actos e Procedimentos da Inquisição em Portugal.* Ed. João Palma-Ferreira. Biblioteca de Autores Portugueses. Lisbon: Imprensa Nacional. Reprint 1980.

Paulo, Amílcar. "Os Marranos em Trás-os-Montes (Reminiscências Judeo-Portuguesas)." *Douro Litoral*, no. 7.5-6 (1956): 523-60; 7-8: 627-59.

_____. "Freixo de Espada-à-Cinta: Subsídios para o Estudo Antropológico e Etnográfico do Concelho." *Douro Litoral*, no. 4.9 (1959): 779-810.

_____. *Romanceiro Criptojudaico: Subsídios para o Estudo do Folclore Marrano.* Bragança: Escola Tipográfica, 1969.

_____. *Os Criptojudeus.* Oporto: Athena, 1971.

_____. *Os Judeus Secretos em Portugal.* Oporto: Labirinto, 1985.

_____. "O Ritual dos Criptojudeus Portugueses (Algumas Reflexões Sobre os Seus Ritos)." In Yosef Kaplan ed., *Jews and Conversos. Studies in Society and the Inquisition*, 139-48. Jerusalem: World Union of Jewish Studies and the Magnes Press, the Hebrew University of Jerusalem, 1985.

Primav. See Wolf and Hofmann *Primavera y flor de romances*, 1945.

Rodrigues, Samuel. "Tradições Cripto-Judaicas: Orações de Pinhel." *Ha-Lapid*, no. 7.51 (December 1932): 2-4.

Rodríguez-Moñino, Antonio, ed. *Silva de romances (Zaragoza 1550-1551)*. Zaragoza: Cátedra Zaragoza, 1970.

Roth, Cecil. *A History of the Marranos*. 2d ed. New York: Meridian Books and the Jewish Publication Society of America, 1960.

RPI. See Fontes. *O Romanceiro Português e Brasileiro*, 1997.

Saraiva, António José. *Inquisição e Cristãos-Novos*. 5th ed. Imprensa Universitaria, 42. Lisbon: Estampa, 1985.

Schwarz, Samuel. *Os Cristãos-Novos em Portugal no Século XX*. Lisbon: Empresa Portuguesa de Livros, 1925.

Shapiro, Haim. "They're 'Secret Jews' No Longer." *Jewish Exponent* (March 1991): 5, 15.

Tavares, Maria José Pimenta Ferro. *Os Judeus em Portugal no Século XV*. Lisbon: Universidade Nova de Lisboa, Faculdade de Ciências Humanas, 1982.

_____. *Judaísmo e Inquisição: Estudos*. Lisbon: Presença, 1987.

TM. See Fontes. *Romanceiro da Província de Trás-os-Montes*, 1987.

Valle, Carlos. "Tradições Populares de Vila Nova de Gaia: Orações Tradicionais." *Revista de Etnografia*, no. 3 (1964): 138-81.

Vasconcellos, José Leite de. "Cristãos-Novos do Nosso Tempo em Trás-os-Montes e na Beira; Suas Práticas Judaicas." In *Etnografia Portuguesa. Tentame de Sistematização*, 162-235. Written according to the materials of the author. Expansion with new information by M. Viegas Guerreiro. Introduction, notes, and conclusion by Orlando Ribeiro. Vol. 4. Lisbon: Imprensa Nacional, 1958.

Vasconcellos, José Leite de. *Romanceiro Português*. 2 vols. Acta Universitatis Conimbrigensis. Coimbra: Universidade, 1958-1960 (cited in text as VRP).

VRP. See Vasconcellos *Romanceiro Português*, 1958-1960.

Wolf, Fernando J., and Conrado Hofmann. *Primavera y flor de romances*. Ed. Marcelino Menéndez Pelayo. Antología de poetas líricos castellanos 8. Edición Nacional de las Obras Completas de Menéndez Pelayo 24. Santander: CSIC, 1945 (cited in text as Primav.).

◆ Chapter 3

A Collusion of Gardens: Continuity of Memory in Medieval Sephardic Poetry

Libby Garshowitz and Stacy N. Beckwith

"In the days of Ḥasdai Ibn Shaprut the Nasi (905-970) they began to chirp, and in the days of Samuel the Nagid (993-1056) they sang aloud." In these words the medieval chronicler of early Andalusian Jewry Abraham Ibn Da'ud (1110-1180) described the "Golden Age" of Jewish Andalusian Poetry.[1] More apt imagery could not have been chosen to depict the explosion of Jewish poesy during the Muslim caliphate of 'Abd al-Raḥmān III (912-961). It was at this time that Dūnash Ibn Labraṭ (d. ca. 990), a native of Fez, Morocco, arrived in Córdoba and introduced Arabic meter into Hebrew poetry. With this he launched the era of the "exquisite song birds" (Ashtor 1973, 252-53; Schippers 1993, 50). Indeed, for the next two centuries (roughly 950-1150), the Jews of southern Spain, concentrated mainly in the cities of Granada, Córdoba, Seville, and in the border city of Toledo, produced exquisite poetry, both secular and sacred, that reflected well the influence of their Muslim domicile. At the same time, these poets also inculcated the tropes and signifiers through which they would later mourn and recall the loss of this domicile, with the Jews' incremental departure as professing Jews, first from areas in southern Spain, and then from the entire Iberian Peninsula.

Hebrew meter and poetic form in medieval al-Andalus were indubitably outgrowths of contemporary Arabic poetry. So, too, were many of the thematics in Hebrew verse, including the splendor of gardens, the delicacies of nature, and the delights of wine, women, cameraderie, and revelry. That the inspiration for these subjects was identifiably local is apparent in the works of Andalusian Arab and Hebrew poets alike. It is also manifest in nostalgic poems by Muslims who traveled abroad while al-Andalus still marked the height of their empire, in Arab verse dating from the displacing Berber-Almohad invasion of Iberia in the mid-1100s, and in Arab poetry dating from the collective loss of al-Andalus in 1492 to the present day. Much of the vivid and sensuous garden imagery in Arab Andalusian poetry, medieval or modern, was either coterminous with lived experience in al-Andalus, or else it looks back with an eye to recapturing the essence of that zenith.

In other words, when Arab Andalusian poetry was flourishing in Islamic Spain, the Arab national tragedy entailing and surrounding the loss of this paradise had yet to occur. By contrast, the mnemonic strains in Hebrew poetry composed in al-Andalus, in Christian Spain, and in the Spanish Jewish (Sephardic) diaspora post-1492, reveal the most about Jewish memories of Spain when they are examined in the context of a series of Jewish national tragedies which, by 70 C.E., had already occurred. As outlined briefly below, these include the twice decreed loss of homeland and national, spiritual anchor: the divinely endowed Temple in Jerusalem. A need for the Jewish homeland to become essentially portable, with the expansion of two consecutive Jewish diasporas (from 586 B.C.E. and 70 C.E.), focused attention on all aspects of the thirty-nine books of the Hebrew Bible, not just as a reservoir of comfort and teachings, but also as a source of communicative tools with sacred and popular national resonance.

If the Jews' initial period of stability in al-Andalus seemed a modified echo of national stability in Canaan under the biblical kings David and Solomon, and if their flight into Spanish Christian territories at the time of the Almohad invasion recalled the instability of the subsequent division of Canaan into northern and southern Jewish kingdoms, their respective surrender to foreign conquerors, and the first mass expulsion of Jews from their national territory, this was due in no small measure to the diachronic signifying capacities of the garden and nature imagery in biblical prose and poetry, which correlated closely with Andalusia's abundant verdure. The Song of Songs, in particular, which only joined the biblical canon when its suggestive depictions were identified as a collective metaphor for Israel's conjugal, at times perfidial, relationship with the Jewish God, was a poem replete with flowers, fruit, and animals which could simultaneously evoke the natural abundance in Jerusalem's ancient hills and in Spain's medieval gardens. Similarly, biblical storm images could be tapped not only in foreboding and mourning for the single old man facing sickness and death, but also for the Spanish Jews as a whole, well ensconced in Andalusia as they had been in Zion, facing another two-staged displacement.

One Spanish Jewish figure who managed to rise to unprecedented political heights in Granada, despite his early flight from Berber-invaded Córdoba, was Samuel

Halevi, who eventually earned the Hebrew title, Hanagid, "the leader," in 1030, when he became a vizier in the Granada court. Throughout a tumultuous and multifaceted career, Samuel Hanagid also composed Hebrew poetry. Being so close to the winds of political change, it follows that the biblical images through which Hanagid extended Israel's dialogue with God, and her self-interrogation over the loss of her ancient homeland, should also register thanks for bounty and premonitions of depravity on the Spanish scene.

For allegorical purposes, and also, as Hebrew medievalist Raymond Scheindlin has suggested, quite possibly for some "literary funmaking as part of [an] evening's entertainment" Samuel Hanagid wrote a series of poems about fawns, "*'ofer*," and gazelles, "*ṣevi-ṣeviyya*," both male and female (Scheindlin 1986, 75; Schirmann 1961, 1:167, n. 18). Quite often the gender lines in these poems appear blurred.[2] In one, the male fawn is transformed into a musician, a foil for the poet, who urges him to drink up and kiss his bloodred lips to the sound of harps and lutes, against the backdrop of a moonlit night. As Scheindlin notes, ". . . this is not a love poem, only a poem replete with pleasure and beauty" (70). The literal beauty of Zion's vineyards and their produce, everywhere in Andalusian Hebrew poetry, become metaphors for physical comeliness. In another poem the gazelle is depicted as a beautiful but treacherous woman, offering, along with a crystal goblet of bloodred fiery wine, her lips, while her fingertips are stained with the blood of her victims. In yet another poem, Samuel Hanagid himself is ravished by the gazelle's eyes (Schirmann 1961, 1:167, n.18). He is consumed with unquenchable passion, and is prepared to flee with the animal anywhere in the countryside to enjoy a romp in the glories of nature. In his artfully crafted love poems, of which these are only a miniscule number, Samuel Hanagid reveled in his observation of God's abundance, as seen in his literary recollections of Zion which also connote his own Andalusian surroundings.

The gazelle is also a metaphor for the robust and rigorous. Another poet, Joseph Ibn Ḥasdai composed an elegy for his friend and contemporary, Samuel Hanagid. In the poem the latter appears to Ibn Ḥasdai in a dream.[3] Ibn Ḥasdai praises Hanagid's fame, erudition, generosity of spirit, art, and Jewish priestly descent, intimating that Hanagid is perhaps on a par with the exalted status of his namesake, the prophet Samuel. (Samuel Hanagid quoted in Schirmann 1961, 1:173-74, lines 15-33). Extending national memory, Ibn Ḥasdai's panegyric to Samuel Hanagid, couched in sensual language reminiscent of the Song of Songs, ends with a plea to God to assist in Israel's rebirth, much as the prophet Samuel had been instrumental in forging Israel's early, ancient monarchy.

Ibn Ḥasdai did not exaggerate Samuel Hanagid's distinctiveness, for among the latter's many achievements were his actual and/or envisaged skills in battle. These Hanagid recorded in many of his own poems,[4] mainly as a vehicle, again, for remembering the loss of Zion and Jewish independence there.[5] The warrior poet's descriptions of battles against the enemies of al-Andalus are perhaps but a pale reflection of those fought by his eponymous ancestors in the land of Israel against, for example, their eternal 'Amaleqite enemy.[6] To them Hanagid added contemporary Christian, "*benei edom*," and Arab, "*benei qeturah*," adversaries (Samuel Hanagid, "Battle at Alfuente" quoted in Schirmann 1961, 1:83-92, line 41). In contrast to serene gardens, fiery constellations, and fragrant aromas, Hanagid's battles won and lost emphasize the traumas of war: upheavals, like those wrought on Sodom and Gomorrah, cunning battle maneuvers, rampaging horses, scorpion and bee-like weapons, menacing skies, bloodied warriers, and bloody ancient sacrifices (Samuel Hanagid, "The Battle at Alfuente," quoted in Schirmann 1961, 1:83-92, lines 55-65).[7] Hanagid's ultimate abhorrence of war is best summed up in his brief poem by that name:[8]

War's beginnings resemble a beautiful wench with
whom every man yearns to play, but its end is like
a repulsive whore whose fans wail and mourn.
(Hanagid, Schirmann 1961, 1:142, No. 21)

From here Hanagid's victories in Zion and/or Andalusia, either imagined or real, are recognized for what they are: futile, and the cause of both flight and exile. No matter how admiring Spanish Jewish poets were of their immediate habitat, nor how comfortable some appeared in their important positions in royal courts, exile was never far from their minds or pens. The varying protection which Jews enjoyed under Moslem hegemony came with the acceptance of taxes and official minority status (*dhimmis*). Samuel Hanagid lamented his and his people's longstanding exile and grief in these words:

A bejeweled dove in precious ornaments coos
among the myrtle branches,
I asked her: "For whom and why do you weep?"
She answered: "for turtledoves and swallows."
I replied: "As do I my friends lament, who, laden
with my love are gone."
They left me and my eyes gush blood
on my palms to them outstretched,

I behold their cheeks as they weep
Like roses the shards scattered them.
(Hanagid, Yarden 1966, 310, No. 196; Schirmann 1961, 1:83-84, No. 23)

Despite the beauty of this poem, a sense of the macabre hovers over all; the poet feels abandoned, as a lover abandons his beloved. On the other hand, Hanagid and his contemporaries turned local, natural bounty into spokespieces for the fullness of life. A veritable cornucopia of ripe fruits, budding vines, and aromatic spices, all symbols of productivity, affluence, and eroticism, are depicted in both Hebrew and Arabic Andalusian poetry. The comely "apple" in the Song of Songs takes on a life of its own, especially in the talented hands of Samuel Hanagid.[9] For him, the sight of a bowl of apples, real or ornamental, was an opportunity to entertain his companions, both Muslim and Jewish, with witty discourse, challenging riddles, and apt truisms, all suffused in biblical nuances (See Yarden 1966, 275-78, Nos. 116-29). Red and green apples are metaphors for the jewels in the breastplate of the high priest in the ancient Jewish Temple; the *'urim ve-tumim* (oracle), and the personification of wisdom. For Hanagid the apple was to be admired for its beauty, its fragrance, and its delicacy—but it was not to be eaten.[10] Intrinsic to the poet's entertaining ditties about the apple, which well reflect enjoyment of life in Andalusian high circles, is a message that speaks, among other things, to managing such a lifestyle: be wise, discreet, cautious in choosing one's friends, and especially one's mate. Like the apple, she must be fragrant, sweet, smooth, and comely.[11]

When Solomon Ibn Gabirol (1021-1058) was lifted from poverty by a later Jewish *Nagid*, or "vizier," in the Arab court in Granada (Samuel ibn Nagrela), his years as a regal poet, though transitory, allowed him to give free rein to his imagination, and to sing the praises of lush milieux in Zion and Andalusia, in tandem. In his poem "The Palace and the Garden,"[12] Ibn Gabirol mimicks the setting for the lusty lovers in the Song of Songs, who call to each other as they frolic amidst beautiful gardens and cavorting fawns and gazelles.[13] The beautiful grounds, courtyards, and palace of the Alhambra, with which Ibn Gabirol was familiar, may very well have been the model for these gardens in his poem.[14] In this composition the author heralds the end of winter and its rainy season, the return of songbirds, and the appearance of budding flowers and burgeoning fruit trees, all governed by the heavenly constellations. Movement is rampant in the joy of renewed life as the visual and the olefactory fuse, in flowing streams, moving clouds, full foliage, fragrant flowers, orchards, and vineyards, among which are nestled houses and a majestic palace.

Solomon Ibn Gabirol is carried aloft on eagles' wings, and fantasizes that this palace, tiled and marbled, and surrounded by insouciant stone-carved animals, may have been similar to that built in Jerusalem by his royal namesake, the biblical King Solomon. Here, in a Spanish/biblical setting that evokes the sovereignty of the Jewish God and of Israel, Ibn Gabirol finds solace. A range of flowers, birds, and animals compete to present themselves as the most glorious of creatures, as do the heavenly constellations and the dazzling sun. All are outshone, however, by the poem's recipient, before whose radiance earthly kings and rulers pale. Upon him is lavished praise for his incessant benefactions, and what began for Ibn Gabirol as a romp amid the wonders of renewing nature, and a profuse tribute to a benefactor (likely the poet's contemporary patron), ends as a paean to "God toward whom all rivers flow. Truly, He is unique in heaven and on earth" (Ibn Gabirol, "The Palace and the Garden" quoted in Schirmann 1961, 1:223-25, lines 33-44).

Accolades to God, service in his Temple, and in ancient/contemporary royal courts are frequently echoed in Ibn Gabirol's other poems through imagery of aromatic gardens, wet, fluid fields, gushing rains, and the virginal sun adorned in jeweled ornaments and prancing intermittently over paved courtyards like a royal, horse-drawn chariot clothed in regal colors of purple and gold.[15] From finely detailed descriptions of such gardens, Ibn Gabirol and his contemporaries also produced sketches of individual flowers. With personification of natural phenomena a classic feature in medieval Arabic and Hebrew poetry, various flowers take on human attributes and discourse among themselves, spinning out the intrigues of contemporary and ancient/sacred courtly life, in metaphor.

Surpassing them all, not surprisingly, is the rose, "*ha-shoshan*," (also pale rose or lily). This flower is visually magnificent and majestic, comparable to the beloved in the Song of Songs who triumphantly proclaimed: "I am the lily of Sharon, the wildflower of the valleys."[16] For Moses Ibn Ezra (1055-after 1135), the practitioner par excellence of medieval Hebrew poetry, the *shoshan* was more than a beautiful flower: it was conceivably the strongest of all the flowers, "a stately warrior" and king of the garden,[17] leading a "procession" of rejuvenated, richly colored spring flowers. For Ibn Ezra and his contemporaries, nature's rebirth, which was signified by this recurring procession of flowers from their wintry prison through cyclical renewal, recalled Israel's ancient glories, including territorial sovereignty and submission to God (the *shoshan*) alone, not to foreign rulers.[18] Metaphorically, release from prison/exile leads to the poet's challenge to "drink up [and] enjoy." Inasmuch as drinking wine is a toast to freedom and deliverance, and not necessarily to hedonism, the poem ends, nonetheless, with a caution to avoid errant ways and to be loyal to the observance of the rituals of Judaism.[19] Likewise, in Solomon Ibn Gabirol's poem "A Rose on the Branch," contemplation of a single rose in the company of the blazing sun and a blushing doe whose tears metamorphose into rain, becomes a plea for restoration of the priestly service that administered the Jewish Temple in Zion and Judaism's ancient sacrificial rites, and for communication with God.

In an entourage other than that of the caliphal court of Granada, or of the Jewish sacred court in Jerusalem (God's Temple), the majestic rose stood not only for physical beauty and enjoyment, but also for wit and acuity. At the court of Alphonso the Wise, in Christian Toledo, Todros ben Judah Halevi Abulafia (1247-after 1298), gave the rose center stage in a "flowers' debate." Todros Abulafia, a scion of an illustrious, but somewhat impecunious Toledan family, revived the art of Hebrew poetry in Christian Spain even prior to the Catholic Reconquest.[20]

As can be expected from changed historical circumstances, that is, the flight of many Jews in the wake of the Berber-Almohad invasion of southern Spain, Todros Abulafia's poetry differed in many ways from that of his Andalusian Jewish predecessors. Nonetheless, in Todros Abulafia's hands Toledan gardens received the same effusive descriptions as those in Andalusia. The poet wrote his "flowers' debate" in honor of Ibn Shoshan, a Jewish newcomer to Toledo from Morocco (See Schirmann 1961, 4:421-23, No. 367). In his verse, the author's tapestried earth, encircled by a jeweled necklace of flowers, frames the rivalry of a group of prominent flowers: the red rose, "*vered*," the pale rose, "*shoshan*," and the narcissus, "*ḥavaṣelet*." The flowers mockingly debate their respective characteristics and differences, but none can compare with the original *shoshan*, which stands for the Ibn Shoshan family; righteous, courageous, humble, philanthropic, and praiseworthy. Hyperbole was a necessary component in both Arabic and Hebrew medieval poetry.[21]

Among Jewish writers in Moslem and Christian Spanish territories alike, praise was lavished not only on friends and benefactors (the latter, in Solomon Ibn Gabirol's case, at least, being vital), but also on the poets' own writing skills. Such encomiums can often be considered in contrast to a poet's mortality and bodily afflictions. For Ibn Gabirol, "tormented" all his life by a "skin ailment," ". . . poetry was more than the expression of a dazzling literary talent. It was emotional therapy in every sense of the word" (Sachar 1994, 11). The ailing Ibn Gabirol, beset by real or perceived enemies, celebrated his own creative talents in "perfumed, honeyed and jewelled words that outweighed even precious silver" (Solomon Ibn Gabirol quoted in Schirmann 1961, 1:227-28, No. 87, lines 1-3, *'al-shirato*, "about his poetry"). Prone to melancholy and conscious of his own mortality, he visualized his immortal soul as a bird freed from the prison of its body, "fluttering like a dove," and longing to return to its Maker, "like a bird to the nest." He was notably proud of his ability to create poetry:[22]

I am the Song[23]—and the Song is my Serf
I am a Lyre for all singers and strummers.
(Ibn Gabirol, Brody-Schirmann 1974, 77, No.129)

"Boasting," as we have seen above, was a distinctive feature in both Arabic and Jewish poetry. It could be applied to one's own skills, or it could be used in the poetic immortalization of benefactors and patrons. Poems enrobe the latter in sizzling scarlet and princely purple during their lifetimes. Death, even in laudatory verse, is accompanied by a lack of ornament, however. In death benefactors and poets alike are eclipsed by shadows, night skies, and barren earth. Life, unlike nature, is depicted as brief and transitory. Only nature is cyclical;[24] only flowers march in processions that assert as much.

Humans, meanwhile, take their cue from the pathetic fallacies suggested by stormy weather and changing seasons. Samuel Hanagid's "Death of Av and Elul,"[25] mark not only the waning of summer and fall, and the approach of wintry, foreboding skies, but also the recurring theme of approaching senescence, accompanied by the vain hope that wine might dispel its attendant gloom.[26] Hence the urgency in this poem to seize the moment: "drink up, all night and day, from cup and jug" (See Samuel Hanigid quoted in Schirmann 1961, 1:6). Cold descends, flames rise, and hope soars that the pressures of old age might be alleviated by fellowship and cameraderie. Wine is described as fiery and red; its fragrance was celebrated from Spain to India. However much it signifies God's burning bush in the Book of Exodus, and acts as a reminder of God's covenant with the Jews, though, wine can numb, but it cannot dispel an aging man's personal malaise, nor an exiled people's liminality.

There are instances, reflecting as yet little disturbed Andalusian Jewish lifestyles, where the best is made of storms and winter, as in one of Solomon Ibn Gabirol's most celebrated poems, "The Writing of Winter":

The winter writes with the ink of its rain and its showers
with the nib of its lightning, with the hand of its clouds.
A message upon the garden, of violet and purple
No human being can perform acts such as these

And when the earth becomes jealous of the skies
It embroiders its garments with flowers like the stars.
(Ibn Gabirol, Goldstein 1982, 78)

Before the age of the Andalusian "songbirds" drew to an ignominious close, Moses Ibn Ezra also depicted a personal paradise, blending the fellowship of humans, local/biblical flora, and fauna:

A handsome face,[27] a cup of wine, a garden,
birds warbling, sounds of rushing water—are
balm for the beau, joy for the jittery, verse for the
vagabond, wealth for the wretched,
and salve for the sick.
(Ibn Ezra, Schirmann 1961, 2:378, No. 11)

Instability and a premonition of comfortless suffering are inherent in this poem, however, whose content contrasts starkly with the fragrant, wafting spices, the sun-tinted, embroidered fields, the all night festivities, and their attendant, temporary physical setbacks in Ibn Ezra's "wine poems." Indeed, elsewhere Ibn Ezra depicts himself and his companions as powerless and deprived of weapons of self-defense (See Moses Ibn Ezra quoted in Schirmann 1961, 2:372-73, Nos. 1, 3-5). This poet experienced first hand the destruction of Spain's southern Jewish communities, and their inhabitants' flight from invading Almohad Berbers into Christian territories. Thus expelled himself, Ibn Ezra's physical loneliness magnified palpably his spiritual solitude as he sought metaphysical, if not real refuge in mountainous terrain in Castile. Here his proximity to the heavens evoked plaints of pain and alienation. In his poem "In the Fortress on a Castillian Mountaintop,"[28] Ibn Ezra depicts himself as a wandering, wounded bird surrounded by still bigger birds who empathize with him in his isolation. Far from family and friends, he compares his solitude and that of his people, far from Zion and soon to be far from Andalusia, with the solitude of the dove, which is symbolic of Jewish national suffering.

Along these lines, a different poet from Christian Gerona, Meshullam ben Shelomo de Piera (d. 1260),[29] who was a contemporary of the celebrated rabbi and philosopher Moses ben Nahman, also harnessed transient seasons, spectacular but fleeting dawns, warbling birds, and musical diversions, to communicate plaint and ill ease. De Piera's setting in one of his poems is still another wine banquet. Just as depictions of such scenes registered bounty and contentment, and then jitters and premonitions in Andalusian Hebrew poetry, so do the main visitors in de Piera's gathering extend this downward trend. The guests in this latest scene seem to be storm clouds, thunder, fog, and rain-harnessed chariots.[30] Joy and mirth are absent. Instead, the thunderous skies rumble, the mighty, biblical cedars of Lebanon are exfoliated, mountaintops are banded in snow and ice like a necklace of crystal beads, and fields are denuded.

There is no shelter for either the poet or his wine-numbed companions, who had gathered to enjoy bubbly drink, good music, and beautiful bejeweled women. In his dreamlike trance the poet remembers that "God is all he has, his future (his cup) is in divine hands." From God de Piera awaits wonderful gifts. Whether or not these are ever bestowed is left unresolved by other poems, such as one replete with biblical and midrashic references, beautiful pastoral imagery, and descriptions of the mating season. In this poem de Piera conversely harrasses his enemies—cheats, hedonists, and sinners, who are all jealous of his literary activities. The poet vows nonetheless to remain true to his artistic calling, honest in his business dealings, and faithful to God.[31] What may be a commentary on contemporary society may also be a reflection on the breakdown of Spain's southern Jewish communities and on the larger crisis already threatening and being felt in the Christian north.

That Spain's migrating Hebrew poets began recalling their abundant lifestyles and surroundings in Andalusia in language and imagery identical to familiar and hallowed signifiers of national sovereignty and security amid the beauties of ancient Zion was by now a matter of inherently explicable tradition. Abandonment was a constant refrain among those poets who witnessed the slaughter that befell much of Andalusian Jewry at the hands of the marauding Berbers. One writer, Isaac Ibn Ghiyyat (1038-1098), mourned the fragrant orchards and profuse vineyards that were laid waste. The heavenly stars were dimmed with the dispersal of Andalusia's Jewish inhabitants who had been raised in the lap of luxury like their Davidic and Solomonic ancestors.[32] Solomon Ibn Gabirol complained to his "beloved" (i.e., God), "How could you have enslaved me? Let me go to the Land of the Gazelle (*'ereṣ ha-ṣevi*),[33] and drink its wine." This beverage, of course, could neither dull nor dissipate the impact of further pillaging and expulsion from southern Spain at the hands of the Almohads in the years surrounding 1140.

One of Moslem Spain's most famous surviving Jewish scholars, Abraham ben Meir Ibn Ezra (b. Tudela 1093-1167, place of death undetermined) recorded his reaction to the outrages which had visited Andalusia. Upon his arrival, as an exegete, in Rome, "with terrified heart" he wrote: [34]

I'll shave my head
and bitterly bewail
Seville's travail,
Its slain dignitaries
and their captive children
Its genteel daughters
delivered to an alien creed[35]
Córdoba abandoned, like a desolate sea—
There the mighty
and powerful
died hungered
and parched
Not a Jew left in Jaén or Almería
No sustenance in Majorca
or Malaga,
Surviving Jews smitten anew,
This I shall grieve and bitterly glean
And dolefully lament in my groans and griefs,
And as they melt like water
My eyes drip tears.
(Abraham Ibn Ezra, Brody-Albrecht 1906, 138-40)

Despite such verse, now singly recalling specific sites in Andalusia and a contemporary, fallen civilization, as glimpsed already, a renewed era of Jewish literary creativity began in Spain's Christian kingdoms to the north. This lasted from roughly 1150 to 1492. In the communities of Aragon, Castile, and Navarre, Jews flourished, engaged in commerce, studied, wrote, and became influential in royal courts. Religious and secular poetry highlighted their creative activities and they elaborated many of the themes of their southern forebearers: love, beautiful surroundings, the joys of wine—and exile. Despite lengthy periods of affluence and social and political influence, these Jews in

Zaragoza, Barcelona, and throughout northern Iberia, still retained and expressed their people's traditional hope for collective liberation and submission to God's sovereignty alone.

The relative quiet which the Jews of northern Spain had enjoyed since the beginning of the Catholic Reconquest of the Peninsula ended when brutal persecutions in 1391 ravaged and subsequently erased many Jewish communities. There followed mass conversions to Christianity and the flight of many Jews who refused to compromise their religious beliefs. Simon ben Ṣemaḥ Duran (b. 1361 in Majorca, d. 1444 in Algiers), was a philosopher, polemist, and a Talmudist who was among those who sought refuge in Algiers, where he later resumed his career as a community leader, adjudicator, and recorder of Spanish Jewry's lost glory. His poems memorialize the destroyed Sephardic communities in tandem with Zion, now overrun by spiritual and cultural orphans or foreigners ("foxes") such that the two homelands intertwine:

> Absolute destruction awaited me
> when the enemy destroyed my mansions.
> On desolate Mount Zion
> parade before me little foxes,
> Remnants of Zion's beloved children
> my oppressors devoured.
> My consolation—my redeemed will yet return
> and all my foes will flee,
> All who devour them will be arraigned:
> "I will utterly consume them," says the Lord![36]
>
> (ben Ṣemaḥ Duran, Schirmann 1961, 4:589)

Scenes of persecution, captivities, baptismal fonts, and chaos, as well as enemies' taunts to worship a foreign God, "*'el zar*," Jesus, haunted ben Ṣemaḥ Duran's memories as he encapsulated the Jews' recollections of remote Zion and proximate Spain (Ṣemaḥ Duran quoted in Schirmann 1961, 4:589-91, *Teḥinah*). The cries for divine help in his poetry clash with a recurring refrain of *shalom*, "peace." These scenes of destruction were of naught, however, when compared with the havoc wrought on the millenium-long Jewish entity in Spain when its conquerors, Ferdinand and Isabella, banished professing Jews from within its territories in 1492. The Spanish Jewish exiles who then successfully made their way to Italy, Greece, Turkey, the Netherlands, and more distant destinations, carried with them, along with their meager belongings, memories not only of the physical beauty of their beloved Spain, but also of a glorious, now defunct school of Hebrew poetry. In the latter's place was a vacuum that would never be filled again.

Solomon ben Reuben Bonfed (d. after 1445), "the last Hebrew poet in Spain" (Schirmann 1997, 628) and witness to many forced and voluntary religious conversions (Schirmann 1946, 35-36) wrote,

When I die so will die
Jeduthun and Heman[37]
My generation with my passing
Will resemble a widower

(Bonfed, Schirmann 1946, 4:35-36)

Jeduthun and Heman were musicians in the ancient Jewish Temple in Jerusalem. Their evocation in this poem once again brings ancient and contemporary glory and tragedy into an expressive synergy. Bonfed's dirge for the loss of "those who hungered for sweet songs," is tempered by the contempt he felt for his fellow Jews who had converted to Christianity, especially after the disastrous Tortosa

Disputation (1413-1414), in which he himself had been a participant.

While it signaled the end of a comprehensive literary school, the expulsion of the Jews from Iberia did not entail the end of their writing of poetry. The talents of the Sephardim (Spanish and Portuguese Jews and their descendants) accompanied them into this, the latest Jewish exile. For one of the most prominent emigrés, Judah Abravanel (b. ca. 1460, in Lisbon, d. after 1523, in Naples), scion of the illustrious Abravanel family that had moved intermittently between Spain and Portugal, the memories of Spain recounted by his famous father, Isaac Abravanel,[38] reflected neither glorious gardens nor insouciant wine soirees, but the horrors of exile and the physical pain of decades of wandering and dispersion. In a lengthy historical-autobiographic poem, "Complaint about Fate,"[39] Judah Abravanel mourns the destruction of Spanish Jewry, the flight of thousands of survivors, and his forced alienation from his elder son, Isaac, "my beloved fawn," and "my soulmate," who, at the age of one year, in 1492, had been sent to Portugal in the care of a Christian nurse and there was possibly forcibly converted.

Judah Abravanel mourned as well the death of his younger Genoese-born son, Samuel, when the latter was only five. The horses and chariots that had metamorphosed into the forces of nature for the earlier Spanish Jewish poets became for Judah Abravanel his own personal demons. His "spring (*'aviv*) was over, his friends and contemporaries exiled . . . his parents and siblings scattered" ("Complaint about Fate," lines 9-12). For Judah Abravanel and his inconsolable wife, the loss of this son signified that,

> the moon will ever be dark before me
> my star concealed in my gloom

My sun's spark will neither illumine my dwelling
nor shine on my roof or window
my narcissus of Sharon (*ḥavaṣelet sheroni*)
will never bloom
nor will rain shower upon my grass.
(Judah Abravanel, Schirmann 1934, 218)

Here immediate personal tragedies meld into the admixture of recent and ancient national disasters—and landscapes. While the moon will be dark, the poet's personal star concealing, and his grass parched, their inclusion in this stanza, even in the negative, continues the tropes of nature long familiar in Hebrew poetry, from the Bible through a millenium of postbiblical composition in Spain. Underscoring this continuity are the only items that are specifically named in Judah Abravanel's poem: the narcissus, of biblical, and now Sephardic, reknown, and the ancient landscape of Sharon, which, through his possession of the flower, the writer also owns personally. Abravanel again displays his combined biblical and Sephardic literary heritage in directly recalling his lost son:

My friend, what are you amid a corrupt people
like an apple inside carob woods.
Your pure soul among the profane
is like a rose among thorns and grass
. . . .
Flee and be like a fawn and gazelle
(Judah Abravanel, Schirmann 1934, 218)

Implicit in this injunction is the understanding that the boy/animal will flee not to a place where he will remain the solitary apple, soul, or rose among adversaries, but to a homeland where he will find himself in like company, just as the gazelle joins the fawn in his father's verse. Given the steadiness with which the lyrics of medieval Spanish Jewish poetry evoked and created a nexus of national homelands: the ancient Israelite, the Andalusian, and the Christian Spanish, one can conclude that the young fawn Abravanel is being urged to find freedom in remembered spaces at both ends of the Mediterranean. A history of ancient territorial sovereignty won and lost, the annals of which abound with ecological descriptions and imagery that befit many aspects of a new, nurturing milieu, are the underwriters of medieval Sephardic poetry's modes of designating Iberia a *shoshan* among other flowers in an ongoing procession of collective memory.

Notes

1. See Ibn Da'ud 1967, 102. For good background on Medieval Sephardic poetry, see Brann 1991, 1-22.
2. See Hayyim (Jefim) Schirmann 1961. 1:151-56, n. 50-51, and pages 167-68 for a series of poems dealing with fawns, deer, and gazelles. See also Scheindlin 1986, 60, 61, 68-71, 74, 75.
3. Joseph Ibn Ḥasdai lived in Zaragoza during the first half of the eleventh century. See Schirmann 1961, 1:171-72 for brief details on his life and this sole remaining poem of his; see 172-75 [*shirah yetomah*] *ha-la-ṣevi ḥen,* "the lovely gazelle," for this poem, especially lines 4-14. See also Carmi 1981, 302.
4. For an analysis of Arabic and Hebrew "war poems" also see Schippers 1994, 217-43, especially 221-22 and bibliography.
5. See Samuel Hanagid in Schirmann 1961, 1:112, "A Dirge for Zion's Destruction: The War at Yaddir" (Hebrew).
6. For the uniqueness of Samuel Hanagid's war poems see Schirmann 1961, 1:85-92, line 12 of "The Battle at Alfuente"; 1:93, "A Prayer on the Battlefield"; 1:94, "The Defeat of Seville's Battalions," especially lines 47-48; 1:117-18, "The Victory at Lorca" (Hebrew). See also Doron 1989, 56, and Mirsky 1992, 164-65.
7. See also Schippers 1994, 225-29.
8. Samuel Hanagid quoted in Schirmann 1961, 1:142, No. 21 "war's beginnings resemble a beautiful wench" (Hebrew). See also Carmi 1981, 291, and Goldstein 1982, 72. All translations of Hebrew poems from here

forward by Libby Garshowitz, except for Ibn Gabirol, "The Writing of Winter," translated by Goldstein 1982, 78.

9. See Song of Songs 2:3; 5, 7:9; 8:5. On the prevalence of the different "fruit crops" depicted in Arabic poetry also see Schippers 1994, 34-35. For the translation "apricot" rather than "apple" for the *tapuaḥ* in the Song of Songs, see Bloch and Bloch 1995, 149; for the translation "quince," see Falk 1990, 151.

10.Yarden 1966, No. 120: *ve-tapuaḥ le-hariaḥ*; No. 125, *ve-tapuaḥ-yefeh to'ar ve-tov reiaḥ ve-tov piryo*. See also Song of Songs, 2:3.

11. Yarden 1966, No. 128: *requhah kemo reiho, metuqah kemo ta'amo, halaqah kemo gildo, ve-yafah kemar'ehu.*

12. See Ibn Gabirol, quoted in Schirmann 1961, 1:223-25, No. 84: *ha'armon veha-bustan*, and Song of Songs 1:14; 2:11-13 for a description of the garden flowers. On Ibn Gabirol also see Schippers 1994, 56-59.

13. Song of Songs 4:1-6. See also Bloch and Bloch 1995, 3-5.

14. On a partial analysis of this poem, also see Scheindlin 1986, 8.

15. Ibn Gabirol, *Shirei ha-ḥol*, quoted in Yarden 1975, 338-39, No. 181,*'et niṣṣevu kha-ned resiseha*, "when the dew piled up in a heap"; Ibn Gabirol op. cit. quoted in Brody-Schirmann 1974, 84, No. 138, especially lines 6-12. Also see Schippers 1994, 192.

16. Song of Songs 2:1, *ḥavaṣelet ha-sharon, shoshanat ha'amaqim*. For different interpretations of the flowers see Bloch and Bloch 1995, 148-49, and Falk 1990, 173-74. Throughout this essay we may vary the translations of these flowers in keeping with the context of the specific poem.

17. See Moses Ibn Ezra quoted in Schirmann 1961, 2:371, *kotenot passim lavash ha-gan*, "the garden wears a multicolored coat." Also see Scheindlin's analysis 1986, 34-39, and the biblical allusions quoted there. For details of Moses Ibn Ezra's writings, also see Schippers 1994, 59-62. Solomon Ibn Gabirol also writes about the "rose's" strength in his poem, *be-shoshanei leḥayyekha*, "your rosy cheeks are bulwarks," See Ibn Gabirol, *Shirei ha-ḥol*, quoted in Yarden 1975, 136, No. 65.

18. This is based on 2 Kings 25:29, King Jehoiachin's release from his Babylonian prison.

19. Based on Numbers 9:13, where the context adjures the Israelites to proper Passover observance.

20. Brann 1991, 145-57, discusses Todros ben Judah Halevi Abulafia's penchant for sexual escapades, his composing poems about them, and then, as he aged, his writing of quasi-penitential verse about his regrettable adventures, a recurrant theme among his Andalusian predecessors, both Arabs and Jews.

21. For different genres in both Arabic and Hebrew poetry see Schippers 1994, 72-104, 287-95.

22. Ibn Gabirol quoted in Schirmann 1961, 1:192, No. 61; Ibn Gabirol quoted in Brody-Schirmann 1974, 77, No. 129, *'ani ha-shir ve-ha-shir li le-'eved*. In his poem *'ate hod va-'ade u-levash ge'onim*, Schippers 1993, 79-82, No. 132, lines 11-14, 32-63, "don glory and excellence," Ibn Gabirol contrasts his poetry with that of his contemporaries and finds their

creations lacking. On his long illness, see his poem *ke'evi rav u-makkati 'anusha*, "my pain is great and my wound mortal," quoted in Schirmann 1961, 1:193.

23. In Schirmann's 1961 version of this poem he reads *'ani ha-sar*, "I am the Prince," whereas in Brody-Schirmann 1974, 77, the reading is *'ani ha-shir*, "I am the Song." Yellin 1975, 36, also reads "song" whereas Schippers 1994, 300, reads "Prince." The reading "song" is used here. See the preceding note.

24. See Solomon Ibn Gabirol quoted in Schirmann 1961, 1:109-11, "Reflections on his status in the state—the war at Yaddir," lines 38-40 (Hebrew). See also Mirsky 1992, 166-67. On the discussion of the literary genre of "boast" or "self-praise poems," see Schippers 1994, 241-43.

25. See Schirmann 1961, 1:167, No. 16, *met 'av u-met 'elul*. See also below on Meshullam de Piera's poem and Schippers 1994, 112-13.

26. The examples are too numerous to list. For one, see Todros ben Judah Halevi Abulafia quoted in Schirmann 1961, 4:427, No. 375 *sa'arot ha-sevah*, "hoary old age," and *hilbin se'ari 'et 'asher 'ahavti*, "I became prematurely gray."

27. The Hebrew masculine form *yefeh to'ar* is used in this poem.

28. Moses Ibn Ezra quoted in Schirmann 1961, 2:380, *ba-mivṣar 'al 'eḥad meharei qastiliyah.*

29. For a description of some of his poetry, see Schirmann 1961, 3:295-98. On the qualitative decline of poetry in Christian Spain, see Mirsky 1992, 183-87.

30. See Meshullam ben Shelomo de Piera, quoted in Schirmann 1961, 3:299 *Ha-setav*, "The Winter," *be-yom sagrir*, "On a Rainy Day."

31. Meshullam de Piera, quoted in Schirmann 1961, 3:307-10, No. 346, *ke'or boqer be-ruaḥ ṣaḥ shefa'im*, "like morning light in a scorching wind on high hills," lines 16-35. On the poem's title, see Jeremiah 4:11.

32. Isaac Ibn Chiyyat quoted in Schirmann 1961, 2:325-26, [*Qinah le-tish'ah be'av*], *gerushim mi-beit ta'anugeihem*, "banished from their pleasure palaces," lines 12-17, and Schirmann's 1961 introduction, 2:301-2.

33. The Land of Israel. For this expression see Daniel 11:16. The poem is found in Ibn Gabirol quoted in Schirmann 1961, 1:215-16, No. 8.

34. See *Shema' 'Imerei Shefer* in his introduction to his commentary on Ecclesiastes and quoted in Schirmann 1997, 19, n. 26. For excerpts of this poem see Schirmann 1997, 20, and for the complete poem with the poet's name in acrostic, see Brody-Albrecht 1906, 138-40.

35. That is, Muslim.

36. Jeremiah 8:13. See Schirmann 1961, 4:589, *qinah*, "dirge."

37. Musicians in the ancient Jewish Temple in Jerusalem. See 1 Chronicles 25:1, 3-7.

38. Isaac Abravanel, whose family had originated in Spain, had been born in Lisbon, as were his sons, but had relocated to Castile, where he achieved as much prominence in the Spanish court as he had in Portugal. With the expulsion of the Jews from Spain, he and his family fled again to

Portugal, where his son Judah had been born. From there they went to Naples. On the Abravanel family, see Leone Ebreo (Giuda Abarbanel) 1983, 15-43.

39. *Ha-telunah 'al ha-zeman*. See Schirmann 1934, 217-22, and Ebreo 1983, 37.

Works Cited

Ashtor, Eliyahu. *The Jews of Moslem Spain*. Vols. 1 and 2. Philadelphia: Jewish Publication Society, 1973.

Bloch, Ariel, and Chana Bloch, eds. *The Song of Songs: A New Translation with an Introduction and Commentary*. Berkeley: U of California P, 1995.

Brann, Ross. *The Compunctious Poet*. Baltimore: Johns Hopkins UP, 1991.

Brody, Haim (Heinrich), and Karl Albrecht. *The New-Hebrew School of Poets of the Spanish-Arabian Epoch*. Leipzig and New York: n.p., 1906.

Brody, Haim (Heinrich), and Hayyim (Jefim) Schirmann. *Shelomo Ibn Gabirol: Shirei ha-ḥol*. Jerusalem: Schocken Institute of the Jewish Theological Seminary of America, 1974.

Carmi., T., ed. and trans. *The Penguin Book of Hebrew Verse*. New York: Penguin Books, 1981.

Doron, Aviva. *Todros ha-Levi Abulafia: A Hebrew Poet in Christian Spain*. Tel Aviv: n.p., 1989. (Hebrew).

Ebreo, Leone (Giuda Abarbanel) *Dialoghi D'Amore*. Ed. and trans. Menachem Dorman. Jerusalem: n.p., 1983 (Hebrew).

Falk, Marcia. *The Song of Songs: A New Translation and Interpretation*. San Francisco: Harper Row, 1990.

Goldstein David, ed. and trans. *The Jewish Poets of Spain: 900-1250*. New York: Penguin Books, 1982.

Ibn Da'ud, Abraham. *Sefer ha-qabbalah*. 2 vols. Ed. and trans. Gershon D. Cohen. Philadelphia: Jewish Publication Society, 1967.

Mirsky, Aharon. "Hebrew Literary Creation," in ed. Haim Beinart, *The Sephardi Legacy*, Vol. 1. 147-87. Jerusalem: Magnes Press of the Hebrew University of Jerusalem, 1992.

Pagis, Dan. *Change and Tradition in Secular Poetry: Spain and Italy*. Jerusalem: n.p., 1976 (Hebrew).

_____. "Trends in Medieval Hebrew Literature," *Association for Jewish Studies Review*, no. 4 (1979): 125-41.

Sachar, Howard M. *Farewell España: The World of the Sephardim Remembered*. New York: Random House, 1994.

Scheindlin, Raymond. *Wine, Women and Death*. Philadelphia: The Jewish Publication Society, 1986.

Schippers, Arie. "Arabic and the Revival of the Hebrew Language and Literature," in Julie-Marthe Cohen, ed., *Jews Under Islam, A Culture in*

Historical Perspective," 75-93. Zwolle and Amsterdam: Waanders/Jewish Historical Museum, 1993.

_____. *Spanish Hebrew Poetry and the Arabic Literary Tradition.* Leiden: Brill, 1994.

Schirmann, Hayyim (Jefim). *Mivḥar ha-shirah ha-'ivrit be-'italyah.* Berlin: n.p., 1934.

_____. "Solomon Bonfed's Polemic Against Saragossan Dignitaries," *Qoveṣ 'al Yad*, no. 4 (1946).

_____. *Hebrew Poetry in Spain and Provence.* 4 vols. Jerusalem and Tel Aviv: 1954; reprint 1961.

_____. *The History of Hebrew Poetry in Christian Spain and Southern France.* Ed. Ezra Fleischer. Jerusalem: Magnes Press of the Hebrew University of Jerusalem, 1997.

Yarden, Dov, ed. *Shirei ha-ḥol le-rabi Shlomo Ibn Gabirol.* Jerusalem: Hebrew Union College Press, 1975.

_____. *Diwān Shmuel Hanagid 993-1096.* Jerusalem: Hebrew Union College Press, 1966.

Yellin, David. "The Influence of Arabic Poetry on Hebrew Poetry in Spain." In A.M. Habermann, ed., *The Writings of David Yellin: Hebrew Poetry in Spain*, 30-43, Vol. 3. Jerusalem: Ruben Mass, 1975.

◆ Chapter 4

Al-Andalus and Memory: The Past and Being Present among Hispano-Moroccan Andalusians from Rabat

Beebe Bahrami

A postcard for sale in the streets and shops of Rabat shows a cartoon sketch of a man walking out of an ancient gate of a Moroccan city toward the beach, wearing only swimming trunks and a Fez hat, carrying a towel and an ice-cream cone, accompanied by the caption, "*C'est l'Orient, c'est l'Occident, c'est le Maroc!*" This is a popular depiction of a widespread sentiment among Moroccans that they are both from the East and from the West. King Hasan II had a famous saying: "Morocco is like a tree with roots in Africa and its branches in Europe" (Laurent 1993, 66). This saying refers to a nation founded in both a transnational past and present.

Transnationalism is not a recent phenomenon for Moroccans, whose history and culture carry the influences of the Arab, African, and European peoples that have passed through this northwesternmost African nation. One group of Moroccans in particular, the Andalusians,[1] represent the multiple historical and cultural influences of the past on contemporary Moroccan society. Andalusian Moroccans in the country's capital, Rabat, are descendants of families from medieval Spain who were expelled from Iberia between 1492 and 1614, and who resettled in Morocco. This essay makes manifest the construction of a contemporary Andalusian Moroccan context, in the city of Rabat. It also addresses the inherent multidimensionality and multidirectionality of global phenomena touching this social context, by examining the transnational identity dynamics among Andalusians of Rabat, as guided by the ways in which they remember their historic roots in al-Andalus.

Introduction: Globalization, Complex Identities, and Localization

Among the major theoretical concerns in anthropology during recent years have been those involving global flows and transnationalism. The ideas of Hannerz (1992, 261-67) on cultural flows and creolization have elicited special attention as have Appadurai's notions of globalization, ethnoscapes, and deterritorialization (1990 and 1991). Erikson (1992), Foster (1991), Friedman (1990), Falk Moore (1989), and Smith's (1990) positions on globalization, localization, pluralism, and multiple traditions have also been significant. This essays especially concerns itself with Ulf Hannerz's ideas of global creolization and with Arjun Appadurai's understanding of ethnoscapes and processes of global territorialization in order to illuminate the syncretic dynamics of Andalusian identity in Rabat.

Hannerz argues that the world is undergoing cultural creolization through complex and dynamic multidimensional flows of political, economic, and cultural influences to and from global cultural centers and peripheries (1992, 217-67). He concludes that the global flows are not only extremely complex, but that they are also likely to bring forth unpredictable and new cultural centers and peripheries as new creolized cultures emerge in the world. In the context of contemporary Nigeria, for example, Hannerz also addresses the divergent access to global cosmopolitan knowledge and the experiences of "Beentos" (1992, 228-31). These are Nigerians who have literally, *been to* places abroad and who possess knowledge of the world from related experience, versus those Nigerians from the "Bush." The latter include Nigerians whose access, knowledge, and experience of the world have been restricted more to local cultures, but who nevertheless possess an imagination of the social lives of those going abroad (Appadurai 1991, 193).

Appadurai examines the flow of people, ideas, media, money and finances, and technologies, while emphasizing the importance of taking into consideration the flow of peoples or ethnoscapes, in contemporary ethonographies (1990 and 1991). Both Appadurai and Hannerz address the idea that what we are looking at is complex, multidirectional and multidimensional. Moreover, Appadurai emphasizes the important role that historical reconstructions of contemporary local situations can offer in understanding how each situation developed with the influence of people, ideas, and commodities not originally from the locale in question.

Memory is one of the critical elements that can render an identity multidirectional and multidynamic. Moreover, it is further argued here that all individuals possess both simple identities, identities that serve only one context or that are neither resilient nor relevant to several contexts, and complex identities. The latter are said to have multiple potentials and modes of expression and manipulation in changing contexts. Again, memory, in adding the great expanse of time and past events and diverse groups of origin, contributes significantly to a complex identity's potential for broad expression in shifting contexts.

Moroccan Andalusian identity is complex, with a multifacted and selectively remembered past: it is one identity label with multiple contextual relevances. For example, during a train ride to Tangier I was sitting in a train car with nine other people. A young Moroccan woman asked me why I was in the country. On mentioning my research on the Andalusians of Rabat, all nine people mentioned a range of diverse ideas as to what it meant to be Andalusian. None of these people was, in fact, Andalusian, and yet they all harbored diverse notions of what such an identity connoted. Some mentioned the widespread idea that Moroccan Andalusians have fairer skin coloring and have more children with blond hair and blue eyes than do other Moroccans. When I asked why this was so, everyone in the car said it was because Andalusians were more European than other Moroccans. Then one of the Moroccans added that Andalusians were also descended from Arabs who came from the eastern Mediterranean and the Arabian Peninsula. Because of this, he said, Andalusians also possessed many Arab as well as Andalusian features. In this vein, Arab features were defined as classical Middle Eastern expressions in music, poetry, and handicrafts that had influenced Spanish and other European societies during the Islamic period in Spain. These features are also important to Moroccans in general, for they compose an important part of Moroccans' cultural values and influences.

According to my train companions, and commonly expressed by many Moroccans I met, a person who is

Andalusian has a broad social universe in which to negotiate with diverse others, while always calling himself "Andalusian." There are other identites in Morocco that are also complex, such as Arab, Berber, and Jewish. Within these, Andalusian identity is among one of the most complex because of the many varied relational contexts that can come into play in an Andalusian's contact with a wide range of people. Andalusian identity owes much of its complexity to the fact that its remembered past spans not only several centuries, but also several cultures and contexts, including the European, the Arab, and the West African. I propose that in the globalization of the world, it is the complex identites with their complex memories that are surfacing, toward the localization and adaptability of global influences in both core and peripheral culture areas. This can be demonstrated through an examination of the Andalusians in Rabat.

The Andalusians of Rabat

The Andalusians of Rabat are people who claim descent from families forced out of Spain by Philip III, between 1609 and 1614. The refugees from this last mass expulsion from Spain were known as *moriscos*. This marks the fact that they were among the Hispanic Muslims who had submitted to Christian baptism over a hundred years earlier in order to stay in Spain. The *moriscos*, despite their distinction from other Andalusian Muslims because of forced baptism, possessed a continuity of historical identity along with those Andalusians in North Africa who were expelled from Spain between the thirteenth and fifteenth centuries. Today, the Andalusians of Rabat are among the cultural elite of the city, and in many cases, of the country. The collective historical and transnational Hispanic inheritance of the Andalusians in Morocco is comprised of the contemporary knowledge and memory of the following: diverse religious communities that once lived together in the Iberian Peninsula; the movements of peoples and ideas within the Islamic world to and from Iberia; the mass expulsions from Spain and the subsequent creation of immigrant communities around the Mediterranean and the New World; and the explosive commercial activities of those worlds in the sixteenth and seventeenth centuries.

Using Hannerz's terminology (1992, 261-67), the Andalusians of Rabat can be viewed as the product of a creolized culture; a blend of European, Arab, and African cultures, as evidenced by the use of these cultural labels in both Andalusians' and other Moroccans' discussions about what elements comprise the Andalusian identity. Today Andalusian families throughout Morocco draw upon this rich heritage in securing a position for themselves in the rapidly changing world of economic opportunities, national politics, migration patterns, and international relations. In Rabat there are between forty-five to sixty Andalusian families whose Moroccan origins stem back to the city's settlement by *moriscos* in the early seventeenth century. There are several other Andalusian families in Rabat today who have moved there from Tetouan and Fez. Many members from the Andalusian families of Morocco are in service to the king as advisors, ambassadors, diplomats, and administrators, to name but a few positions that they occupy within the national government. Not all Andalusians are involved in large business concerns and in politics. A number of Andalusians in Rabat are artisans, musicians, small business proprietors, and scholars. In any event, it is noteworthy that a common link in the occupational diversity of the Andalusians is that their chosen professions are often dictated by those that fall within a range of pursuits that have been traditionally Andalusian, first in Spain, and later in Morocco.

In describing their identity as complex, therefore, I refer to Moroccan Andalusians consistently as such. This would seem to signal that they possess, in anthropological terms, a single identity, which might be understood as an identity that is salient in many contexts. The Andalusian identity is one that can be a part of religious, political, and secular international spheres of interaction, for example, without the necessity of a name or label change. What changes in the case of Andalusians in Morocco are their memories and their references to the Iberian past, and the relevance of these in different social situations.

Andalusians' identity is complex because it involves multiple dimensions of self-perception, and consequently a more complex range of possible responses and reactions to varied circumstances. Greater adaptability to change is inherent. Finally, a complex identity is one that is more likely to be passed on from one generation to the next, provided that the society of which one is a part continues to recognize this identity as integral to itself. The fundamental and overall complexity of Moroccan Andalusian identity draws significantly on ancestral experience in medieval Spain as diverse and multivocal, and on the ways in which Andalusians have remembered this to the present day.

The Complexity of the Historical and Geographic Setting of the Andalusians of Rabat: Several Centuries of Global Locales

It is common for an Andalusian from Rabat to present his family history in two parts. The first part represents the period that his family resided in Spain. This Spanish half of the history brings up less detail, since it is in the more distant past. Sometimes the only known fact about an Andalusian's Spanish heritage is the name of the city or town in Spain from which his or her family came. I learned that much of what is forgotten of a family's Spanish history is made up for with a set of "collapsed" historical episodes in the mind of the person engaged in remembering. This is to say, where there is no specific memory, a general memory of the history of Islamic Spain is collapsed into the person's family history. I discovered a common thread in the ways Andalusian descendants tend to recall their Spanish roots. This was visible in the case of people I spoke with whose ancestors were refugees to Morocco from the thirtheenth-century Christian Reconquest of Seville (as was the family of the prominent medieval philosopher and social historian Ibn Khaldūn). The pattern of collapsing and generalizing memories and history was also exhibited by Andalusians whose predecessors were exiles from Granada before, during, and after 1492, or were *moriscos* who remained in Spain until later. Andalusians' memories of Spain also tend toward the metonymic. All Moroccan Andalusians take the total Andalusian heritage as their own heritage. So even if one family came from Castile in 1610, the Alhambra and the glory of Córdoba, Seville, and Granada are also a part of their identity attachments.

For example, one of the families I interviewed may have come from León, in northern Spain, in the early seventeenth century. Yet León, being associated more with Christian Spain than with Muslim Spain, meant less to this family than did the Spanish cities more famous for their Muslim history, especially Granada. Spain's multifaceted past, therefore, offers a Moroccan Andalusian of today an identity with profound depth and broad historic reference. This is especially so in light of the resonance which the esteemed Islamic Andalusian heritage has in wider Arab and Muslim contexts, in and beyond Morocco. This wide ranging resonance, in turn, is compounded by the high degree of contemporary Arab and Muslim imagining regarding al-Andalus. All of this imparts a legitimacy which underpins the Andalusian and his/her history's adaptability and relevance to several social contexts, again confirming Moroccan Andalusian identity as anthropologically "complex."

An example of the broad applicability of the "imagined" Andalusian identity came in the Second International Meeting of Muslim Preachers held in Marrakesh on January 23, 1993. One of the participants at the conference, praising the king of Morocco's position in support of Bosnian Muslims, stood up and said, "Bosnia-Herzegovina will never be a new Andalusia . . ." (*Le Matin*, 1993). This historical reference was to the treatment of the Muslims of Granada, as well as the later persecution and expulsion of the *moriscos*, at the hands of the Christian monarchy of Spain. In this case al-Andalus was used as the chosen metaphor for Muslim suffering in the contemporary world. It would not have worked, however, to refer in this case to the Arab and Berber invasion of the Iberian Peninsula, another part of the same broad history, since that would also have evoked a time when Jews and Christians came under Muslim hegemony. Nor would it have worked to refer to the ups and downs of *convivencia* (coexistence, a common term used in historical writings on medieval Spain) as it varied, retreated, and realigned itself under different rulers throughout the nine hundred years of Iberian cohabitation.

On the other hand, the Arab and Berber conquest of Spain can be tapped as a good metaphor for the glory of Islam, for Arab unity, and for the transfer of knowledge from Arabs to Europeans. *Convivencia*, too, is a useful image on which to draw when informing others that Muslims, Jews, and Christians lived in peace on and off at one time. When and where appropriate, historical allusions geared in these ways have been made, so that the Andalusian heritage offers Arabs and Muslims over all, and Moroccan Andalusians in particular, identity components that have *varied* and *variable* cultural, ethnic, linguistic, artistic, historical, and transnational qualities.

Returning to Moroccan Andalusians in Rabat, much of the early portion of their history, therefore, has become a nostalgic and generalized picture of Islamic Spain. The second part of this history begins in the year 1609. From this date forward specific memories correlate more closely with veritable historical facts often found in written documents. The commonalties that link the Spanish and the Moroccan parts of a family history are the facts that being Andalusian in Spain and in Morocco is central, and that the family's experience in both locales was and is rich in transnational elements. The latter reinforce the international focus that many Andalusians in Rabat hold today.

The History of the Rabati-Andalusian Families in Spain

In 1492, unlike the Spanish Jews, the Spanish Muslims had not yet received the ultimatum to either convert to Christianity or leave the Peninsula. As early as 1499, however, Muslims in Spain knew that the same prospect presented to the Jewish communities would come to apply to them. The choice of religious conversion or exile was a difficult one. Conversion meant abandoning one's religious community for that of one's conqueror. Exile not only meant leaving the land one considered home across eight centuries of one's family history and abandoning much of one's possessions, but it also meant leaving one's younger children in Spain (Boase 1990, 9-28; Friedman 1983, 10-23). Many adults did go, though it appears that many more stayed and converted. This latter group of Muslim converts were thereafter called either *moriscos*, meaning both "little Moors" and "Moorish," or *cristianos nuevos*, "new Christians."

These terms indicate a separation of the new Christians from the old: the *moriscos* were seen as a minority in Spain up to their final expulsion in the early seventeenth century. Many *moriscos* were suspected of retaining loyalty to Islam and of practicing Muslim sacred rituals in secret. Other *moriscos* had fully left behind their Muslim past and embraced the Catholic Church with the hope of complete assimilation into Spanish Christian society. Owing to many factors—the threat of the Ottoman Empire's expansion in the Mediterranean, the rise of the Protestant Lutherans in France, and internal paranoia about Islam and Muslims bred throughout centuries of military skirmishes between northern Christians and southern Muslims—by the early 1600s both the king and the Church wanted a resolution to what was now termed the "*morisco* problem." The potential disloyalty of the *moriscos* as perceived by the Spanish Empire at this time led to a severe final solution: mass expulsion of all *moriscos*. Estimates of the number of *moriscos* expelled range between 275,000 to 300,000. The total number of *moriscos* in early-seventeenth-century Spain, with a total populace of approximately 7.5 million, is placed somewhere between 300,000 and 500,000 (Ackerlind 1989, 35; Boase 1990, 12; Chejne 1983, 13, 279; Harvey 1992, 231; Hess 1989, 154; Lapeyre 1959, 204).

It is clear that not all of Spain's *moriscos* were expelled. Some were never noticed, having assimilated into the Catholic population over generations. Other *moriscos*, mostly land laborers, were considered necessary by their lords to keep the land going, and were thus protected from expulsion. A smaller number of expellees smuggled themselves back into Spain and resettled, unnoticed, in another part of the Peninsula than the one from which they originated. The vast majority, however, appear to have been permanently expelled (López Martinez 1935, 67-69). It is estimated that approximately 80,000 of the 275,000 to 300,000 exiled *moriscos* went to Morocco. Around half this number settled in Tetouan and the other 40,000 continued on to Fez or Rabat (Friedman 1983, 23-26; Epalza 1992, 146-48).

The History of the Andalusian Families in Rabat

By the sixteenth century the city of Rabat, on Morocco's Atlantic coast, was mostly in ruins following the abandoned building campaigns of the Almohad Dynasty in the twelfth century. Rabat was founded in 1150 as an Almohad fortress from which campaigns against twelfth century Spain were to be launched. The offensives against Spain were never carried out from Rabat, though, since Almohad concerns quickly turned to internal problems. From 1184 to 1199, however, the Almohad ruler, Yacub al-Mansur, the grandson of Rabat's founder, turned attention back to Rabat and began ambitious building projects which would never be completed. It was during this brief period that the most prominent architectural features in the city were built, including the famous Ḥasan Mosque, whose minaret was a cousin to the Kutubiya Minaret in Marrakesh, and to the Giralda Tower in Seville.

Upon Al-Mansur's death in 1199, all major building projects in Rabat came to a halt. Some people continued to inhabit the city over another fifty years. By the mid-thirteenth century Rabat was absorbed under the new dynastic rule in Morocco, the Marīnids, and it is estimated that nine-tenths of Rabat's population fled during the fighting (Abu-Lughod 1980, 58). From this time until the arrival of the *moriscos* in the early seventeenth century, Rabat was mostly overgrown by vines and occupied by a small population of some one hundred households which were within sight of the original Almohad fortress (Abu-Lughod 1980, 58-59). Salé, the city across a river from Rabat, was the more flourishing from the thirteenth to the sixteenth centuries.

The first *moriscos* to arrive in the region of Rabat and Salé in 1608 were all from the village of Hornachos in the Spanish province of Extremadura. This group had managed, through bribes, to leave Spain before the decreed expusion order took effect a year later and to resettle in Morocco as a whole village. The Hornacheros, as they were called, were unusual in that they left Spain with their wealth intact, and were able to resettle with their familes. When the Hornacheros first arrived in the Rabat-Salé river valley, they had hoped to settle in the inhabited and thriving city of Salé. However, the inhabitants of this city were wary of these newcomers, since they were new and because the residents of Salé were not convinced that these *moriscos* were indeed Muslims. They appeared to the people of Salé to be Christian and Spanish because of their style of dress and the fact that they spoke Castilian Spanish (Razzūq 1989, 302-3). Consequently, the Hornacheros crossed the river and rebuilt and refortified the old twelfth-century Almohad fortress of Rabat, known as the Qasbah.

With the Hornacheros settled in the Qasbah, word spread to other *moriscos* coming from all over Spain that there was a *morisco* settlement in Rabat. Many *moriscos* from the Spanish regions of Castile, Valencia, Murcia, Andalusia, and Extremadura came to Rabat and built below the Qasbah what is today called the *medina* (city) of Rabat. The history of the relations between the Hornacheros and the other *moriscos* in Rabat is one of brief periods of peace in which corsair activity thrived, and periods of three-way civil war between the two new settlements and the old city of Salé. The periods of strife and civil war also marked periods when corsair activity, and its lucrative profits, declined. Historian Bookin-Weiner (1990) has corelated the periods of thriving corsair activity with periods of internal peace, as well as with significant independence from the central rule of the Moroccan sultan. Likewise, periods of decline in pirate activity were accompanied by internal strife and increased control from the central government (1990, 164).

In addition to the *moriscos*, other international elements in the refounding of Rabat were the European and North African corsairs, as well as the European diplomatic missions that were attracted to the region. Corsairs from Europe, Algeria, and Tunisia found Rabat the ideal port of entry after launching raids on ships in the Atlantic Ocean. Stopping in Rabat broke up a long journey home for North African corsairs who had shifited their activities from the Mediterranean to the Atlantic. For European corsairs, many of whom had been expelled from their own countries, Rabat was a strategically located destination.

In the year 1666 the Alawite Dynasty came into power, and with this shift in central power, the city of Rabat lost any independence it had held heretofore. Instead of free enterprise piracy, the corsairs came under state control and large proportions of their profits went to the Moroccan Alawite state. The most significant aspect of Rabat's absorption into the central government was that it began a process of assimilating the *moriscos*, then mostly Spanish-speaking, and a blend of past Hispano-Islamic and Christian Spanish cultures, into a more Moroccan, Arabic, and Islamic culture (Abu-Lughod 1980, 73). Throughout the latter half of the seventeenth century, Rabat continued to operate, together with Tetouan in the north, as one of Morocco's most important ports and links to the outside world. By the middle of the eighteenth century, corsair activity began to diminish because of increasing European power over the activities along the Moroccan coast. At the same time, all European consuls were removed to the port of Essouira, far south of Rabat, thereby reducing Rabat's European population until very few foreigners resided there by the end of the eighteenth century.

The start of the nineteenth century marks the slow beginning of greater and greater European control over the Moroccan people. As Morocco's economic and political dynamics changed with the tighter grip of European powers, Rabat, too, experienced changes in its economic life. By 1912 the French Protectorate was set up in Morocco, and when plans to make Fez the Protectorate's capital were abandoned, Rabat became the obvious choice because of its coastal location and its central access to the other urban centers of Morocco. The French preserved Rabat's traditional Moroccan quarters, including the still largely Spanish Andalusian *medina*, and they built separate European residential areas and commercial districts. All these quarters were, and still are connected by broad boulevards and avenues. During the French Protectorate period the Andalusians of Rabat lived in the *medina* as they had always done. Because of Rabat's central role as the colonial capital, European diplomats as well as immigrants seeking employment, set up residence there. There was also a large delegation of Spanish and Portuguese officials living in the city. Oral accounts of this time describe the Andalusians of Rabat as interacting a great deal with the Spanish and Portuguese, who considered each other to be cultural and historical brothers.

When the French left Morocco in 1956, their administrative positions and their residences were taken up by the small Moroccan elite, which included a large number of Andalusians from Rabat, as well as from Fez and Tetouan. All members of this Morrocan elite had in common a more European educational background, and its members were operating successfully within the French administration before independence, indicating both a greater proximity to the foreigners in Rabat and also a higher income level. In the 1960s Rabat's *medina* was becoming crowded from the rural immigration into the city. Feeling that the *medina* was no longer exclusively Andalusian, many Andalusian families began moving out to farmland that surrounded the city. Today large portions of this land have developed into several suburbs of Rabat. Many Andalusian families, still living near each other, are now leading suburban lives, though a few of the wealthier

Andalusians have retained their old family homes in the *medina*.

A strong feature of the Andalusian families of Rabat today is that they pride themselves on their European style of doing things. This "Europeanness" is seen as going back to their origins in Spain, yet in the present era it is also redirected as stemming from French culture, a shift which many Andalusians consider both easy and natural. This shift also issues from the assumption that the most European native of peoples in Morocco are those descended from ancestors in Spain. Given the dominant French cultural influence in Morocco, and because of twentieth-century politics, many Moroccans, Andalusian and non-Andalusian alike, told me that they see the Spanish and the French sides of their heritage as closely intertwined, allowing them to claim dual provenance. The logic of intercultural identity formation and transfer underlying this tendency toward self-Europeanization further enables an attitude which states, "because my heritage is Spanish I am more European, and therefore I can understand the French culture better than a non-Andalusian Moroccan is able to."

Many Andalusians see themselves as natural intermediaries between these European cultures and Moroccan culture. Moreover, whether non-Andalusian Moroccans do or do not accord the Andalusians themselves the status of cultural intermediaries, they do privilege the Andalusians' Iberian or "mixed European" heritage. As a self-promoting strategy, the success of "Europeanization" is clearly observed in the high social status enjoyed by Moroccan individuals who have a French education (this includes *many* Andalusian Moroccans), and by those who behave in ways that are consistent with European customs or behavior. Nonetheless, these same members of the Andalusian elite also engage in behaviors that are considered traditional North African and Arab, and which also stem from their Andalusian background. Thus, again, the Andalusians can be both European since they are descended from a culture(s) grown in Europe, as well as traditionally Arab. Islamic Spain was largely a product of their diverse ancestors who were both Iberian and Middle Eastern, culturally and geographically. It is through these rich and diverse contexts of historic origin, and through their flexible and context-sensitive reiteration in contemporary tropes that Moroccan Andalusians are assisted in preserving their high social status and their complex identity in an overall culture that deeply values their history.[2]

Finally, the Andalusians of Rabat have lived through times when forces from the outside world intenseley engaged with and/or occupied their city, as well as through times when Rabat had peripheral importance and shrinking economic activity. Such fluctuation notwithstanding, what has persisted are the Andalusians' Spanish-sounding names, such as Díaz, Marino, Bargach (Vargas), Kilito (Quilito), Baris (Pérez), and Torres. Marriage alliances have remained almost exclusively Andalusian, and the styles of their residences recall medieval Spain. Inspiration for these homes has been taken from artistic and architectural styles seen in the Alhambra palace in Granada, from stucco carved wall designs to central courtyard arrangements. Along with Andalusians' acknowledgement of their own social exclusivity, all of the above is testimony to the fact that the Andalusian's complexity of identity and memory is based in its broad and international past, and to the fact that it has been a tool for confronting change.

The Complexity of the Andalusian Moroccan Identity in Rabat

It is a strongly held belief of many Moroccans that it is Andalusian descent which gives Andalusians their political and cultural clout. Romanticization of al-Andalus by its exiles was already taking place in the fourteenth century (Rosenthal 1958, 1:xxxvi; 2:24, 290, 386; 3:302). The Andalusians carried, and still carry, the prestige associated with being better educated, more cosmopolitan, and better off financially than the average North African. Historically, some Andalusian refugees went into advisory and diplomatic positions for the sultan, or into military service, religious education, local government administration, and large-scale mercantile trade. Others continued developing the crafts by which they had lived in Spain, and they carried over Hispano-Muslim styles of music, poetry, calligraphy, cooking, embroidery, wood carving, and painting. All of these skills and crafts are still practiced in Rabat, as can be seen in the stories of two Andalusians, one from a family of diplomats and the other from a leading performer of Andalusian music in the city.

Muḥammad (name withheld)[3] is a historian, though at one time he was involved in commerce. Many of the men in his family have worked in the service of the king, especially in diplomatic and advisory roles. Muḥammad's family came from Castile, the north central region of Spain. His family name is Spanish in etymology, bearing only minor phonetic changes in transferring from a Spanish-speaking to an Arabic context. Muḥammad's family name is both a famous name in Morocco today and also a very common name, in its Spanish form, in contemporary Spain. Muḥammad's ancestors were among the Muslims who lived in Castile as *mudéjars*, or Muslims under Christian rule, during the period in which the kingdom of Granada was still in Muslim hands. Therefore, Muḥammad's family was accustomed to Christian Spanish culture and was most likely more assimilated in this direction than were the family's Muslim counterparts in Granada, before the latter's fall in 1492.

Muḥammad told me that between 1492 and 1609, his ancestors were well established and successful in Castilian society. Some of his ancestors were in the service of the Catholic king. One ancestor was a bishop, thus placing a *morisco* in one of the highest offices possible within the Church in Spain. Muḥammad's family's occupational history is known from the medieval period in Spain and it demonstrates a continuity of professional roles up to the present day in Morocco. My informant's ancestors were councilors, advisors, and diplomats to royalty, first in Spain and later, from 1609 on, in Morocco. Given the generations in Muḥammad's family that have continued to hold such positions, he claims that diplomatic speech and cross-cultural understanding are well-honed skills among his relatives. What is most striking about Muḥammad is that he is extremely self-conscious and fiercely proud when it comes to the Andalusian past of his family and his city. He is currently writing the history of his family in Spain, Morocco, and also the New World, since he has evidence that his ancestors, like many Spanish Muslims and Jews, sought new lives during the explosive period of New World exploration by the Spanish Empire.

Muḥammad's first ancestor in Rabat of whom there is knowledge was among the early *morisco* settlers in the seventeenth century. What Muḥammad knows of this first ancestor in Rabat is that ". . . he had an alliance with England, between the Republic of the Qasbah and England, in 1627," and that ". . . this was the [occupational] structure of our family at that time." During the first half of the seventeenth century in Rabat, the business of having alliances with European powers translated into two possible occupations which were often combined and symbiotic: diplomacy and piracy. Interestingly, Muḥammad discusses only diplomacy. (Indeed, only one Andalusian with whom I spoke directly mentioned his family having been involved in piracy. Other familes described the early settlement's economic activities as, "being in the shipping business.")

From the historical work done on Rabat in the first fifty years of *morisco* settlement, it is clear that piracy could not be distinguished from "legal"commerce since often the pirated goods fed the trade and commerce in the city. Among the most famous relatives in Muḥammad's family is a great-grandfather who lived during the latter half of the nineteenth century. This relative had been appointed to a diplomatic mission to Spain, and while he was there he acquired an official document, notarized by the Spanish government and signed by the king of Spain, which states that the family bearing the name of his family is of Spanish origin. This notarized document, which is also a who's who of the family, was created 277 years after this Andalusian family left Spain, indicating the persistent importance of the family's Spanish roots.

Muḥammad's family today is, and has been for several generations, among the most famous and well-to-do families of the Moroccan urban elite. He and other Andalusians attribute this success to the cross-cultural skills they inherited from their medieval Spanish past, as well as the high status Moroccans generally place on someone from this esteemed background. Muḥammad sees the Andalusian families of Rabat as a distinct group; distinct from other Moroccans both in physical appearance and in cultural manner. To him, Andalusians today are more "European and Cartesian" in their thinking *because* they are originally from Spain. In his words,

> Our ideas are a little European, Cartesian. We're from the bourgeoisie. Our thoughts are not like the thoughts of other people of Morocco. Our ideas are not within the heads of non-Andalusians. We do not share the same industry, we do not agree, we do not mesh. My family is in politics, with the Monarchy. We are like the Hornacheros who settled in the Qasbah. We have money. We have *jāh* (rank, standing, dignity, honor, glory, fame). We have these things so we are not like the others. It is in our blood, under our skin. We are *khayr* (good). We have good *akhlāq* (character, temper, nature). Also, we worked with foreigners, Germans, French, Italians, English, etc., because we know how to talk with them, that is, we can go across boundaries, be diplomatic, appreciate different cultures. In the nineteenth century my family was in the *qaṣr* (palace). (Bahrami 1993)

Later Muḥammad went on to elaborate this point of being distinct and more European: "When I was twelve years old I went to live in France. I found that it was easy to be there, that there was no difference between my ideas and the French ideas." (Again, the Europeanization strategy is operating here: he sees himself as Spanish, hence more European than other Moroccans and as a result, more capable of feeling that French ideas are naturally akin to his own.)

> Then my mother and father came [to France] and they found it the same. The ideas we all shared with the

> French are the same . . . I think like Europeans. When I returned from France I found that my family and I thought alike, but that my friends, non-Andalusians, and I did *not* think alike; we were distinct. This is not the case with a French educated friend of mine from the Qayrawan in Fez. This friend and I understand each other even though he speaks differently (Muhammad mimics the religious scholars in their slow, exact classical Arabic). We think alike, as if we were both from an Andalusian family. In fact, he's found that his thoughts are not like those of people who are not from this background. "*Andana fī dam*" (It is in our blood). We understand each other. When we meet other Andalusians it does not take long to realize that we understand each other. When we meet, we understand. Others do not." (Bahrami 1993)

In these statements Muḥammad is implying that Andalusians are a distinct group within Morocco, and that they are more European by virtue of having descended from Spanish "blood." This makes sense because he sees few contradictions between Andalusian and French styles of thinking. In his parlance above, Muḥammad is also using his Andalusian heritage from Spain to argue that he is, in tandem, more French. Again, the utility of this sidestepping relates to the strong influence of French culture and lifestyles on Morocco's elite society.

Despite the rhetoric Muḥammad uses to express the distinctiveness of the Andalusians, he then summons Andalusian identity as one reason in an explanation of why no one should be divided along religious or ethnic lines. Here he draws on the general memory of *convivencia* in Islamic Spain, stating that there, Muslims, Jews, and Christians lived together in relative harmony compared to elsewhere in the known world. During one meeting Muḥammad philosophically asked, "Why are the differences between people used to insist on divisions between them? Why is the world like this?" He elaborated this point turning to Muslim diversity: "Culturally, Muslims are distinct from each other, and yet we all have one religion and are one in this way" (Bahrami 1993).

In sum, on the one hand Muḥammad argues that Andalusians are special, and a class apart, and he is comfortable with this distinction. On the other hand, Muḥammad musters the same identity to argue for the tolerance of social difference. Here he reveals that his family's actual *mudéjar* provenance, from Christian Castile, melds almost imperceptibly with an assumed, attendant legacy from a romanticized Islamic Spain. Coupled with the Spanish persecution of his ancestors, this amalgamate personal and family background allows Muḥammad to play the two sides of transnational Moroccan interests: belonging to an exclusive group with social and political hegemony in Rabat, and presenting oneself as open-minded and tolerant.

Another Andalusian man with whom I spoke also demonstrates the centrality of the Andalusian identity and memory in defining himself and his group as both distinct, yet at the same time, open-minded. The difference between Aḥmad, as I shall call him, and Muḥammad above, is the style in which he expresses these sentiments. The content is the same while the form of expression varies. The memory of specific details of Aḥmad's family's history does not come up to that of Muḥammad, although, as with all of the Andalusians with whom I spoke, scant detail-specific memory is compensated for by one's familiarity with the general cultural memory of al-Andalus. With Aḥmad, as with others, it is clear that specifics are not necessary for one to posit one's Andalusian identity as central to one's self-conception, nor to feel that remembering one's ancestral past is a challenge.

The few known details of Aḥmad's family history are that the family came from the territory in Spain between the cities of Toledo and Seville. Subsequent conversations with Aḥmad placed his family origins in one of the two cities rather than in the rural terrain in between. This is significant because scholarship today reveals that rural *moriscos* were land laborers, whereas before and during the time of the *moriscos*, the more respected Andalusian occupations were urban based, including musical performance, letter writing, and craft making (Busto, 1974, 1992; Epalza, 1992). Given the greater prestige associated with the latter pursuits, in remembering his family as urban based, Aḥmad was endowing himself with a more respectable background. This is a good example of selectively remembering, as well as possibly borrowing from recent, locally known scholarly studies of medieval Spain, to present a family history in tune with contemporary values and attitudes.

In Morocco today, as well as in the past, urban centers and lifestyles have been esteemed as more lofty and learned than rural ones. From Aḥmad's recollection of his family's geographic origins in Spain, he then jumps forward many generations and speaks of his own extended family, recalling times when he was young and when his grandparents were still alive. At that time the family still lived in Rabat's *medina*, which was, again, the traditional place of residence of Rabat's Andalusian families. For Aḥmad this temporal jump is not a break in continuity. Whether he remembers everything or not of the last centuries of his family's history, he *feels* the connection is perpetually there, allowing him to articulate remembered specifics when contemporary contexts and circumstances oil the wheels of memory. In actual fact, speaking of continuity, it is remarkable that until his own youth, Aḥmad's family had lived in the same space in Rabat since his ancestors' arrival there early in the seventeenth century.

When Aḥmad married he moved to a neighborhood next door which had housed Portuguese and Spanish workers in Morocco during the time of the Protectorate. What Aḥmad's family did know all along, and what is definitely a persistent memory, is the rich closeness of all the relatives and their lifestyles. Specific activities recalled in this light are cooking, embroidery, and musical performance. The first activities fall within the domain of the women of the family, while music is a man's pursuit. All three activities are considered to be medieval Andalusian in provenance. The culinary tradition in Aḥmad's home, as in other Andalusian homes, is believed to go back as early as the thirteenth century in Spain. Many of the traditional meals are also common to Moroccan cooking in general, and many people believe that Moroccan cuisine overall has major Andalusian influences.

The Andalusian embroidery styles are floral, and they closely resemble the floral silk embroidery seen on Spanish silk shawls, or *mantones*. As for Andalusian Moroccan music, it is described as a blend of Middle Eastern melodies and tones, performed in an orchestral structure simlar to a string ensemble, with lyrics that praise "Andalusian themes of love, beauty, and nature" (Bahrami 1993). These different elements and forms are seen as coming together because of the diverse people and communities living in Islamic Spain. For many, including Aḥmad, the music he plays today harkens back to those Iberian peoples and to their diversity.

Thus, actual memories or ties to being Andalusian emerge, for Aḥmad, in their clearest forms while he is doing things related to tradition and handed-down practices. Such activated memory is a part of daily life, and it reinforces, in turn, Aḥmad and his family's sense of being Andalusian. Possessing this identity, born of the hybrid and unique cultures of al-Andalus, seems to reinforce, here, a contemporary open-minded and universalist worldview, and this brings Andalusians such as Aḥmad and his children into closer contact with the international elements in their city. In this way, unlike Muḥammad, above, Aḥmad interprets the Andalusian past as an impetus toward connectivity, instead of a means of distinguishing oneself and standing apart.

Aḥmad's modes of relating to his inherited Andalusianness are more deferential and humble than are Muḥammad's. This is in spite of the fact that Aḥmad's family, too, has a long history of important governmental roles, even though he is a greengrocer. He is also a very respected and talented *'ūd* (Arabic lute) player and he performs in an amateur orchestra that specializes in Andalusian music from the old city of Granada. Aḥmad speaks of the *'ūd* as a prime example of the Andalusian influence in Morocco and its European counterpart, the lute, as an Arab Andalusian element that similarly influenced Europe. The musician has also taught his son to play both the *'ūd* and the guitar; the latter is also associated with Aḥmad's Andalusian memory of things Spanish.

Aḥmad insists not on personal distinction by virtue of his Andalusian bloodline, but on the universality in his and fellow musicians' outlook. They have come to this through their backgrounds and their positions in their community. Aḥmad characterizes the ancestral Andalusian experience as teaching one to transcend differences in religion, financial and economic status, music and dress and to be widely accepting. He goes on to claim that music is one of the purest ways to achieve universal spiritual experience. This he accesses through playing the old Andalusian music of Granada. For both Muḥammad and Aḥmad, their Hispano-Islamic heritage has shaped much of who they are and what they do, even today when the connections between the past of al-Andalus and the present in Morocco may not be clearly perceived by the non-Andalusian. To these two men and to many other Andalusian, being of this descent has given them privileges and opportunities in Moroccan society that are not necessarily available to everyone in that society.

Conclusion: The Andalusian Identity as a Transnational Traditional and Modern Identity

The complexity and situational flexibility of the Moroccan identity labeled "Andalusian," as seen, offers many alternatives to its possessor, within Rabat's many international social contexts, alone. Moroccan Andalusian identity renders one highly international, by dint of family roots in Spain, cultural and behavioral associations with France which thence become feasible and naturally explained, and a large stake in Rabat's diversified history. By contrast, the Andalusian identity also serves to anchor its possessor in the local setting of his or her city through the fact that being Andalusian is significant in Moroccan culture overall. Andalusians thereby receive national confirmation and endorsement of their particular sense of self.

I have also shown that being Andalusian allows the individual to be Arab, European, or a distinct hybrid. This, in turn, gives the Moroccan Andalusian a foot in what is traditional and what is modern. Anthropologist Jonathan Friedman writes in 1992, that what is modern for different people is "a contrast [that] is one of symmetrical inversion: consumption versus production of tradition, other-centered versus self-centered, pilgrimage to Paris versus struggle for land rights. The contrast in strategies of identity . . . is not simply a question of cultural difference, but of global position" (1990, 324). Friedman states this in the context of summarizing trends on local levels that are emerging as a result of increased worldwide contact between cultures, mostly prompted by economic activities. Friedman posits two basic local responses to processes of sociocultural globalization. Some people choose to participate in the "consumption of modernity" and to abandon tradition, while others choose a grassroots "production of tradition" strategy.

By way of conclusion I offer a third possibility. The Andalusians are a group of individuals whose strategy is actually a combination of the modernist and traditionalist strategies observed by Friedman. Andalusians are producers of tradition, and the Andalusian tradition(s) are among the most influential in Morocco. Moreover, since Andalusianness, as a complex identity, is rooted in both European and Arab cultures, it also enters into definitions of people's consumption of modernity by creating new ways of being classically traditional in a modern setting. By virtue of being Arab the Andalusians are rooted in tradition(s), and by virtue of being European they have a strong foothold in contemporary Moroccan interests in European commodities and cultures.

Put another way, much like Ulf Hannerz's Nigerian "Beentos," these Andalusians claim access, knowledge, and exprerience in conjunction with the wider cosmopolitan world and this offers them advantages in the local context of Rabat. However, even more to their advantage in global creolization is the fact that Andalusians can claim well-heeled, "Beento" knowledge of the world not only through recent personal and family experience abroad, but through widespread ancestral and intergenerational continuity, as well. Andalusians have ancestrally "been to" the culturally famous and important sites of Islamic Spain, including Granada, Seville, and Córdoba, even if they have never been there individually. In other words, the Andalusians' historical reconstruction of the present, in the Appaduraian sense (1991, 208-9), draws heavily on medieval places and events that, given the value Moroccans place on these references, accords Andalusians "Beento" status not only in contemporary time and space but also in past time as it is made present and globally relevant in the twentieth century. Like the exclamation on the postcard described at the beginning of this essay, which indicates Morocco's position between East and West, there is a parallel with how Morocco is being portrayed by its nationals to outsiders, and how Andalusians portray themselves to other Moroccans. One could accurately rewrite that postcard and say, "*C'est l'Orient, c'est l'Occident, c'est l'Andalusien.*"

Notes

1. The term "Andalusian" has many meanings and has been used in a variety of contexts by scholars of Spanish and Moroccan history. J.D. Latham states, "In the present context I shall follow the old Arab custom of designating as 'Andalusian' (a) the inhabitants of Muslim Spain (al-Andalus), (b) Muslims inhabiting reconquered territories under treaty with their Christian conquerors, (c) those Muslims who have remained in Spain after the completion of the Reconquest in 1492, were later denied their religion, language, and culture and compelled to submit to baptism and practice of the Christian faith—in other words, the *moriscos*" (1986, 189). I

add to these three definitions of Andalusians the following: (d) those individuals residing today in North Africa, who claim Andalusian ancestry, and (e) the inhabitants of the present-day southern province of Andalucía, in Spain. While this essay focuses on the descendants of the *morisco* Andalusians, all five definitions of Andalusians above are relevant and come into play because of the way the individuals (*morisco* Andalusian descendants) collapse their memory of al-Andalus.

2. It is significant that the Berber identity is not a strong part of the composition of the Andalusian's identity because the Berbers are not as powerful a group in Morocco. There is a general sentiment that I found expressed by many Moroccans from diverse backgrounds, which is that Berbers are romanticized, but at the same time, are not as respected as Arabs and Europeans. The public debate (casual conversation, newspaper articles, public policy) over Berber identity and who the Berbers are exactly, has been wide-ranging and heated. It is nonetheless clear that the Berber identity does not carry the same prestige as the aforementioned identities in Morocco.

3. I have chosen to call my informants by two common Moroccan first names. The family names of these individuals are Spanish and distinct, and therefore easily recognizable to other Moroccans.

Works Cited

Abu-Lughod, Janet. *Rabat: An Urban Apartheid.* Princeton: Princeton UP, 1980.

Ackerlind, Sheila. "Moriscos." In *Patterns of Conflict: The Individual and Society in Spanish Literature to 1702*, 35-36. New York: Peter Lang, 1989.

Appadurai, Arjun. "Disjuncture and Difference in the Global Cultural Economy." *Public Culture*, Spring, no. 2.2 (1990): 1-24.

_____. "Global Ethnoscapes: Notes and Queries for a Transnational Anthropology." In R.G. Fox, ed., *Recapturing Anthropology*, 191-210. Santa Fe: School of American Research Press, 1991.

Bahrami, Beebee. Personal Interviews with Muḥammad and Aḥmad (names withheld). Rabat, Morocco, Spring and Summer 1993.

Boase, Roger. "The Morisco Expulsion and Diaspora: An Example of Racial and Religious Intolerance." In David Hook and Barry Taylor, eds., *Cultures in Contact in Medieval Spain: Historical and Literary Essays Presented to L.P. Harvey,* 9-28. King's College London Medieval Studies III. Exeter: n.p., 1990.

Bookin-Weiner, Jerome B. "The 'Sallee Rovers': Morocco and the Corsairs in the Seventeenth Century." In R.S. Simon, ed., *The Middle East and North Africa: Essays in Honor of J.C. Hurwitz*. New York: Columbia UP, 1990.

Busto, Guillermo Gozalbes. *La republica andaluza de Rabat en el siglo XVII*. Tetouan: Imprenta Minerva, 1974.
_____. *Los moriscos en Marruecos*. Granada: T.C. Arte, Juberías & CIA, 1992.
Chejne, Anwar. *Islam and the West: The Moriscos*. Albany: State U of New York P, 1983.
Epalza, Mikel de. "Al-Andalus et le Maghreb: Frontiére de l'Islam dans la Conscience Musulmane, Medievale et Moderne." *Horizons Maghrebins: le Droit a la Mémoire* (January 1988): 28-32.
_____. *Los moriscos antes y después de la expulsión*. Madrid: Mapfre, 1992.
Erikson, Thomas H. "Multiple Traditions and the Question of Cultural Integration." In *Ethnos* (Oslo: Scandinavian UP), no. 57. 1-2 (1992): 5-30.
Falk Moore, Sally. "The Production of Cultural Pluralism as a Process." *Public Culture*, Spring, no. 1.2 (1989): 26-48.
Fiske, Susan T., and Taylor, Shelley T. *Social Cognition*. 2d ed. New York: McGraw Hill, 1991.
Foster, Robert J. "Making National Cultures in the Global Ecumene." *Annual Review of Anthropology*, no. 20 (1991): 235-60.
Friedman, Ellen G. *Spanish Captives in North Africa in the Early Modern Age*. Madison: U of Wisconsin P, 1983.
Friedman, Jonathan. "Being in the World: Globalization and Localization." In M. Featherstone, ed., *Global Culture: Nationalism, Globalization, and Modernity*, 311-28. London: Sage Publishing, 1990.
_____. "Myth, History, and Political Identity." *Cultural Anthropology* (Spring 1992): 194-210.
Goffman, Erving. *Presentation of Self in Everyday Life*. Woodstock: Overlook Press, 1973.
Hannerz, Ulf. *Cultural Complexity: Studies in the Social Organization of Meaning*. New York: Columbia UP, 1992.
Harvey, Leonard, Patrick. "The Political, Social, and Cultural History of the Moriscos." In Salma Khadra Jayyusi, ed., *The Legacy of Muslim Spain*, 201-34. Leiden: E.J. Brill, 1992.
Hess, Andrew C. *The Forgotten Frontier*. Chicago: U of Chicago P, 1989.
al-Karīm, Krīm. *Rabat al-Fāṭḥ: ʻāṣimat al-mamlaka al-Magribiyya*. Rabat: Mutabiʻāt al-Muaʻriq al-Jadīda, 1986.
Latham, John Derek. "Towns and Cities of Barbary: The Andalusian Influence." In *From Muslim Spain to Barbary*, 189-205. London:Variorum Reprints, 1986.
Lapeyre, Henri. *Geographie de l'Espagne morisque*. Paris: n.p., 1959.
Laurent, Eric. Personal Interviews with King Hassan II of Morocco. *Hassan II: La Mémoire d'un Roi*. Paris: Plon, 1993.
Lewis, Bernard. "The Cult of Spain and the Turkish Romantics." In *Islam in History: Ideas, People, and Events in the Middle East*, 129-33, 433-34. Chicago: Open Court Publishing Company, 1993.

López Martinez, Celestino. *Mudejares y moriscos sevillanos*. Seville: Rodriguez, Gimenez y Companía, 1935.

_____. "Poursuite des travaux de la recontre internationale des precheurs du vendredi." *Le Matin*, Rabat. January 27, 1993.

Razzūq, Muḥammad. *Al-Andalusiyyūn wa-hijratūhūm ilā al-Maghrib khilāla al-Qarnayn 16-17*. Casablanca: Ifrīqyā al-Sharq, 1989.

Rhodes, A., trans. "The Tree." In *The Challenge: The Memoirs of King Hassan II of Morocco*, 169-77. Paris: Editions Albin Michel, 1978.

Rosenthal, Franz. Translation of Ibn Khaldun's *The Muqaddimah: An Introduction to History*. 3 Vols. New York: Bollingen Foundation, 1958.

Smith, Anthony D. "Towards a Global Culture?" *Theory, Culture, and Society*, no. 7 (1990): 171-91.

Souissi, A. *Tarīkh Rabāṭ al-Fatḥ*. Rabat: Maṭba'at al-Bilād, 1979.

◆ Chapter 5

Voices from the Past: Judeo-Spanish (Ladino) Nicknames among the Israeli-Sephardic Jews from Salonika

Shmuel Refael

(Translated by Stacy N. Beckwith)

The last decades of the twentieth century will undoubtedly be considered among the most fruitful in terms of research on the culture of Ladino-speaking[1] Sephardic Jews. The literature, language, music, and history of Ladino speakers are all expanding fields of inquiry, while other areas of research, obscure in the eyes of scholars until only a few years ago, are slowly gaining more attention as well. When philologists began taking a new interest in the cultural world of Ladino-speaking Sephardim over a hundred years ago, they ushered in a new era in the life of the culture involving and surrounding this language. Scholars began to focus on the linguistic and literary heritage shared by Sephardic Jews throughout communities in the Mediterranean basin and North Africa, wishing to examine the degree to which Ladino culture has kept faith with ancient Spanish tradition, as well as the strength and nature of its Iberian ties.

These were heady years for Ladino culture, which at that time stood at a crossroads. In this initial period of interest, researchers began gathering and examining Sephardic Jews' folk and literary traditions. No one could have imagined the importance of this scholarly activity, which was then gaining momentum. No one foresaw that the popular and folkloric texts collected from elderly informants around the Balkans would become, or would eventually be on a par with, museum pieces attesting to a splendid culture which only began to fade as a result of unpreventable historical processes. It would have occurred to no one that an unfathomable Holocaust would tear tens of thousands of the Ladino-speaking tribe from the face of the earth. Subsequently, the enormous importance of every inch or piece of text collected in the early days of research has become widely recognized. Every Spanish ballad, poem, and folktale that was recorded and collected before the Holocaust provides raw material for current research on the culture, literature, and language of then extant Ladino-speaking communities, and much of this research is conducted from various Hispanic perspectives.

An exemplary scholar in the Spanish tradition is Ramón Menéndez Pidal, justifiably considered the father of research on the Ladino *romansa.* Indeed, Pidal has found in Sephardic *romansas* echoes of Spanish tradition, as have other scholars of his and following generations. All have found the challenge of researching the *romansas* of Ladino speakers to be fascinating, symbolic, and best pursued from broad and multidimensional vantages. Approached in this way, examination of Sephardic materials uncovers cultural treasures of past eras while drawing increased attention to more contemporary Ladino traditions. What began with Menéndez Pidal's pioneering research has definitely gained momentum over the years, such that today hundreds of researchers focus on the *romansa* in Ladino, again examining both its Ladino tradition and its ties to different Hispanic traditions.

Without entering into the thick of these activities, I will point out that it is not only the popular character of the *romansa* that has gleaned the attention of researchers. Other genres, such as folktales, proverbs, and even the *coplas* have also been graced with such attention. Recently, Ladino lyrical tradition, a genre too often forgotten but one that also has clear folkloric characteristics, has also begun to be examined. Research on lyrics in Ladino is based on the classification and cataloging of hundreds of traditional texts in the language. Many of these texts have been collected under the auspices of the Informants' Cataloging Project of the Ladino broadcasting program at Voice of Israel radio, in Jerusalem, under the direction of Moshe Sha'ul. Likewise, such cataloging is ongoing at the Menéndez Pidal archive in Spain, involving colleagues such as José Manuel Pedrosa and Iacob Hassán. Hassán is the director of the Arias Montano Institute for Sephardic Studies at the Consejo Superior de Investigaciones Científicas in Madrid. All of these projects constitute experiments of great importance, since they involve not only cataloging, but also identifying and/or characterizing the different findings on Ladino lyrical tradition from multiple perspectives and literary traditions.

Despite the fact that the importance of the classic Ladino literary genres is not earth-shattering, I will point out that in recent years scholars have endeavored to open additional venues of research likely to shed light on the tie that Ladino speakers maintained with Spanish culture over the hundreds of years in which they have been physically separated from Spanish soil. As research into these literary genres proceeds, so does Sephardic ethnography, since ties between various periods of Sephardic and Spanish dress, cuisine, popular or folk medicine, and supernatural belief all come to the fore. The many details in these areas of overlap or commonality point to a wealth of potential discoveries in the ambit of Ladino-Spanish ties.

My focus in this essay is on an additional venue through which examination of such linkages is possible and fecund: the composition of Ladino speakers' names. While this study includes both first and family names, I will concentrate specifically on names of endearment and nicknames, which became very widespread among Ladino speakers. In order to focus my discussion I chose to examine a relatively small group of names and nicknames that circulated among Ladino speakers in Salonika, and whose traditional application continues in contexts which have followed the city's demise in the Holocaust as a significant center of Sephardic life, culture, and commerce. I assembled all the names in this study through personal fieldwork in 1996 and 1997, with a group of Israeli informants who are all resettled Ladino speakers from Salonika. I asked my informants to recall names and nicknames that were common in Greece, as well as those their community has continued to use in Israel.

Identifying and understanding the dynamics of Salonikan Sephardic attachment to Spanish culture contributes uniquely to one's examination and interpretation of the nicknames that have circulated among the Greek city's Ladino speakers. The etymology of the names certainly foregrounds ties to Spain, though over time Ladino speakers infused their daily spoken language with names and nicknames whose origins are not precisely Spanish, but are of regional Mediterranean provenance. This attests to the Salonikan Jews' contact with different local populations. The blending of names from different linguistic sources is particularly illustrative of the character and the dynamism of Ladino culture, which simultaneously managed its unique ties to Spanish culture and carried on a dialogue with Greek, Turkish, Italian, Arab, Hebrew, and other cultures of the Mediterranean basin.

Judeo-Spanish Onomastics

Research on the terms of endearment and the nicknames that Ladino speakers have used and guarded falls within the general field of onomastics. This has produced informative and intriguing studies in Jewish and broader cultural areas, alike.[2] Beyond its pertinence to the linguistic field, onomastic research is a branch of study which enables the history of different peoples to be tracked, along with their geographic wanderings and their multilateral ties to other cultures. In terms of Judeo-Spanish culture, one can identify many interesting convergences through an onomastic lens. Those that come to the fore in this study are indicative of the importance of this type of research to Sephardic scholarship focused broadly or particularly, as on the pet names which a richly historic community preserved and still use *en famille*.

It is first necessary to contextualize this study within an overview of wider research on Jewish names, as this has developed from the 1920s to the present, and has come to involve direct consultation of census recordings from Spanish archives. An early pioneer in the area of Jewish onomastics was Samuele Schaerf, whose examination of the family names of Jews in Italy is very instructive regarding the techniques and principles which guide onomastic research overall. Schaerfe's study, published in Firenze in 1925, is perhaps too broadly based, for it extends for some ninety detailed pages. In his introduction the researcher notes a shortage of general, collateral information on Jewish family names in Italy, but he expresses the hope that his work will nonetheless round out knowledge of Jewish Italian life, and will constitute an important milestone on the road to publishing a dictionary of Italian Jewish family names.

The database which Schaerf had at his disposal included some ten thousand family names of Italian Jews as they were listed in *Keren Hayesod* (local community organization) files. In his introduction Schaerf writes that through analysis of the names one can construct an exciting mosaic of Jewish history, of the wanderings of specific Jewish populations, and their professions. Significant events in Jewish lives also begin to stand out, including riots and the onset of diseases or plagues, from which a portion of individuals suffered. On a more personal level, bodily defects or deformities can also be seen as the basis for particular family names. Apart from "uncovering" stories behind the different names he studied, Schaerf indicates that he was confronted by an additional challenge: attempting to locate the geographic origins of the names. One can deduce that the researcher was well equipped for this endeavor because he divides the names he lists in his work by origin: German, Spanish, Eastern, Hebrew, and Greek. In terms of the Sephardic names he includes, Schaerf mentions that they are from Livorgno, particularly from the region of Tuscany. In his list of Spanish surnames Schaerf includes Franco, Navarra, Fernandez, (H)Enriques, (H)Errera, Roquez, Díaz, and more (1925, 37).

Two other studies that share conceptual elements and presuppositions with Schaerf's work focus on the names of Bulgarian Jews. These reports were published respectively by Isac Moscona in 1967, and by Ivan Kunchev in 1977. Moscona's research, which was published in Bulgaria, aimed at uncovering the origins of the family names of local Jews. It bears many resemblances to Schaerf's study, both in intent and methodology. Moscona was the head of the cultural organization of Jews in Bulgaria and an important researcher on their history. His official capacity lent additional weight to his local onomastic research of the Ladino speakers of Bulgaria.

The person who set out to broaden Moscona's scope was Ivan Kunchev, who in the late 1970s sought to find not only the origins, but also the meanings of family names among Bulgarian Jews. Kunchev's study is not, in fact, onomastic in the accepted sense of the term, since it also involves deeper dimensions of Bulgarian Sephardic-Ladino culture. Kunchev's main concentration is on the nicknames of the Jews of Sofia, largely because he was unable to obtain information on Jewish nicknames in other cities.

All of the information which Kunchev brought to his study is actually the fruit of fieldwork conducted by one Albert León Niño, which the latter recorded in a research log. Niño was a sixty-five year old who succeeded in combing his memory and filling his diary with a few hundred Ladino nicknames. Drawing on Niño, Kunchev (like Schaerf), divides his list of names into several classifying sections, such as nicknames of Turkish, Greek, or Bulgarian origin, nicknames which point to personal characteristics, to a person's behavior in society, to an individual's physiological features, to the types of foods he/she enjoyed, and to other similarly intriguing individual characteristics. Subsequent researchers accord unique importance to Kunchev's study because he attempted to roll back and uncover several layers of Judeo-Spanish folklore and popular life, all of which have underpinned the creation of family names and nicknames among Ladino speakers.

The list of nicknames which I will present following this overview of Jewish onomastic research will bear many similarities to Kunchev's list. Both this study and his foreground the special roles that nicknames have played in identity formation among Ladino speakers. Humor and mockery can be found in these names in abundance. Through their breakdown of cultural barriers, such elements enable the researcher's unmediated contact with specific name bearers, as personalities in a community. In a great many cases nicknames have replaced surnames and even first names, to the point where the nickname bearers themselves have often come to call and present themselves thus, instead of using their original name(s) as registered in an official census or on their birth certificates.

Another example of an onomastic study with Sephardic nicknames at its core is one conducted by the Spanish scholar Rodrigo Pita Merce, in 1975. This researcher provides an interesting look at the invention, and some permutations of, Balkan Sephardic surnames that belonged to Jews whose ancestors inhabited the regions of medieval Lérida and Huesca. In keeping with his Spanish, rather than Sephardic perspective, in the midst of his research Merce tried to flesh out the roots of these names in their Spanish ancestral contexts. He examined period rosters and historical accounts in which several Jewish names are inscribed, after which he studied how these names have persisted in the repertoire of Sephardim in Bucharest, Sofia, Salonika, Athens, Istanbul, Adrianopolis, Alexandria, and Cairo. Through this research Merce was able to substantiate the histories of various Sephardim in these contemporary locales as indeed originating in the Spanish regions of Lérida and Huesca. He includes in his study some one hundred and thirty surnames. Besides identifying their geographic Iberian beginnings, sometimes to the city, he also traces the names to traditional Spanish/Sephardic vocations, to nuanced linguistic sources, and to any nickname substitutes that took hold in Iberia or in the diaspora.

Moving again to a more narrow diasporic perspective, a study that focuses solely on the Jews of Greece was published by Rachel Dalven, first as an article in 1977 and then as a chapter in her book on the Jews of Iaonina (1990). Dalven's research brings together a number of important topics in onomastic research on Greek Jews. She documents the continuing tendencies to nickname people after their physical characteristics, their personality traits, and their vocations. She also discusses Ladino nicknaming as a gendered process, comparing names given to male and female children and examining attendant rationale or impulse. Dalven notes the widespread use of nicknames in the Greek region of Epirus, and that the substitution of nicknames for officially given names varied (1990, 17).

In her descriptions of nicknames derived from professions she explains how *Konduratzis*, "cobbler" went by this epithet because of his shoemaking. *Sakis* (Turkish for "one who limps") was conferred on a lame person. Some of the most amusing nicknames were those bestowed in recognition or blunt announcement of personal characteristics or legendary behavior. *Kaokas* was the baker who burned the fare he had prepared for a festival. The nickname has its origins in the word *Kaio*, which means burning or incineration in Greek. Even though Dalven's work is not accompanied by a range of etymological or linguistic data, its distinction lies in the multiplicity of stories about lifestyles and folkways which it brings to the fore. All of these have been, and continue to be, vital and indispensable in the creation of human nicknames overall, and Sephardic Ladino epithets in particular.

A more programmatic examination of naming practices among Greek Sephardim followed Dalven's initiative. In the fall of 1990 a Greek researcher, Nikos Stavroulakis, published an article in a newsletter from the Jewish Museum of Greece, in Athens, which presents not only onomastic findings on the Jews of Greece, but genealogical research as well. Indeed, the article presents a brief list of Jewish Greek names and aligns them with possible origins along genealogical, rather than onomastic lines (Stavroulakis 1990, 1-3). In his bid to paint as well rounded a genealogical picture as possible, Stavroulakis enumerates several obstacles which confronted him including the destruction of most of Greece's Jews in the Holocaust, and the lack of earlier research in the genealogical arena. Even so, the author indicates several possible sources which can fuel credible genealogical research, such as periodicals, old books, and even addresses and dedications that were preserved from Jewish synagogues in Greece.

Stavroulakis's article in the Jewish Museum newsletter was eventually followed by another authored by an American undergraduate at Amherst College, who was writing a research paper on Spain and the Jews of Salonika. In issues 31 and 32 of the Museum newsletter (1991, 1992), more in the line of Pita Merce, Sari Meyer focuses on correlations between Jewish Salonikan names and elements of Spanish tradition. Meyer's research led her to examine an official Spanish roster from 1949 of Sephardic Jews and Spanish citizens visiting or residing in Greece and Egypt. Included in the list were several names of Jews and/or contemporary Spaniards of Jewish or *converso* origin. Meyer recognized the name of the Spanish dictator,

Francisco Franco. Out of 144 of the Greek Jews listed, she found 27 whose names have a clear connection with Spanish tradition, of which 15 belonged to Jews from Salonika. In the latter category Meyer attempted to sketch past connections with medieval Spain, as preserved in family names such as Arditi, Benveniste, Motton, Ezrati, and a few others.

Some of Meyer's findings, and brief narrative explanations of a few of the more widespread Salonikan Ladino names, precede similar findings and explanations which I will include shortly in this essay. *Gattegno* was a common nickname among Salonikan Jews, derived from the Spanish word for cat "*gato.*" What Meyer brings out in her study is the significant fact that Ladino nicknames in Salonika were not only devised for people. *Gattegno* was also the common name for the synagogue of Salonikan Jews who had originally come from Aragon. Exhibiting even more precise popular memory, the name *Saltiel* is a Salonikan Ladino name which recalls a personal incident in medieval Spain. Meyer estimates that the name originated in 1410, when a Jewish woman who answered to the name María jumped from the wall of a monastery in Segovia in order to escape a blood libel. The woman, Meyer found, became known as *María del Salto*, whence the later Ladino surname *Saltiel*.

Three basic trends in researching the names of Sephardic Ladino speakers from the Mediterranean basin emerge from the different onomastic and/or genealogical studies I have presented here. The first tendency is toward building a base that classifies and catalogs the nature and characteristics of Jewish names. This trend is manifest in the studies by Schaerf (1925), Moscona (1967), and Dalven (1977, 1990). These researchers' projects sprang from the need to construct lists of Jews and Jewish customs in

Mediterranean communities (Livorgnian, Sofian, Iaoninan, and more), that would be as well-rounded as possible.

Dalven's study also exhibits signs of the second research trend, that is, that which seeks to present the historic and linguistic origins of Ladino names as elements that illuminate a particular nature these names have about them, and tend to exude. In addition to Dalven's research, Kunchev's study is instrumental along these lines. It also discusses several nicknames' linguistic and historical origins, by way of clarifying the types of names in the Bulgarian Jewish repertoire, which is its main focus.

The third trend in the research, clearly orienting the later studies, is the genealogical direction. At its core this seeks to highlight the potential genealogical information embodied in so many Spanish Jewish names, and inherent in their socially informed examination. This research pattern evinces itself in studies whose basic goal is to reconstruct genealogical dynasties through their focus on the names. The Spanish scholar Pita Merce's work (1975), exemplifies this process, as do the later studies of Nikos Stavroulakis (1990) and Sari Meyer (1991, 1992). Merce and Meyer worked in the Spanish arena directly, and show that it has much to offer by way of information that further explains and substantiates Sephardic names as mnemonic and cultural links.

An Entrée to Nicknames in Salonika: Synagogue Titles, and Humor and Mockery in the Press

Before embarking on a presentation of Salonikan Jewish nicknames for individuals, it is more illustrative to contextualize these within the widespread custom of bestowing Ladino nicknames on local, communal synagogues and on individual newspapers in a highly active journalistic environment. These papers in turn perpetuated popular fun-making. Lest they be considered overly formal and a poor indicator of their congregations' geographic provenance, let alone of their creative tendencies, on one level the synagogues in pre-Holocaust Salonika took the name of the cities or lands from which their expelled Iberian founders had come after 1492. Hence Salonika was home to the *Aragon* Synagogue, the *Catalan*, the *Italia*, and so on. On a level of greater familiarity, the synagogues also had nicknames drawn from fruits, plants, animals, and even popular insults. In addition to its religious name in Hebrew, the *Etz Haim*, "Tree of Life," Synagogue was affectionately called the *Ajo*, "garlic." The Lisbon Synagogue bore the name *Mangrana*, "pomegranate," and the Portugal Synagogue went by *Calabasa*, "pumpkin." Animals' names for the Salonikan synagogues also abounded. The Oranto Synagogue was the *Gallo*, "rooster," the Aragon Synagogue was also the *Gato*, "cat," and other syagogues were referred to as *Gamello*, "camel," and *Raton*, "mouse." Names of objects also played a role, such that the *Nave Tzedek*, "Herald of Justice," Synagogue went by the name of *Cuerno*, "horn," the Pulia Synagogue was called *Macaron*, "noodle," and the Qiana Synagogue was popularly named after a tray or flat dish.

This is but a taste of the nicknaming culture that flourished in Salonika and applied unstintingly to the sacred and the profane, alike. Much like the synagogues, the city's Jewish humoristic newspapers also went by names consistent with the bite of their typical content. There was daily or regular fare called *El Kirbač*, "the whip," *El Gante*, "the glove," *El Shamar*, "the slap on the face," *El Culevro*, "the serpent," *La Gata*, "the female cat," *El Punčon*, "the thorn/sting," *La Vara*, "the rod," *El Rezon*, "the smiler," *El Azno*, "the donkey/ass," and *El Burlon*, "the joker/prankster." Many newspapers were similarly grounded in humoristic, sarcastic, and/or thorny ways of relating to different issues arising in Salonikan Jewish society, and their titles also reflected as much.

Such journalism presents a view of Salonika's Ladino-speaking Sephardim that is unique in its canted access to popular life. Journalistic creativity in the city projected, and continues to project, in surviving newspapers and ongoing writing and broadcasting, the humoristic and "smiling" tone that flavors Ladino culture and is so familiar to its intimates. Moreover, the myriad of Judeo-Spanish newspapers in Salonika constituted a special forum for literary exchange, as well as a linguistic workshop in which Ladino was constantly evolving; taking in new words in local and colonial languages (Turkish, Greek, and French), remixing some Hebrew elements, and bringing forward its Spanish base.

Tel Aviv 1996-1997: Nicknames among Ladino Speakers from Salonika

At this point the personal nicknames which Ladino speakers from Salonika still confer, answer to, and internalize in Israel, can be examined as dynamic remnants of Sephardic naming practices in Greece that not only wove, but also inculcated the multicast fabric of daily life. The individuals whose nicknames are described below were born in Salonika and now reside in Tel Aviv. They still speak Ladino, although modern Hebrew has generally taken precedence. It is in these speakers' instincts to confer a particular Ladino nickname on a certain person for a specific reason, to render the bond between nickname and bearer lifelong, and it is in the deeply ingrained names themselves, that one finds manifold cultural and linguistic preservation. The Hebrew linguistic environment represents a complete change from the Ladino environment in Sephardic Salonika. Nonetheless, the transplanted Salonikans in Tel Aviv continue to use the Ladino nicknames with which they are innately familiar. They often use them to open interpersonal communication and to punctuate it, thereby encapsulating someone's character and legendary or contemporary behavior in society in a multifarious signifier that slides between pasts and present.

Turning to my list of nicknames itself, I must point out that there is nothing in it to enable statistical conclusions; the names and brief explanations are intended purely to serve as an illustration of the popular Sephardic practices and processes of memory I have discussed thus far. What cannot be understated is the uniqueness of this list. The names were assembled from first generation Salonikan Israelis, that is, from Ladino-speaking informants who are still accustomed to using the names and nicknames they describe in their everyday spoken language. This, again, points to the dynamism and multireferentiality in this aspect of their speech. Moreover, my informants told me that they use modern Hebrew for their everyday communication, "but," in their words, "when it is possible to mix in a word in Ladino we do so, and this tints the Hebrew with nostalgic Ladino." The latter is clearly the language of long-standing individual and collective memory.

In this vein, I should underscore that a majority of the names (thirty-five) that I am presenting here show clear ties between Ladino and Spanish, and this indicates the continued dominance of Spanish within Ladino. In descending order Turkish is represented in seven of the names, Greek in four, Italian in four, Hebrew in one, and French in one. Interestingly, two nicknames also derive from Yiddish, which further evidences Ladino's capacity for absorbing words from various linguistic sources. It is clear that the Yiddish made its way into the Ladino when speakers of both languages came into contact in Israel, especially after the state's political establishment in 1948, and the influx of large waves of immigrants from Yiddish and Ladino backgrounds and cultures in the 1950s.

As with the names of the synagogues and newspapers in Salonika, the sources of Ladino nicknames used in Israel continue to vary and to emphasize personal qualities and predilections, as well as animate or inanimate elements in one's everyday world. The names described by my informants can be categorized by type in the following manner. A nickname may have been, or may be, conferred and perpetuated in recognition of (1) a personality trait and/or social behavior; (2) a visible or outstanding physical defect or quality; (3) a food which an individual enjoys or favors; (4) a person's profession; and (5) a resemblance to a particular animal. Nicknames also derive from a play on given names, and from other nouns and linguistic elements, constituting a sixth category. The list of nicknames resembles that in Kunchev's Bulgarian based study from 1977. It will be followed by a brief conclusion.

Nicknames Remembered and Currently Used by Salonikan Ladino Speakers in Israel[3]

(1) Personality Trait or an Individual's Behavior in Society

Balabaya Preta[4]—a female "owner of a black house."—"I remember that this is what they nicknamed a woman who owned a house of ease." (E.G.)
Source: Hebrew (housewife) and Spanish (?)

Boračon—"drunkard."—"We have a neighbor who likes drinking wine so much that his name is *Isaac el boračon.*" (H.R.)
Source: Spanish (*borracho*)

Bovo—"fool."—"This is a widely accepted nickname in Ladino overall, not just among the Jews of Salonika. Everyone who has behaved like a fool is called by this name. A woman is called by the female version, *Bova.*" (E.G.)
Source: Spanish (*bobo*)

Coqueta—"a coquettish woman."—"Every woman who loves to show off we call by this name." (E.G.)
Source: Spanish (*coqueta*)

Čuflaculo—"inflated backside."—"It's not nice to explain the personal source of this name, but everyone understands that we give it to someone who passes wind in the company of men." (H.R.)
Source: Spanish (*chuflaculo*)

Favlastina—"chatter box."—"The most accepted nickname for a woman who is a gossip or talks nonstop." (E.G.)
Source: Spanish (*habla*)

Fishurento—"pest," "snoop," or "curious one."—"Term of endearment for pests and snooping types". (H.R.)
Source: Spanish (*fisgón*—?)

Fisuna—"bellows" or "a man inflated with self-importance."—"This was someone who was accustomed to making an impression on his surroundings, though not everything he said was true, so we called him this." (I.M.)
Source: Greek (?)

Medio Griego—"half Greek."—"Someone who didn't know Ladino very well we called "half Greek." (I.M.)
Source: Spanish (*medio griego*)

Nono—"Grandfather."—"When we were liberated from the Nazi concentration camps Moshe Shmuel was the old man among the Holocaust survivors from Greece. We were relatively young so we called him by the nickname *El Nono*." (H.R.)
Source: Italian (*nanno*)

Pantuflero—"skirt chaser."—"This was a very common nickname in Salonika for someone who chased women even if he was wearing slippers. Even in Israel we still use this nickname." (I.M.)
Source: Spanish (*pantufla*)

Partal—"sloppy," or "negligent."—"Who didn't know Dario Partal. There is no one who didn't know that this name stuck to him. I think the source of the word is Greek. I also know the word *partalada*, which means heaps of sloppiness." (H.R.)
Source: Greek (?)

Esterina Pelestrina—"Esterina the arguer."—"This Esterina was so argumentative that we decided that she needed to be called by this name." (H.R.)
Source: Spanish (*peleona*)

Pilisco—“pinch.”—“He really loved to eat fish with his hands, and would get a great deal of pleasure from pinching the flesh of a fish.” (I.M.)
Source: Spanish (*pellizco*)

Tonto—“fool.” Another—“accepted nickname for someone who behaved like a fool.” (E.G.)
Source: Spanish (*tonto*)

(2) Outstanding Physical Defects or Bodily Features

Alto—“tall.”—“No one knew this person by his first name, but by this name that stuck to him: *El Alto David* (David the Tall).” (H.R.)
Source: Spanish (*alto*)

Bashico—“short.”—“Everyone who was short was called this.” (H.R.)
Source: Spanish (*bajito*)

Bučiča—“a fat woman, of heavy body.”
Source: ?

Caraderia—“smiling face/face full of laughter.”—“This name we gave to a young Salonikan man who frequently wore a smile on his face.” (H.R.)
Source: Spanish (*cara de reír*)

Caranegra—“dark brown face—someone who frightens.”—“Dario had an ugly face. It was dark and threatening, so they called him *Dario Caranegra*.” (H.R.)
Source: Spanish (*cara negra*)

Cosho—“crippled.”—“People who were crippled were always called *El Cosho*.” (H.R.)
Source: Spanish (*cojo*)

Kambur—"hump," or "hunchback."—"This was for someone with a stoop and because of his hunch back we called him this all his life." (I.M.)
Source—Turkish (*kambur*)

Kyor—"blind." "Yes, I remember the man whose name was *Kyor Nissim* (blind Nissim)." (H.R.)
Source: Turkish (*kyr*)

Langada—"tall."—"The word *Langer* in Yiddish means "tall," and from there it mixed with Ladino and everyone who was particularly tall we called by this nickname" (I.M.)
Source: Yiddish, German.

Mavraqi—"dark skinned."—"Someone who had dark hair was called by this name." (H.R.)
Source: Greek (*mavros*)

Nanico—"dwarf."—"We called someone this because he was very, very small, just like a midget." (I.M.)
Source: Italian (*nano*)

Oreja—"ear."—"He had gigantic ears so we called him by this name." (H.R.)
Source: Spanish (*oreja*)

Preto—"black."—"I have a friend whose name is Shabtay Hanoca, but because he has a dark face we call him *Shabtay el Preto*." (H.R.)
Source: ?

Sodro—"deaf."—"A deaf person is called this name, and we sometimes apply it to someone whose hearing is good, but who pretends that he does not hear a thing in order to get out of his duties." (H.R.)
Source: Spanish (*sordo*)

Tiniozo—"sick with chatterbox disease."—"He always suffered from this disease, and because of it his hair fell out." (E.G.)
Source: Spanish (*tiñoso*)

Tripuda—"a fat, big-bellied woman," "intestine," or "stomach."—"This was a common nickname for such a woman."(E.G.)
Source: Spanish (*tripa*)

(3) Names of Foods

Almendra—"almond."—"We call a particular man *Nathan Almendra* because whenever he is out in the streets he eats almonds. There is never a time when Nathan doesn't have almonds in his pockets. It's come to the point where everyone substitutes this for his real name." (I.M.)
Source: Spanish (*almendra*)

Kartoshke—"potato."—"In Israel we learned this word from the Ashkenazi Jews. In Yiddish and perhaps in German it means "potato." I have a good friend that I call *Haim Kartoshke* because he's very heavy." (I.M.)
Source: Yiddish, German

Kaysi—"apricot."—"I know why they called *Natan Kaysi* this—maybe because he sold apricots." (I.M.)
Source: Turkish (*kayisi*)

Macaron—"macaroni."—"I had a friend whose name was Abraham Sustiel, but because he was so thin we called him *Abraham Macaron*." (I.M.)
Source: Italian (*macaron*)

(4) Professions

Bakal—"owner of a corner grocery store."—"The name of my good friend Haim is *Haim Bakal* because he has a

store that all the Ladino speakers from Salonika come to and shop in." (I.M.)
Source: Turkish (*bakal*)

Bañador—"a person who bathes the dead before burial."—"Everyone was afraid of the person in this line of work, and we called him *Moshon el Bañador*." (I.M.)
Source: Spanish (*bañador*)

Berber—"barber."—"Who doesn't know Eliyahu Teva, the barber? His name among our friends is *Lieto el Berber*." (I.M.)
Source: Italian (*barbiere*)

Boyadji—"painter/dyer."—"This is what we call a painter, not necessarily by his first name. For example, we might call someone *Aron (Aharon) el Boyadji*." (E.G.)
Source: Turkish (*boya*)

Čaush—"officer."—"I know why they call him this, maybe it's because he was an officer and maybe it's because he went around like an army officer." (H.R.)
Source: Turkish (*cavus*)

Handrajon—"rag vendor."—"A nickname for somenoe who sold rags and who also looked bedraggled." (I.M.)
Source: Spanish (*andrajo*)

Kapelo—"cap," or "hat."—"He was a haberdasher, so we nicknamed him this. Everyone knew *Isaac Kapelo*." (I.M.)
Source: Greek (*kapelo*)

Naranjero—"orange juice vendor." "He earned his living in Tel Aviv by selling squeezed orange juice, so we called him this." (H.R.)
Source: Spanish (*naranjero*)

Pipenero—"pickle man."—"It's clear, of course, why we used this name. Haim had a pickle stand so we called him *Haim Pipenero*." (H.R.)
Source: Spanish (*pepino*)

Pulis—"policeman."—"No one knew him by his real name, but called him this because he worked as a policeman in Israel." (H.R.)
Source: Spanish (*policía*)

(5) Animals

Čaka—"jackal."—"He was accustomed to spending many nights on the prowl, and he looked like a threatening bandit, just like a jackal out at night. His name was *Nathan Čakal*." (I.M.)
Source: Turkish (*čakal*)

(6) Nouns, Pronouns, and Wordplays

Cadavez—"every time."—"His name was Haim Zion. He worked as a coachman and every time he was seated in his coach he made the same round by the same route. So we called him *Haim Cadavez*, which in Ladino means 'every time Haim.'" (I.M.)
Source: Spanish (*cada vez*)

Colčona—Taken from the Spanish word for "blanket."—"It's not clear to me why, but there was a woman called *Colčona*. (I.M.)
Source: Spanish (*colcha*)

Copa—"cup," or "goblet."—"I don't know why he's called that, but his name is *Sion de Copa*." (H.R.)
Source: Spanish (copa)

Čagania—a Greek name.—"In my childhood I loved to play football in Salonika and in those days there was a

Greek player who was very well known and admired and his name was *Čagania*. Since everyone calls me by this name they don't even know my real name, which is Isaac Levy." (I.L.)
Source: Greek; proper name

Čuflet—"whistle thin."—"This was a common name for an extremely thin person." (I.M.)
Source: French (*sifflet*)

Čupa—"lip licking," or "lip smacking."—"The lemonade that David sold tasted so good that we all called him *David la Čupa*." (I.M.)
Source: Spanish (*chupa*)

Pantalon—"trousers."—"I have a good friend whose family name is Petilon. But we jokingly call him *Pantalon*." (I.M.)
Source: Spanish (*pantalón*)

Radio—"radio."—"Since he loved to listen to radio programs all day long we called this person *Dario Radio*." (H.R.)
Source: Spanish (*radio*)

Tranca—"clothes peg."—"A nickname for someone who behaves like a parasite and clings to another person like a clothes peg." (E.G.)
Source: Spanish (tranca)

Conclusion

Even if the number of nicknames here is not large, and even if this collection does not lend itself to statistical analysis, it underscores the modes in which the names are ensconced in the daily speech and habits of Ladino speakers in Israel, even on the threshold of a new millenium. If, as I fear may happen, use of Ladino per se fades more in Israel, the nicknames will continue to be an inspiration, extending their folkloric importance, which is both linguistic and cultural. As can be seen, it is not just the nicknames and their linguistic sources in this collection that speak volumes. The Sephardic informants' casual explanations do so as well, both in their content, and especially in their unfettered navigation between the present day and individually/ collectively experienced pasts.

Just as the Iberian-named synagogues in Salonika, and family names like *Saltiel*, were vivid reminders of homes and mishaps in medieval Spain, the above nicknames still used in Tel Aviv also enable a straddling of worlds. In a referential community that encompasses a girl jumping from a Spanish monastery, coachmen making repetitive rounds in Greece, and men and women continuing to foreground their identity-laden quirks in Israel, insider status has been constructed and perpetuated to a great extent by language and attendant memory. The "half-Greek" was the newcomer in Salonika whose Ladino was not fluent, and neither, by inference, were the Spanish dimensions in his cultural literacy. As the keynote in Ladino, Spanish continues to render coeval remotely distant neighborhoods, and to blend the "friends" who walk their streets, through such instinctual Sephardic traditions as name giving.

Notes

1. I refer to Ladino, rather than Judeo-Spanish in this essay in accordance with the Van Leer Research Institute in Jerusalem, and its practice of using this shorter term.

2. Here I wish to note a few studies involving research on names and their trajectories. These include the *Proceedings of the Ninth International Congress of Onomastic Sciences* (Louvain: International Center of Onomastics, 1969), and Jennifer Mossman, ed., *Pseudonyms and Nicknames*

Dictionary (Detroit: Gale Research, 1980). Also worth mentioning are Joseph Oppenheimer's *Name Giving in Israel: Customs of Calling Children by Particular Names* (Buenos Aires: n.p., 1975) (Hebrew); Aharon Damaski et al., *These Are Names: Studies on the Treasury of Jewish Names*, (Ramat Gan: Bar Ilan UP, 1997) (Hebrew).

3. The names of the informants from the Tel Aviv area, Erella Gattegno, Isaac Levy, Ino Medina, and Haim Refael, are abbreviated according to the convention set by the Van Leer Research Institute in Jerusalem.

4. Ladino has a long tradition of being written in Hebrew. However, in this essay and in the list of personal names I am presenting here, all of the Ladino appears in Roman letters, in italic type. Writing Ladino in Roman letters is not normative but, rather, is fueled by changing research considerations and personal taste. I endeavored not to write the Ladino names and words in this essay in a phonetic style, in the narrow sense of the word. Therefore, the reader will discover that the written Ladino here resembles normative Spanish writing, while the characteristic and distinguishing sounds of the language are emphasized. It should be noted that syllables of words that would normally carry a written accent in modern Spanish are not so designated in this form of Ladino writing **[editor's note]**. The type of Ladino orthography that I use in this essay is very close to that used by scholars in Spain's Consejo Superior de Investigaciones Científicas, and its Arias Montano Institute for Sephardic Studies in Madrid. For some of the Institute's guidelines, see pages xiii-xv of the *Proceedings of the First Symposium on Sephardic Studies* edited by Iacob Hassán in 1970, following the Conference in Madrid in 1964.

Works Cited

Dalven, Rachel. "The Names of the Iaoninan Jews." *The Sephardic Scholar*, no. 3 (1977-78): 9-23.

_____. *The Jews of Iaonina*. Philadelphia: Cadmus Press, 1990.

Damaski, Aharon, Joseph A. Reif, and Joseph Tabouri. *These Are Names: Studies on the Treasury of Jewish Names*. Ramat Gan: Bar Ilan UP, 1997 (Hebrew).

Hassán, Iacob M., ed. *Proceedings of the First Symposium on Sephardic Studies*. Madrid: Arias Montano Institute, 1970.

Kunchev, Ivan. "On the Problem of the Origin and Meaning of Sephardic Names in Bulgaria." n.p.: Unpublished typescript, 1977.

Merce, Rodrigo Pita. "Apellidos sefardíes de los Balcanes y del Oriente Medio existentes entre los judíos medievales de Lérida y Huesca." Instituto de estudios ilerdenses de la diputación provincial de Lérida. Comissioned by the Consejo Superior de Investigaciones Científicas. Lérida: 1975.

Meyer, Sari. "A Study Tracing Salonikan Surnames to Spain." *The Newsletter of the Jewish Museum of Greece*, no. 31 (1991): 1-3.

_____. "A Study Tracing Salonikan Surnames to Spain." *The Newsletter of the Jewish Museum of Greece*, no. 32 (1992): 1-3.

Molho, Michael. *Les Juifs de Salonique à la fin du XVIéme siècle: Synagogues et Patronymes*. n.p.: Tarason, 1991.

Moscona, Isac. "On the Origin of Family Names of the Bulgarian Jews." *Annual*, nos. 1-2 (1967): 111-37.

Mossman, Jennifer, ed. *Pseudonyms and Nicknames Dictionary*. Detroit: Gale Research, 1980.

Oppenheimer, Joseph. *Proceedings of the Ninth International Congress of Onomastic Sciences*. Louvain: International Center of Onomastics, 1969.

_____. *Name Giving in Israel: Customs of Calling Children by Particular Names.* Buenos Aires: n.p., 1975 (Hebrew).

Refael, Shmuel. Conversations with research informants in 1996 and 1997, Tel Aviv, Israel. Informants: Erella Gattegno, Isaac Levy, Ino Medina, and Haim Refael.

Schaerf, Samuele. *I Cognomi degli ebrei d'Italia*. Firenze: Casa Editrice Israel, 1925.

Stavroulakis, Nikos. "Tracing Family Names in Greece." *The Newsletter of the Jewish Museum of Greece*, no. 30 (1990): 1-3.

◆ Chapter 6

Spanish Balconies in Morocco: A Window on Cultural Influence and Historical Persistence in the Mallāḥ (Jewish) Community[1]

Hsaïn Ilahiane

Introduction

The Islamic City continues to be the focus of a number of scholars in the West as well as in the Middle East and North Africa. Most of this literature has dwelt on sorting out the pre-Islamic and Islamic attributes of urban centers through time and how these places have changed in response to cultural, economic, and religious currents. Despite the voyeurist and ahistorical nature of much of this debate, it has contributed enormously to our understanding of the historical development of urbanization in the Islamic world and before. This is not another attempt to sort out the non-Islamicness or Islamicness of the city.[2] Instead, this essay traces the influences of Medieval Muslim Spain on the urban and physical layout of the *Medina*. Specifically, it critiques ahistorical readings of the Islamic City, and argues that the pronounced distinction between *mallāḥs* (Jewish quarters) with and without balconies correspond to

Medieval Islamic Spanish influence not colonial influence. It is suggested that unlike the rest of the *Medina*'s (old Islamic City) urban layout and built environment, the Jewish quarter's urban layout attests to the cultural memory of Medieval Spain preserved by the Jewish communities of Moroccan cities.

Western readings and examinations of the urban layout and built environment of the Islamic City have been used as the point of entry to diagnose the Arab-Islamic cultural ethos. The sprawling nature of Islamic Cities, and their perceived dark, tortuous, and irregular urban design has led some Western observers to classify the Arab-Islamic civilization as "a civilized architecture without architects" (quoted in Brown 1973). Unlike the European gridiron pattern and despite the decontextualized nature of this debate, the Arab-Islamic urban design by analogy has come to be viewed as the product of the irrational, crooked, and confused mind of the Muslim.

Eickelman summarizes this debate succinctly in stating that "it is not cities, then, which are being compared, but problems of social order in the setting of what, in our own cultural tradition, are regarded as cities" (Eickelman 1974, 275). Lapidus rightly complains about the lack of historicity in the analysis of the urban morphology of the Islamic City and disparages the neglect of the organization of quarters (Lapidus 1973, 50; 1967, 91). Others have emphasized the evolution and development of ethnic clustering and formation of quarters in Middle Eastern and North African cities. For example, Greenshields (1979, 121) argues that "ethnic clusters within cities must originate and grow through population redistribution, that is either through migration to a town or redistribution within it. Explanation of cluster formation must therefore lie in the relationship between these population movements and the socioeconomic environment in which they take place."

Indeed, a great deal has been written about the causes behind ethnic formation, clustering, and interaction between the non-Muslims and Muslims in the Arab-Islamic world. While most of this scholarship has emphasized social and spacial relationships among different ethnic and religious groups, it has paid little, if any attention to the relationship between the historical movement of populations, especially the non-Islamic groups, and its implications on the organization of the physical urban layout of such communities. This essay traces some of the influences of population movement on the built form of the urban outline of the North African city. I argue that unlike the rest of the *Medina*'s urban built form, the *mallāḥ*'s outline expresses a strong relationship between migration and production of new patterns of urban design. I also suggest that the emergence of the balcony feature in the *Medina* could be perceived as one way the New Spanish immigrants were also remembering or reinventing their Iberian communities.

The Mālikī School as the Framework for Urban Design in North Africa

It is first necessary to briefly examine the Mālikī School of Islamic Law and its role in shaping the urban development of North African cities. Unlike most scholars concerned with the development of urbanization in the Arab-Islamic world, Hakim (1989) sees the Arab-Islamic City as the outcome of a long historical process intertwined with Islamic Law after the arrival of the Prophet Muḥammad. Hakim's innovative contribution to the theme is vital, going well beyond the interpretive methodologies that have characterized previous literature. Hakim discusses the essential underlying factors that have shaped the traditional built environment in Islamic culture:

> Viewing the city as a process and a product is an effective analytical-evaluation and planning tool, and is indispensable for the study of the Islamic city. The process encompasses the decision making in building activity as guided by Islamic values. Looking at the city as a product clarifies how a complex, heterogeneous, and sophisticated built form is achievable with a simple set of physical organizational components, and a related mechanism of verbal communication used in building decisions. (Hakim 1989, 89)

We can best understand the process of Islamic urbanization by considering the city on two scales: the whole city and the neighborhood. Decisions at the citywide scale were usually made by the ruler or government; these decisions concerned the foundation, growth, and revitalization of an urban center, and would usually include the location of the Friday Mosque, the distribution of the land in the projected frontiers of the city to various ethnic, familial, or tribal affiliations, and the location and configuration of the city's walls and gates. These were decisions which would typically be made during the first years of a city's foundation. On the neighborhood or quarter scale, decisions tended to be of a different nature and results were of immediate significance. Since building activity affected both the initiator and his/her immediate neighbors, the development of guidelines became the concern of the science of *fiqh* (Islamic jurisprudence), from the earliest development (Hakim 1988, 19).

In the theoretical framework of the Mālikī School of Islamic Law, a corpus of guidelines are identified as vital to building activity. These guidelines, implemented in a society that lacked wheeled transport (Bulliet 1975), include the following, as reported by Hakim (1989, 90): (1) avoid harm to others and oneself; (2) accept the concept of interdependence; (3) respect the privacy of others, particularly avoiding the creation of direct visual corridors; (4) respect the right of original or prior usage; (5) respect the right of building higher within one's air space; (6) respect property of others; (7) respect the rights of preemption by adjacent neighbors; (8) maintain seven cubits as the minimum width of public through-streets; and (9) avoid locating the sources of unpleasant smells and noisy activities adjacent to or near mosques. All the latter activities are located and practiced outside the walls of the *Medina*.

In addition, the *Sunnah* (saying and deeds of the Prophet Muḥammad, peace be upon him) is replete with additional guidelines that restrict the behavior of the individual and the community. A prime example is the idea of "beauty without arrogance." The concept of simplicity in the Islamic public sphere contrasts sharply with the private one in the sense that the interiors of much of the Islamic housing were decorated with facades of courtyards and loggias. The expressed or felt need to "fill up" the house with furniture and to decorate it from the inside in the form of façades and balconies opening onto the courtyard and loggias, still factors prominently in planners' concern, in urban and rural Morocco today, for the built form which well-to-do families will occupy.

One of the shortcomings of Hakim's work, despite his appropriate emphasis on *fiqh*, is his neglect of the distinctive built form of ethnic quarters, especially *Ḥārat al-Yāhud*, "Jewish quarter," the Jewish quarters in Tunisian cities and throughout North Africa. Given the historical role of these communities in the social and economic development of the North African cities, Hakim's reconstruction of Arab-Islamic architecture falls short in the sense that he does not integrate the distinctive built form qualities of the *mallāḥs*. Furthermore, Hakim does not discuss the impact of population movement on changes of urban architecture as the *mallāḥs* of Moroccan cities suggest.

The Mallāḥ, the Balcony, and the Spanish-Jewish Connection

The word "*mallāḥ*" is closely associated with the history of the Moroccan Jewish community, most especially the community of the city of Fez. The *mallāḥ* was the original name given to the site due south of Fez-Jadīd (New Fez) on which the first Jewish quarter of its kind in Morocco was founded around 1438 (Corcos 1976, 87).[3] As to the origin and meaning of the term, the literature concerned with the *mallāḥ* institutions suggests discredited and credible etymologies. Some of the refuted etymologies are those that maintain that the word is derived from the root *m-l-ḥ* meaning salt in Arabic. This false interpretation holds that the *mallāḥ* is a "salted, cursed ground" and Jews were responsible for "salting the heads of the decapitated rebels" (Zafrani 1987, 293). The term "*mallāḥ*" has nothing to do with salt or Jews salting the heads of the rebels, rather it was the original name of the territory on which part of Fez-

Jadīd was established. The same place is referred to as "*Mallāḥ* of the Muslims" even before the transfer and establishment of the Jewish quarter there in 1438 (Corcos 1976, 76).

In North Africa and the rest of the Arab world, Jewish quarters and settlements carry different names. For instance, in Syria the Jewish quarter is known by the name *Ḥayy al-Yahūd* (Khoury 1984, 512). In Algeria, it goes by the name of *Darb al-Yahūd* or *shari'* and by *Ḥārat al-Yahūd* in Libya and Tunisia. In the city of Tetouan, in northern Morocco, the Spanish term "*judiría*," is used to designate the Jewish quarter. In the rest of Morocco, the word "*mallāḥ*" means the part of town, village, or streets that used to be inhabited by Jews. Given their status as the People of the Book, Jews are entitled to the protection of the government and have a right to a special quarter where they can practice and preach their beliefs without any hindrances (Fattal 1958, 91-93).[4]

For Eickelman (1974, 1981) the concept of the quarter in the Muslim city is that it is an ensemble of households cemented by what he calls *qarāba*, or "closeness," and sustained by a wide net of personal ties and similar concerns anchored in a common morality and shared space. The point is that the quarter has a cultural logic to its function. This logic lies not in its urban layout but rather in its constellation of social relations. Based on his work on the social history of urban Salé, Brown contends that in Salé "the notion of quarter had no social significance" (1976, 39). However, Greenshields correctly notes that the "term has been used rather loosely . . . representative of a certain pattern of social organization, and possessing a certain structure and set of distinguishing characteristics which it shares with other quarters" (1979, 124). True as this may be, Greenshields's analysis falls short of analyzing the distinctive characteristics of quarter formation and development and their impact on social organization.

Not every town or village in Morocco has a Jewish quarter, or *mallāḥ*. Furthermore, it is essential to discern the urban *mallāḥs* from the rural ones. The urban *mallāḥ* constitutes an integral part of the urban fabric of major *Medinas* in several large cities; it is adjacent to the *Medina*, integrated into its urban layout or found on its periphery, yet in some places it is enclosed within a walled and fortified enclave. Unlike the *mallāḥs* of the major urban centers, most of the rural *mallāḥs* do not make up separate enclosed enclaves or *quṣūr* (sing. *qsr*, "fortified village") but rather point to a long tradition of coexistence and religious tolerance within the ethnic diversity that permeates the Moroccan society as a whole in pre- and postcolonial times. *Quṣūr* are walled self-contained settlements, and form agglomerations of connected houses made of packed earth mixed with hay and stone. Typical *quṣūr* have as their center a mosque with a well, a marketplace or square, a caravanserai for traveling petty traders and their beasts, and threshing fields used also for social and religious ceremonies. Another feature is the cemetery found outside the walls of the village, and usually located near the tomb of the local saint. Narrow and covered streets run from the square in several directions leading to the houses.

In southeast Morocco the term "*mallāḥ*" applies to both the streets and villages that the Jewish community occupied. In the fortified villages of the Ziz River Valley, for instance, the Jewish population used to live in what is called in Berber *l'lu n'udayn*, "Jewish streets," and in some cases in separate fortified Jewish villages, "*tighremt*," or "*ighram n'udayn*," in Berber. In the village of Rissani, for example, the *mallāḥ* resembles both Arab Black, and Berber fortified villages. However, in some regions of Morocco, such as the valleys and mountains of the Atlas and the Rif ranges, the *mallāḥs* are open and do not constitute self-contained fortified villages, as is the case in other rural regions of Morocco.[5]

The *mallāḥ* of Fez is, par excellence, the oldest and most important in Morocco. In the middle of the eleventh century, al-Bakri described the town of Fez as the town with the most Jews in the Maghreb, which gave rise to the popular rhyme: "*Fas blad bilā nās*": "Fez, a town where there are no people worth mentioning" (al-Bakri quoted in Colin 1987, 460). Between 1492 and 1496, large waves of Spanish and Portuguese Jews fled the wrath and persecution of the Catholic kings to settle in major cities of Morocco.[6] The arrival of these communities, after the Inquisition, had far-reaching implications for the indigenous Jewish communities of Morocco, ranging from religious studies to the built form of their environment. These immigrants are known as *megorashim*, a Hebrew term meaning "expellees." They have been referred to in local, colloquial Arabic as *rūmīs*, meaning Romans or foreigners. Their rabbinical order went by the name of "the sages of Castile." Native Moroccan Jews have been called *toshavim* (Hebrew, meaning "residents," or Arabic, "*beldyin*"). These native Jewish residents were believed to be *berberiscos* (partly assimilated into Berber culture), and *forasteros*, "foreigners," (Kenbib 1986, 275). Deshen states that:

> Various particular practices of the *toshavim* were rejected in most parts of Morocco in favor of customs that the newcomers had brought with them from Spain. Once the refugees established their authority Moroccan

> Jewry became significantly different from what it had been before. (Deshen 1989, 8) [editor's translation]

The "expellees" who made the *mallāḥs* their final refuge were, for the most part, more complexly developed in cultural, economic, and intellectual terms than the native communities. Using rabbinical writings from the eighteenth and nineteenth century, Deshen (1989, 119) claims that the *megorashim* held eminent distinction and solid leverage in the administration of day-to-day affairs of the community. One can further this claim and suggest that this influence also led to a radical transformation of the organization of the community and to a refurbishment of its decayed, stifled, and overcrowded built environment deplored by the cosmopolitan *megorashim*. This cultural transformation, I suggest, led to the emergence and appendage of the full-blown outward-looking architectural feature of the balcony in Jewish housing encountered only in northern and central Moroccan cities. These cities are indeed the ones most influenced by Spanish Jews.

Indisputably, before the eighteenth and nineteenth centuries the Spanish Jews dominated the cultural and social activities of the Moroccan *mallāḥ*. Reading the urban fabric of the *Medinas* that accommodated mass migrations of Spanish Jews such as Sefrou, Fez, Rabat, Salé, and Tetouan, one is struck immediately by the *mallāḥ*'s iron balconies and windows looking upon straight and parallel streets leading to gates that until recently had been locked at night (Brown 1976, 38).

Wirth (1991, 23), in his study of the urban morphology of the city of Fez in 1912 and 1913, categorizes the *mallāḥ*'s balconies as "Western, fin de siècle architecture, standing in radical contrast to the classical model of the Islamic city" [editor's translation]. The architecture and the urban elements of the *mallāḥ* may deceivingly strike the eye as a relic of French colonial design, but its fin de siècle motifs probably go back further than the nineteenth century suggested by Wirth. Unlike the rural Jewish *mallāḥs*, whose built form and outline resemble their Muslim counterparts, the urban *mallāḥs*, especially those located in northern and central Morocco, contrast with the built environment of the rest of the Islamic City or *Medina*. The urban *mallāḥs* I have in mind are those of Fez, Salé, Rabat, Sefrou, and Tetouan. Even the segregationist and paternalistic colonial policies of urban design in Morocco, those associated with Lyautey and his entourage, evince an understanding of the cultural and religious differences of different quarters (Abu-Lughod 1970; Rabinow 1989; Wright 1991).

In 1912, when France finally established its control over the Moroccan state, Lyautey was appointed Head of the Military as well as "Résident Général," a post he held until 1926. Lyautey is known for being the individual to have single-handedly directed town planning in colonial Morocco. He had a poignant disdain for the disruptive, Roman-inspired military architecture in Algeria, which, coupled with his colonial experience in urban design and planning in Madagascar in the late 1880s, led him to emphatically insist that city planning should be broached through its contextualization within the history of Morocco and the particulars of the indigenous environment. This is not as yielding as it may sound. Indeed, Royer ostentatiously asserts that "among all the North African countries and perhaps among all colonies, Morocco was at the head of the urbanist movement. Morocco had the good fortune to be governed by a man [Lyautey] who had full power and who combined, in this capacity, artistic insight and a gift for action . . . He was the soul of this work" (quoted in Dethier 1973, 209). Unquestionably, one does not have to tax his/her imagination to perceive the underlying ideological and psychological footing of Lyautey's urban worldview; his was one of a sly double-edged political strategy: to uplift and refurbish the urban environment and, therefore pacify and stupefy the rebellious elements of colonial society (see Abu-Lughod 1970, 131-49; King 1995).

The Lyautey approach to urban design, then, consisted of respect for the old form and innovation without disturbance. In this context the Jewish *mallāḥ* was a good example to copy in designing a new type of city "*à la Française*." Imitating the *mallāḥ* would allow for "harmonization" with the Islamic *Medina*, though what has remained visible is the degree to which the colonial architects were history and tradition bound. The colonial approach to urbanization drew much of its inspiration from ethnic and quarter separation that had ancient roots in Moroccan history, going back to *mallāḥs* for Jews and *funduqs* for Christians. The latter were medieval Islamic hotels where traders and their beasts of burden rested, and also a place for commodity information and exchange. In their search for urban order and beauty, or ironically, "beauty without arrogance," colonial architects under Lyautey's mandate became the "servants of art, the faithful guardians of tradition" and were obliged to carry out their designs in the spirit of the formula: "Intervene everywhere, but change nothing" (Wright 1991, 130).

To achieve their goals, the colonial architects, especially those close to Lyautey, drew a great deal upon the Hispano-Moorish architecture to the point that, in 1924, the modernist French architect, Julien Borély, criticized this method as ". . . pseudo-Moroccan style . . . of trumped-up little Alhambras" (Wright 1991, 137). Lyautey's appreciation of the Hispano-Moorish architecture of Muslim Spain and ethnic quarters, especially the urban design of the *mallāḥ*, went beyond the fin de siècle characteristics of the *mallāḥ* of Fez-Jadīd, as described by Wirth above.

Just as Fez was the major urban Jewish settlement in the Maghreb, in the middle of the tenth century, Granada, in al-Andalus, according to al-Razi, went by the name of "*villa de los judíos*" and "*la ciudad de los judíos,*" *Madīnat al-Yahūd*, "City of the Jews" (Torrès Balbas 1971, 214). The city of Toledo is reported to have also its *mallāḥs* or *judirías* in the ninth century:

> . . . the Jews resided in Toledo, in a "City of Jews" (*Madīnat al-Yahūd*), apart from the Muslims and Mozarabs, surrounded by a wall built in 850 by Muhayir ibn al-Qatil, against the Umayyad authority . . . Various internal gates linked different parts of the city and there was an external gate for the Jewish quarter (*Bāb al-Yahūd*) . . . The Jewish quarter was nestled among various neighborhoods. One of its areas which bordered San Román and was separated from the Christian sector by a dividing parapet, was called the high or outer quarter. (Ibn Ḥayyān quoted in Torrès Balbas 1971, 212) [editor's translation]

Indeed, Granada, Seville, Toledo, and Fez shared a great deal in common as major Jewish urban centers. However, this common thread that ran through all of these communities, on both sides of the Mediterranean, would come to an end during the Catholic Kings' reign, only to reproduce itself later in major Moroccan cities in the fifteenth century.

Andalusian architecture and its offshoots in Maghrebi medieval architecture cannot be fully understood unless we situate the historical forces that shaped the incessant exchange and borrowing, on both banks of the Mediterranean, within the tumultuous ninth through fifteenth centuries. The golden age of Maghrebi architecture thrived between the eleventh and fifteenth centuries, a period dominated politically by a string of Berber dynasties, the Moslem Almoravids and the Almohads. These dynasties did not emanate from an urban environment. Rather, they stormed the Maghreb and al-Andalus from their religious strongholds in the Sahara Desert and the Anti-Atlas range.

The Almoravid and the Almohad dynasties were strictly concerned with the religious concerns and matters of the time, and can hardly be seen as urban and town-planning aficionados. They saw themselves as religious reformers engaged in ridding North Africa, as well as Muslim Spain, of religious impurities, "*al-fasād*," by any necessary means (Abun-Nasr 1971). In so doing, they forcibly converted non-Muslim populations, and in some cases eradicated them (Stillman 1976; Gerber 1980; Hirschberg 1981). The work of these two Berber dynasties was fundamental to the establishment of the total hegemony of the Mālikī legal rite throughout the Maghreb. Members of the Marīnid dynasty that followed did not model themselves as aggressive religious reformers. Deficient in Sharifian genealogy and symbolic capital, they instead launched a massive program of *madrasa*, "religious school," construction, conceivably in an effort to display their allegiance to Islamic orthodoxy and to ward off other religious and power-hungry competitors. However, in spite of these dynastic efforts to act as sponsors of urbanism and architecture, the conclusive built environment was always anchored and situated within the Spanish Islamic architecture that stemmed originally from Ummayad Syria (Abun-Nasr 1971; Guedes 1979; Hill 1976).

Medieval Maghreb compromised its cultural and architectural styles only to be dominated later by the Islamic Spanish tradition, which was condemned to remain religious at its crux.[7] Repeated immigration from Andalusia in conjunction with the dominance of Maghrebi dynasties there, secured regular contact with the Maghreb, especially Morocco, until the last decade of the fifteenth century (Chouraqui 1968; Stillman 1976; Goitein 1974). This uninterrupted contact was a backdrop to the height of Maghrebi medieval architecture and town planning under the Almoravids, the Almohads, and the Marīnids. In conjunction with large waves of Jewish immigrants, who "carried" ideas and technologies across the Mediterranean, there existed the appropriate mechanisms for the transfer and implantation of the Spanish-designed balcony feature in the *mallāḥs* of Morocco. It is in this context, given the cultural hegemony of the "expellees" over the *mallāḥ*'s affairs, that the new immigrants strived to rearrange and imagine their social and urban fabric in Morocco by recalling and tapping into their ongoing memory of Spain.

The intensified settlement of Spanish Jews in Morocco, through their immigration, is itself a dynamic historical event that reshaped, refurbished, and molded the Moroccan Jewish heritage. The refugees restructured the cultural milieu of the indigenous communities and in practical terms, extended a hegemonic cultural umbrella over the *mallāḥs*. Not only did the hegemony of the "expellees" give them control over the organization of the *mallāḥ*, but they may well have dictated principles guiding the physical building of the *mallāḥ* as well. The transfer of the balcony to the *mallāḥs*, I suggest, in association with the Jewish immigration to Morocco, is the fitting context from which to start reconstructing the history of the balcony in North Africa, particularly Morocco.

Torrès Balbas contends that the balcony did not exist and was not known in Morocco before the fifteenth century, stating that "in Morroco the balconies (*las aljimeces*) [were] unknown" (1971, 406).[8] He goes on to say that the balconies that appeared in the urban fabric of major Andalusian cities at the end of the fourteenth century came from Cairo and Alexandria in Egypt. In Egypt, Syria, and Arabia these balconies carried the name of *mashrabiyyat* or *al-shamasa* (colloquial) (Torrès Balbas 1971, 404).[9] Moreover, Torrès Balbas makes the case that balconies existed in Cadiz, Córdoba, Seville, Granada, Malaga, and Murcia, in the last years of the fifteenth century and into the sixteenth. This is highlighted in particular decrees of the period that prohibited further construction of these balconies and ordered existing ones to be destroyed (Torrès Balbas 1971, 406). In Portugal these balconies were known as *adufa* from the Arabic word "*al-duffa*," (plural *al-difāf*) meaning a door, or a window, or a wooden venetian blind. Clearly, these Spanish cities had their *judirías* or even separate *Madinat al-Yahūd*, "Jewish quarters." It is not surprising that the architecture of most *judirías* was reproduced in the *mallāḥ* once the Jewish population fled from the Iberian Peninsula at the end of the fifteenth century. This preliminary analysis of the Andalusian balconies and *adufas* in their reproduced and evolved form in the *mallāḥs* supports the postulated linkage between Jewish population movement and urban built-form transfer and reproduction of the balcony found in the *mallāḥs*.

Conclusion by Way of Discussion

The Mālikī School of Islamic Law which dominated North Africa and Muslim Spain in the early Middle Ages, stressed the principle of upholding the private life of Muslims. This is illustrated in the closed-in, urban architectural fabric of the Islamic City, the *Medina*, as distinct from its adjacent Jewish quarter. The regular, open, and parallel streets of the Jewish *mallāḥ*, punctuated by balconies, clearly stand in radical contrast with the cul-de-sac and the justified "irregularity" of the Muslim residential sector. The latter's features owe much to the absence of wheeled transportation and ecological adaptation (Bulliet 1975; Bonine 1979).

These sharp differences between the Jewish *mallāḥ* and the Muslim *Medina* stem in part from the different religious beliefs of the two communities. The regularity of the *mallāḥ*'s streets and the abundance of balconies, as distinct from the Muslim part of town, can also be understood as reflecting a different conceptualization of private and public spheres, particularly regarding standards of gender segregation in association with the dynamics of population movement. This does not mean that the Muslim built environment lacked the feature of a balcony. The Islamic version is not as wide, nor as open as the one encountered in the Jewish quarter; basically it consists of a window-balcony from which the members of the household could look out, but could not be seen by the outside world. Under the *sharīʿa*, "Islamic Law," the privacy of the household led, as Torrès Balbas observed (1942), to an intensified dichotomization of urban social space. On the one hand, inward-looking, private social life revolved around the domestic courtyard, and not the streets. These, on the other hand, along with the *sūqs*, "markets," and mosques, were where social activities were governed by local and higher levels of government. Households' spheres of activities "touched externally without mingling to form a *civitas*" (Hourani 1970, 24).

In conclusion, this essay has argued that there is a relationship between Spanish Jewish immigration to North Africa and its absorption of some elements of Andalusian architecture. This is particularly illustrated in the balcony attribute encountered in the *mallāḥs* of northern and central Morocco. An historically informed approach, embedded in the realities of Islamic society and the existence and lay out of its minorities' urban quarters, promises a better future for research on the Islamic City. Collapsing the urban plan into pieces and tracing its provenance through time is vital in order to better understand urban landscapes as products of local and exterior cultural processes. Only through examination of the historical impact of national and international population movements on the built form of different quarters that make up most cities in North Africa and the Middle East will the long-imagined fascination with the (neo) orientalist tradition eventually wither away.

In this context the phenomenon of the balcony found in the Jewish *mallāḥs* in northern and central Morocco (and absent in southern Morocco) indicates that the Muslim *Medina* is an active preserver of remembered spaces. It contains a store of architectural wealth that informs the present about the cumulative human influences and memories of the past; in this case one clearly marked by flows of cultural exchange between North Africa and medieval Islamic Spain.

Instead of dwelling on interpretive readings of the Islamic urban vistas, extant material culture in the shape of the *Medina*'s built outline and in its distinctive attributes from quarter to quarter, offers more that will enrich inquiry. The

Jews' immigration from Muslim Spain, following the Catholic Inquisition, and their settlement among the Muslims, *en plein Medina*, made the *mallāḥ* contrast radically with the rest of the *Medina*'s urban layout. Hence, analysis of the *Medina*'s urban layout and formation in association with historical mutations is both fruitful and significant. It can tell us more about the Islamic City and its imagined and rearranged spaces that testify to ongoing, specifically directed processes of memory, than can the descriptive methods that have colonized most of the region's literature on urbanization.

Notes

1. I would like to thank Professors Michael Bonine and Ted Park for their comments and encouragement. Special thanks also go to Dr. Stacy Beckwith for her help and sustained interest.

2. On the Islamicness and non-Islamicness of the North African and Middle Eastern urban vistas and issues of the Islamic City, see Akbar (1988), al-Sayyad (1988), Berque (1967, 1980), Bonine (1977, 1979, 1990), Brown (1973), Brown (1986), Grunebaum (1955), Hourani (1970), Inalçik (1991), Joseph (1984), Marçais (1945), Pauty (1951), and Serjeant (1980), to cite a few.

3. The Jewish community and the *mallāḥ*'s institutions are one of the most researched themes by anthropologists and historians alike in Morocco. For instance, see Brown (1976), Corcos (1976), Deshen (1989), Eickelman (1974, 1981), Geertz (1979), Gerber (1980), Goulven (1927), Kenbib (1985, 1986), Le Tourneau (1949), Rosen (1972, 1984), Schroeter (1988), Shokeid (1980), and Zafrani (1983), to name but a few. (**editor's note**: The widely used *Hans Wehr Arabic-English Dictionary of Modern Written Arabic* (1976 edition, page 920) lists *mallāḥ* as a Moroccan term for "a ghetto of Moroccan cities." This translation is preceded in the same entry by "sailor," or "seaman," which does derive from the root letters of *milāḥ*, "salt." My choice to follow *Hans Wehr*'s transliterated spelling of the term *mallāḥ* throughout this essay does not constitute an additional statement or reflection on its origins.)

4. The usage varies from city to city and region to region throughout North Africa. Given the diverse ethnic and linguistic makeup of most of North Africa, the term usually takes its local usage. However, the following

list can more or less mean quarter: *ḥayy*, *humma*, *ḥāra*, *darb*, *driba*, *zanqa*, *maḥalla*, *mallāḥ* in Arabic; *l'lu*, *tighremt*, and *ighram* in Berber.

5. As discussed above, Jewish quarters, streets, and villages in urban and rural Morocco, despite their scale and magnitude, are called *mallāḥs*.

6. See Pike (1971) on the situation of the *moriscos* of Seville, and Yerushalmi (1992) on the predicament of the *marranos* in Portugal under the Catholic Kings.

7. This religious architecture was essentially limited to buildings such as mosques, *madrasa*, *ribāṭs*, and *zāwiyas*.

8. According to Torrès Balbas the Andalusian balconies came from Egypt where they were made by the Copts under the Mamluk regime, especially during the reign of Sultan Qayt Bay (1468-95).

9. Torrès Balbas writes that the Spanish word "*ajimes*" is derived from the Arabic word "*al-shamsiyya*," "window," which, in turn, is derived from *al-shams*, "sun."

Works Cited

Abu-Lughod, J. *Rabat: Urban Apartheid in Morocco*. Princeton: Princeton UP, 1970.

Abun-Nasr, J.M. *A History of the Maghreb*. Cambridge: Cambridge UP, 1971.

Akbar, J. *Crisis in the Built Environment: The Case of the Muslim City*. Singapore: Concept Media Pte., 1988.

al-Sayyad, N. *Cities and Caliphs: On the Genesis of Arab Muslim Urbanism*. New York: Greenwood Press, 1988.

Berque, J. *French North Africa: The Maghrib between Two World Wars*. London: Faber and Faber, 1967.

_____. "An Islamic Heliopolis?" In R. Holod, ed., *Toward an Architecture in the Spirit of Islam*, 19-31. Philadelphia: Aga Khan Awards, 1980.

Bonine, M. "From Uruk to Casablanca: Perspectives on the Urban Experience of the Middle East." *Journal of Urban History* 3 (1977): 141-80.

_____. "The Morphogenesis of Iranian Cities." *Annals of the Association of American Geographers* 20 (1979): 208-24.

_____. "The Sacred Direction and City Structure: A Preliminary Analysis of Islamic Cities of Morocco." *Muqarnas* 7 (1990): 50-72.

Brown, C., ed. Introduction to *From Medina to Metropolis: Heritage and Change in the Near Eastern City*, 15-47. Princeton, N.J.: The Darwin Press, 1973.

Brown, K. *People of Salé: Tradition and Change in a Moroccan city 1830-1930*. Manchester: Manchester UP, 1976.

_____. "The Uses of the Concept: The Muslim City." *Middle Eastern Cities in Comparative Perspectives. Points de vue sur les villes du Maghreb et du Machrek*. Franco-British Symposium. London: Ithaca Press, 1986.

Bulliet, R. *The Camel and the Wheel*. Cambridge: Harvard UP, 1975.

Chouraqui, A. *Between East and West: A History of the Jews in North Africa*. Trans. Michael Bernet. Philadelphia: The Jewish Publication Society of America, 1968.

Colin, G. "Mallah." *The Encyclopedia of Islam*, 459-60. Leiden: E.J. Brill, 1987.

Corcos, D. *Studies in the History of the Jews of Morocco*. Jerusalem: Ruben Mass, 1976.

Deshen, S. *The Mellah Society: Jewish Community Life in Sherifian Morocco*. Chicago: U of Chicago P, 1989.

Dethier, J. "Evolution of Concepts of Housing, Urbanism and Country Planning in a Developing Country, 1900-1972." In L.C. Brown ed., *From Medina to Metropolis: Heritage and Change in the Near Eastern City*. 197-243. Princeton, N.J.: The Darwin Press, 1973.

Eickelman, D. "Is There an Islamic City? The Making of a Moroccan Quarter in a Moroccan Town." *International Journal of Middle East Studies*, no. 5 (1974): 274-94.

_____. *The Middle East: An Anthropological Approach*. Englewood Cliffs, N.J.: Prentice-Hall, 1981.

Fattal, A. *Le statut légal des non-musulmans en pays d'Islam*. Beirut: Imprimerie Catholique, 1958.

Geertz, C. "Toutes Directions: Reading the Signs in an Urban Sprawl." *International Journal of Middle East Studies*, no. 21 (1989): 291-306.

Geertz, C., H. Geertz, and L. Rosen. *Meaning and Order in Moroccan Society: Three Essays in Cultural Analysis*. Cambridge: Cambridge UP, 1979.

Gerber, J. *Jewish Society of Fez: 1465-1700*. Leiden: Brill, 1980.

Goitein, S.D. *Jews and Arabs: Their Contacts through the Ages*. New York: Schocken Books, 1974.

Goulven, J. *Les mellahs de Rabat-Salé*. Paris: Librairie Orientale Paul Geuthner, 1927.

Greenshields, H. "Quarters and Ethnicity." In G. Blake and R. Lawless, eds., *The Changing Middle Eastern City*, 120-40. New York: Barnes and Nobles Books, 1979.

Grunebaum, G.E. "The Structure of the Muslim Town." In *Islam: Essays in the Nature and Growth of a Cultural Tradition*, 141-58. London: Routledge and Kegan Paul, 1955.

Guedes, P, ed. *Encyclopedia of Architectural Technology*. New York: McGraw-Hill, 1979.

Hakim, B. *Arabic-Islamic Cities: Building and Planning Principles*. New York: Routledge, Chapman and Hall, 1988.

____. "Islamic Architecture and Urbanism." *Encyclopedia of Architecture Design, Engineering and Construction*. Ed. J. Wilkes and R. Packard. New York: John Wiley and Sons, 1989, 3: 81-103.

Hill, D. *Islamic Architecture in North Africa.* London: Faber and Faber, 1976.
Hirschberg, H.Z. *A History of the Jews in North Africa.* 2d ed. Ed. Eliezer Bashan and Robert Attal. Leiden: E.J. Brill, 1981.
Hourani, A. "The Islamic City in the Light of Recent Research," In A. Hourani and S. Stern ed., *The Islamic City*, 1-24. Philadelphia: U of Pennsylvania P, 1970.
Inalçik, H. "Istanbul: An Islamic City." *Journal of Islamic Studies* 1 (1991): 1-23.
Joseph, R. "The Symbolic Significance of the Moroccan City." In J.C. Vatin, ed., *Connaissances Du Maghreb: Sciences Sociales et Colonisation*, 345-54. Paris: CNRS, 1984.
Kenbib, M. "Les relations entre musulmans et juifs au Maroc 1859-1945." *Hespéris-Tamuda* 23 (1985): 83-104.
_____. Les juifs de Tetouan entre la chronique et l'histoire. *Hespéris-Tamuda* 24 (1986): 273-99.
Khoury, P. "Syrian Urban Politics in Transition: The Quarters of Damascus during the French Mandate." *International Journal of Middle East Studies*, no. 16 (1984): 507-40.
King, A. "Writing Colonial Space: A Review Article." *Comparative Studies in Society and History*, no. 37 (1995): 541-54.
Lapidus, I. *Muslim Cities in the Later Middle Ages.* Cambridge: Harvard UP, 1967.
_____. "The Evolution of Muslim Urban Society." *Comparative Studies in Society and History* no. 15 (1973): 21-50.
Le Tourneau, R. *Fés avant le protectorat.* Casablanca: Société de Librairie et d'Edition, 1949.
Marçais, G. "La conception des villes dans l'Islam." *Revue d'Alger*, no. 2 (1945): 517-33.
Pauty, E. "Villes spontanées et villes crées en Islam." *Annales de l'Institut d'Etudes Orientales*, no. 9 (1951): 52-75.
Pike, R. "An Urban Minority: The Moriscos of Seville." *International Journal of Middle East Studies* 2 (1971): 368-77.
Rabinow, P. *French Modern: Norms and Forms of the Social Environment.* Cambridge: MIT Press, 1989.
Rosen, L. "Muslim-Jewish Relations in a Moroccan City." *International Journal of Middle East Studies*, no. 4 (1972): 435-49.
_____. *Bargaining for Reality: The Construction of Social Relations in a Muslim Community.* Chicago: U of Chicago P, 1984.
Schroeter, D. *Merchants of Essaouira: Urban Society and Imperialism in Southwestern Morocco, 1844-1886.* Cambridge: Cambridge UP, 1988.
Serjeant, R.B. *The Islamic City.* Paris: UNESCO, 1980.
Shokeid, M. "Jewish Existence in a Berber Environment." In *Les Relations entre Juifs et Musulmans en Afrique du Nord. Actes du Colloque International de l'Institut d'Histoire des Pays d'Outre-Mer*, 62-71. Paris: CNRS, 1980.

Stillman, N. *The Jews of Arab Lands: A History and Source Book.* Philadelphia: The Jewish Publication Society of America, 1976.

Torrès Balbas, L. "Les villes musulmanes d'Espagne et leur urbanisation." *Annales de l'Institut d'Etudes Orientales* 6 (1942): 5-30.

_____. *Ciudades hispano-musulmanas.* Vols. 1 and 2. Madrid: Ministerio de Asuntos Exteriores, Direccion General de Relaciones Culturales, Instituto Hispano-Arabe de Cultura, 1971.

Wehr, Hans. *Arabic-English Dictionary: The Hans Wehr Dictionary of Modern Written Arabic.* Ed. J. M. Cowan. 3d ed. Ithaca: Spoken Language Services, 1976.

Wirth, E. *La médina de Fès el-Bali: modèle de ville musulmane traditionnelle.* Unpublished manuscript, 1991.

Wright, G. *The Politics of Design in French Colonial Urbanism.* Chicago: U of Chicago P, 1991.

Yerushalmi, Y. "Les derniers marranes: le temps, la peur, la mémoire." In F. Brenner and Y. Yerushalmi, ed., *Marranes,* 19-44. Paris: Editions de la Différence, 1992.

Zafrani, H. *Mille ans de vie juive au Maroc: histoire et culture, religion et magie.* Paris: Maisonneuve & Larose, 1983.

_____. "Mallah." *The Encyclopedia of Islam,* 292-94. Ed., C. Bosworth, E. Donzel, B. Lewis, and C. Pellat. Leiden: E. J. Brill, 1987.

Chapter 7

Memory: *One Hundred Years of Solitude*

Sultana Wahnón

(Translated by Stacy N. Beckwith)

The renowned Columbian author Gabriel García Márquez has written two works in which he has embedded evidence of a history that has been practically forgotten: that of the Jews who were expelled from Spain. In both works he has created a literary testimony to this history. In his most recent novel, *Of Love and Other Demons* (1994), which deals directly with religious intolerance in the Spanish American colonies, memory of the Jewish expulsion from Spain is explicit. In this novel it is embodied in the character Abrenuncio de Sa Pereira Cao, "a Portuguese Jew who had emigrated to the Caribbean because of the persecution in Spain" (García Márquez, *Of Love and Other Demons*, 1994, trans. Grossman 1995, 18).[1] In his fictional role, Abrenuncio serves to recall a set of facts which is supported by ample historical evidence: "the existence of the Jews in America during the colonial period, from 1493 through 1825" (See Liebman 1984, 3).

More so than any other historian, in his *Requiem for the Forgotten* (1984), Seymour B. Liebman has tenaciously pursued the circumstances surrounding the Jews' arrival in America and the conditions in which they were forced to live for centuries until the abolishment of the Catholic inquisitorial trials. Liebman's work provides excellent historiographic support for the realities which Gabriel García Márqez portrays in a literary mode. Literary representation has its limits, and therefore may not always accord exactly with historical fact. It would be absurd, for example, to try to find an exact historical corollary of the fictional Abrenuncio, though there must have been plenty of Jews in Spanish America who closely resembled him.

García Márquez's other testimony to the history of the Jews in America is much more literary, and hence more fictional. It is woven into his master novel, *One Hundred Years of Solitude* (1967). Here, where memory is more complete and complex than in *Of Love and Other Demons*, it is also cryptic and enigmatic to a far greater degree. The hypothesis that García Márquez's narrative of the Buendías is in large part a tale about the Jewish Iberian expulsion and inquisitorial persecution is merely interpretive; it does not constitute a scientifically provable truth. Still, if this interpretation I wish to advance here is correct, we may well be in the presence of a literary work that is one of the most closely tied to Hispanic-Jewish memory of Spain. Accordingly, the following pages will be dedicated to tracing the signs of the forgotten past in *One Hundred Years of Solitude.*[2]

The Scourge of Forgetting

Macondo is founded in the glow of the Enlightenment, that is to say, in the glow of the idea of progress. At the point when José Arcadio and Úrsula grasp the reins of their fate, the Buendía clan is of a lineage that is predisposed to forgetting historical experience. This hardly implies that the founders of Macondo do not have a past, since the novel makes clear that contrary to mythic forebears who are created ex nihilo, the Buendías come from a tradition and carry a history with them.[3] What happens is that, as Vargas Llosa pointed out in his well-known work on García Márquez, the origins of this breed—the Aragonese merchant, the creole tobacco farmer, and so forth, "lose themselves in a damp vagueness, splintering indistinguishably in the distance" (Vargas Llosa 1971, 502). On the other hand, neither José Arcadio nor Úrsula seem to show any interest in sharpening the contours of that past. Quite to the contrary: they have left the prosperous town whose families intermarried for three hundred years, with the express purpose of forgetting that place. They always proceed away from Riohacha, in the opposite direction, so they will not "meet anyone they know" (García Márquez, *One Hundred Years of Solitude*, 1967, trans. Rabassa, 1998, 26).[4] When they fail in their search for the sea, they will found Macondo simply to avoid "taking the road back" (García Márquez, *Cien Años de Soledad* 1991, 91). José Arcadio is not interested in a route which, like the eastern one, "could only lead to the past" (*Solitude*, 11).

All things considered, the founders' decision is neither completely arbitrary nor capricious: the past they wish to leave behind is a painful one. At a minimum it harbors two deaths: that of the ancient past, in which an interbred relative's "pig's tail that was never allowed to be seen by any woman . . . cost him his life" (*Solitude*, 22), and that of Prudencio Aguilar, whose taunts about José Arcadio's impotence cost him his life in "a matter that was put down as a duel of honor" (*Solitude*, 24). The founders cannot expurgate the "twinge of conscience" in their souls (*Solitude*, 24), and they react to their past's freight of horror by embracing Progress as authentic ideologues. This is to say, they flee forward without looking back, to ensure a bright future for their progeny:

> That was how they undertook the crossing of the mountains. Several friends of José Arcadio Buendía, young men like him, excited by the adventure, dismantled their houses and packed up, along with their wives and children, to head toward the land that no one had promised them. Before he left, José Arcadio Buendía buried his spear in the courtyard and, one after another, he cut the throats of his magnificent fighting cocks, trusting that in that way he could give some measure of peace to Prudencio Aguilar. All that Úrsula took along were a trunk with her bridal clothes, a few household utensils, and the small chest with the gold pieces she had inherited from her father. They did not lay out any definite itinerary. They simply tried to go in the opposite direction to the road to Riohacha so they would not leave any trace or meet any people they knew. (*Solitude*, 25-26)

The road that interests the founders is precisely the one that leads to the future. This is embodied in the civilization that extends to the north: "According to José Arcadio Buendía's calculations, the only possibility of contact with civilization lay along the northern route" (*Solitude*, 11). The clan's patriarch is captivated by dreams of progress and related projects that are all tied to the idea of industrial development and to faith in the possibilities of science:

> He thought that in the near future they would be able to manufacture blocks of ice on a large scale from such a common material as water and with them build the new houses of the village. Macondo would no longer be a burning place, where the hinges and door knockers twisted with the heat, but would be changed into a wintry city. (*Solitude*, 27)

The effects of the plague of forgetting, clearly associated with the *modern consciousness* of the founders, are especially visible in the well-known episode when Rebeca arrives at the Buendía's home. The girl, no more than eleven, has made "the difficult trip from Manaure" (probably one of the locales where the Buendías' past unfolded) (*Solitude*, 44). She brings a "canvas sack" in which she has hauled her "parents' bones" and a letter addressed to José Arcadio Buendía indicating that she "[is] a second cousin of Úrsula's and consequently also a relative of José Arcadio Buendía . . . because she was the daughter of that unforgettable friend, Nicanor Uloa and his very worthy wife Rebeca Montiel . . ." (*Solitude*, 45). Despite the profusion of details, the founders are unable to identify the girl: "*Neither* José Arcadio nor Úrsula *remembered* having any relatives with those names, *nor did they know* anyone by the name of the sender of the letter (*Solitude*, 45, emphasis added). The sourge of forgetting has already damaged Macondo's founders, who have lost all notion of personal identity, including their own. And it is for precisely this reason that when the plague of oblivion is officially declared, José Arcadio Buendía communicates to his son Aureliano, "his alarm at having forgotten even the most impressive happenings of his childhood" (*Solitude*, 5).

The Returns to the Past

As if distrustful of the founders' enterprise of modernity, the narrative of *One Hundred Years of Solitude* steadily manifests to the reader signs and discourses that remit to times and spaces already past and presumably overcome. It is not incidental that critics, particularly Michael Palencia-Roth, have underlined the circularity of the novel's temporal structure as one of its defining characteristics. Even when the diegetic narrative allows one to distinguish a beginning and end to the story, and even when Buendías' tale seems to organize between a Genesis and an Apocalypse, the linearity of the main plot does not occlude an inner unfolding of events and characters that distrust the modern concept of Time. In García Márquez's ingenious work it is the characters who, at given moments, can perceive Time in a linear manner. As a result, at certain points the characters can see in history (their own and general), the continuum of progress that is destined to lead humanity to its ultimate realization. If the founder, José Arcadio Buendía, dreams that smouldering Macondo will convert—thanks to advances in science and industry—into a "wintry city" in the future, this is because history appears to be a process that moves from deficit to gain, from confusion to order, and from darkness to light. However, independently of how the progressive patriarch conceives of the historical march of Time, the narrative slowly keeps presenting us with what Palencia-Roth indicates, is a circular history. This might be better described as a cyclical history (circular, but dynamic) which, instead of proceeding linearly from minus to plenty, moves in circles around an axle and thereby creates the sinister phenomenon of *repetition.*

Palencia-Roth ties this cyclical concept of history in *One Hundred Years of Solitude* to the novel's mythic vision of the world: "From the mythic perspective, time is also cyclical, whence García Márquez becomes a mythic writer" (Palencia-Roth 1983, 125). However, the concept of narrative time that one infers from the story could be equally related to the current *crisis of modernity* and its attendant *critique of historical reason.* This is to say that what evinces itself here is not an attempt to escape modernity through a simple return to myth, but instead an attempt to do so by fathoming the aporias in historical-temporal human experience as this has been understood in modernity.

The crisis of modern experience becomes explicit in the novel for the first time when José Arcadio Buendía—who keeps dreaming of a great future for Macondo—has a strange experience in the course of one of his scientific experiments (which are more philosophic than scientific); an experience that will transport him to a state similar to madness. On close examination one sees that the patriarch stops dividing and perceiving Time in linear fashion, and begins to perceive and conceive of it instead as invariable repetition. What the experience unleashes is memory: José Arcadio Buendía spends a night talking with a ghost from the past, that of Prudencio Aguilar, the man he killed many years earlier for the matter that was "put down as a duel of honor" (*Solitude*, 24).[5]

What is undoubtedly—in the strict Freudian sense—a *sinister* experience, a bad trick of memory that makes José Arcadio live something from the past as if it were completely current, initiates the crisis that will lead the patriarch of the Buendía clan to turn into, what Palencia-Roth terms, "a kind of crazed saint, into a metaphor of atemporal and ahistoric space" (1983, 116). A short section of the decisive passage in which José Arcadio Buendía loses the (modern) sense of time reads as follows:

> A few hours later, worn out by the vigil, he went into Aureliano's workshop and asked him: "What day is today?" Aureliano told him that it was Tuesday. "I was thinking the same thing," José Arcadio Buendía said, "but suddenly I realized that it's still Monday, like yesterday. Look at the sky, look at the walls, look at the begonias. Today is Monday too. (*Solitude*, 84)

From repeatedly feeling that it *keeps being* Monday, and from experiencing diverse returns from the past in the form of ghostly visitors,[6] José Arcadio Buendía reaches an overwhelming conclusion that seems to encapsulate the modern concept of historical temporality in the novel: "The Time Machine is broken!" (*Solitude*, 85). Since there is nothing on hand that shows any signs of a real passage of (historical) Time and its effects on reality, the patriarch senses an evaporation of that ancient faith he had kept many years earlier as he waited for the transforming effects that the passage of time and the development of science and technology would have on his own reality:

> He spent six hours examining things, trying to find a difference from their appearance on the previous day in the hope of discovering in them some change that would reveal the passage of time . . . On Friday, before anyone arose, he watched the appearance of nature

> again, until he did not have the slightest doubt that it was Monday. Then he grabbed a bar from the door and with the savage violence of his uncommon strength he smashed to dust the equipment in the alchemy laboratory, the daguerreotype room, the silver workshop, shouting like a man possessed in some high-sounding and fluent but completely incomprehensible language. (*Solitude*, 85)

The violence with which José Arcadio Buendía reacts to his last discovery does not preclude the patriarch from remaining, as the narrator says, "in a state of total innocence" once he is past the initial surprise, and all of the *equipment* that symbolized technical and scientific progress has been destroyed (*Solitude*, 86). He will remain in such a state of innocence until his death. His last appearances in the novel present the anomaly of a psyche that seems to operate backward, in a "regressive," rather than a "progressive" direction. Think, for example, of that moment in the novel when José Arcadio Buendía—suddenly taking on a strange similarity to García Márquez's recent character in *Of Love and Other Demons* Abrenuncio de Sa Pereira Cao—discusses as minimally modern a theme as the existence of God with the priest Nicanor Reyna in a language as minimally current as Latin (See García Márquez 1991, 178-79, or *Solitude*, 90-92). It is obvious that after receiving the visitors from an earlier time, the Buendía patriarch seems to return to the past himself, on a journey in time which, in my opinion, constitutes what Paul Ricoeur has termed, a *metaphor for the indestructible.*

The rest of the characters in the novel, on the other hand, will keep living by logical and chronological Time, though some of them, little by little and by different routes, will reach the same conclusions as the patriarch about the impossibility of measuring historical Time according to an order with linear succession. For example, Úrsula, the matriarch, will explicitly pronounce the law of cyclical Time: ". . . time was not passing, as she had just admitted, but . . . was turning in a circle" (*Solitude*, 361). With Úrsula as well, this new concept of Time is accompanied by sinister returns from the past. Úrsula herself—when she is about to die—receives visits from loved ones who passed on many years earlier, and she talks with them exactly as her husband conversed with Prudencio Aguilar: ". . . they would find her sitting on her bed talking to herself and lost in a labyrinth of dead people" (*Solitude*, 368). Moreover, the matriarch comes into almost sensory contact with beings who, despite having come from the past and therefore constituting mere memories, enter her experience as if they were current:

> "Fire!" she shouted once in terror and for an instant panic spread through the house, but what she was telling about was the burning of a barn that she had witnessed when she was four years old. She finally mixed up the past with the present in such a way that in the two or three waves of lucidity she had before she died, no one knew for certain whether she was speaking about what she felt or what she remebered. (*Solitude*, 367-68)

The experience of Time that the founders of Macondo come to have at an advanced stage in their lives is precisely that which informs the narrative structure of *One Hundred Years of Solitude*. It is as if the narrator had also discovered that Time moves round in circles, on one hand the novel follows an undeniable logical line, that is, when the most recent events in Columbian history are told one after another. On the other hand, the novel continually mixes and superimposes different times and spaces. These remit to different periods in the past, but they also wind up creating the sensation of an eternal present, or put another way, the sensation of an *eternity* that is always present, always current.

This is precisely what explains how the patriarch, José Arcadio Buendía, can suddenly appear and converse with a priest in Latin without the narrator, who blends past and present in so natural a matter, feeling the need to indicate that here he is relating something that belongs to the past and not the present of the Buendía clan: the religious polemics with Catholicism. Like Melquíades's Manuscripts, which critics consider to be a mirror image of the novel, García Márquez's narrative is written in such a way that it does not obey the rules of chronological Time: "Melquíades had not put events in the order of man's conventional time, but had concentrated a century of daily episodes in such a way that they coexisted in one instant" (*Solitude*, 446).

The Motif of the Wandering Jew

Nonetheless, this is not the first time that characters in García Márquez's fictional universe live past events as if they were current, thereby causing their memories to materialize. It is intriguing to turn to a short story the author wrote years before *One Hundred Years of Solitude*, titled, "One Day After Saturday" (1954). This story is said to contain the nucleus of Macondo. In it García Márquez also distrusts the chronological and linear order of narrated history, and superimposes different times in the same space. Of even greater interest is the fact that this occurs precisely in connection with the motif of the Wandering Jew.

In the story from 1954, several characters from the novel make their debut: Rebeca is already the widow of José Arcadio Buendía, and therefore the sister-in-law of Colonel Aureliano Buendía. A centenarian priest, Father Anthony Isabel of the Holy Sacrament of the Altar, plays a role as does Argenida, Rebeca's maidservant, who is also mentioned in the novel. Above all, however, the story contains one other character from *One Hundred Years of Solitude* who has escaped the attention of many critics and who, in both works, is associated with a strange expiration of birds. In "One Day After Saturday" this character/ motif is related to an obsession of the priest who, in a clear medieval mindset, tends to associate plagues with Jews,[7] and the latter with the devil. What is critical in the story and for our purposes here, is that in an action fully situated in the twentieth century, the priest lives the memory of the Wandering Jew (an image bequeathed to him by his Catholic tradition dawns in his mind's eye), as if it were absolutely in the here and now:

> "I swear to you that I saw him. I swear to you that he crossed my path this morning when I was coming back from administering the holy unction to the wife of Jonas the carpenter. I swear to you that his face was blackened with the malediction of the Lord, and that he left a track of burning embers in his wake." (García Márquez, "One Day After Saturday," 1954, trans. Rabassa and Bernstein, 1991, 174-75)[8]

The same occurs in the case of the widow, Rebeca Buendía, who upon learning from her maidservant that the priest claims to have seen the Wandering Jew, reacts in a strange manner, as follows:

> The widow felt her skin crawl. A multitude of confused ideas, among which she could not distinguish her torn screens, the heat, the dead birds, and the plague, passed through her head as she heard those words which she hadn't remembered since the afternoons of her distant girlhood: "The Wandering Jew." And she began to move, enraged, icily, toward where Argenida was watching with her mouth open.
> "It's true," Rebeca said in a voice which rose from the depths of her being. "Now I understand why the birds are dying off."
> Impelled by terror, she covered herself with a black embroidered shawl and, in a flash, crossed the long corridor and the living room stuffed with decorative objects, and the street door, and the two blocks to the church . . . (*Saturday*, 174)

As seen, Rebeca experiences the materialization of a memory from childhood—that of the Wandering Jew—as well. The memory terrorizes her in the present moment, which is exactly what happens to Úrsula in *One Hundred Years of Solitude* when the latter recalls/relives the burning of the barns. By the same token, the most enigmatic moment in "One Day After Saturday" is when the respective memories of the two characters fuse into a single recollection that ends up causing the Wandering Jew *to materialize*. This occurs when the priest, who has just looked toward the central nave of the church and has seen "Rebeca, pathetic, showy, her arms open, and her bitter, cold face turned towards the heavens . . . advancing," resumes his sermon and says, *while Rebeca approaches him*,

> Then he walked toward me . . . He walked toward me and he had emerald eyes and shaggy hair, and the smell of a billy goat. And I raised my hand to reproach him in the name of Our Lord, and I said to him:
> "Halt, Sunday has never been a good day for sacrificing a lamb." (*Saturday*, 175)

The priest's sermon mixes the past with the present and converts what was a memory from the past—the relation between the Jews and the Catholic Church—into something fully current. This occurs when Father Anthony takes on the typical attitude of the inquisitor before Rebeca, the widow whose faith he distrusted.[9] Even though, with her arms open and her face turned toward the heavens, Rebeca herself resembles the image of Christ crucified, the priest accuses her directly of having sacrificed "the lamb." It is impossible to know, as a result—and the story does not clarify—whether these characters are talking about what they are feeling or what they are remembering.

Something similar occurs when the motif of the Wandering Jew, again associated with the death of the birds and with the figure of Rebeca Buendía, reappears in *One Hundred Years of Solitude*.[10] In the few cases where this episode has received some critical attention, it has been treated as one with mythical or legendary significance. This was Mario Vargas Llosa's approach, for example, in his otherwise thought provoking essay on the Columbian author. At a point very late in the novel Úrsula, the Buendía matriarch, dies and burns herself in the intense heat that is causing the birds to die. This is followed by the sudden, unexpected, and "*achronic*" appearance of a character whom the narrator himself identifies as the Wandering Jew, and who, in an absurd, illogical, and apparently inexplicable manner is hunted down by the residents of Macondo. Like medieval inquisitors they hang him from his ankles in an almond tree and immolate him in a pit.

For Vargas Llosa—always loyal to his idea that *One Hundred Years of Solitude* is above all the creation of a "fictitious reality"—this strange irruption of the Wandering Jew in the novel would not amount to anything more than a kind of intertextual play. García Márquez would have been limiting himself to reappropriating a "literary tradition," that of the mythical character of Ashaverus, without intending anything other than the creation of an absolutely imaginary world. In Vargas Llosa's words,

> The real imaginary figure of the Wandering Jew in the streets of Macondo, where he is seen by Father Anthony Isabel and then hunted like a dangerous animal is not a "miracle" but a prodigy of a mythic-legendary type: the Wandering Jew has more to do with a literary tradition than with a religious creed and he constitutes an appropriation by *this* fictitious reality, of an element that belongs to *other* [fictitious realities], in this case to a mythical-legendary reality present in different cultures and nourished by various literatures. (Vargas Llosa 1971, 534)

However, the appearance of the Wandering Jew in Macondo could have much more to do with a conception of history in crisis than with the mere literary appropriation of a myth. As I have already advanced, the Wandering Jew also appears in connection with the character of Rebeca Buendía, who will exit the narrative action of *One Hundred Years of Solitude* to return to it later, accompanied on every occasion by the fantastic historical figure. Indeed, Rebeca disappears from the plot of the novel at the very moment when the narrator chooses to announce for the first and only time, the future passing of the Wandering Jew through Macondo. It is immediately after the description of the mysterious death of her husband, José Arcadio Buendía (eldest son of the founders), and the fabulous tour made by the "thread of [his] blood" (*Solitude*, 144-45), that the narrator informs us that Rebeca will close herself off in her house for many years and will only venture out to the street on one occasion—precisely when the Wandering Jew will pass through the town.

> She went out into the street on one occasion, when she was very old, with shoes the color of silver and a hat made of tiny flowers during the time that the Wandering Jew passed through the town and brought on a heat wave that was so intense that birds broke through the window screens to come to die in the bedrooms. (*Solitude*, 146)

This passage contains the novel's *only* mention of the Wandering Jew before he appears in the present, many years later, in Macondo. In this way the strange figure of the Wandering Jew appears on two occasions over the course of the narrative: he is associated with the mystery of José Arcadio Buendía's death in the first part, and with the mystery of the death of the birds in the second. In his excellent annotated edition of the novel, Jacques Joset has indicated that the death of José Arcadio Buendía is a kind of "detective story's enigma" that is never resolved in the novel (See García Márquez 1967, 235, n. 26). What caused the birds to die will never be elucidated either, even though in the episode on which we are focused, Father Anthony Isabel will attribute the mass expiration to precisely the bad influence of the Wandering Jew, whose flagrant breath, in the priest's words, would have produced the intense heat.

When Úrsula dies on the same symbolic date of Holy Thursday, the phenomenon García Márquez described in "One Day After Saturday" reproduces itself in *One Hundred Years of Solitude*, namely: the intense heat that causes the strange death of the birds. In the novel as in the story, this type of catastrophe (natural or social) on various occasions is called a "plague." In the novel the priest, Anthony Isabel, makes assurances in the pulpit on the Sunday of Resurrection that the death of the birds has been brought on by the bad influence of the Wandering Jew, whom he describes—blending his memories with the present—"as a cross between a billy goat and a female heretic, an infernal beast whose breath scorched the air and whose look brought on the birth of monsters in newlywed women" (*Solitude*, 369).

In contrast to what transpires in the short story, however, the matter is not left here in the novel. Instead, the town of Macondo proceeds to chase down the monster the priest has described. One woman finds the *tracks* of a "biped with cloven hoof" (*Solitude*, 370), which compels the people of Macondo to take the confabulation of the priest for the truth: ". . . those who went to look at [the tracks] had no doubt about the existence of a fearsome creature similar to the one described by the parish priest and got together to set traps in their courtyards" (*Solitude*, 370). When the Macondians hang the beast they capture by its ankles and burn it in a pit they too will be causing a memory to *materialize*, reliving an episode from the past and giving it full presence in the current moment.

In the course of the capture, the Wandering Jew is described anew in the novel, though now by the narrator instead of the priest. This new description of the monster has correctly reminded many critics of what the anonymous author of *Amadis of Gaul*—one of García Márquez's preferred novels (See Mendoza 1983, 49)—did in his day with the figure of Endriago. The latter was the infernal beast whom the Knight of the Green Sword fought and killed in one of the most famous chapters of the chivalric novel. The physical similarites between Endriago and García Márquez's Wandering Jew are highly noticeable, as Olga Carreras González underscores (1974, 65). These resemblances are not coincidental, nor are they a mere literary whim, (as Carreras González holds, for example). In the final analysis, the literary character of Endriago has something in common with the Wandering Jew from literary tradition: the fact that in medieval thinking he appears as the very incarnation of evil and the devil.

As it happens, the criticism that has underlined the similarities between the two monsters has not considered their differences. In *Amadis of Gaul* the reader can harbor no doubt as to the infernal character which the author attributes to this creature of his imagination, given that the very same devil emerges from Endriago's mouth when the latter finally expires at the hands of the heroic knight. By contrast, in *One Hundred Years of Solitude*, when all is said and done, the Wandering Jew whom the Macondians kill in the manner of late-fifteenth-century inquisitors (hanging him by his ankles over a fiery pit), is not as evidently guilty as was Endriago. This is so even in the eyes of the novel's narrator, who makes known to the reader his doubts on the subject.

First of all, in Endriago's case there is no doubt that he was really a *beast*, whereas with the murdered Wandering Jew this is not at all clear: ". . . they could not determine whether its bastard nature was that of an animal being thrown into a river or a human being to be buried" (*Solitude*, 370). Secondly, the novel's narrator distances himself from the literary model of Endriago, and thus from the medieval values of Father Anthony Isabel, the priest. In *One Hundred Years of Solitude* it is not at all certain that the Wandering Jew is a devil. Instead, in the narrator's words, he has much more in common with an *angel*: ". . . unlike the priest's description, its human parts were more like those of a sickly angel than a man . . ." (*Solitude*, 370). Finally, and by the same token (the devil does not emerge from his mouth), the death of the Wandering Jew does not serve—as it did in Endriago's case—to put an end to the evil said to originate in him, just as it does not resolve the mystery of the birds: "It was never established whether [the murder of the Wandering Jew] had really caused the death of the birds, but the newly married women did not bear the predicted monsters, nor did the intensity of the heat decrease" (*Solitude*, 370).

With all of this what is important is to observe that in the cyclical structure of *One Hundred Years of Solitude*, the death of the Wandering Jew who passes through Macondo can be read as a sinister return of the past. And is this not exactly how one can read the permanent reactualization of this motif in global political history? In making present an episode from the forgotten past, García Márquez seems to suggest that it is not summoned from a past that has been overcome, but rather from one that can become current time and again, in the very same way in which the memories and ghosts have become present and have been turning themselves over in Úrsula's memory since the earliest days of her childhood.

Melquíades's Keys

All of this becomes even clearer if we move to another, much more important character in the narrative. The Wandering Jew turns out to be no more than a mirror reflection of the extravagant Melquíades, and he is not present throughout the novel as is the latter (literally or symbolically, through his Manuscripts). Even though García Márquez chose to present him as a gypsy, there are many features in Melquíades's personality and in his fabulous history that enable an association with the figure of the Wandering Jew. Melquíades appears to be ageless: he is, like the Wandering Jew who passes through town when Úrsula dies, a transhistoric character, and therefore "achronic." He does not belong to a determined time or space, but seems to traverse human history in its entirety. As Melquíades himself tells José Arcadio Buendía (senior), on that suffocating noon when he decides to reveal "his secrets" to him,

> . . . death followed him everywhere, sniffing at the cuffs of his pants, but never deciding to give him the final clutch of its claws. He had survived pellagra in Persia, scurvy in the Malayan archipelago, leprosy in Alexandria, beriberi in Japan, bubonic plague in Madagascar, an earthquake in Sicily, and a disastrous shipwreck in the Strait of Magellan. (*Solitude*, 6)

Clearly Melquíades embodies a people persecuted throughout history; one that has been associated with plagues and catastrophes and which nonetheless has managed to survive as a people, outliving others. In Melquíades then, more so than in any other character in the novel, different moments of the historic past of the clan converge and superimpose themselves on one another. Even when he appears as a contemporary of the founders and accompanies them (in the nineteenth century) when they begin a new life in the light of progress and science, Melquíades is, as was Prudencio Aguilar, a ghost of the past. He is a character who returns from the dead and is therefore a memory, but he is also more than this. Melquíades embodies history itself: if he comes back from the dead it is precisely to return memories to the forgetful characters of Macondo who have lost these in succumbing to the plague of oblivion. Melquíades is the only one who can accomplish this since, ". . . it was evident that he came from the world where men could still sleep and remember" (*Solitude*, 53). The decisive passage in which Melquíades reinvests his old friends with memory reads as follows:

> He opened the suitcase crammed with indecipherable objects and from among them he took out a little case with many flasks. He gave José Arcadio Buendía a drink of a gentle color and the light went on in his memory. His eyes became moist from weeping even before he noticed himself in an absurd living room where objects were labeled and before he was ashamed of the solemn nonsense written on the walls, and even before he recognized the newcomer with a dazzling glow of joy. It was Melquíades. (*Solitude*, 53-54)

It is not by chance, moreover, that Melquíades, who is presented in the fabulous writing of *One Hundred Years of Solitude* as a chatty wizard and a nomadic gypsy, has in the other—secret—writing all the features that enable his association to an ancient cast of wisemen and scientists. (The suitcase contains "many flasks," for example). Indeed, Melquíades possesses knowledge that pertains not to a wizard but to a real scientist from early periods in history. Within his ken are the powers of the Imam, which he himself refers to as "the eighth wonder of the learned alchemists of Macedonia" (*Solitude*, 1), a telescope and a magnifying glass, which he himself "exhibit[s] as the latest discovery of the Jews of Amsterdam" (*Solitude*, 2), the Portuguese maps and navigation instruments (an astrolabe, a compass, and a sextant) that were so useful in Columbus' day . . . and above all, alchemy . . . In the same passage in which Melquíades reveals his secrets to the Buendía patriarch, he gives José Arcadio the famous alchemy laboratory. This is also the passage in which the narrator first ties the figure of Melquíades to the historic persona of Nostradamus and to his secret "keys."

Nostradamus's real name was Michel de Notre-Dame. Today we know only his most esoteric side that is mainly related to his famous *Prophecies*, and this we know hardly at all. Nostradamus was a great physician-alchemist of the sixteenth century. He had the distinction, moreover, of having descended from Jews expelled from Spain in 1492, and of belonging to a family that, once established in France, converted to Christianity.[11]

As someone conscious of his origins, Nostradamus was unswerving in his dedication to being a physician. He carried on in his profession in times that were difficult for the exercise of science, spending his life in search of a cure for the plague while his prodigious ability to heal stirred the suspicions of the inquisitors. Nostradamus also had an extraordinary and inexplicable capacity for premonitions and was said to be capable of reviving the dead. (See Balducci 1991, and Corvaja 1994). For my part, I am convinced that when García Márquez associates the figure of Melquíades with that of Nostradamus, in the famous phrase in which he refers to the gypsy as "that prodigious creature said to possess the keys of Nostradamus" (*Solitude*, 6), the author is trying to orient the reader so that he/she discovers the *secret keys* of Melquíades in his own encoded writing.

As a result, it is not at all surprising that Melquíades should dedicate the years in which he resides among the Buendías—until he definitively dies—to writing his renowned Manuscripts. It is in these, at the end of the novel, that the last of the clan, Aureliano Babilonia, will be able to read aloud "the history of the family" (*Solitude*, 446). The Manuscripts, conceived as a mirror reflection of the novel (in a characteristic *mise en abîme*), are described as enigmatic literature; as "impenetrable writing" (*Solitude*, 78). In spite of this they will be *decoded* at the end of the narrative by Aureliano Babilonia. A long and "patient manipulation" of ". . . the material that had become attenuated with months of manipulation" (*Solitude*, 42) is necessary for the Manuscripts to reveal their secrets to their interpreter. Prior to him, Aureliano's great uncle José Arcadio the Second enclosed himself in Melquíades's room to dedicate himself exclusively to "perus[ing] the manuscripts" (*Solitude*, 336). Herein lies the tenacity that will permit the only survivor of the slaughter on the farm "to classify the cryptic letters of the parchments" and to further discover that the letters "corresponded to an alphabet of forty-seven to fifty-three characters, which when separated looked like scratching and scribbling . . ." (*Solitude*, 375-76).

It will be José Arcadio the Second, himself, who "initiates" Aureliano Babilonia in the "study of the parchments" (*Solitude*, 375). And this José Arcadio will also transmit to the boy the charge to remember that will inspire the final and definitive reading of the manuscripts: "Always remember that they were more than three thousand and that they were being thrown into the sea" (*Solitude*, 380). Obeying the mandate, Aureliano will not leave Melquíades's room for a long time. He will memorize all the knowledge that the legendary alchemist bequeathed to the family: "the notes on the science of demonology; the keys to the philosopher's stone, Nostradamus' *Centuries*, and his research concerning the plague" (*Solitude*, 383). On many occasions Aureliano will believe he is conversing with Melquíades himself, whose memory seems to be materializing in everything he reads:

> Santa Sofia de la Piedad thought that Aureliano was talking to himself. Actually, he was talking to Melquíades. One burning noon, a short time after the death of the twins, against the light of the window he saw the gloomy old man with his crow's-wing hat like the materialization of a memory that had been in his head since long before he was born. (*Solitude*, 384)

For by then the young interpreter has already discovered that the parchments are written in Sanskrit, and that Melquíades himself will reveal to him that the parchments will be deciphered when they are a century old:

> Melquíades revealed to him that his [Melquíades's] opportunities to return to the room were limited. But he would go in peace to the meadows of his ultimate death because Aureliano would have time to learn Sanskrit during the years remaining until the parchments became one hundred years old, when they could be deciphered. (*Solitude*, 384)

From another angle, an evident similarity exists between Nostradamus's *Prophecies*, written in an intricate hotchpotch of idioms, and on quartos inscribed from right to left that oblige the reader to use a mirror in order to interpret them; and Melquíades's Manuscripts. These are also written in an extraordinary admixture of languages and codes[12] that Aureliano Babilonia deciphers "as if he were looking into a speaking mirror" (*Solitude*, 447).

If the hypothesis I have put forward here is correct, and Melquíades/Nostradamus is a symbol of the learned Jew or *converso* persecuted by the Inquisition, then it is obvious that his character relates significantly to that of the Wandering Jew who passes through the town when Úrsula dies, and is unable to escape either his fate or his death in the fiery pit. In this episode the structural relation between Melquíades and the Wandering Jew is revealed in various clues that the author provides over the course of the novel. The first and foremost of these is given in the relation that Úrsula, the matriarch, establishes between the scientist and the devil in the passage discussed earlier, wherein Melquíades gives the Buendías the gift of the alchemy laboratory. Indeed, when Melquíades "carelessly" breaks a "flask of bichloride of mercury," Úrsula thinks she recognizes the "smell of the devil" (*Solitude*, 7). Throughout the novel only one figure (apparently very secondary compared with the centrality of Melquíades), is explicitly associated with the devil, and this is the Wandering Jew. It follows that he and Melquíades are both related and share a feature that is very significant in the semantic structure of the work.

The second clue along these lines lies in the way Melquíades is described, and how the structural setup of the novel ensures that his description also recalls that of the Wandering Jew.The extended wings on Melquíades's large, black hat irremediably bring to mind the potent wings on the Wandering Jew, that had to be hacked off with a farmer's ax. Moreover, just like what is ultimately a hybrid monster, despite his fabulous and extravagant gypsy dimension, Melquíades, too has some human aspects that make him resemble angels more than devils. Here is the full portrait of the "achronic," learned heretic:

> That prodigious creature, said to possess the keys of Nostradamus, was a gloomy man, enveloped in a sad aura, with an Asiatic look that seemed to know what there was on the other side of things. He wore a large black hat that looked like a raven with widespread wings, and a velvet vest across which the patina of the centuries skated. But in spite of his immense wisdom and his mysterious breadth, he had a human burden, an earthly condition that kept him involved in the small problems of daily life. (*Solitude*, 6)

In García Márquez's most recent novel, *Of Love and Other Demons* (1994), where the theme of the Jews persecuted by the Inquisition is made explicit, the mythic figure of the Wandering Jew is concretized in the character of Abrenuncio de Sa Pereira Cao. Just like Nostradamus, Abrenuncio would be descended from Jews; a physician and an alchemist endowed with an exceptional bent for healing and premonitions. He would be someone presumed to be capable of reviving even the dead, and an individual under the strict watch of the Inquisition. Abrenuncio's physcial and moral profile immediately remnd us of Melquíades's own portrait not only because—like him, Abrenuncio wears a "broad-brimmed hat for the sun" (*Of Love*, 18), but also because for most of his life he has been a fugitive too, searching for medical remedies for sourges and plagues while having to evade suspicions of being their cause. In Abrenuncio's case, as in that of Melquíades, the eternal persecution leads him to take refuge in the New World:

> On Tuesdays he offered his services at the Amor de Dios Hospital, treating the lepers who suffered from other diseases. He had been an outstanding student of the physician Juan Méndez Nieto, another Portuguese Jew who had emigrated to the Caribbean because of the persecution in Spain, and had inherited his evil reputation for necromancy and a loose tongue, but no one cast doubt on his learning. (*Of Love*, 18)

The similarities to Melquíades's persecution stand out. All the extravagances of the gypsy in *One Hundred Years of Solitude* seem less so, and more understandable if we understand the symbolic role this character plays in a novel on the history of Latin America. This is to say, if we understand that his role is to represent those persecuted by the Inquisition in a country and a continent whose history has been marked by the existence of the Sacred Office of the Inquisition and consequently by "an obscurantist model of racial discrimination and pupated violence," to which García

Márquez referred not long ago in his article "A Country in Reach of the Children" (1994a).

The Buendías' Keys

In their configuration as charcters who lie somewhere between the historical and the symbolic, the Wandering Jew and Melquíades, then, provide allusions to the past that has been forgotten in America: they serve as actualizers of memory. However, once again they are not the only ones in *One Hundred Years of Solitude* who have this function. Still other, more or less indirect or metaphoric, allusions to this same chapter of history can be found interspersed throughout the novel, and in relation to its protagonists, the Buendías. In my reading of the novel that I have elaborated since 1992, I consider the Buendías themselves, from their origins, and from the moment they appear in Spanish-American history in the sixteenth century, to be bearers of that ethnic, religious, and cultural diversity that will come to constitute Latin American identity. The Buendías are far from genuine representatives of a cleanness and purity of blood which later mixes, nonetheless, with the diverse populations of America (according to the traditional reading of the novel). Instead, they are better seen as representatives of Otherness; as carriers of a differentiated cultural identity that will wind up integrating and losing itself in Latin America's hybridization.

The signs of this Otherness are scattered throughout the novel, like the hints the author keeps dropping. The end result is that we can solve the detective/Oedipal enigma around which the narrative turns: the identity of the Buendías. Above all, these tracks and clues are concentrated in the magnifacent second chapter of the novel, in which the first signs of the clan's strangeness present themselves and suggest the family's identification with the same tribe of fugitives and persecuted people to which Melquíades and the Wandering Jew belong.

Indeed, all the references to the Buendías' past are found in the second chapter of *One Hundred Years of Solitude*. Although most criticism has overlooked them, taking them once more as a mere whim of the author's fantasy, the data that allow us to recognize José Arcadio Buendía and Úrsula as wandering Jews are all laid out here in an organized manner. The second chapter opens by stating that Úrsula's great-grandmother had "something strange . . . [in] her way of walking," owing to "burns [that] changed her into a useless wife for the rest of her days." This ancestor *renounced* "all kinds of social activity," including "walk[ing] in public." She lived "obsessed with the notion that her body gave off a singed odor," and she had nightmares in which "the English and their ferocious attack dogs . . . submit[ed] her to shameful tortures with . . . red hot irons" (*Solitude*, 21-22).

These terrors and obsessions date to the sixteenth century, and have their origin in the "pirate," Francis Drake's attack on Riohacha, whereby the great-grandmother "became so frightened" that "she lost control of her nerves and sat down on a lighted stove" (*Solitude*, 21). So odd a woman is, quite simply, the wife of an "Aragonese merchant" (*Solitude*, 21), who, one can infer, had recently arrived in America. In seeking a way to "alleviate [his wife's] terror," he liquidated his business and took his family to live in a "settlement of peaceful Indians" (*Solitude*, 21).[13]

At a minimum, then, in the origin of the Buendías one finds the features that make them resemble the Jewish people who emerged from the Expulsion from Spain in 1492. First, there is the fear of burnings and tortures. Second, one has the constant displacement: first from Aragon to America, and then within the continent, from one locale to another, just as Liebman relates in his *Requiem for the Forgotten*. Here the historian describes how the Jewish *conversos* who opted to seek refuge in the New World were obliged to stay on the move. Therefore, there is nothing surprising in the fact that in finding umbrage in the "*hidden* settlement" (*Solitude*, 21, emphasis added), the Aragonese husband should meet someone who had come there for the same purpose long ago: "a native-born tobacco planter, Don José Arcadio Buendía" (*Solitude*, 22).

Other facts or clues seem to confirm the hypothesis that the origin of the Buendías is possibly Crypto-Jewish. One example is the tradition of intermarriage, of which full account is given in the novel's second chapter (*Solitude*, 22-23). For three hundred years the two families who took refuge in the hidden and tranquil settlement, the Iguaráns and the Buendías, intermarried exclusively, becoming "two races that had interbred" by the time the action in *One Hundred Years of Solitude* begins (*Solitude*, 22). This custom is followed precisely up to this point, because Úrsula and José Arcadio still wed for the same reason their ancestors adhered to since they arrived in the settlement: ". . . because actually they were joined till death by a bond that was more solid than love: a common prick of conscience. They were cousins" (*Solitude*, 22).

Nonetheless, something has changed recently (when the novel opens we are in the nineteenth century), since the family tries to dissuade the betrothed from actually marrying, for fear that they will ". . . suffer the horrible shame of breeding iguanas." There exists a "horrible precedent" in the family's history: one relative had been born with "a pig's tail" that "was never allowed to be seen by any woman" and that "cost him his life when a butcher friend did him the favor of chopping it off with his cleaver" (*Solitude*, 22). (The same will happen years later to the wings of the Wandering Jew). José Arcadio Buendía and Úrsula disobey their family and run the risk of engendering children with pigs' tails.[14]

With the casual attitude of his nineteen years, José Arcadio reassures his wife that he does not care ". . . if [he] has *piglets* . . ." (read: *marranos*) (*Solitude*, 23). Úrsula, however, lives in *terror* of the "sinister predictions about her offspring" (*Solitude*, 23) until, following the death of Prudencio Aguilar—who indulges in taunting the Buendías' fertility—her husband decides to put an end to that "twinge in their conscience" (*Solitude*, 24) that has bound them to their ancestors' home. They embark on the journey that will lead them to found Macondo, where they will break with their predecessors' secular habit by endeavoring, above all else, to make certain that their children do not marry one another.

Nevertheless, the rational decision taken by Macondo's founders will not save their descendants. There are other key episodes that substantiate the repetitive and cyclical structure of the novel, namely the death of Colonel Aureliano Buendía's seventeen sons, who are ". . . hunted down like rabbits by invisible criminals at the center of their crosses of ash" (*Solitude*, 257), and above all the massacre of the workers in the station (who are driven in a death train to the sea).

It is in the light shone by the Wandering Jew, and his fleeting, perilous existence in America, that the novel is cyclically structured, just as the two episodes above pull in all the semantic density in the novel. This is especially so because at the end of the novel the same risk of oblivion also threatens the protagonists of these episodes, as one can deduce from the efforts of the last of the Buendías, Aureliano Babilonia, to save the memory of the new victims. Like the memory of the victims of the Catholic Inquisition, this is a memory that is also threatened by the manipulated versions of official history and by the indifference of the survivors.

> Even the proprietress, who normally did not take part in the conversations, argued with a madam's wrathful passion that Colonel Aureliano Buendía, of whom she had indeed heard speak at some time, was a figure invented by the government as a pretext for killing Liberals. Gabriel, on the other hand, did not doubt the reality of Colonel Aureliano Buendía because he had been a companion in arms and inseparable friend of his great-great-grandfather Colonel Gerineldo Márquez. These fickle tricks of memory were even more critical when the killing of the workers was brought up. Every time that Aureliano mentioned the matter, not only the proprietress, but some people older than she would repudiate the myth of the workers hemmed in at the station and the train with 200 cars loaded with dead people . . . (*Solitude*, 419)

Notes

1. **Translator's note**: In this essay citations from this novel are drawn from Gabriel García Márquez, *Of Love and Other Demons*, translated by Edith Grossman (New York, Alfred A. Knopf, 1995). Hereafter their documentation is abbreviated as (*Of Love*, pp.).

2. I have advanced this hypothesis on the Jewish origins of the Buendías in previous publications, including, "Un réquiem por los judíos

olvidados de América," *Raíces. Revista judía de cultura*, no. 15 (1993): 37-41, and "Las claves judías de *Cien años de soledad*," *Lenguaje y Literatura* (Barcelona: Octaedro, 1995), 103-23. Although some details from these two articles may be repeated here, in furthering my thesis, this essay presents a reflection on the temporal structure of the novel and its relation to the crisis of historical reason.

3. As we are told at the start of the novel's second chapter, this history would have commenced in sixteenth-century Spain (more concretely in Aragon), and would then have continued in colonial America, in scenes that were typically Columbian, such as those in Riohacha.

4. **Translator's note**: In this essay citations from this novel are drawn from Gabriel García Márquez, *One Hundred Years of Solitude*, translated by Gregory Rabassa (New York: Harper Collins, 1998). Hereafter their documentation is abbreviated as (*Solitude*, pp.). In addition, in this translation of the novel the Spanish spelling of the name Rebeca is retained. This is not the case in Gregory Rabassa and J.S. Bernstein's translation of "One Day After Saturday" (García Márquez 1954, in *Gabriel García Márquez: Collected Stories*, New York, Harper Collins, 1991, 154-76). This essay will consistently use Rebeca, as the name is spelled in the translation of the novel.

5. "The fever of insomnia fatigued him so much that one dawn he could not recognize the old man with white hair and uncertain gestures who came into his bedroom. It was Prudencio Aguilar. When he finally identified him, startled that the dead also aged, José Arcadio Buendía found himself shaken by nostalgia . . . José Arcadio Buendía conversed with Prudencio Aguilar until dawn" (*Solitude*, 84).

6. "That night Pietro Crespi found him on the porch, weeping for Prudencio Aguilar, for Melquíades, for Rebeca's parents, for his mother and father, for all of those he could remember and who were now alone in death" (*Solitude*, 85).

7. During the Middle Ages, and especially from the fourteenth century on, following the great Black Death in 1347, the Christian West frequently blamed the Jews for plagues and other natural calamities that decimated populations. This occasioned the first great pogroms, "killings" of the Jews in medieval Europe (See Poliakov 1986, 107-13).

8. **Translator's note**: In this essay citations from this short story are drawn from Gabriel García Márquez, "One Day After Saturday" in *Gabriel García Márquez: Collected Stories*, translated by Gregory Rabassa and J.S. Bernstein (New York: Harper Collins, 1991). Hereafter their documentation is abbreviated as (*Saturday*, pp.)

9. ". . . the truth was that Father Anthony Isabel of the Holy Sacrament of the Altar did not feel at ease in this house, whose only inhabitant had never shown any signs of piety and who confessed only once a year but always replied with evasive answers when he tried to pin her down about the puzzling death of her husband" (*Saturday*, 161).

10. The coinciding of these characters and motifs in García Márquez's story from 1954 and in his great novel of 1967 has led the Spanish scholar

José María Pozuelo Yvancos to support my thesis on the central role of the Wandering Jew in the constitution of *One Hundred Years of Solitude* (See Pozuelo Yvancos, 1995).

11. "The first ancestor of Michel de Notre-Dame . . . is Amauton de Velorgues, a grains merchant of Jewish origin. An influential person from the [Hebrew] tribe of Issachar, Amauton de Velorgues married a handsome Jewish woman in 1449, called Venguenosse, whom he had met when he was on business in Geneva" (Balducci, 1991, 9). As this specialist on Nostradamus writes, the latter always lived the double life of the *converso*: "A Jew in the depths of his convictions—and a Christian of pacifying religion" (Balducci 1991, 411).

12. "He had written it in Sanskrit, which was his mother tongue, and he had encoded the even lines in the private cipher of Emperor Augustus and the odd ones in a Lacedemonian military code" (*Solitude*, 446).

13. Note that Úrsula's great-grandmother's fear of the burns, and the strange habits that derive from this, such as not walking in public and renouncing a social life, originate when Francis Drake attacks Riohacha. This is to say, the female ancestor's fear commences on the same dates, toward the end of the sixteenth century, when the Sacred Office, the first tribunals of the Inquisition, are being established in America. This occurs in Lima in 1590, and in Mexico and Cartagena de las Indias in 1610. Furthermore, the first significant auto-da-fé also occurred in new Spanish America at the end of the sixteenth century, in 1596: "The Auto of 1596 signaled the moment of the most intense persecution of the Jews at the end of the sixteenth century. All the public auto-da-fé's had the purpose of sewing fear in those attended, and this was the largest and grandest Auto held in the New World up to that time" (Liebman, 1984, 43).

14. The Jews have been represented in various ways in anti-semitic tradition: from the image of the Jew with horns to that of the Jew with a tail and a kid or mature goat's beard, to the least known images of Jews with pigs' ears. There is nothing singular about the way in which these last two images fuse into one representation, to create the picture of the Jew with a *pig's tail*, which Úrsula invokes when she expresses an ancient fear that her children might be identified with the Jewish devil.

Works Cited

Balducci, Richard. *La fabulosa vida de Nostradaums*. Madrid: Ediciones del Prado, 1991.

Corvaja, Mirella. *Las profecías de Nostradamus*. Barcelona: Editorial de Vecchi, 1994.

Carreras González, Olga. *El mundo de Macondo en la obra de Gabriel García Márquez*. Barcelona: Ediciones Universal, 1974.

García Márquez, Gabriel. "Un día después del sábado" (1954). In Márquez, *Todos los cuentos*. Bogotá: La Oveja Negra, 1986.

_____. *Cien años de soledad.* (1967). Ed. Jacques Joset. Madrid: Cátedra, 1991.

_____. *Del amor y otros demonios*. Barcelona: Mondadori, 1994.

_____. "One Day After Saturday." In *Gabriel García Márquez: Collected Stories*, 154-76. Trans. Gregory Rabassa and J.S. Bernstein. New York: Harper Collins, 1991.

_____. "Un país al alcance de los niños." *El Espectador* (Santa Fe de Bogotá) July 23, 1994.

_____. *Of Love and Other Demons*. Trans. Edith Grossman. New York: Alfred A. Knopf, 1995.

_____. *One Hundred Years of Solitude*. Trans. Gregory Rabassa. New York: Harper Collins, 1998.

Liebman, Seymour B. *Réquiem por los olvidados. Los judíos españoles en América 1493-1825*. Madrid: Altalena, 1984.

Mendoza, Plinio Apuleyo. *Gabriel García Márquez. Conversaciones con Plinio Apuleyo Mendoza. El olor de la guayaba.* (1982) Bogotá: La Oveja Negra, 1983.

Palencia-Roth, Michael. *Gabriel García Márquez. La línea, el círculo y las metamorfosis del mito*. Madrid: Gredos, 1983.

Poliakov, León. *Historia del antisemitismo. De Cristo a los judíos de las Cortes*. Barcelona: Muchnik, 1955; reprint 1986.

Pozuelo Yvancos, José María. "García Márquez y el estilo del cuento tradicional." In Peter Frölicher and Georges Güntert, eds., *Teoría e interpretación del cuento: estudios*, 488-509. Berna: Peter Lang, 1995.

Vargas Llosa, Mario. *García Márquez. Historia de un deicidio*. Barcelona: Barral Editores, 1971.

◆ Chapter 8

Musical 'Membrances of Medieval Muslim Spain[1]

Dwight F. Reynolds

Scattered throughout the modern Arab world are a number of regional musical traditions commonly referred to as "Andalusian" and generally thought to have developed, through different historical paths, from the vibrant musical culture of al-Andalus, medieval Islamic Spain. Their relationship to the medieval music of the Iberian Peninsula and to each other is problematic, however, for not only are they quite distinct from one another in musical terms, but they also fulfill vastly different social roles. In some areas Andalusian music is performed by small ensembles in strictly traditional attire as formal entertainment at public festivities and social gatherings; in other regions Andalusian music functions primarily as dance music for weddings; in some regions it is performed by Sufi dervishes in religious rituals as a means of achieving trance states; in neighboring regions it is performed by orchestras wearing tuxedo and black tie in expensive concert halls; and elsewhere it is featured in costumed stage reenactments of medieval Iberian scenes reminiscent of low-grade Hollywood movies. Yet all of these are experienced, to varying degrees, as Andalusian, a term that invokes many different, often conflicting, social values. This essay is an exploration of the historical circumstances that have led to the formation of these related but divergent regional traditions, the ways in which they are perceived to be Andalusian by their audiences and practitioners, and the variety of social meanings they have come to embody as musical 'membrances of medieval Muslim Spain.

General History

Al-Andalus bequeathed to the world a rich heritage in poetry, literature, architecture, philosophy, science, theology, and landscape design, as well as music. These achievements, however, have remained beyond the immediate experience of most Arabs. The intellectual legacy of al-Andalus was studied only among a highly educated elite and images of even those architectural sites most familiar to us today, such as the Alhambra palace, were completely unknown in the Arab Middle East until the advent of the modern mass media. Al-Andalus survived in the popular imagination primarily as a site of nostalgia, its beauties and wonders celebrated by authors who had never laid eyes on them. For centuries Arab poets composed elegies for the fallen cities of al-Andalus by deploying a mixture of motifs drawn from the repertory of classical Arabic lamentations for fallen heroes, descriptions of the beloved, and portrayals of lush gardens and abandoned ruins. For Arabs in eastern Mediterranean lands, al-Andalus was already being "remembered" before it was entirely lost.

Until the twentieth century, most Arabs experienced Andalusian culture directly through a single medium: song. The song tradition of Islamic Spain, based on the Andalusian poetic forms of the *muwashshaḥ* and *zajal*, was distinct from those of other regions, yet was clearly appreciated by audiences almost everywhere, for it was quickly adopted and imitated by poets, composers, and singers throughout the Arab Middle East. More than any other cultural form, Andalusian music has existed for Arabs as a tangible, living legacy of medieval Islamic Spain.

The *muwashshaḥ* and *zajal* were strophic vocal genres that emerged uniquely in Muslim Spain. Although sometimes portrayed as a tradition of the Muslim elite, their popularity extended across sectarian and social boundaries. Jewish musicians performed in Muslim courts and Jewish poets composed Hebrew and Arabic *muwashshaḥāt.* The tradition was probably also popular among Arabized Christians, Berbers, and the less elite Arab social classes, but historical evidence for this is sparse. In contrast to the classical mono-rhymed ode that had dominated Arabic poetry in previous centuries, the primary structural element of both the *muwashshaḥ* and *zajal* is that the text moves back and forth between two distinct elements: one maintains the same rhyme throughout the poem (the common rhyme *a*) while the other presents a new rhyme in each stanza (the independent rhymes *b*, *c*, etc.). This alternating movement is shown in the following structural diagram:

Rhyme Pattern:	Arabic Term for Each Stanza:
---------------------------------*a*	*maṭla'*
---------------------------------*a*	
---------------*b*	
---------------*b*	*ghuṣn/bayt/dawr*
---------------*b*	
---------------------------------*a*	*simṭ/qufl/khāna*
[---------------------------------*a*]	
---------------------*c*	
---------------------*c*	*ghuṣn/bayt/dawr*
---------------------*c*	
---------------------------------*a*	*simṭ/qufl/khāna*
[---------------------------------*a*]	

This pattern is repeated until a final mono-rhymed verse which is termed differently.

---------------------------------*a*	*kharja/qafla*
[---------------------------------*a*]	

Medieval Arabic terminology for the parts of strophic poems differed from writer to writer. The opening common-rhyme section is usually called the *maṭla'* and the final common-rhyme section the *kharja* (in later centuries, *qafla*).[2] The commonly cited differences between the two genres are: (1) the *muwashshaḥ* is normally composed in classical Arabic and the *zajal* in colloquial dialect; (2) the *zajal* requires an opening *maṭla'* whereas this is optional in the *muwashshaḥ*; and (3) in the *muwashshaḥ*, the common-rhyme section repeats the full rhyme scheme of the *maṭla'* while the *zajal* repeats only one verse of the common rhyme (i.e., minus the verses bracketed above). These supposed distinctions, however, were often disregarded by poet-composers, resulting in a multitude of hybrid forms.

The most common themes of these new strophic song genres were the pangs of yearning love, ornate description of garden scenes, and the depiction of intimate drinking parties where the poet and his companions compete for the favors of the cup bearer. A related but separate body of songs drew upon religious themes such as praise for the Prophet Muḥammad, usually couched in the standard motifs of love poetry, and spiritual themes depicting the central ideas of Sufism, the mystical branch of Islam that emerged in the early Middle Ages.

Historical records concerning the rise and spread of Andalusian music contain biographical information about famous musicians and singers, many song texts, occasional descriptions of musical performances and styles, and even the details of musical instruments, but not the melodies themselves. Although various types of musical notation were used by medieval Muslim scholars in treatises on music theory, actual compositions were not transcribed in premodern Islamic culture, but were instead taught and learned aurally. What can be reconstructed from the available sources, however, does allow a basic understanding of the distinctiveness of the Andalusian tradition and how so many branches came to evolve from it, each maintaining certain elements that the performers within that tradition perceive as Andalusian.

In the ninth century, Córdoba began to flourish as the capital of the newly established Umayyad dynasty of Iberia, a branch of the eastern Umayyad dynasty that had been defeated by the 'Abbasids in 750. The wealth and rising fame of the Cordoban court soon attracted singers and musicians from eastern cities, particularly from Baghdad and Medina (al-Maqqarī 1967; Touma 1987). For a time, due to the constant influx of Eastern performers, there were few differences among the musical styles of these three great centers. Ziryāb, a brilliant singer and composer who arrived in Córdoba in 822, is credited with the first efforts to create a regional song style distinctive to al-Andalus (Wright 1992); his contributions, however, have not lasted until the present. The body of song texts he worked with was later completely supplanted by the *muwashshaḥ* and *zajal* forms that did not appear, even according to the earliest estimates, until well over a century after his death. The thirteenth-century North African writer al-Tīfāshī (d. 1253) states that Ziryāb's musical style fell out of favor in the eleventh century and was replaced with the style of another musical luminary, Ibn Bājja (d. 1139), known as Avempace to the Latins. Ibn Bājja is also credited by al-Tīfāshī with having combined "the songs of the Christians with those of the East, thereby inventing a style found only in [al]-Andalus, toward which the temperament of its people inclined, so that they rejected all others" (Liu and Monroe 1989, 42), a statement that is equally as intriguing as its vagueness is frustrating. It is almost certainly this later style that provided the foundation for most of what is now known as Andalusian music in the Arab Middle East. Nevertheless, Ziryāb remains the more famous of the two figures and is cited in oral traditions in many parts of the Arab world as the "father of Andalusian music."

At nearly the same time al-Tīfāshī was writing his treatise, the "new music" of al-Andalus was making its presence felt in Egypt and the Levant. In Egypt Ibn Sanā' al-Mulk (d. 1212) wrote a now famous treatise on the *muwashshaḥāt* entitled *Dār al-Ṭirāz* [The House of Brocade], working entirely from those he had heard sung in

Cairo while bemoaning the fact that he had never had the opportunity to travel to al-Andalus and hear this music at its source (Ibn Sanā' al-Mulk 1977). Nevertheless, he himself composed a large number of *muwashshaḥāt* imitating the models he heard, many of which have survived.

Great *muwashshaḥ* poets from Iberia such as al-Sushtarī (d. 1269) and Ibn al-'Arabī (d. 1240) also traveled through Aleppo, Damascus, Mosul, Medina, and Mecca and it was not long before locally composed *muwashshaḥāt* began to appear in those regions as well. The first *muwashshaḥāt* composed in the eastern Mediteranean may have appeared as early as the 1160s (Raḥīm 1987). In later centuries songbooks (sing. *safīna*, pl. *safā'in*) were compiled that included *muwashshaḥ* and *zajal* texts organized into the distinctive "suite" form of Andalusian music in which the songs are grouped according to their melodic mode and rhythm.

Comparative study of historical texts and modern musical traditions reveals that different lyrics often can be found sung to the same melody and the same text may also be found set to different melodies. The mid-nineteenth-century compiler Shihāb al-Dīn al-Misrī, for example, was careful to notate these variant versions in his songbook, *Safīnat al-mulk wa-nafīsat al-fulk* [The ship of state and the treasure of the ark], first written in the 1840s. It is clear from this and other historical evidence that contrafactum creation, the setting of new words to a known melody or a new melody to a known text, has been a part of the Andalusian musical tradition from its earliest period.

Given this fluidity and the fact that the majority of the song texts performed in modern Andalusian traditions cannot be traced to medieval Iberia (determining the age of the melodies is all but impossible), some scholars almost scoffingly point out that the traditions can therefore not be considered Andalusian. The question in these cases, however, should be in what way these traditions were and are perceived as "Andalusian" both at their outset and now. Seen from the musical perspective, for example, a new song style that first emerges by setting local poetry in the Andalusian style to well-known melodies from the "classical" Andalusian tradition could easily be referred to as "Andalusian" by dint of the melodic repertory it has adopted. Al-Tifāshī states as much already in the thirteenth century when he notes that audiences in his day appreciate new songs only if the new lyrics are set to well-known melodies (Liu and Monroe 1989, 37). The Syrian term for a branch of Andalusian music associated primarily with the city of Aleppo, *qudūd*, provides another indication that this may be the case since it refers to a mold or model; modern musicians explain the term as the setting of poems in local Syrian dialect *'alā qadd*, "to the model of," ancient Andalusian tunes.[3]

Equally likely is the possibility that a tradition may have become known as "Andalusian" not due to its use of Andalusian texts or even specifically Andalusian melodies, but because it used the melodic modal system and/or the rhythmic system of the Andalusian repertory in contrast to an extant local folk music, particularly if the local musical structures were quite different, as is the case with regional musics marked by strong African features, for example. In the end, what is "Andalusian" is in the ear of the listener or musician, and the scholar's task is to discover how and why it is perceived as Andalusian, and what that attribution means in both historical and social terms.

Modern Andalusian Traditions

In the following brief portraits of six modern Andalusian performances from Algeria, Morocco, Tunisia, Egypt, Los Angeles, and Bahrain, a brief description of each musical event is followed by a historical sketch of that tradition and its modern social role. All are based upon firsthand fieldwork observations and interviews with the exception of the 1975 Tunisian example, which is drawn from the dissertation of the late Jafran Jones (1977) and the description of the Fayrūz performance in Bahrain which is taken from a videotape of that concert.

Tlemcen, Algeria, July 3-5, 1991

Violence broke out again this week in the capital of Algiers and government tank columns made their way through the central boulevards there. The atmosphere in Tlemcen is subdued and even grim. Although no serious violence has yet taken place here, significant changes have occurred since the summer of 1990. The large billboard at the end of the main square that last year presented portraits of the most famous Andalusian musicians of Tlemcen has been replaced with a single quotation from the Qur'ān enjoining fair government. There is a nearly tangible sense of foreboding in the air. The Andalusian music festival that opens with tonight's performance was originally planned to last several nights and to include the participation of nearly two dozen orchestras from Morocco, Algeria, and Tunisia. It was deemed unsafe for any of the groups to travel, however, so the festival has been reduced to a series of performances by Tlemcen's own local youth orchestras spread over two evenings, with a third evening devoted to music by the local ʿĪsāwīya Sufi ensemble.

Tlemcen is a rare town, however, and although the population scarcely exceeds 150,000, there are six full Andalusian orchestras here, indeed a festival unto themselves. Each group rehearses two or more times a week, and for the festival they have each learned a full *nūba*, "suite," of about an hour's duration. Teenagers and college-aged youths dominate, but there are a few younger faces. Some of the orchestras have both male and female musicians, a few are all male groups. Several of the ensembles' names reflect the popularity of Andalusian imagery: the al-Qurṭubiyya [Cordoban] orchestra, Riyāḍ al-Andalus [The gardens of al-Andalus], and the Orchestra of Gharnāṭa [Granada].

Andalusian music in Tlemcen is called *ṣanʿa* meaning "art" or "craft." The instruments in the orchestras include traditional lutes of both a larger variety from Egypt and a smaller local variety. The lute is originally an Arab instrument and was introduced to Europe via Islamic Spain and Sicily in the Middle Ages; the European names for the instrument all derive from the Arabic word *al-ʿūd*, "the wooden instrument." Several of the groups, but not all, include a *rabāb*, a small boat-shaped instrument with a half-leather, half-metal face and short, arched bow. It, too, entered Europe in the Middle Ages, as the rebec, and was a popular instrument there for several centuries. The *rabāb* is considered the Andalusian musical instrument par excellence for, unlike the other instruments, it is used only in the performance of Andalusian music. It is normally played by a group's leader, seated at the center of the ensemble. The *rabāb*, lutes, drums, and tambourines are all instruments that might have been found in an ensemble a thousand years ago in Córdoba or Seville. But these orchestras also include violins, violas, fretted mandolins, and mandoles (the slightly larger cousin of the mandolin) that have all been introduced from Europe in the last century or so.

As a security precaution the festival has been moved into an auditorium rather than being held outside in the gardens as in the past. The front central section of the auditorium has been reserved for women, most of whom are wearing the Tlemcenian traditional white head covering. Some women, however, sit with friends and family members in the other sections of the hall. The audience listens intently and quietly to the opening sections of the first *nūba*. After the first three sections there is a series of vocal solos, the *istikhbārāt*, that rouse the audience to more vocal approval. When the ensemble breaks into the lively six-beat rhythm of the final movement, the *mkhlas*, the audience begins clapping along to the music, some of the men stand up and clap, some of the women ululate. The end draws a loud cheer and a sustained round of applause. A few minutes later, the next orchestra is in place, and the mood has returned to the somber, lyrical feel of the opening moments of a Tlemcenian *nūba*.

Tlemcen is a city in which several different origins have been brought together: Berbers and Arabs of the region (the *ḥaḍar*), a large Jewish community whose forefathers are thought to have immigrated to Tlemcen in the Middle Ages by way of Fez, Morocco, and families of partially Turkish ancestry, the *kouloughli*, descendants of marriages between Ottoman bureaucrats and military men with women of local origin. Unlike certain other urban centers of North Africa, there is no distinct group that lays claims to Andalusian identity. Although certain families, particularly among the Jewish community, assert their descent from medieval

Andalusian refugees from the Christian conquest of Iberia, they do not form a cohesive social class.

The French invasion of Algeria in 1830 ushered in a period of cultural suppression that lasted over 130 years and only ended with Algerian independence in 1962. The French language displaced Arabic in education, and local cultural traditions were at times banned outright. In the nineteenth century, master musicians of the Andalusian tradition kept Tlemcenian music alive through traditional forms of transmission. Songs, melodies, and instrumental techniques were taught almost exclusively by ear directly from teacher to pupil. Promising young musicians were incorporated into their teacher's ensemble when they became proficient enough to perform publicly. Performances occurred at weddings and, on a more regular basis, in cafés and in private gatherings. In addition to these semiprofessional musicians, some families performed Andalusian music within the privacy of their own homes. As one Tlemcenian declared even in 1991 in an outburst of love for the Andalusian tradition, "Every family in Tlemcen is an orchestra ready to perform at a moment's notice!"

When French control over Algeria began to extend outward from the urban centers into the provincial towns and countryside, Tlemcen's historical tradition of Andalusian music aquired a new, anticolonial aura. In the early twentieth century small associations were formed to preserve this heritage that was now threatened by French cultural hegemony. The first of these in Tlemcen was the Societé littéraire, artistique et musicale, referred to as l'SLAM in a not-so-veiled reference to the Arabic word for peace *salām* and the religion of Islam. The SLAM established the first of Tlemcen's institutionally based youth orchestras and was eventually joined by five other such ensembles. These groups became a publically recognized focal point for cultural life in Tlemcen. Maps of the city distributed by the municipal tourist office in the early 1990s prominently displayed images of traditional Andalusian musical instruments in their margins and the location of each musical association was marked with the symbol of a treble clef.

Throughout the twentieth century, the doyen of Andalusian music in Tlemcen was the revered figure of Shaykh al-'Arabī Ben Ṣārī (1872-1964). His prodigious age, remarkable memory for repertory, and decades of teaching and performing made him quite simply the grand old man of Tlemcenian music. Many musicians in Tlemcen state categorically that the town's musical life has never truly recovered from his departure. One of the more recently founded orchestras is in fact called the *Aḥbāb shaykh al-'arabī ben ṣārī* [Lovers of Shaykh al-'Arabī Ben Ṣārī].

Throughout North Africa, the Andalusian musical heritage is organized into a series of "suites," or *nūbāt* (sing. *nūba*), each based upon a different melodic mode. Each suite is divided into five main vocal sections or movements with each movement distinguished by a particular rhythm. In addition there are a number of purely instrumental compositions performed as overtures and intermezzi. The *nūba*, however, takes slightly different forms in different regions. In Tlemcen the *nūba* has remained, until very recently, a fluid, even spontaneous, unit of performance. The maestro often selects the songs for each of the five movements during the performance itself, and the musicians follow his lead. Every rendition of a *nūba* thus turns out differently with the Shaykh following the inspiration of the moment in selecting one or more songs of the proper mode and rhythm to create the first movement of the *nūba*, then one or more songs for the second movement, and so forth until the fifth and final movement. But there are fewer and fewer musicians with the finely honed performance skills and the vast memorized repertory needed to follow the onstage decisions of a great maestro. The youth orchestras select the pieces that they will perform months in advance and rehearse them diligently. The tradition thus lives on, but the degree of spontaneity that kept Tlemcen's Andalusian music so vibrant is declining.

The most remarkable characteristic about Andalusian music in Tlemcen, however, is the abundant enthusiasm and devotion demonstrated by its young people for this tradition. In the 1990s, however, this music that was once endangered by French cultural hegemony is again threatened, but from an entirely different direction. The reactionary religious groups that have thrown Algeria into a state of virtual civil war have attacked this "secular" musical tradition, with its lyrics of gardens, wine drinking, and lovers' trysts, and called for a ban on public performances. No music festival has been held in Tlemcen since that of 1991, and although no reliable information has been available for some time, it appears that public performances in general have indeed become rarer and rarer. In contrast with other branches of Andalusian music, however, Tlemcen's tradition has survived with its popularity intact (albeit with a certain loss of repertory and in somewhat reduced circumstances), perhaps precisely due to the struggle that has been necessary to keep it alive against such heavy odds.

Fez, Morocco, July 1993

This evening's wedding party is held in the garden of a spacious home in the new section of Fez. Tables set up on the lawns provide seating for perhaps two hundred guests while others stroll among the tables and stream in and out of the main house. The male guests are for the most part dressed in western clothes, though a few are wearing versions of the traditional caftan or *jubba*; the women are in brightly colored dresses based on traditional patterns, many of which are ornately decorated with needlework. The food is abundant and lavish.

Fifteen musicians are seated in a covered patio in a half circle, all in traditional white attire, some wearing the red felt hat known to English-speakers as a "fez." The instruments include lutes, violins, a drum, a tambourine, and a *rabāb*. The lute and the *rabāb*, as mentioned above, were introduced into Europe during the Middle Ages. The violin on the other hand, migrated in the other direction over the last century and a half, from Europe to the Middle East where it fully replaced an indigenous spike-fiddle called the *kamānja*. Its role as a recent substitute is still evident from the playing technique of Moroccan and Algerian musicians, for it is held vertically on the knee while the bow, grasped from underneath, is moved horizontally across the strings, precisely as if it were a *kamānja*.

In the center of the semicircle sits the venerable Shaykh 'Abd al-Karīm Rāyis, at eighty years old nearly a living legend among music connoisseurs. Flanking him are several of the music teachers from the small conservatory in Fez that specializes in Andalusian music, a tradition which is known in Morocco as *āla*, or "instrumental," music, in contrast to the Andalusian traditions of neighboring Algeria, for example, that are here referred to as *gharnāṭī*, or "Granadan," music. It is a mark of the social standing of the families involved in this marriage that the Shaykh himself is performing.

The audience members listen at times but are primarily occupied with the ongoing festivities. When the orchestra launches into a faster section, many of the guests visibly redirect their attention to the orchestra and some even begin to snap their fingers, but they soon turn back to their conversations. There is no dancing.

Morocco, perhaps more than any other region in North Africa, maintains a clear cultural identification with al-Andalus. For centuries there was a constant flow of population—including scholars, poets, and musicians—back and forth between the Iberian Peninsula and what is now Morocco. For nearly two centuries, from the late eleventh century to the mid-thirteenth, Morocco and al-Andalus were jointly ruled first by the Almoravid and then the Almohad states. Even during periods of political separation the ties between the two regions were always strong. As the Northern Christian Iberian states pushed their conquest southward in the Middle Ages, many Andalusians relocated to Morocco. Their presence in cities such as Fez was felt quite early and has continued to be felt even in modern times. A large section of the old city of Fez is still known as "the Andalusian Quarter" and families of Andalusian descent throughout Morocco have been able to establish themselves as a distinct social group, closely tied to the current monarchy. In Morocco, the term "Andalusian" refers not just to a musical tradition, but also to a still powerful social identity (Chapter 4). The degree to which the two are intertwined has not yet been well documented.

The Andalusian musical tradition of Morocco is popularly conceived of in terms of regional styles based in key urban centers such as Tetouan, Meknes, Fez, and Rabat. Oujda, in the far northeast of modern Morocco, is understood to practice the musical traditions of neighboring

Algeria rather than those of western and northern Morocco. Fez, in particular, has been associated with the performance of Andalusian music for centuries. Here the social identity of "Andalusian" mixes freely with the musical tradition of the same heritage. Andalusian music is commonly performed at weddings, indeed in some circles this is almost obligatory, and, as the regional "art music," it is performed for public and government functions such as receptions for visiting political figures as well. Few studio cassette recordings, however, are sold in the shops of the new quarters of Fez. To buy recordings of Andalusian music, one goes into the Old City, into the areas of the market that sell equipment and paraphernalia for weddings such as tall candles, incense, and decorations, and there one finds dozens of recordings, some of which are from other weddings. These recordings are sold by the name of the lead musician, but often with the name of the family and the date of the performance marked carefully on the cover. Andalusian music in Fez, even in its recorded cassette form, remains rooted in the social systems of patronage that have kept it alive.

In Morocco the form of the *nūba* as a unit of performance differs from that in Algeria. Here, instead of playing through the sequence of five movements and performing a few songs from each, it is now common for musicians to perform only one of the five movements, a single *mīzān*, and to perform all of the known songs in the local repertory that are of that rhythm and melodic mode in a set, canonical order (Schuyller 1978). Even one *mīzān* takes well over an hour if played in this manner, so, in Morocco, musicians in modern times sometimes perform only half a *mīzān* at a time. Each *mīzān* or half *mīzān* is an exploration of a single mood, tempo, and rhythm with little internal variation. Over an evening, a group such as Shaykh 'Abd al-Karīm Rāyis and his troupe will therefore usually present a series of *miyāzīn* (pl. of *mīzān*) from different *nūbāt* chosen for their contrasting moods.

Elsewhere in North Africa, Andalusian orchestras create variation in mood and tempo by moving through the five vocal sections which are organized roughly from the slowest to the fastest. Thus a performance of Andalusian music in Tlemcen, for example, traditionally implied the presentation of a single *nūba* which moved from a slow, lyrical pace to a fast, driving rhythm at the finale with the maestro making the decisions every few minutes about what song to play next, while in Fez a performance in recent times most often consists of the presentation of large blocks of repertory such as a full *mīzān*, lasting from a half hour to two hours, in which the order of the songs is predetermined. In Tlemcen audience members must wait to hear what song the maestro decides to play next, while in Fez audience members familiar with the tradition may begin humming or singing the next song before the ensemble has finished the present one.

This distinctive Moroccan practice appears to derive from the powerful influence wielded by the late-eighteenth-century songbook compiled by al-Ḥā'ik that came to be widely accepted as the primary articulation of the Andalusian tradition, including even the order in which the songs were presented. In more recent times in Fez, a work derived from al-Ḥā'ik's work, called *al-Kunnāsh al-jāmi'i*, [collective songbook], became an authoritative treatment which was further refined in a publication by Shaykh 'Abd al-Karīm Rāyis himself under the title, *Min waḥī al-rabāb* [To the inspiration of the *rabāb*] (Rāyis 1989). This work is now used as a definitive text and is studied by all students of the tradition and memorized, line by line, in precisely the order laid out in the printed book. Andalusian music in Fez stands as a remarkable example of the multiple and complex effects that writing can have on an oral tradition.

On the whole, Andalusian music still thrives in Fez for it has a strong social base and a continuing performance context in traditional weddings and other celebrations. But young musicians view it more and more as a "fossilized" tradition in which there is no room for innovation, change, or even interpretation. Paradoxically, the growing authority of the written text, originally created to help preserve the tradition, has helped suppress all impetus for change or innovation, and thus may eventually condemn it to neglect. Andalusian music in both Tlemcen and Fez is a symbol of social conservatism, long-standing tradition, and an idealized heritage, but in Fez, unlike in Tlemcen, is not a symbol embraced widely by young people.

Qṣībet Sūsa, Tunisia, August 22, 1975

It is late summer and the musicians of the 'Īsāwīya Sufi Brotherhood are booked for performances of Andalusian music nearly every night. On Friday afternoons they perform the *ḥaḍra* ceremony in the brotherhood's *zāwiya*, "lodge," and occasionally they perform a full *kharja*, a street procession, for special events such as the birthday of the Prophet. During the day they perform at funerals, but most evenings they are occupied with weddings, family gatherings, and private parties. Performances of Andalusian music in Tunisia presented by non-Sufis include a variety of melody instruments such as violins, lutes, *rabāb*, reed flute, and zither. The 'Īsāwīya, however, perform with only five singers and five drummers, all of whom are active members of the brotherhood, and a single instrumental soloist, the *zakkār*, who performs on the double-reed *zukra*, a type of folk oboe, and is hired from outside the brotherhood for specific occasions. When the ʻĪsāwīya members perform for themselves, even this one melody instrument is absent and the music consists entirely of voice and percussion; together these provide accompaniment for the members' ritualized dancelike movements during the *dhikr* ceremony that eventually bring some of the brothers to a state of trance or *takhmīr*, "intoxication."

Tonight's wedding performance is led by Shaykh ʻĀmir Qasmī. All of the singers and percussionists are from the village of Qṣībet Sūsa; the *zakkār*, however, has been brought in from another town. The evening opens with a solo improvisation on the *zukra*, which is followed by the *qaṣīda* in which a solo vocalist sings a poetic text in musically ornate improvised lines each of which are then echoed by the *zukra*. With these two introductory sections over, the chorus and percussionists begin the first *nūba*, "suite," the main element of the performance. As soon as the *nūba* begins, a dance line or *ṣaff* is formed by men and boys from among the guests and is constantly replenished with new participants throughout the evening. Male guests not already wearing the traditional *jubba* outer garment borrow one and put it on before taking a place in the *ṣaff*. The ʻĪsāwīya ensemble has even come equipped with extra *jbāyib* (pl. of *jubba*) to accommodate guests who did not bring their own. The women are all in traditional attire; they clap and ululate from the sidelines, but never participate in the dance line.

Over a period of two and a half hours the Sufi brothers perform a series of six *nūbāt* (pl. of *nūba*) lasting from ten to thirty minutes each, in the order traditionally maintained by the 'Īsāwīya brotherhood. Almost all of the singing is performed in unison, with the chorus and the *zakkār* alternating back and forth in a call-and-response pattern. The most heightened emotional moments are when the *zakkār* makes a *khurūj*, "exit," and performs a solo instrumental improvisation. During his *khurūj* he abandons the traditional Andalusian repertory and improvises, at times without reference to known melodies, but at other times incorporating local folk tunes and even popular hit songs from the radio. The audience is enthusiastic throughout the performance. Their comments and applause ebb and flow with each new section and swell at the conclusion of each *khurūj* solo (Jones 1977, 62-64).

Musical life in the courts of Tunisia was already flourishing by the ninth century. The legendary "father" of Andalusian music, Ziryāb, sought patronage there first before traveling on to Córdoba in 822. From that time to the year 1100, however, there is little evidence from which to construct a portrait of the regional style, though it is safe to assume continued contact with the more prestigious centers of Iberia. The origin of a distinctive Andalusian style in Tunisia is sometimes attributed to the arrival of Ummaya Ibn 'Abd al-'Azīz Abū al-Ṣalt of Seville, ca. 1100. He is said to have founded a school of music in the first half of the twelfth century and to have established the Andalusian musical tradition of Tunisia.

In recent centuries Andalusian music in Tunisia has existed in two distinct though related forms: a primarily nonreligious form, called *malūf*, a term that means "customary" or "familiar," that exists as an art music tradition, and an overtly religious form performed by Sufi brotherhoods in religious rituals, but which is also found in other contexts such as entertainment at weddings. Although the "secular" Tunisian repertory contains many song texts that are overtly spiritual, such as poems of praise to the Prophet Muḥammad, it has been a repertory most often performed by professional musicians, many of whom were Jewish, and at times privately by upper-class connoisseurs, but not in specifically religious contexts. The parallel tradition of a decidedly Sufi nature was apparently first developed by Andalusian poets such as Abū l-Ḥasan 'Alī al-Shushtarī (1213-1269) and was brought to North Africa and then adopted by certain Sufi brotherhoods in Tunisia. Indeed this music is sometimes referred to in Tunisian Arabic as *shishtrī* (from al-Shushtarī). The most prominent of the Sufi brotherhoods in Tunisia in their use of Andalusian music is the 'Īsāwīya. Since the 'Īsāwīya trace their origins only as far back as the early-sixteenth-century Moroccan spiritual leader Sīdī Ben 'Īsā (ca. 1467-1526), it is clear that the tradition of Sufi-oriented Andalusian music in the form of sung *muwashshaḥāt* poems predates their adoption of this music as a primary element of their characteristic rituals.

There is little evidence concerning the degree of contact or separation between the secular *malūf* tradition and Sufi Andalusian music until the late nineteenth and early twentieth centuries, and by that time the two branches had developed characteristic differences not only in their choice of texts and melodies, but in the very structures of their performances. Though both traditions are based on the performance of "suites" known as *nūbāt* (sing. *nūba*), the 'Īsāwīya *nūbāt* are much shorter in length (ten to thirty minutes) and are almost always performed in the same order (Jones 1977, 69-70). Only one of the suites, *al-gharbī*, is used in achieving the trance state or *takhmīr*, literally intoxication or fermentation, that is associated with the 'Īsāwīya. This trance ceremony along with the eating of broken glass or scorpions, piercing the body with metal skewers, and feats of phenomenal strength are the most (in)famous traits of the brotherhood and those most often condemned by other groups. The twentieth century has seen a decline in the social status and power of the Sufi brotherhoods, particularly in the period after Tunisian independence from French colonial rule in 1956. The independent Tunisian government has viewed the Sufi brotherhoods as a phenomenon to be suppressed both as a political force and as an embarrassing element of superstitious backwardness. 'Īsāwīya music has been disappearing at a steady rate over the past two decades. Where they once were a common feature at weddings, they and their music are more likely to be perceived as a quaint "folk" tradition or even downright objectionable by many modern Tunisians.

The nonreligious Andalusian music of Tunisia has also undergone a drastic transformation in this century. Already in the 1920s a French enthusiast and scholar, Baron Rodolphe d'Erlanger, had begun the process of transcribing the *malūf* tradition into western musical notation for the purposes of preserving it. He also helped introduce western-style theory and music education (Davis 1992). During the ensuing decades transcriptions of the *malūf* that were drawn in part from the 'Īsāwīya tradition were created by combining and editing out the regional distinctions between different styles and versions. The eventual result was a conservatory mindset that now promulgates a single homogenized, though composite, version of Tunisia's musical Andalusian heritage (Davis 1986). Thus the nonreligious Andalusian tradition of Tunisia has followed a path in some ways parallel to that of Fez, Morocco. The creation of a written, authoritative version of the tradition for the purpose of preservation has been followed by a decline in the popular base of support for its performance. On the one hand, this heritage is a source of national pride, while on the other, is has been transformed into a museum piece that in the 1990s can claim little popularity beyond a limited circle of aficionados.

Cairo, Egypt, June 1995

On the grounds of Cairo's glistening white new opera house about two hundred people are seated on folding chairs set up in rows in an area that is for most of the year an unused courtyard. It is midsummer, however, the heat is sweltering, and many evening performances are being held outside rather than in the opera house itself. The outside location works to counteract not only the heat but also the formal dress code of the main opera hall (coat and tie for men) for official performances—only a few men in suits are to be seen in the audience. An orchestra of sixteen musicians and a choir are performing from atop a wooden platform covered in cloth. The male musicians and singers are wearing tuxedos while the women are in full-length dresses in a variety of bright colors decorated with gold-threaded embroidery. The instruments include one lute, several violins, a stand-up bass viol, a reed flute, a large zither (Ar. "*qānūn*"), and a tambourine, but no drum. (The North African *rabāb* is not found in the eastern half of the Arab world; the name is used, but for an entirely different instrument.)

This is one of the few spots left in Cairo where one can hear Andalusian *muwashshaḥāt* performed. It is a style that appeals only to a small circle of modern listeners and the repertory is kept alive almost entirely by state-supported ensembles. This evening's program ranges from traditional repertory dating back to the nineteenth century or earlier, including some *muwashshaḥāt*, to mid-twentieth-century compositions that were considered quite "popular" in their day, but in the fast-moving world of Egyptian music have already acquired a "classical" patina due to the datedness of their style. Six *muwashshaḥāt* are included in the program; of these, my companions agree that only one is widely known even among listeners who like the "old" music. All six are performed in the same sedate manner.

The audience listens intently and with evident pleasure to these pieces; heads sway gently back and forth with the music. They applaud each one, but with restraint. Their responses become noticeably more enthusiastic in the second half of the program as the selections become progressively more recent and modern in style, although whether this is due to greater appreciation or simply to the faster, more upbeat rhythms of these songs is hard to say.

Egypt has been home to a tradition of *muwashshaḥāt* since the late twelfth century. The above-mentioned writer Ibn Sanā' al-Mulk, author of the treatise *Dār al-Ṭirāz* [The house of brocade] on the composition of *muwashshaḥāt* states clearly that he himself was never able to visit al-Andalus and that all of his knowledge of this exciting, new genre of song was derived from the examples he heard performed in Cairo. His treatise remains the single-most important extant medieval text on the subject of the *muwashshaḥāt* and his testimony provides significant, though indirect, evidence of the continuous flow of musical performers back and forth between the Iberian Peninsula and the eastern Mediterranean.

Seven hundred years later another major work on the *muwashshaḥ* was composed in Egypt: *Safīnat al-Mulk wa-nafīsat al-fulk* [The ship of state and treasure of the rrk] compiled by Muḥammad Shihāb al-Dīn in the 1840s. The title and structure of the work play with the image of a ship since the Arabic word *safīna*, originally a ship or vessel, had by then become the traditional term for a songbook of *muwashshaḥāt*. Shihāb al-Dīn's collection of texts is particularly valuable since it includes indications for the melodic mode and rhythm of each song, as well as occasional comments on variant versions of the songs. When a song had only one or two stanzas, Shihāb al-Dīn frequently added several more of his own devising and notated these additions in his collection. In nineteenth-century Cairo the repertory of *muwashshaḥāt* was clearly not a closed corpus of songs to be notated for preservation, but rather a living body of music to which gifted poets and musicians were welcome to make their own contributions.

In nineteenth-century Egypt, *muwashshaḥāt* were performed primarily in sequences or suites similar to those of North Africa, but with one very important distinction: in North Africa, all of the vocal sections of the *nūba* suite consisted (and do to this day) of *muwashshaḥāt*, whereas in the Egyptian suite, or *wasla*, the *muwashsḥah* was but one of several genres of song performed. The Andalusian element was thus assimilated into the larger frame of the *waṣla* alongside a number of other genres and styles, including for example, instrumental compositions from the Ottoman Turkish art music tradition and vocal genres of local Egyptian origin.

By the mid-twentieth century, however, the popularity of the *waṣla* was fading rapidly and was being replaced by newer genres of song that evolved in the Cairene musical theater of the 1920s and 1930s and the new "concert song" format pioneered by singers such as Umm Kulthūm in the 1940s and 1950s (Danielson 1997, 126-38). Even in the courtyard of the Cairo opera, where such obvious efforts are being made to preserve a classical repertory despite its loss of popularity, the *waṣla* is no longer found. Instead of the complex sequence of elements that distinguished the *waṣla* form (Racy 1983), *muwashshaḥāt* are now offered up piecemeal, one or two at a time, amid a far more arbitrary collection of compositions in a preplanned concert program. Thus, individual items of the Andalusian repertory survive, but not the performance structure in which they used to appear.

The role of the modern Egyptian state in patronizing public musical events has been prominent at least as far back as the building of the first Cairo Opera House by the Egyptian Khedive Ismā'īl as part of the flamboyant celebrations that accompanied the opening of the Suez Canal in 1862. In the 1960s, when the older repertory of Egyptian music appeared to be disappearing, the government of Gamāl 'Abd al-Nāṣir created the first in a series of government orchestras dedicated to the performance of this musical heritage (El-Shawan 1980). During the 1970s and 1980s the main government ensemble, *firqat al-mūsīqā al-'arabiyya* [The Arab music ensemble], performed a repertory primarily drawn from the Arabo-Turkish classical repertory of instrumental pieces and older Arabic-language songs, including *muwashshaḥāt*. In sharp contrast to performances in North Africa, however, though aficionados might comment that such-and-such a piece is a *muwashshaḥ*, the sense of Andalusian origin or style is very vague among audience members and musicians. When asked about Andalusian *muwashshaḥāt*, many Cairenes are more likely to mention the popular recordings by the

Lebanese superstar, Fayrūz see Manama, Bahrain, below), than the performances that take place in their own city.

Los Angeles, California, April 5, 1996

The main floor of the Los Angeles Palladium has been furnished with large round tables seating eight to ten people each where the guests have been served dinner. Most of those present are Syrian-Americans who have come to hear the man who for many simply *is* Syrian music: Ṣabāḥ Fakhrī. A diminutive figure dressed in a tuxedo, as are his musicians, he steps up to the microphone to loud applause after the conclusion of several warm-up performances by other singers. Before he even begins to sing, the mood has begun to crackle with festivity. By the time he has finished his first set many of the young men in the audience have climbed onto their chairs, and, holding the two ends of twisted white cloth napkins in their hands, are swaying and singing to the music. The women remain seated.

Ṣabāḥ Fakhrī's set consists of a *wasla* of *muwashshaḥāt* from the city of Aleppo in northern Syria. At first he sings with restrained demeanor and gestures, though often breaking into a beaming smile. The audience frequently sings along. Toward the end of the set he has clearly warmed up; at one point he moves away from the microphone and, in dancing steps, spins around in a small circle on stage. The audience goes wild with approval.

Ṣabāḥ Fakhrī sings a repertory of songs of which he is the single-most popular and best known interpreter. In addition, this is an immigrant audience, people who have left their homeland to come to America and have come to this evening to hear songs they have known since childhood, and for many, to hear them sung by the same voice, in the same manner, and by the same performer that they have listened to all their lives.

Syria, like the North African countries and Egypt, claims a proud heritage of *muwashshaḥāt* (Raḥīm 1987; Poché 1995). As mentioned above, famous Sufi composers of *muwashshaḥāt* such as al-Shushtarī and Ibn al-ʿArabī began settling in Syria as early as the twelfth century and Syrians soon after began producing *muwashshaḥāt* on their own. The city of Aleppo is particularly renowned as a musical center for *muwashshaḥāt*. Unlike in Egypt where *muwashshaḥāt* became integrated into the *waṣla* "suite" form along with a variety of different song genres, Aleppo has preserved a local version of the *waṣla* in which all of the vocal pieces are *muwashshaḥāt*, similar to the North African *nūba*. The *muwashshaḥāt* is far more prominent a genre in Syria than in Egypt; however, the question of how "Andalusian" Syrians have felt this genre to be over the centuries is problematic. The historical record is uneven and there are almost no written references to this music as being Andalusian prior to the nineteenth-century revival of this connection. This may mean that Syrians saw this tradition as being wholly and truly of their own making, or it may mean that this association was simply taken for granted. In the twentieth century, scholars and musicians alike conceive, or have reconceptualized, the Syrian *muwashshaḥāt* tradition as a branch of the greater Andalusian heritage while at the same time accepting it as an authentic element of Syrian culture. In Los Angeles the *muwashshaḥ* can still command large audiences and high prices, and, paradoxically, for this audience, nothing could be more Syrian than Andalusian music.

Manama, Bahrain, 1970s

A wide outdoor stage has been erected in front of the historic mud fort of Bahrain. A full orchestra of thirty or more musicians can be heard from the orchestra pit consisting of many violins, several cellos, and a bass that provide the basic sound texture, while a reed flute, a single lute, and a zither are individually amplified and occasionally featured in solo sections. There is a brief musical overture and then, when the drums launch into a faster rhythm, a line of female dancers moves to the center of the stage. They are dressed in flowing, brightly colored synthetic fabrics in a manner guaranteed to bring the 1960s American television series *I Dream of Jeannie* to the mind of anyone who ever watched it. The dance production is choreographed to highlight the flowing costumes. Suddenly a thundering wave of applause all but drowns out the orchestra. Fayrūz has walked out onto the stage. She too is dressed in a flowing costume meant to evoke medieval Islamic Spain. She assumes her characteristic statuesque stance in front of the microphone, her unchanging facial expression betraying no emotion whatsoever.

At the end of the first dance number, the orchestral music drops to a sustained drone. Fayrūz pauses, then lifts her head to the microphone and begins singing a nonrhythmic, almost improvisatory, version of a *muwashshaḥ*. But for audience members it is clear that although she is singing in a seemingly unmeasured manner, this is a very precise replication of her fabulously popular 1966 recording *Andalusiyyāt* [Andalusian Songs]. After this follow in rapid succession a series of short *muwashshaḥāt* punctuated with instrumental interludes and dance numbers. Male dancers garbed in equally exotic attire join the women dancers and Fayrūz on stage. The overture and the dance sequences were composed especially for Fayrūz's *Andalusiyyāt* and act as a frame for the handful of traditional *muwashshaḥāt* scattered throughout the show. The whole concludes with a combined musical, vocal, and dance finale to tremendous applause.

For many Arabs of the eastern Mediterranean countries, this is the most readily available image of Andalusian music, a popular production drawing on the style and feel of the Andalusian tradition by incorporating old songs into new settings. In fact the process of composing "in the Andalusian style" seems never to have ceased in the Arab world. The thirteenth-century treatise of the Tunisian al-Tifāshī examined above testifies to this. His Egyptian contemporary Ibn Sanā' al-Mulk proudly presented his readers with selections from his own compositions. The nineteenth-century compiler Shihāb al-Dīn al-Miṣrī added freely to traditional songs and had no qualms about noting which stanzas were of his own composition. In the early twentieth century, the Egyptian composer Sayyid Darwīsh (d. 1923) composed new *muwashshaḥāt* for performances in Cairene music halls. Many of these, such as the song *Yā shādī al-aḥān* [O singer of songs] became so famous that many Egyptians believe them to be of much older origin. The theatrical extravaganzas of Fayrūz with their popular tone and their mixture of old and new elements, though musically distant from other Andalusian traditions, are in many ways an authentic extension of an aesthetic found in the Andalusian tradition from the earliest period onward.

Conclusion

Scholars may continue to seek "true" Andalusian origins by attempting to trace specific lyrics or musical features back to medieval Islamic Spain. The term "Andalusian," however, functions in the Arab musical world as a classification that defines not so much a regional or historical origin, such as German music or Italian music, but rather a stylistic category more akin to the concepts of jazz or classical music, that is, categories defined by the features that distinguish them from other types of music rather than by their geographic provenance.

The Andalusian musical traditions of the Arab world are rich and highly complex social constructs. On the one hand musicians and audience members often argue for the authentic qualities of their own Andalusian tradition in historical terms (claiming direct transmission from medieval Iberia, for example, in contrast to "less authentic" traditions in neighboring regions), while at the same time, in social terms, claiming those traditions as a powerful marker of local identity. Hence, paradoxically, nothing indeed could be more Moroccan, or Algerian, or Syrian, than good Andalusian music. There is a constant interplay between the element of nostalgia for an Andalusian golden age of which these musical traditions are the most accessible representation and a celebration of local artistic achievement; in some contexts the two are equally present while in others one of the two poles is far stronger. The current popularity, or lack thereof, of modern Andalusian traditions is tightly interwoven with many issues such as social identity, oral versus written techniques of transmission, the history of the colonial encounter, the institutionalization of music education, and even Islamic resurgence movements. What is clear is that in all of these branches of the far-reaching family of Andalusian musics there is an in-dwelling of both historical and social symbolism, a dual nature that manifests itself in a rich variety of forms.

Notes

1. Support for field research in Tlemcen, Algeria in 1991 and in Fez, Morocco in 1993 was provided by travel grants from the American Institute for Maghrib Studies.

2. A corpus of, now renowned, *kharjas* were found in 1948 to be composed in popular amalgams of Hebrew, Arabic, and/or Spanish. The popular themes treated in these *kharjas* also tend to differ from those on which the main body of each *muwashshaḥ* focuses.

3. Oral communication, Los Angeles, California, April 5, 1996, with musicians of Ṣabāḥ Fakhrī's ensemble.

Works Cited

Danielson, Virginia. *The Voice of Egypt: Umm Kulthūm, Arabic Song, and Egyptian Society in the Twentieth Century*. Chicago: U of Chicago P, 1997.

Davis, Ruth F. "Modern Trends in the Ma'lūf of Tunisia, 1934-84." Ph.D. Diss., Princeton University, 1986.

_____. "The Effects of Notation in the Performance Practice of Tunisian Art Music." *The World of Music* 34, no. 1 (1992): 85-114.

El-Shawan, Salwa. "Al-Mūsīkā al-'Arabiyyah: A Category of Urban Music in Cairo, Egypt, 1927-1977." Ph.D. Diss., Columbia University, 1980.

Ibn Sanā' al-Mulk. *Dār al-ṭirāz fī 'amal al-muwashshaḥāt*. Ed. Jawdat al-Rikābī (1st ed., 1949). 2nd Edition. Damascus: Maktabat Dār al-Fikr, 1977.

Jones, Lura Jafran. "The 'Isāwīya of Tunisia and Their Music." Ph.D. Diss., University of Washington, 1977.

Liu, Benjamin M., and James T. Monroe. *Ten Hispano-Arabic Strophic Poems in Modern Oral Tradition*. Berkeley: U of California P, 1989.

al-Maqqarī, Aḥmad ibn Muḥammad. *Nafḥ al-ṭīb min ghuṣn al-Andalus al-raṭīb*. "Analectes sur l'histoire et la littérature des Arabes d'Espagne". Ed. R. Dozy, et al. Leiden: 1855-61; Report. Amsterdam: Oriental Press, 1967.

Poché, Christian. *La musique arabo-andalouse*. Musiques du Monde. Arles: Cité de la musique, 1995.

Racy, Ali Jihad. "The Waslah: A Compound-form Principle in Egyptian Music." *Arab Studies Quarterly*, no. 5 (1983): 396-403.

Raḥīm, Miqdād. *Al-muwashshaḥāt fī bilād al-shām mundhu nashatih ḥattā nihāyat al-qarn al-thānī 'ashar al-hijrī*. Bayrūt: Maktabat al-nahḍa al-'arabiyya, 1987.

Rāyis, 'Abd al-Karīm. *Min waḥī al-rabāb*. 3d Edition. Casablanca: Maṭba'at al-najāḥ al jadīda, 1989.

Schuyller, Philip D. "Moroccan Andalusian Music." *The World of Music* 20, no. 1 (1978): 33-46.

Shihāb al-Dīn, Muḥammad b. Ismā'īl. *Safīnat al-mulk wa-nafīsat al-fulk.* Cairo: n. p., 1864.

Touma, Habib Hassan. "Indications of Arabian Influence on the Iberian Peninsula from the 8th to the 13th Centuries." In *Alfonso X el Sabio y la Música. Revista de Musicología* 10, no. 1 (1987): 137-50.

Wright, Owen. "Music in Muslim Spain." In ed. Salma Khadra Jayyusi, *The Legacy of Muslim Spain*, 555-79. Leiden: Brill, 1992.

◆ Chapter 9

"Al-Andalus Arising from Damascus": Al-Andalus in Modern Arabic Poetry[1]

Reuven Snir

For Dick, the humanist

Violins are weeping over the Arabs leaving al-Andalus

Maḥmūd Darwīsh

In the mid 1980s, the Palestinian poet Maḥmūd Darwīsh (born 1941) asks himself what he would do if he were given the chance to start his life all over again. He has no doubts:

> If I were to start all over again I'd choose what I have chosen
> now: the roses on the fence
> I'd set out again on the road that may or not lead to Córdoba

Andalusian Córdoba here is the paradise whence the poet was driven out, the mythological homeland to which he longs to return. Reaching this homeland, however, may always remain an illusion:

I will return, if I can, to my roses, to my steps
But I will never go back to Córdoba
(Darwīsh, *Ward Aqall*, 1987, 9)

Darwīsh is among the numerous Arab poets who, since the nineteenth century, have steadily invoked the image of Muslim Spain in their poetry. As such they are part of a wider phenomenon: a conscious effort on the part of contemporary Arab poets and writers to highlight the benefits that modern, that is, Western, civilization has gained through its interaction with Arab civilization. The al-Andalus experience is seen as the epitome of that interaction; the Arabs' greatest and most enduring period of success on European soil. Moreover, when poets recall the cultural achievements of the Arab heritage in al-Andalus during nearly eight hundred years of Muslim rule in Iberia, they do so to remind their audience that their present bitter state is only transitory; a temporary clouding of the skies between a glorious past and a splendid future. Modern Arab writers and artists also revive the Andalusian past. In particular they scale literary and musical heights to counter those who claim that Arab culture has westernized excessively.

When we look more closely at the way al-Andalus figures in Arabic literary works, we find that they reflect a number of aspects of Muslim Spain's historical developments from the time Arabs and Berber troops crossed the Straits of Gibraltar into the Iberian peninsula in C.E. 711 and overthrew the Visigoths there. Though the period that followed was one of political fragmentation and a proliferation of local dynasties (known as *Mulūk al-Ṭawā'if* [Petty kings], it was also a period of great cultural efflorescence which lasted without interruption until the fall of Granada in 1492 to the Christians. Inspired by nostalgia, the picture that most frequently appears in modern Arabic literary writings is that of al-Andalus as the lost paradise, "*al-firdaws al-mafqūd*," or as God's paradise on earth, "*jannat Allāh 'alā al-arḍ.*"

Undoubtedly, the Arabs left their mark on Spain: "in the skills of the Spanish peasant and craftsman and the words with which he describes them, in the art, architecture, music and literature of the Peninsula, and in the science and philosophy of the legacy of antiquity faithfully guarded and increased" (Lewis 1970, 130). Since Muslim Spain is generally associated in modern Arabic literature with images intended to play off Arab culture against Western culture, it is not surprising that most literary expressions of al-Andalus appear in poetry, as poetry is the sole literary genre that was not introduced into the Arabic literary system as a result of interference from or interaction with Western culture. Poetry recorded the very appearance of the Arab nation and has been the principal channel through which Arabic literary creativity has flowed from the pre-Islamic period through the Middle Ages, when it peaked both in the East and in al-Andalus, up through the 1950s. Poetry functioned as the true "annals" or as the "public register" of Arab cultural and political history, "*al-sh'ir dīwān al-'Arab.*"[2]

That we see a change in the second half of the twentieth century is partially explained by the universal decline of the status of poetry in modern society together with the increasing influence of the mass media. Still, in the Arab world it is overwhelmingly poetry to which people turn when they seek a vehicle for expressing their national sentiments, their trials and frustrations, their hopes and aspirations, and it is in connection with such content that we find the image of al-Andalus appearing in Arabic poetry, much more frequently than in moden Arab prose and drama, where the Andalusian theme is instead more marginal.[3]

In the nineteenth and early twentieth centuries, neoclassical poetry set out to cleanse impurities that had come to cling to it over the course of previous centuries, and to revert to the grand poetic style that had characterized the golden age of Arabic poetry during the Middle Ages.[4] Adhering to the rigid structure of metre, "*wazn*," and rhyme, "*qāfiya*," of the ancient Arabic poetic form, the *qaṣīda*, traditional poets include many direct as well as indirect allusions to al-Andalus. Among them we find Maḥmūd Sāmī al-Bārūdī (1839-1904), Aḥmad Shawqī (1868-1932), Ḥāfiz Ibrāhīm (1871-1932), Aḥmad Muḥarram (1878-1945), ʻAlī al-Jārim (1881-1949), Ismāʻīl Ṣabrī (1885-1923), Maʻrūf al-Ruṣāfī (1875-1945), Jamīl Ṣidqī al-Zahāwī (1863-1936), and Muḥammad Mahdī al-Jawāhirī (1900-1997). Al-Andalus's contribution, the neoclassical poets claimed, was not confined to the Arab civilization, but, in the words of Ḥāfiz Ibrāhīm "through it the world acquired the garb of civilization" (Ibrāhīm n.d., 1:99). Of significance is the tendency among the neoclassical poets to frequently engage in *mu'āraḍa*, or writing a poem for which rhyme, metre, and sometimes even the topic, are borrowed from a particularly well known classical, and in our case, Andalusian, poem (on the *mu'āraḍa*, see Nawfal 1983).

One of the prominent poets who frequently called up the image of al-Andalus in his poetry was Aḥmad Shawqī (1868-1932), the "prince of poets" [*amīr al-shuʻarā*] in the first quarter of the twentieth century. As a court poet closely associated with the Khedive of Egypt, ʻAbbās II, he was given the title of "bey." When, at the start of World War I, the British ousted ʻAbbās II and prevented him from returning to Egypt from Istanbul, Shawqī remained loyal to the Khedive. Following a poem he wrote in honor of the deposed ruler, he was himself exiled from Egypt in 1915. Shawqī preferred to go to Spain, where he stayed until 1920. During his Andalusian exile Shawqī spent much of his time visiting the great ancient Arab monuments and reading the works of famous Andalusian writers. Especially remarkable was the influence on him of *Nafḥ al-Ṭīb fī Ghuṣn al-Andalus al-Raṭīb* [The breath of perfume on the fresh branch of al-Andalus] by the Moroccan man of letters al-Maqqarī (1591-1632), which many regard as the source for all subsequent works on Andalusian music (al-Maqqarī 1968; al-Makkari 1967).

While in Spain, Shawqī wrote a series of poems in which he commemorated the glories of the Andalusian Arab civilization and described its enduring heritage.[5] He gave these poems the collective title *Andalusiyyāt*. Among them is a *mu'āraḍa* of the well-known poem which the Andalusian poet Ibn Zaydūn (born in Córdoba in 1004, deceased in Seville in 1070) wrote to his beloved Wallāda after he had escaped from prison in Córdoba and was heading toward Seville. Ibn Zaydūn's poem opens with one of the better-known hemistichs in medieval Arabic poetry: *Aḍḥā al-Tanā'ī badīlan min tadānīnā* [The great distance between us replaced our intimate relationship] (Ibn Zaydūn 1958, 141-48). Aḥmad Shawqī's poem opens with the words, *Yā nā'iḥ al-ṭalḥ ashbāhun 'awādīnā* [O mourner of bad luck, our evil days are so similar] (Shawqī, n.d., 2:104-108). Ibn Zaydūn's influence on Shawqī's poetry is evident not only in form, but also in content. When the *Dīwān*, "anthology," of this medieval Andalusian poet first appeared in print, Shawqī published a poem praising Ibn Zaydūn's eloquent lines (Shawqī, n.d., 4:78-79; Boudot-

Lamotte 1977, 376). In *al-Riḥla ilā al-Andalus* [Journey to al-Andalus] (Shawqī, n.d. 2:44-52), Shawqī describes the great Andalusian sites by borrowing through techniques of *mu'ārada* from a famous poem by the classical poet al-Buḥturī (d. 897), about the ruins of Khosrau's palace.

Shawqī's poems became so well known that in a poem written on the eve of his return to Egypt from Spain, his compatriot, Ḥāfiz Ibrāhīm coined the term, "Andalusiyya Shawqiyya," that is, a poem containing an image of al-Andalus composed by Aḥmad Shawqī (Ibrāhīm n.d., 1:98-103). Subsequently, the term "Andalusiyya" was applied to poems by other poets as well and it now stands for the general use of Andalusian themes in Arabic poetry (e.g., al-Bur'ī 1978, 67-68).

While most of Shawqī's *Andalusiyyāt* describe the poet's longing for Egypt, his contemporary homeland, it was the rich heritage of al-Andalus that fired his creativity. When he describes the great Arab Andalusian remains, he finds in them proof that the ancient glory they evoke will be revived in the near future, so much so that the adjective "Andalusī" becomes synonymous with glorious: "Time would become Andalusian" (Shawqī, n.d., 1:242). This alludes to the splendor that al-Andalus's medieval culture and society connotes in the minds of modern Arabs. In this vein Shawqī imports the figure of the first Ummayad king in al-Andalus, 'Abd al-Raḥmān I (731-88), later called *al-Dākhil* [The Incomer], in his poem *Ṣaqr Quraysh* [The Hawk of Quraysh], which is the epithet of the Andalusian king (Shawqī, n.d., 2:171-78). Shawqī praises 'Abd el-Raḥmān al-Dākhil with the following words:

In the book of praises al-Dakhīl has a chapter
No one of the sons of the kings can enter into.

Significantly, Shawqī chose to write this poem in the form of a *muwashshaḥ*, a postclassical poetic form arranged in specifically rhymed stanzas, which flourished in medieval al-Andalus but never entered the overall Arabic poetic canon from there.[6] We can assume that this is Shawqī's way of showcasing the unique literary heritage of al-Andalus.

The image of al-Andalus in neoclassical Arabic poetry finds typifying expression in Ahmad Shawqī's Andalusian poems, abounding as these do in sensuous descriptions of the Muslim Spanish heritage. Shawqī's poems also use referential patterns that the poet consciously imported from medieval Andalusian poetry. Indeed, most neoclassical modes in Arabic poetry that refers to al-Andalus derive from ties of cultural memory to Iberian medieval contexts. The latter include the production and performance of Andalusian Arabic poetry, the composition and dissemination of medieval historical chronicles, as well as coeval and variously inspired, subsequent veneration for famous Andalusian sites such as those that inspired many modern poets. Some neoclassical poets even used remnants of the Andalusian past as rhetorical figures. A case in point can be seen in a poem by the Egyptian poet Isma'īl Sarā al-Dahshān (1882-1950), taken from his collection *Bayna al-Jidd wa-l-Jayyid* [Between seriousness and excellence] (al-Dahshān 1983, 107). In al-Dahshān's poem, instead of alluding to a medieval Andalusian theme, such as splendor or fortitude, *al-Ḥamrā'*, "the Alhambra," the Citadel of Granada, stands paradoxically for contemporary poverty, the inverse of grandeur, as captured in the word *kūkh*, "hovel," or "hut."

On the whole neoclassical Arabic poetry is backward-looking and evinces few attempts on the part of its composers to use the sensuous impressions generated by al-Andalus as vehicles for broaching new and complex realms of human experience. Such moves came about in the late 1940s, when poets began deviating from classical metrics, adopting *al-shi'r al-ḥurr*, "free verse," and thus breaking the patterns of ancient, heretofore sacrosanct Arabic poetic form.[7] Influenced by English poetry, the crux of Arabic free verse is a reliance on the free repetition of the basic unit of conventional prosody, that is, the use of an irregular number of single feet, "*taf'īla*," instead of on a fixed number of feet. This was innovation not just with regard to metrics—writers and literary critics from the center of the literary system claimed that the new poetry was not a superficial reflection of modern life, but a profound expression of the new age. The new aesthetic concept sprang from the heart of the literary work itself, which sought to explore the essence of life and to reflect the culture of the age on a universal basis. Now that changing perceptions had inspired new forms and techniques, poetic experiences were no longer limited to personal emotions.

These new forms were, in turn, seen as the only way in which Arabic poetry could be reivived and could move beyond neoclassical orientation toward direct importation of Andalusian images and their use in one-to-one contemporary/medieval analogies. Acceptance of these new forms was vital if poetry was to remain for the modern Arab world the vehicle of artistic and intellectual expression it had been in the past. Hence, the image of al-Andalus, together with the innovations which poets now incorporated, proved crucial in shaping the development of the new genre of poetry. It was descriptive al-Andalus which now served as a tool for gaining access; for enabling the new Arabic poetry to rediscover the actual cutting-edge dimensions within its own heritage. The employment of

Andalusian figures as literary masks, or as filters for cross-temporal and complexly human metaphors, created the so-called *qaṣīdat qinā'*, or mask poem. This has become a favorite artistic technique among modernist poets, especially since the late 1950s. In this mode the poet elaborates an artistic mask, which means that he quite literally assigns a medieval face (of a known historical persona) to a modern problematic, to reconcile "the mortal and the eternal, the finite and the infinite."[8] Thus, the modernist Syrian poet 'Alī Aḥmad Sa'īd, better known as Adūnīs (b. 1931), in his *Kitāb al-Taḥawwulāt wa-l-Hijra fī Aqālīm al-Nahār wa-l-Layl* [The book of changes and migration in the regions of night and day] (Adūnis 1965; 1988, 431-597) invokes the figure of 'Abd al-Raḥmān al Dākhil to express the contemporary human condition. However, Adūnīs makes no attempt to imitate the narrow correlative use which neoclassical Arabic poetry often made of the same historical persona:

The Hawk in his labyrinth, in his creative despair
Builds on the peak at the end of depths
Andalus of the depths
Andalus which is arising from Damascus
Bearing to the West the harvest of the East

For Adūnīs, *Ṣaqr Quraysh* [The Hawk of Quraysh], 'Abd al-Raḥmān al Dākhil, is one of the links in the chain of transmission through which the achievements of medieval Arab civilization reached the West.[9] Another such figure is that of the conqueror of al-Andalus, Ṭāriq b. Ziyād (d. 720), who has become popular in Palestinian poetry. For example, Mu'īn Bsīsū (1927-1984) uses it in both his poetry and his poetic drama. In his *Qaṣīda min Faṣl Wāhid*

[A poem with one chapter] Ṭāriq b. Ziyād is in prison (Bsīsū, *al-A'māl al-Shi'riyya al-Kāmila*, 1988, 331-32), and in Bsīsū's verse drama *Thawrat al-Zanj* [Revolution of the negroes], Ṭāriq is called to particpate in the *Jihād*, "Holy War," (Bsīsū, *al-A'māl al-Masraḥiyya*, 1988, 285).

In his poem *Ziryāb* (*al-Dustūr*, July 31, 1989, page 52; reprinted in al-Bayyātī 1995, 123-25), the Iraqi poet 'Abd al-Wahhāb al-Bayyātī (b. 1926) speaks through the character, or artistic mask, of the gifted Baghdadian musician 'Alī ibn Nāfi, also known as Ziryāb (d. 857). The latter's jealous teacher had driven him from the Baghdadi court of Hārūn al-Rashīd. Ziryāb subsequently reached the Cordoban court of 'Abd al-Raḥmān II in 822. He then introduced artistic innovations which the monarch and his entourage had not heard before, whereupon he became chief court musician (Shiloah 1995, 74-75). The figure of Ziryāb, as the musician who transplants himself with great success from the eastern end of the Islamic Empire to the western, is that which the contemporary Iraqi poet al-Bayyātī harnesses to represent a continuum of progress leading from the past through to the present and future, unifying "all man's experience throughout history . . . [and] proving the endless capacity of human experience for reproducing itself" (Jayyusi 1977, 745).

O Andalus of the unknown
What is hidden behind that voice?
Have the lovers returned from the journey?
Or is it warnings uttered by the fortune teller of fate?
Was Ziryāb her voice,
Her other voice and nightmare?

That one of the great contemporary Arab poets chose to avail himself of Ziryāb as an artistic mask through which to communicate his own emotional and intellectual aspirations is again testimony to the great cultural impact the Andalusian past has had on Arab culture. This does not mean that alongside this new technique, neoclassical techniques are no longer used by contemporary poets. For example, ʻAlī al-Ḥusaynī's poem *Sifr ʻAbd al-Raḥmān al Dākhil* [The book of ʻAbd al-Raḥmān al Dākhil] from the collection with the same title (al-Ḥusaynī 1980, 107-14) reflects in clear neoclassical style the longing of contemporary Arabs to see the ancient glory of the past revived through the medieval figure of ʻAbd al-Raḥmān al Dākhil:

> You are the Arab man coming in East and West
> And you are the fire hidden among the people.
> (al-Ḥusaynī 1980, 114)

Likewise for the Israeli Palestinian poet Fārūq Mawāsī (b. 1941) the impressions that a visit to Spain left on him led to a long poem called *Andalusiyyāt* included in his colection, *al-Khurūj min al-Nahr* [The exodus from the river] (Mawāsī 1989, 51-79). Written in August 1987, the poem consists of seven parts which correspond to the stages of his visit: (1) "A Smell of Perfume"; (2) "Córdoba"; (3) "Seville"; (4) "Malaga"; (5) "Far from Gibraltar"; (6) "Alhambra"; (7) "All Over Again." Most poems that concentrate on the kind of sensuous employment of Andalusian sites evinced in Mawāsī's composition are usually written, again, as in this case, during or after contemporary visits to Spain.

In addition to their manifold use of historical Andalusian figures, contemporary modernist poets also incorporate Andalusian sites into their works, not to imbue them with sensuous external descriptions, but to again give voice to deeper, more inner experiences. In the last collection he published, *Kitāb al-Marāthī* [The book of elegies], al-Bayyātī, for example, who spent many years in Spain, when he was exiled from Iraq, includes a poem entitled *al-Dukhūl ilā Ghranāṭa* [Entering Granada] (al-Bayyātī 1995, 99-104). In this poem an emotional attachment to the streets of that Andalusian city moves beyond the sensual into the realm of myth:

> I did not enter Granada, but I was a ghost there
> Wandering in Alhambra
> Listening to the weeping water
> And the wailing roots of the trees
> Climbing the towers of the destroyed walls
> What did the fortune teller say?
> You will never enter Granada
>
> Here I am falling from high above the tower
> I am flying for some time
> I am entering Granada through all its gates

Granada, here, is no longer the actual Andalusian city. Rather, it has become a symbol of the longed-for utopian city which the poet realizes he will never enter during his earthly life. In this sense Granada is mentioned by many other poets for whom the distant past serves as a backdrop to their current emotional experiences (Shalḥat 1989, 51). It is therefore eminently understandable that for these contemporary Arab writers the legendary image of the Spanish poet and dramaturge Federico García Lorca (1898-1936), who gained posthumous fame with his murder by the Nationalists at the start of the Spanish civil war, should have become for them a powerful, major link connecting

Granada's past and its present. Lorca is frequently described by Arab authors as the son of Granada:

> Lorca, before anything else, is the son of the ancient Arab city of Granada, which once upon a time was one of the radiant cultural oases, that is, he is the son of al-Andalus. This is al-Andalus the myth, whose civilization and culture were created by the Arabs, especially since Lorca's poetry is so highly influenced by the Arabic writings of al-Andalus. (Rafīq al-Akhdar in *al-Sha'b* [May 15, 1986]: 4)

The figure and image of Lorca has captivated Arab poets not only because of his reputation as a revolutionary poet, or because he was the son of Granada, but especially because of the Arab "Andalusian" nature of so many of his poems. Aware of the close relationships between Lorca's poetry and Arabic poetry, in his arabesque *Casidas* and *Gracelas del Diván de Tamarit* (published in 1940), for example, some Arab poets even detect links between Lorca and Andalusian Arab culture.[10] In fact the hold Lorca has had on the minds of poets in the Arab world, over the past decades, has turned him into a symbol for their struggle of freedom and justice, as in the case of the Egyptian poet Ṣalāḥ'Abd al-Ṣabūr (1931-1981) in his poem *Lorca*:[11]

> Lorca
> Is a fountain in the square
> A shelter and resting place for the poor children
> Lorca is gypsies' songs
> Lorca is a golden sun
> Lorca is a tender summer's night
> Lorca is a woman bearing twins

Lorca is a white lily
Rinsing her cheeks in water
Lorca is bells of domes
Dwelling in the midst of the fog
Near the lone star
Sometimes singing, sometimes sighing
Lorca is the green palm of the feast day
Lorca is sweet candy
Lorca is a heart filled with pure light
(ʻAbd al-Ṣabūr 1972, 228-30)

The Lebanese Druze poet Fu'ād al-Khashin (b. 1925) concludes his *Qamar Ghranāṭa wa-l-Haras al-Aswad* [Granada's moon and the black patrol] (al-Khashin 1972, 155-57: see also 213-16) with the following lines:

Who silenced the poet's voice
With treacherous nightly bullets
O Lorca the adored features
O soul, the clearest of mirrors
Vanished from the lands of al-Andalus

In a poem entitled *Layālī Ghranāṭa* [Granada's nights], the Egyptian poet Faṭhī Sa'īd says:

Lorca's fountain in the square
Is weeping of the poet and laughs at the corners
Its [water] scattering about as an Arabic letter
As Andalusian metre
Lorca exists in my Arab blood even if he belongs to Spain
(*al-Ahrām*, January 21, 1983: 11)

In his collection *Andalusiyyāt Miṣriyya* [Egyptian *Andalusiyyāt*], Sa'īd published the same poem under a new title, *Ḥānat Lorca* [Lorca's tavern], together with several textual changes (Sa'īd 1994, 47-50). This anthology also includes other poems that recall al-Andalus and connect it with the Arab present and the poet's own experiences. For example, in *Layl Ghranāṭa* [Granada's night], he describes the latter as:

Breaking into tears
Flowing like speckled sneak
Into my blood
. . . .
Granada's river
A line uttered by the writer of *al-Iḥāṭa*[12]
Water streams on its green pastures
Braids on its silent domes
Covering part of its nakedness.

(Sa'īd 1994, 39-40)

For Palestinian writers, and especially poets, Lorca has become a catalyst, triggering widespread use of al-Andalus as a metaphor for lost paradise. As a mythical figure, Lorca has inspired them to search the rich Andalusian Arabic heritage for connections between past and present that could serve as links in the cross-temporal and contextual chain asserted in and by their own collective and cultural memory. The glory of the Andalusian past and the fame of the modern Spanish poet, as products of the same spatial context, have made the mythologization of Lorca almost self-explanatory. For example, after he visited Spain Samīḥ al-Qāsim (b. 1939), one of the most important Palestinian poets of our day, wrote a poem entitled *Laylan, 'alā Bāb Federico* [At night, at Federico's door].[13] The poem does not allude directly to al-Andalus at any point, but rather to a sense of the splendor that was Arab Andalusia, such that the atmosphere that pervades several ages of Andalusian Arabic poetry hovers unmistakenly over al-Qāsim's lines:

Federico
The guard turned off his flashlight
Come down
I am waiting in the square

Fede—ri—co
The lamp of sadness is a moon
The fear is trees
Come down
I know, You are hiding in the house
Gripped with fever

Burning with death
Come down
I am waiting in the square
Burning with the flame of the rose
My heart is an apple

A rooster calls on a tiled roof
Federico
The star is a wound
And the blood is screaming on the strings
And the guitar is aflame

Fede—ri—co
The black patrol threw its weapons in the well
Come down to the square
I know, You are hiding between the wings of an angel
I see you

A lily behind a curtain
And between your lips trembles a butterfly
And your hands caress the hair of the night
Come down, Federico
And open the door for me
Quickly
I am waiting on the doorstep
Quickly

At the street corner
The din of an approaching militia
The clatter of rifles
And the clanging of lances
Open the door for me
Quickly
Hide me
Federico
Fede—ri—co!

Moon, trees, rose, apple, strings of a guitar, lily, butterfly; all of these allude to earlier Andalusian nature poetry, while black patrol, weapons, militia, rifles, and lances all allude to the powers of darkness responsible for "that crime in Granada" (Machado 1973, 252-53). Death reigns in the poem's image of Lorca: he is hiding "between the wings of an angel", a butterfly trembles between his lips; his soul is about to quit his body (cf. al-Bayyātī 1979, II, 258-61).

The literary annals of the history of the Palestinian people, especially after their defeat and the establishment of the State of Israel in 1948, evidence a wide range of neoclassical and modernist techniques that incorporate al-Andalus. These are in addition to, and apart from the image of Lorca and the special connective agency with which he is endowed. For this reason one of the first comprehensive studies of the presence of al-Andalus in modern Arabic poetry concentrates solely on Palestinian literature.[14] For Maḥmūd Darwīsh, the main Andalusian sites (Córdoba, Granada, Toledo, and Seville) are icons that stand for experiences that continue to play themselves out beyond the historical, external meanings, or the sensuous dimensions of these places. In a poem entitled *Idhā Kāna Lī an U'īda al-Bidāya* [If I were to start all over again], he says:

> If I could but start all over again I'd choose what I have chosen now: the roses on the fence
> I'd travel again on the road that may or may not lead to Córdoba.
> I'd hang my shadow on two rocks for fugitive birds to build a nest on my shadow's branch
> I'd break my shadow to follow the scent of almonds as it wafts on a cloud of dust
> And feel tired at the foot of the mountain; come and listen to me. Have some of my bread
> Drink from my wine and do not leave me on the road of years on my own like a tired willow tree
> I love the country that's never felt the tread of departure's song, nor borrowed to blood or woman.
> I love women who in their desire conceal the suicide of horses dying on the threshold.
> I will return, if I can, to my roses, to my steps
> But I will never go back to Córdoba
>
> (Darwīsh, *Ward Aqall*, 1987, 9; translation is based on al-Udhari 1984, 23)

Again, Córdoba as the famous center of Andalusian learning and culture, is not just the historical Andalusian city, but a vehicle for the "Palestinian" experience of the 1980s, signifying the lost Palestinian paradise, or even Jerusalem, as the Palestinian critic Muḥammad ʻAbd Allāh al-Juʻaydī says: "If the circumstances prevented the poet from reaching Jerusalem, and he was forced to go to Córdoba, the idea is that his journey stopped on the boundaries of his creative work and that it remains a dream with no chance of ever being fulfilled" (al-Juʻaydī 1997, 9).

Córdoba, like other Andalusian sites, appears in Darwīsh's poetry on the same level as "tears, dance, and the long embrace of a woman. Al-Andalus is a universal aesthetic and artistic property, whereas Jerusalem is an aesthetic, spiritual, and juristic property" (al-Juʻaydī 1997, 25). In Psalm 16 from his *Mazāmīr* [Psalms] (Darwīsh 1988, 396-97), Darwīsh says:

I flirt with time
As a prince caresses a horse
And I play with the days
As children play with colored beads.

Today I celebrate
The passing of a day on the previous one
And tomorrow I shall celebrate
The passing of two days on yesterday
I drink the toast of yesterday
In remembrance of the day to come
And thus I carry on my life!

When I fell from my indomitable horse
I broke an arm

My finger, wounded a thousand years ago,
Caused me pain!

When I commemorated the passing of forty days on the city of Acre,
I burst out weeping for Granada
And when the rope of the gallows tightened around my neck
I felt a deep hatred for my enemies
Because they stole my tie.

(translation following Darwīsh 1989, 50)

This poem is about the attention modern Arabs pay to marginal matters while neglecting the essence, as illustrated by Acre of the East (on the northern coast of Israel/Palestine) and Granada of the West. The most prominent motive in Darwīsh's poetry, as in the entire corpus of modern Palestinian poetry in general, and the one that is specifically in evidence in works composed between the 1982 Lebanon War and the outbreak of the *intifāḍa* in the West Bank and the Gaza Strip in December 1987 is the use of al-Andalus as a mirror for Palestine. The despair and frustration that formed the psychological background for the outbreak of the *intifāḍa* have been deeply etched into the poetry and writings of Maḥmūd Darwīsh, whose own fate may equally be seen as a metaphor for the Palestinian tragedy.

Darwīsh's series of poems entitled *Aḥada 'Ashara Kawkaban 'ala Ākhir al-Mashhad al-Andalusī* [Eleven stars on the end of the Andalusian scene], from the collection *Aḥada 'Ashara Kawkaban* [Eleven stars] is one long repetition of the equation al-Andalus equals Palestine, equals Paradise Lost. The general title illustrates the tragedy which the eclipse of the Arab Andalusian scene represents in the overall history of the Arabs, within global history. Significantly, Darwīsh published this anthology in 1992, that is, five hundred years after the end of Arab rule in al-Andalus. It was on the second of January, 1492, that the combined armies of Castile and Aragon captured the city of Granada. Afterward followed a royal edict that decreed the expulsion of all non-Catholics from the Peninsula. Darwīsh sees himself as one of the last kings in the Andalusian era; the fourth "star poem" is called *Anā Wāḥid min Mulūk al-Nihāya* [I am one of the kings of the end]:

> And I am one of the Kings of the end, jumping from
> My horse in the last fall, I am the last Arabs' sigh
> . . . .
> There is no present remaining for me
> So I could pass near my past. Castile is raising her
> Crown over Allāh's minaret. I am hearing the rattling of keys in
> The door of our golden history, good-bye our history, will it be me
> Who will close the last gate of heaven? I am the last Arabs' sigh
>
> (Darwīsh 1992, 15-16)

As against the glory of the past which elicits the image of al-Andalus in the present, the only remaining hope is survival (Darwīsh, *Dhākira li-l-Nisyān*, 1987, 45), but, as the poet describes in an earlier collection, there will be harder days ahead:

> There will be blacker night. There will be fewer and fewer roses
> The trail will split even more than we have seen till now, the plains will be sundered

The foot of the mountains will heave upon us, a wound will break down over us, families will be scattered
The slaughtered among us will slaughter the slaughtered, to forget the slaughtereds' eyes, and to erase memory
We will know more than we knew, we will reach an abyss beyond the abysses, when we rise above
A thought which the tribes worshipped, then roasted on the flesh of its originators, when they had grown fewer
We will see among us emperors etching their names in wheat in order to refer to ourselves.
Haven't we changed? Men who slaughter with faith in their daggers, and increasing sand
Women with faith in what they have between their legs, and a shadow to lessen shadows
Still, I will follow the poems, even if I have fewer and fewer roses.

(Darwīsh, *Ward Aqall*, 1987, 45)

In the poem *al-Kamanjāt* [Violins], memory of the lost paradise also becomes that of the lost territory of love:

Violins are weeping seeing the gypsies coming to al-Andalus
Violins are weeping over the Arabs leaving al-Andalus

Violins are weeping over lost time which will never come back
Violins are weeping over a homeland that could return

Violins are burning the forests of that very far darkness
Violins are causing knives to bleed and smelling my blood in the veins

Violins are weeping seeing the gypsies coming to al-Andalus
Violins are weeping over the Arabs leaving al-Andalus

Violins are horses on the string of a mirage, and weeping water
Violins are a field of wild lilacs to-ing and fro-ing

Violins are a wild animal tortured by a woman's fingernail
Violins are an army building a cemetery of marble and music

Violins are a chaos of hearts maddened by the wind blowing at the dancer's foot
Violins are groups of birds escaping the missed flag

Violins are the complaint of the curled silk during the beloved night
Violins are the voice of distant wine on a former desire

Violins are walking after me, here and there, to take revenge on me
Violins are looking for me to kill me, wherever they can find me

Violins are weeping over the Arabs leaving al-Andalus
Violins are weeping seeing the gypsies coming to al-Andalus.

In another poem, Darwīsh asks a friend to "tear the arteries of my ancient heart with the poem of the gypsies who are going to al-Andalus/ and sing to my departure from the sands and the ancient poets" (Darwish 1985, 23).

Before concluding it is necessary to cast a wider net and to mention that al-Andalus was, of course, a temporal and spatial territory shared by Muslims, Christians, and Jews; one generally characterized by cooperation. Given a political reality in which one culture seeks to maintain its dominance over the other, this tripartite image of al-Andalus rarely occurs in modern Arabic poetry. Here and there we can find Arabic allusions to Muslim-Christian cooperation, such as those penned by the Egyptian poet Fārūq Shūsha, who, after participating in the second Muslim-Christian Conference in Córdoba in March 1977, wrote a poem entitled *God's Sun in Córdoba* (Shūsha 1980, 129-35). The poem complements the ancient glory of the Arabs in al-Andalus with sensuous descriptions of the Arab monuments, in order to illuminate a new path on which Muslims and Christians might embark:

On this road Jesus and Muḥammad are planting stars
in the hearts
They are embracing each other . . .

Al-Andalus also appears in the works of Jewish authors writing in Arabic (e.g., Sha'shū' 1979), as a radiant image of tripartite religious coexistence. Here we can find allusions to the famous line of the Andalusian Ṣūfī, "mystic," Muḥyī al-Dīn ibn al-'Arabī (1164-1240) in *Tarjūmān al-Ashwāq* [The translator of desires]:

My heart is capable of every form,
A pasture for gazelles, and a cloister for monks,
A place for idols, and the pilgrim's *Ka'ba*,
The Tables of the Torah, and the Koran

Love is the faith I hold wherever turn its camels,
Love is my belief and faith.[15]

(Ibn al-'Arabī 1996, 43-44)

These famous lines, which express above all the oneness of mystical experience in all religions, have evoked further interpretations, also characterized by "the 'tolerance' of the mystic" (Schimmel 1982, 38). Jewish writers in Arabic as well as Arab Israeli poets who have gone through the Israeli formal education system, all regard these images as calling for cooperation between the three monotheistic religions.[16]

As an overall desire, in and between the lines of Arabic poetry that allude to al-Andalus, we find the hope that one day, in the not too distant future, there will emerge in the West an eminent intellectual figure who, like Alvaro of Andalusian Córdoba, will be able to say that many of his friends

> . . . read the poetry and tales of the Arabs [and] study the writings of Muhammadan theologians and philosophers, not in order to refute them, but to learn how to express themselves in Arabic with greater correctness and elegance . . . [and a day when] All the young Christians noted for their gifts [will] know . . . the language and literature of the Arabs, [will] read and study with zeal Arabic books, building up great libraries of them at enourmous cost and loudly proclaiming everywhere that this literature is worthy of admiration. (Lewis 1970, 123)

In sum, al-Andalus survives in Arab living memory to this day. In North Africa, there are many descendants of Arab exiles from medieval Spain who still "bear Andalusian names and keep the keys of their houses in Córdoba and

Seville hanging on their walls in Marrakesh and in Casablanca" (Lewis 1970, 130). Alongside such "physical" memories, Arab national consciousness preserves memories that are of a cultural, spiritual, and intellectual nature. In this essay I have tried to show how the use and remembrance of al-Andalus in Arabic poetry can be tellingly examined by placing it within a developmental historical context. For the Arab poet the image of al-Andalus has long resonated along two intertwined tracks, and continues to do so. The first of these tracks is spatial; extending from the modern Arab world into specific geographic regions of Spain. The second track is temporal; reaching from a painful present to a medieval golden age. The Andalusian theme has expressed itself in many guises, including direct allusions to al-Andalus as the glory and splendor of the Arab past, images of al-Andalus as the lost paradise, and representations of medieval sites. The latter have been, and still are, tapped to create sensuous impressions and to broach, in tandem, a range of complicated human experiences. This function has also been filled by several medieval Andalusian figures, while in the second half of this century the contemporary Spanish poet Federico García Lorca has gained eminence in the inherently understandable role of catalyst and connector, linking the Andalusian past with the Arab present and future.

Notes

1. I thank my friend Dick Bruggman for his numerous insightful suggestions for improvement of both content and presentation.

2. This saying can be found in many different guises in various works dealing with ancient Arabic poetry (e.g., al-Suyūṭī, n.d., 2:470; Lyall 1930, xv).

3. For exceptions, see, for example, the novels *Fath al-Andalus aw Ṭāriq b. Ziyād* [The occupation of al-Andalus or Ṭāriq ibn. Ziyād] and *'Abd al-Raḥmān al-Nāṣir* by Jurjī Zaydān (1861-1914) (Zaydān 1905; Zaydān 1910). Also see the plays *Fatḥ al-Andalus* by Muṣṭāfā Kāmil (1874-1908) (on this play, see Najm 1956, 310-14) and *Amīrat al-Andalus* (al-Andalus's Princess) by Aḥmad Shawqī (Shawqī 1932; on the play, see Boudot-Lamotte 1977, 296-302). An interesting employment of the figure of 'Abd al-Raḥmān al-Dākhil is found in the play *al-Muharrij* by the Syrian poet and dramatist Muḥammad al-Māghūṭ (b. 1934) (al-al-Māghūṭ 1981, 495-614). We also find images of al-Andalus in Arab comic strips (e.g., Douglas and Malti-Douglas 1994, 143-49). On the limited presence of al-Andalus in Palestinian prose, see al-Ju'aydī 1997, 2.

4. On the neoclassical trend in Arabic poetry, see Moreh 1973, 155-79; Badawi 1975, 14-67; Moreh 1976, 1-2; Boudot-Lamotte 1977; Jayyusi 1977, 46-54; Brugman 1984, 26-56; Somekh 1992, 36-81, 491-94.

5. On Shawqī's exile and the poetry he wrote in Spain, see Mandūr 1971, 60-65; Badawi 1975, 29; and Boudot-Lamotte 1977, 53-64. On the poet's attitude toward al-Andalus before and after his exile, as well as on the circumstances that led to his writing these poems, see al-Miṣrī 1994, 85-193.

6. The noncanonical status of the *muwashshaḥ* is illustrated by the fact that by the mid-twelfth century knowledge of early *muwashshaḥāt* had already disappeared (Ibn Bassām 1979, 1:469. See also Jones 1988, 11-13, and Abu-Haidar 1991, 115-16). Moreover, it was not customary to include *muwashshaḥāt* in literary or historical works of higher regard (al-Marrākushī 1963, 146. See also 'Abbās 1985, 217-18). The noncanonical status of the *muwashshah* should be viewed in the framework of the canonical status of Arabic literature in the East which Andalusians themselves saw as the model of excellence. Ibn Hazm (994-1064) illustrates this attitude when he writes, "I am the sun shining in the spheres of sciences,/but my shortcoming is that I rise in the West" ('Abbās 1969, 321. See also Nykl 1946, 102). We can also learn about the noncanonical status of the *muwashshaḥāt* from the popular models (whether Eastern, according to M. Hartmann, or Spanish, according to García Gómez) which inspired the Andalusian poets that composed them (see Kennedy 1991, 68-69; Monroe 1974, 30-33). Monroe considers the *muwashshaḥ* the daughter of the noncanonical genre of the *zajal* (Monroe 1993, 413). On the close relationship between these two genres, see Einbinder 1995, 252-70. On the intimate association of the *muwashshaḥāt* with Arab folk music, see Shiloah 1995, 77. On the *muwashshaḥāt* in general, see also Stern 1974.

7. On the issue of terminology regarding the "free verse," see al-Tami 1993, 185-98.

8. Al-Bayyātī 1968, 134; see also Badawi 1975, 214.

9. See al-Qāsim 1986, 481-82. On the use of the figure 'Abd al-Raḥmān al-Dākhil in Palestinian poetry, see also al-Ju'aydī 1997, 6-12.

10. For example, the Iraqi poet Buland al-Ḥaydarī (1926-1996) in his essay in *al-Majalla* (London) September 19, 1989, page 75.

11. For other poems using the image of Lorca, see al-Bayyātī 1979, 1: 605-09; 2:225-27, 249-51, 258-61, 332-37, 344-54; 3:221-42, 321-27, 331-40, 407-19; al-Sayyāb 1971, 1:333-34, 355-58. See also Moreh 1976, 268; Badawi 1975, 210, 224, 250, 262; Jayyusi 1977, 565, 577, 691-92, 749; Shukrī 1978, 49, 149; 'Abd al-Azīz 1983, 271-99; Badīr 1982, 129, 177; 'Abd al-Ṣabūr n.d., 167-75.

12. The allusion is to *al-Iḥāṭa fī Akhbār Ghranāta* [The comprehension of the news of Granada] by Lisān al-Din ibn al-Khaṭīb (1313-1374), a historical lexicon including biographies of famous men of Granada.

13. Al-Qāsim 1986, 49-53. On this poem see also the interpretation of Fārūq Mawāsī in *al-Ittiḥād*, January 5, 1996, 20-23. Cf. the poem *Lorca* by Maḥmūd Darwīsh (Darwīsh 1988, 68-70).

14. Muhammad 'Abd Allāh al-Ju'aydī *Ḥudūr al-Andalus fī al-Adab al-Filasṭīnī al-Ḥadīth* [The presence of al-Andalus in modern Palestinian literature], paper presented during the International Conference on Palestinian Literature, Birzeit University, 17-19 May 17-19, 1997. The author is professor of Arabic Studies at the Universidad Autónoma de Madrid (for this essay I have used the text that was distributed to the participants during the conference [al-Ju'aydī 1997]).

15. The translation is according to Schimmel 1982, 38-39, with some corrections.

16. See, for example, *Mifgash* 3 (May 1968): 287; Khalīl 1967, 75-76.

Works Cited

'Abbās, Iḥsān. *Ta'rīkh al-Adab al-Andalusī: 'Aṣr Siyādat Qurṭuba*. Beirut: Dār al-Thaqāfa, 1969.

_____. *Ta'rīkh al-Adab al-Andalusī: 'Aṣr al-Ṭawā'if wa-l-Murābiṭīn*. Beirut: Dār al-Thaqāfa, 1985.

'Abd al-'Azīz, Ahmad. "Athar Federico García Lorca fī al-Adab al-'Arabī al-Mu'āsīr", *Fuṣūl* 3, no. 4 (July—August—September 1983): 271-99.

'Abd al-Ṣabūr, Ṣalāḥ. *Dīwān*. Beirut: Dār al-'Awda, 1972.

_____. *Madīnat al-'Ishq wa-l-Ḥikma*. Beirut: Iqra', n.d.

Abu-Haidar, Jareer. "The *Muwashshaḥāt* in the Light of the Literary Life that Produced Them." In Alan Jones and Richard Hitchcock, eds., *Studies on the Muwashshaḥ and the Kharja*, 115-22. Reading: Ithaca Press, 1991.

Adūnīs ('Alī Aḥmad Sa'īd). *Kitāb al-Taḥawwulāt wa-l-Hijra fī Aqālīm al-Nahār wa-l-Layl*. Beirut: al-Maktaba al-'Asriyya, 1965.

_____. *al-A'māl al-Shi'riyya al-Kāmila*. Beirut: Dār al-Ādāb, 1988.

al-Akhdar, Rafīq. "Lorca fī al-Dhikrā al-Khamsīn li-Mawtihi." *al-Sha'b*, 15 May 1986: 4.

Badawi, M.M. *A Critical Introduction to Modern Arabic Poetry*. Cambridge: Cambridge UP, 1975.

Badīr, Ḥilmī. *al-Mu'aththirāt al-Ajnabiyya fī al-Adab al-'Arabī al-Ḥadīth*. Cairo: Dār al-Ma'ārif, 1982.

al-Bayyātī, 'Abd al-Wahhāb. *Tajribatī al-Shi'riyya*. Beirut: Manshūrāt Nizār Qabbānī, 1968.

_____. *Dīwān*. Beirut: Vols. 1, 2, 3. Dār al-'Awda, 1979.

_____. *Kitāb al-Marāhtī*. Beirut: al-Mu'assasa al-'Arabiyya li-l-Dirāsāt wa-l-Nashr and Amman: Dār al-Fāris li-l-Nashr wa-l-Tawzī', 1995.

Boudot-Lamotte, Antoine. *Aḥmad Shawqī L'Homme et L'Oeuvre*. Damas: Institut Français de Damas, 1977.

Bsīsū, Mu'īn. *al-A'māl al-Masraḥiyya*. Acre: Dār al-Aswār, 1988.

_____. *al-A'māl al-Shi'riyya al-Kāmila*. Acre: Dār al-Aswār, 1988.

Brugman, J. *An Introduction to the History of Modern Arabic Literature in Egypt*. Leiden: Brill, 1984.

al-Bur'ī, Muḥammad. *'Awdat al-Ams*. Cairo: Dār al-Fikr al-'Arabi, 1978.

al-Dahshān, Isma'īl Sarā. *Bayna al-Jidd wa-l-Jayyid*. Cairo: al-Hay'a al-Miṣriyya al-'Āmma li-l-Kitāb, 1983.

Darwish, Mahmoud. *The Music of Human Flesh*. Trans. Denys Johnson-Davies. London: Heinemann, and Washington D.C.: Three Continents Press, 1989.

Darwīsh, Maḥmūd. *Ḥiṣār li-Madā'iḥ al-Baḥr*. Beirut: Dār al-'Awda, 1985.

_____. *Dhākira li-l-Nisyān*. Acre: Dār al-Aswār 1987.

_____. *Ward Aqall*. Acre: Dār al-Aswār, 1987.

_____. *Dīwān*. Acre: Dār al-Aswār, 1988.

_____. *Aḥada 'Ashara Kawkaban*. Beirut: Dār al-Jadīd, 1992.

Darwīsh, Maḥmūd, and Samīḥ al-Qāsim. *al-Rasā'il*. Haifa: Dār Arabesque, 1990.

Douglas, Allen, and Fedwa Malti-Douglas. *Arabic Comic Strips: Politics of an Emerging Mass Culture*. Bloomington and Indianapolis: Indiana UP, 1994.

Einbinder, Susan. "The *Muwashshaḥ*-Like *Zajal*: A New Source for the Hebrew Poem." *Medieval Encounters*, nos. 1-2 (1995): 252-70.

al-Ḥusaynī, 'Alī. *Sifr 'Abd al-Raḥmān al-Dākhil*. Baghdad: Dār al-Ḥurriyya, 1980.

Ibn al-'Arabī, Muḥyī al-Dīn. *Tarjumān al-Ashwāq*. Beirut: Dār Ṣādir, 1996.

Ibn Bassām, Abū al-Ḥasan 'Alī. *al-Dhākhīra fī Maḥāsin Ahl al-Jazīra*. Ed. Iḥsān 'Abbās. Vol. 1. Beirut: Dār al Thaqāfa, 1979.

Ibn al-Khaṭīb, Lisān al-Dīn. *al-Iḥāṭa fī Akhbār Ghranāṭa*. Cairo: n. p., 1901.

Ibn Zaydūn. *Dīwān Ibn Zaydūn wa-Rasā'iluhu*. Ed. 'Alī 'Abd al-'Aẓīm. Cairo: Maktabat Nahdat Misr, 1958.

Ibrāhīm, Ḥāfiẓ. *Dīwān*. Vol. 1. Beirut: Dār al-'Awda, n.d.

Jayyusi, Salma Khadra. *Trends and Movements in Modern Arabic Poetry*. Leiden: Brill, 1977.

Jones, Alan. *Romance Kharjas in Andalusian Arabic Muwashshaḥ Poetry*. London: Ithaca Press, 1988.

al-Ju'aydī Muḥammad 'Abd Allāh. *Ḥuḍūr al-Andalus fī al-Adab al Filasṭīnī al-Ḥadīth*. International Conference on Palestinian Literature, Birzeit University, May 17-19, 1997.

Kennedy, Philip F. "Thematic Relationships between the *Kharjas*, the Corpus of *Muwashshaḥāt* and Eastern Lyrical Poetry." In Alan Jones and Richard Hitchcock eds., *Studies on the Muwashshaḥ and the Kharja*, 68-87. Reading: Ithaca Press, 1991.

Khalīl, Jūrj Najīb. *al-Shi'r al-'Arabī fī Khidmat al-Salām*. Tel Aviv: Dār al-Nashr al-'Arabī, 1967.

al-Khashin, Fu'ād. *Sanābil Ḥazīrān*. Cairo: Dār al-Ma'ārif, 1972.

Lewis, Bernard. *The Arabs in History*. London: Hutchinson, 1970.

Lyall, Charles James, ed. *Translation of Ancient Arabian Poetry*. London: Williams and Norgate, 1930.

Machado, Antonio. *Poesías*. Buenos Aires: n.p., 1973.

al-Māghūṭ, Muḥammad. *al-Āthār al-Kāmila*. Beirut: Dār al-'Awda, 1981.

al-Makkari. *Analectes sur l'Histoire et la Littérature des Arabes d'Espagne*. (Published by M.M. Dozy, G. Dugat, L.Krehl, and W. Wright). Amsterdam: Oriental Press, 1967.

Mandūr, Muḥammad. *A'lām al-Shi'r al-'Arabī al-Ḥadīth*. Beirut: Manshūrāt al-Maktab al-Tijārī li-l-Ṭibā'a wa-l-Nashr wa-l-Tawzī', 1971.

al-Maqqarī, Aḥmad b. Muḥammad. *Nafḥ al-Ṭīb fī Ghuṣn al-Andalus al Raṭīb*. Ed. Iḥsān 'Abbās. Beirut: Dār Ṣādir, 1968.

al-Marrākushī, 'Abd al-Wāḥid. *al-Mu'jib fī Talkhīṣ Akhbār al-Maghrib*. Ed., Muḥammad Sa'īd al-'Iryān. Cairo: Lajnat Iḥyā' al-Turāth al-Islāmī, 1963.

Mawāsī, Fārūq. *al-Khurūj min al-Nahr*. Kafr Qara': Dār al-Shafaq, 1989.

al-Miṣrī, Ḥusayn Mujīb. *al-Andalus bayna Shawqī wa-Iqbāl*. Aleppo: Dār al-Wa'y, 1994.

Monroe, James T. *Hispano-Arabic Poetry*. Berkeley: U of California P, 1974.

_____. "*Zajal* and *Muwashshaḥa* Hispano-Arabic Poetry and the Romance Tradition." In Salma Khadra Jayyusi ed., *The Legacy of Muslim Spain*, 398-419. Leiden: E.J. Brill, 1992.

Moreh, Shmuel. "The Neoclassical *Qaṣīda*: Modern Poets and Critics." In Gustave E. von Grunebaum, ed., *Arabic Poetry: Theory and Development*, 155-79. Wiesbaden: Harrassowitz, 1973.

_____. *Modern Arabic Poetry 1800-1979*. Leiden: Brill, 1976.

Moreh, Shmuel, and M. 'Abbāsī. *Biographies and Bibliographies in Arabic Literature in Israel*. Shfaram: al-Mashriq, 1987.

Najm, Muḥammad, Yūsuf. *al-Masraḥiyya fī al-Adab al-'Arabī al Ḥadīth 1848-1914*. Beirut: Dār Bayrūt li-l-Ṭibā'a wa-l-Nashr, 1956.

Nawfal, Muḥammad Maḥmūd Qāsim. *Ta'rīkh al-Mu'āradāt fī al-Shi'r al-'Arabī.* Beirut: Mu'ssasat al-Risāla and Dār al-Furqān, 1983.
Nykl, A.R. *Hispano-Arabic Poetry and Its Relations with the Old Provençal Troubadours.* Baltimore: J.H. Furst Company, 1946.
al-Qasīm, Samīḥ. *Dīwān.* Beirut: Dār al-'Awda, 1971.
_____. *Persona Non Grata.* Dālyat al-Karmil: al'Imād, 1986.
Sa'īd, Fatḥī. *Andalusiyyāt Miṣriyya.* Cairo: al-Hay'a al-Miṣriyya al-'Āmma li-l-Kitāb, 1994.
Schimmel, Annemarie. *As Through a Veil: Mystical Poetry in Islam.* New York: Columbia UP, 1982.
Shalḥat Anṭwān. *Samīḥ al-Qāsim min al Ghaḍab al-Thawrī ilā al-Nubū'a al-Thawriyya.* Acre: Dār al-Aswār, 1989.
Sha'shū,'Salīm. *al-'Asr al Dhahabī: Safahāt min al-Ta'āwun al-Yahūdī al-'Arabī fī al-Andalus.* Tel Aviv: Dār al-Mashriq, 1979.
Shawqī, Aḥmad. *Amīrat al-Andalus.* Cairo: Dār al-Kutub al-Miṣriyya, 1932.
_____. *al-Shawqiyyāt.* Vols. 1, 2, 4. Cairo: n.p., n.d.
Shiloah, Amnon. *Music in the World of Islam: A Socio-Cultural Study.* Aldershot: Scholars Press, 1995.
Shukri, Ghālī. *Shi'runā al-Ḥadīth ilā ayn.* Beirut: al-Āfāq, 1978.
Shūsha, Fārūq. *Fī Iniṭẓār Mā Lā Yajī'.* Cairo: Madbūlī, 1980.
Somekh, Sasson. "The Neoclassical Arab Poets." In M.M. Badawi, ed., *Modern Arabic Literature,* 36-81, 491-94. Cambridge: Cambridge UP, 1992.
Stern, Samuel Miklos. *Hispano-Arabic Poetry.* Oxford: Clarendon Press, 1974.
al-Sayyāb, Badr Shākir. *Dīwān.* Vol. 1. Beirut: Dār al-'Awda, 1971.
al-Suyūṭī. *al-Muzhir fī 'Ulūm al-Lugha wa-Anwā'ihā.* Cairo: Dār Iḥyā' al-Kutub al-'Arabiyya, n.d.
al-Tami, Aḥmed. "Arabic 'Free Verse': The Problem of Terminology." *Journal of Arabic Literature,* no. 24 (1993): 185-98.
al-Udhari, Abdullah, ed. and trans. *Maḥmūd Darwīsh, Samih al-Qasim, Adonis.* London: Al Saqi Books, 1984.
Zaydān, Jurjī. *Fath al-Andalus aw Ṭāriq b. Ziyād.* Cairo: al-Hilāl, 1905.
_____. *'Abd al-Raḥmān al-Nāṣir.* Cairo: al-Hilāl, 1910-11.

◆ Chapter 10

American Sephardim, Memory, and the Representation of European Life

Jack Glazier

Introduction

The extensive historical and social scientific literature on American Jews devotes little attention to the formation and organization of the Sephardic communities that emerged in several American cities in the early years of the twentieth century. Scholarly concerns and conventional understandings about American Jewish communities have of course reflected the numerical preponderance of Ashkenazim. In the era of the great eastern and southern European immigration to the United States over the four decades prior to its statutory restriction in 1924, annual arrivals of Ashkenazic Jews usually numbered in the tens of thousands. The total Sephardic immigration from the Ottoman territories in the twenty years after its onset in the first decade of the century was approximately twenty-five thousand. Until recent years, a scholarly indifference to American Sephardim relegated them to little more than a footnote to twentieth-century American Jewish history.

The Sephardim were well established in the New World in the seventeenth and eighteenth centuries and indeed formed some of the first Jewish communities in what would become the United States. Famed for their wealth, influence, and achievement, these first American Sephardim ultimately faced a thoroughgoing assimilation into the wider society following extensive intermarriage with their Christian neighbors. Consequently, these early settlements bear no relationship to current American Sephardic communities. The latter derive exclusively from the immigration of Sephardic Jews leaving the Ottoman territories in the early part of the twentieth century in the wake of economic and political instability, particularly the Balkan wars.

In cultural terms the migration to America was costly, for it ruptured the generational continuity of Sephardic life. The largest Sephardic settlements formed up in New York, Los Angeles, Atlanta, and Seattle; smaller numbers of Sephardic newcomers established communities in such places as Indianapolis, Rochester, and Portland. While America promised economic opportunity and personal security, it also placed the fledgling Sephardic communities in an entirely new sociopolitical context that would quickly diminish their distinctiveness. At the same time, momentous linguistic shifts in the course of a generation substituted English for Ladino among the second generation. All of this insured that the Sephardic communities of the United States could not successfully reproduce themselves in the same way that they had managed to do for four centuries in the Ottoman territories. This does not suggest that the European Sephardic communities were in any way static; quite the contrary. They evolved over time, subject to the cultural influence of their Balkan neighbors. But the nature of the changes there were more steady and gradual, constrained in important ways by the self-governing nature of the Jewish communities and Ottoman policies that did not aim at the cultural absorption of minorities.

Focusing on historiographic and ideological issues shaping the portrayal of the European Jewish past, Marcus has called on historians to move beyond the "Sephardic mystique" emphasizing historical breaks such as the expulsion from Spain toward an emphasis on "the structures and continuities of Jewish communal experience" (1985, 36). But the historian or anthropologist examining American Jewish communities can hardly ignore the real historical discontinuities spawned by immigration and the uniqueness of the Jewish experience in America. Regardless of how the scholar may evaluate the significance of this experience, only the most naive could ignore the distinctive refiguration of Jewish lives American citizenship has made possible. American Jews have, in short, undergone a radical shift from obligation to choice—a transformation easily rivaling the most cherished hopes of the nineteenth-century German-Jewish intellectuals who did so much to promulgate the "Sephardic mystique." If we follow Marcus's advice and focus on Jewish communal experience in America, we can only be struck by the enormous historical cleavages between the Old World and the New. Whether American Judaism exemplifies a state of decline from its European past or else embodies new and vital forms of Jewish communal life in the most welcoming society Jews have experienced can only be decided by one's particular visions of Judaism as faith and culture. Still, it seems beyond dispute that, whatever one's interpretation, American Jewish life for both Sephardim and Ashkenazim is something very different from its European sources.

In the early years of their American settlement, immigrant Sephardim were a marginalized segment of Jewish life, owing both to their small numbers and to their cultural and linguistic singularity. Yet it was a marginality that would last little more than a generation. Outside the dominant Jewish world of Ashkenazic culture, the Sephardim spoke Ladino, or Judeo-Spanish, and differentiated themselves further from their Ashkenazic neighbors through cuisine, naming practices, and other customs that had reflected a history quite distinct from the eastern-European Jews. In time, assimilationist values in the early years of the century, the acculturative influence of public schools, and the allure of American culture profoundly transformed the character of American Jewry—Sephardic and Ashkenazic alike. Both traveled broadly similar, convergent routes to their current position at the end of the twentieth century.

As a cultural and linguistic minority amid the Ashkenazic majority, Sephardim were defined both by externally imposed constraints and by self-imposed barriers, especially in the years up to World War II. But over the past five decades, the cultural and institutional divisions between American Sephardim and Ashkenazim have steadily eroded as have the boundaries separating American Jewry from the broader currents of American life. The differences that do exist assume considerably less significance for the second generation and, especially, for their children and grandchildren than they did for the immigrant generation.

In this respect the story of American Sephardim and Ashkenazim replicates the experience of numbers of other European immigrants, despite the many claims of the last thirty years that the ethnic factor remains a powerful influence in the lives of the descendants of the great European immigration. Gans (1979), Steinberg (1981), and Alba (1990) particularly doubt claims that ethnicity is an important means for organizing social life in the contemporary United States. Instead, "symbolic ethnicity"—tenuous linkages to the old country and superficial expressions of ethnicity that are not at odds with middle-class American values and styles of life—represents a dominant feature of the cultural profile of European-derived groups in America (Gans 1979). Excepting the synagogue and its religious and educational focus, Elazar also points to Sephardic institutional decline: "Like contemporary Jewish communities everywhere, associational ties have replaced the organic ties of the past and organizational activity is now the landmark against which Jews measure their commitments" (1989, 180).

Some four generations removed from the immigration era and with only a small number of the immigrant generation remaining, American Sephardim increasingly find themselves with neither a personal experience of European Sephardic life nor the vicarious but still palpable connections to Balkan Jewish communities that immigrant parents and grandparents used to provide. Accordingly, this essay examines the relationship between American Sephardim and the very different European world from which they derive. This examination will focus particularly on how they represent their Balkan homes in the case of the immigrants or how their children portray old-country origins. Toward this end, it will be necessary first to consider the relationship between memory and history. Second, the fundamental problem of American Sephardic cultural continuity is examined in light of the extraordinary acculturative pressures exerted on the immigrant and second generation. Third, the discussion will focus on the

Sephardic community of Indianapolis, which is in many respects an exemplar of the problems of continuity in the open society. The basic dilemma of the Sephardim is a familiar one to other ethnic groups—how to maintain a distinctive cultural and religious identity when the larger society creates social conditions that diminish exclusiveness. Part of the effort to sustain a sense of distinctiveness is through narratives and other representations of the European past, thus investing shared memory with an unusual importance and poignancy amid the many changes coursing through the community.

History and Memory

The Sephardim in America constitute a "minority within a minority" (Lavender 1977). They are the proud heirs of Iberian Jewish culture, both in its fluorescence in Spain and Portugal in the centuries prior to the Spanish Inquisition and in its Diaspora formations in the eastern Mediterranean over the course of four hundred years under a generally benevolent Ottoman rule.

A Sephardic sense of superiority has long been reported and discussed. An early case in point is Isaac de Pinto, a Sephardi from Bordeaux, who responded to Voltaire's anti-Semitism. De Pinto carefully distinguished the Spanish and Portuguese Jews from all others, with whom, through "scrupulous fastidiousness," they would not marry nor even interact. These Jews "do not wear beards and do not affect any peculiarity in their dress, the well-off amongst them carry refinement, elegance and display in this respect as far as the other nations of Europe, from whom they differ only in their forms of worship" (quoted in Poliakov

1968, 4). Non-Jews also remarked about differences between the Ashkenazim and Sephardim, whom they preferred. Von Treitschke, the conservative German historian and no friend to Jewry, thus observed:

> The Israelites of the West and South belonged for the most part to the Spanish Jewish stock, who can look back on a comparatively proud history and who have always adapted to Western ways fairly easily. They have indeed become for the most part good Frenchmen, Englishmen, and Italians in so far as this can be expected of a people with such pure blood and such explicit characteristics. We Germans, however, have to deal with the Polish Jewish stock upon whom the scars of many hundreds of years of Christian tyranny have been deeply inscribed. For these people, the European and especially the German character, is much more foreign." (1987, 112) [author's translation]

Likewise, for a number of German-Jewish scholars of the nineteenth century, the Sephardic elite of Spain represented the apogee of medieval Jewish thought (Marcus 1985, 36). Schorsch identifies this view as the "Sephardic bias." It was a particularly compelling outlook for German-Jewish intellectuals, at once critical of the parochialism of medieval Ashkenazic Jewry and attracted to the accomplishments of the Spanish Jews, especially their success in living both as Jews and as cosmopolitans in a purportedly free society (1983, 436).

In contrast to the historical narratives and analyses of scholars, personal stories and representations of Old World life are a very different genre, both in form and purpose, although common themes may recur. Personal narratives give voice to memory and recreate a past cobbled together from family or community stories, anecdotes, folklore, and the like. Part reclamation and part identity construction, such efforts inevitably tell us at least as much about the present status of American Sephardic communities as they do about the European past. Within this framework, the question of the historical accuracy of such representations—what Lewis (1975, 11-13) designates as remembered or invented history as distinct from the recovered history of the scholar—is at best a matter of secondary importance, a way perhaps of gauging the verisimilitude of memory. What is remembered is often historically questionable and sometimes internally contradictory. While one can easily cast the cold light of historical criticism on the various consoling fictions residing in memory, there is a more important challenge. It is necessary to understand the processes through which the elements of personal and communal experience render memory a ceaselessly active, creative instrument rather than a timeless repository of historical knowledge as real and unchanging as so many objects in a traditional museum display.

Of course few actors representing the past would deny the accuracy of their sharpest personal remembrances or depictions of former times. They know what has happened in their lives. Historians, on the other hand, often discern a sharp break in the relationship between memory and formal, critical historiography. The latter, in the words of Yerushalmi, "continually recreates an ever more detailed past whose shapes and textures memory does not recognize" (1982, 94). Additionally, he tells us that the historian "constantly challenges even those memories that have survived intact" (1982, 94). The historian, in other words, regularly contests memory and the highly selective scheme on which it depends, seeking as he does to recover what has been "winnowed out, repressed or simply discarded by a process of natural selection, which the historian, uninvited, disturbs and reverses" (1982, 95).

What matters here, following Berger and Luckman is the relationship between experience and consciousness—the manner in which "experiences . . . become sedimented, that is, . . . congeal in recollection as recognizable and memorable entities" (1966, 67). Notwithstanding the valuable insights of these sociologists into the social construction of systems of knowledge, their notion of "congealing" recollections implies a fixity in tradition belied by a considerable volume of recent scholarship on invented pasts and related contemporary fabrications in the guise of timeless custom or tradition. Memory, in short, functions "not to preserve the past but to adapt it so as to enrich and manipulate the present" (Lowenthal 1985, 210). As the present itself really is but a moment in a succession of changing circumstances, memory, too, must be seen as equally dynamic in its adjustment to the flux of contemporary life.

The key to understanding memory and its multiple functions lies in comprehending the continually unfolding present, not simply in seeking a putatively objective but only partially retrievable past. In this unfolding process, troubled Sephardic relationships with Ashkenazim, sharp discontinuities between generations with an accompanying sense of cultural loss, and assimilation into a Jewish-American mainstream continually come into view. All combine to challenge Sephardim to shape a cultural self that can ameliorate the injuries of the recent past by glorifying the European experience, but without overtly challenging the wisdom of immigration. It is the latter which set in motion the many changes that have brought a secure, generally prosperous life for most, while deranging communal and personal identity.

Memory is thus much more than a recollection of what has transpired. A means of identity construction, it is both an embellishment and a reduction of events, the transformation of past into present as mediated by lived experience.

American Sephardim and the Problem of Cultural Continuity

The fate of Ladino in the United States offers a particularly telling index of acculturative change since the immigration period. To the considerable extent that language codifies a culture and expresses its fundamental categories and its most subtle and distinctive meanings, American Sephardic life has undergone a major refiguration. Simply put, the grip of ethnicity has loosened. Substantial losses in Ladino fluency have occurred in the course of a single generation, thus mirroring the downward course of ethnic mother-tongue competence among all European-derived ethnics in America. The children of the immigrants are, without exception, more comfortable in English than in Ladino, and many possess only marginal Ladino speaking skills.

The decline in native language ability continues its inexorable course beyond the second generation. Fishman has provided detailed statistics on the general loss of ethnic language competence among the descendants of numerous European groups (1966, "Mother-Tongue Claiming," 1985). Among American Sephardim, in particular, Malinowski reports that the shift from Judeo-Spanish to English was well advanced by the early 1980s (1983, 145).

She also notes that the effects of the renewal of interest in Sephardic cultural preservation on language-maintenance efforts, or perhaps more accurately on language revival, remain to be determined (146). Nonetheless, the weight of evidence strongly suggests that current trends will continue. Judeo-Spanish is also declining in Israel (Harris 1982). In considering ethnic resources capable of enlistment in the cause of maintaining mother tongues across generations, including teaching ethnic languages in private schools, Fishman, Gertner, Lowy, and Milan interpreted "intergenerational linguistic continuity to be not only generally weak but, also unconscious, unfocused, unspotlighted and undramatized" ("Ethnicity in Action: The Community of Resources of Ethnic Languages in the United States" 1985, 274). Ethnic languages are destined, in his view, to remain of minor import, only peripherally related to the question of generational continuity (275). Finding some good news in all of this, Fishman et al. conclude on the hopeful note that linguistic continuity, however meager, has reached an easy accommodation with American society by enabling insiders to feel comfortable and outsiders unthreatened (275). Not surprisingly, no ethnic community school in the United States, as reported fifteen years ago, taught Judeo-Spanish (Malinowski 1983, 143-44). It is highly unlikely that the situation has altered since then.

The linguistic trends index cultural changes within Sephardic communities. Accordingly, two decades ago Angel offered the following gloomy forecast at the conclusion of his survey of American Sephardim: "If there is no reversal in the trends indicated by our data, no viable Sephardi communities may be left in the United States in two or three generations from now. Clearly, synagogue buildings alone cannot insure the survival, let alone growth, of Sephardi culture. The task before the Sephardi community today is to find a meaningful way for their traditions and values to survive" (1974, 136). While there certainly appears to be a revival, at least at the formal institutional and scholarly level, of interest in Sephardic history and culture, its efficacy in turning back the trends Angel identifies is doubtful. That some members of the third Sephardic generation are engaged in "an active search for their roots" in fact attests to the very real transformations of old-country culture that life in the United States has effected (Matza 1990, 354).

Efforts at revitalizing Sephardic culture begun in the 1960s parallel in some respects the so-called ethnic revival of the same period. This revival purportedly swept through the communities of European ethnics two or more generations removed from their immigrant forbears. Any discussion of American Jews, Sephardic or Ashkenazic, and the contours of their communal experience and ethnic identities should thus take account of this new ethnic consciousness. For the Sephardim, the revival has taken several forms. Yeshiva University established a Sephardic Studies Program in 1964. The American Society of Sephardic Studies began in 1967. The American Sephardi Federation was established in 1973. In 1978 Sephardic House, based at Congregation Shearith Israel in New York, was founded in order to advance Sephardic history and culture through various classes, public programs, and exhibits. Still, these initiatives all occur from the top down, so to speak, and are not organic developments springing from community life.

Representing the Past in One Community

The Sephardim of Indianapolis began their settlement of the city in the first decade of this century. Except for two families from Canakale and Aleppo, the Sephardic community coalesced between 1910 and 1920 around a group of immigrants from the town of Monastir (in what was then Turkish Macedonia). They were soon joined by a smaller number of families from Salonika, the large Greek port city. Portrayals of the old country take many forms ranging from self-conscious narratives to more spontaneous remarks in conversation. The various depictions recounted cannot be considered apart from the complex relationship between the Sephardim and the Ashkenazic majority, who set the tone of Jewish life in the city and often excluded their Sephardic co-religionists from formal and informal social networks. Many Ashkenazim simply considered the Sephardim inauthentic Jews. Although the experience of the Indianapolis Sephardim is not unique among American Sephardim with regard to their Ashkenazic neighbors in the early years of contact, the strong nativist, Protestant profile of the city tended to exacerbate the pressures on cultural minorities to spurn heir distinctive Old World practices. In an atmosphere generally unfriendly to the maintenance and public expression of ethnicity, the Sephardim felt doubly vulnerable, first to those broader pressures for conformity and second to the Ashkenazic definitions of Jewishness and its place in a very conservative American heartland community. Such Ashkenazic understandings up until World War II at best diminished the significance of Sephardic Judaism and at worst challenged its legitimacy altogether (Glazier 1988).

Mallah Mordoh arrived in Indianapolis in the second decade of this century. Mr. Mordoh had emigrated from

Salonika, first to Cincinnati in 1912 to join his older brother. In Europe Mr. Mordoh's father had been a successful shopkeeper, and the same entrepreneurial drive for which the Sephardim are well known inspired the son. He lived for a brief time in Detroit before settling in Indianapolis, where he married Oro Cohen just after World War I. Leaving Salonika with her sister, Mrs. Mordoh had emigrated to Indianapolis, where her brothers had previously settled. Mr. Mordoh eventually became a very successful wholesale produce merchant. He died in 1989 at the age of ninety-one, and Mrs. Mordoh in 1997 at the age of ninety-eight. Their passing severs a primary connection of the community to its European past and to its American origins.

Rejection by the Ashkenazim began at the outset of Sephardic-Ashkenazic contact as recounted by Mr. Mordoh in his description of the first Monastir Sephardim to arrive in Indianapolis:

> Well, one more thing I'm gonna tell you is very important. When these people came to this country from Monastir, they had a very hard time. You know, you go to a strange town and you are a Jew or a Greek or whatever you may be, and you need help very very bad. Where will you go? You go to your brothers, won't you? Anyone who belongs to your synagogue is your brother. So those poor guys want to go out and make a little money. They went to those junkyards that there was over here and those people at junkyards they talk Yiddish. They talk to them Yiddish, they don't understand, tell them get away from here, get away. You're not a Jew. And they had a hard time for a good many years until Rabbi Feuerlicht from the

> Hebrew Congregation, the Reform, and he went to all the synagogues wherever they was in the city of Indianapolis and he told them that . . . they are real Jews, and you condemn them because they don't talk your language. And there was the same thing in other towns like in Seattle. (Glazier September 10, 1980)

Immigrants enjoyed a distinct advantage over their children in dealing with such assaults on their self-conceptions and traditions. Most had come of age in flourishing Sephardic communities and, while hardly impervious to the hostility of their eastern-European Jewish neighbors, they were not particularly vulnerable to self-doubt. By contrast, their American-born children, caught between two worlds, responded with a sense of uncertainty and ambivalence.

Observations by members of the Cohen family are particularly illustrative of the generational shifts within the Jewish community in general and the Sephardic community in particular. Yitzhak Cohen, born in Monastir, arrived in Indianapolis in 1906 after a perilous time as a miner in West Virginia. In 1910 he was able to send for his wife, Esther, and two children, in Monastir. Living in the city's old Jewish settlement amidst Ashkenazic newcomers and the very small core of the nascent Sephardic community, Mr. Cohen worked in the needle trade at the Kahn Tailoring Company, a highly successful German Jewish concern which attracted a large number of Sephardic workers. The Cohens had eleven children, the younger ones coming of age in the years spanning the end of the depression and the early postwar period. Three of the Cohens are quoted below. Ben Cohen, a World War II veteran and resident of Chicago since the 1950s left Indianapolis during the McCarthy hysteria. His interest in left-wing politics had brought FBI inquiries and, with some notable exceptions, a disappointing lack of support from much of the community, Sephardic and Ashkenazic alike. He felt that his father's generation—immigrant workmen believing in the rights and dignity of labor—were by and large supportive of his political beliefs or, at least, his right to hold them. His most critical remarks were reserved for members of his own generation, devoted he believes, to climbing upward economically while disregarding the larger lessons of their parents' struggles as immigrants:

> I would say that despite the material success of large numbers of Sephardic people in Indianapolis, I think there still exists a tremendous inferiority complex and a fear of rejection and a lack of confidence in what they could contribute to the Jewish community . . . We used to speak about the Jewish guys, and the Sephardics were different. We didn't speak of ourselves as Jewish guys. Really strange. (Glazier April 18, 1981)

Gladys Cohen Nisenbaum, an energetic leader in a range of activities in the wider Jewish community and in the Reform Temple, offers perspectives on Jewish life in Indianapolis as critical and insightful as those of Ben Cohen. She has been especially interested in renewing commitment to the Sephardic heritage going beyond "gastronomy and music." Here she alludes to the low cost, superficial, uncommitted expressions of ethnicity Gans refers to as "symbolic ethnicity." Agreeing with her brother, she sees uncertainty and diffidence as inhibiting this renewal:

> There was a defensiveness here because the language was different. They [Ashkenazim] didn't believe we were Jewish. It was really hard for them to accept that, but that was their own ignorance because they were ghettoized. They didn't know that we were here in the 1600s. *We* didn't know we were here and that there was a Touro synagogue." [Touro, the oldest synagogue in America, located in Newport, Rhode Island, was completed in 1762 by Sephardic Jews.] (Glazier April 18, 1981)

Here, Sephardic legitimacy is established by connecting contemporary Sephardim to the original Jewish migration to the New World—a Sephardic migration of what would become the first Jewish elite in the Americas, long antedating the appearance of large numbers of German and eastern-European Ashkenazim.

In recollections, redolent with anecdotes, of this hostile atmosphere, every individual of these first two Sephardic generations can provide representations of the Old World which serve as ameliorative devices. They validate and even mythologize a way of life many Ashkenazic Jews, especially the immigrants, only dimly understood. At the same time the shared memory of exclusion ironically helps firm up the weakened boundaries of the contemporary Sephardic community. Representations of Europe additionally reiterate, now without overt challenge, a Sephardic self-conception emphasizing an elite cosmopolitanism in contrast to the perceived provincialism of eastern-European Jewry, a profound and authentic religiosity, and an ease of adjustment to non-Jewish worlds. Sylvia Nahmias Cohen, the nofficial historian of the Sephardic community, thus underscores the multilingual facility of European Sephardim enabling them to flourish commercially amid a diverse and polyglot population (Cohen 1978, i-ii).

The defensive posture assumed by Indianapolis Sephardim in the face of Ashkenazic challenges to their cultural and religious integrity, while very sharply defined, was by no means unique. Angel, for example, refers to Moise Gadol, the influential editor of the Sephardic newspaper *La America*, who reported in 1910: "Many of our Turkinos tell us with tears in their eyes that they are not believed by the Ashkenazim to be Jews" (Angel 1982, 52). Zenner has noted similar patterns of Ashkenazic prejudice in Chicago (1990, 233-34). Writing of Sephardic Jews in Los Angeles, Stern observes that the most popular personal narratives concern the "proving of one's Jewishness to an Ashkenazi" (1980, 98).

In an especially dramatic statement about assimilation, Ben Cohen observed that Sephardic culture "maintained its existence as a tightly knit, developing . . . entity for 400 years in Turkish Macedonia . . . and it was almost wiped out in the U.S. in one generation" (letter to Glazier, March 3, 1981). The decline of distinctive Sephardic ethnic institutions and practices in Indianapolis—such as the *fundo secreto* (an informal welfare fund administered and controlled exclusively by Sephardim), the burial society, and the Sephardic Club—are revealing markers of the radical transformations he laments. Additionally, the attenuation of endogamous Sephardic marriage and the loss of Ladino competence further eroded the boundaries of the Sephardic community.

In Indianapolis, a notable exception to the decline of Sephardic institutions is the continuation of Etz Chaim, the Sephardic synagogue. Whereas the other "ethnic" synagogues formed out of old-country bonds—Russian,

Polish, Hungarian—have either merged with other synagogues or simply disbanded, the Sephardic synagogue continues as the sole ethnic survivor—identity intact—of the various houses of worship that developed in the city's old Jewish immigrant neighborhood. Relocated to the far north side, where virtually all congregants now live, it nonetheless struggles to survive. In so doing, it remains no small symbol of a strenuous effort to maintain cultural continuity against great odds.

Etz Chaim as a small congregation faces the same problems encountered by other Sephardic congregations of limited size (Zenner 1990, 239) It is open only for the Saturday morning service and the High Holidays. Members typically belong jointly to one of the larger synagogues capable of supporting a range of services and functions, including a full-time rabbi and daily worship requiring a quorum of at least ten men. Attendance at the Saturday morning service varies, averaging about twenty people, except when the occasional bar mitzvah is celebrated. Sometimes, meager attendance caused concern over whether a *minyan* would be achieved. Few individuals under the age of forty regularly appear at the synagogue. For the others, the future prospects of the synagogue evoke anxiety tempered by resignation. Especially troubling is the lack of commitment among younger people. The worried sentiment about the future, particularly as expressed by the second generation, indicated that maintaining the synagogue "is more an honorific glimpse backward to the world of their European parents and an acknowledgment of their own past than it is a hopeful look forward to the unbounded world of their children and grandchildren" (Glazier 1988, 60).

Against a backdrop of marginality among the Ashkenazic majority and more recent concerns about the cultural and religious future of the community, representations of

Europe assume significance. They consist of two aspects—the recent and remote past. The former refers to the world into which the immigrants were born during the waning years of Ottoman control of Greece and Yugoslavia. Particularly through the Spanish language and the diffuse meanings and associations embedded within it, recent memory connects to the remote past. The latter refers of course to the golden age—an era of several centuries when Jews prospered in Spain until their expulsion in 1492. The very name is suffused with mythological associations evoking powerful emotive images, nearly as compelling as those of Jerusalem itself.

Contemporary Sephardim feel enormous pride in their connection to Spanish Jewry, noted for its accomplishments in commerce, law, medicine, and philosophy, especially represented by the achievements of the oft-mentioned Moses Maimonides and even Columbus himself. Thus extending Sephardic views of Columbus's alleged Jewish origins, Rabbi Jacob Ott, in the preface to a popular Sephardic cookbook sold by the Sephardic sisterhood in Indianapolis, offers us a vision of the discovery of America through the efforts of a virtual Jewish navy:

> There is good reason to speculate that Christopher Columbus was a descendant of a *marrano* family. Despite the excesses and terror of the Inquisition, the Sephardic Jews served the Spanish crown with distinction and loyalty. Their prowess served Spain in every part of the realm, and very conspicuously in the voyages of exploration. It was Sephardic financial support which made possible the first voyage of Columbus. He relied upon a Sephardic cartographer for

> his maps a Sephardic instrument maker for his navigational instruments, a Sephardic physician was his ship's doctor and the first sighting of landfall in the New World was made by a Sephardic member of his crew (Sephardic Sisterhood Tifereth Israel, Los Angeles, 1971).

Jews were so tightly integrated into the fabric of Spanish society that many people see in the expulsion of a gifted Spanish Jewry the source of Spanish decline, an inevitable slide from the apogee of power and influence heralded by the Columbian voyage. The calamitous end of Sephardic Jewry in Spain is eloquently and emotionally encapsulated in the belief that the final remnants of Jewry departed Spain on the Ninth of Av—the Jewish fast day believed to be the date on which the first and second Temples of Jerusalem were destroyed in conquest. In religious terms the Sephardic catastrophe is nothing less than a collective Jewish tragedy to be commemorated in the physical and spiritual mortification of the obligatory fast on the Ninth of Av.

It matters little that no one can construct a genealogy to include Iberian ancestors whose life experiences they can recount nor does it matter that life in Spain was marked by periodic depredations against Jews, not only by Christians seeking to reclaim the Iberian Peninsula from Islam but also sometimes by Moslems. Nor does it matter that Jewish life in Spain is known only in the broadest outline. As befits representations of a golden age, these allusions and evocations aim to flatten out history in favor of a much simpler but more powerful mythology. Thus Barthes observes:

> Myth does not deny things, on the contrary, its function is to talk about them; simply, it purifies them, it makes them innocent, it gives them a natural and eternal justification, it gives them a clarity which is not that of an explanation but that of a statement of fact . . . In passing from history to nature, myth acts economically: it abolishes the complexity of human acts, it gives them the simplicity of essences . . . (1985, 143)

Such paradigmatic attitudes are counterweights to the unhappy collective experience of exclusion suffered particularly by the children of the immigrants. As another Cohen sibling, Max, a practicing attorney in Gary, Indiana, put it: "Early on, we were always made to feel that we *were* inferior. We *were* the poor Jews of Indianapolis. And we were never made aware of the richness of our culture. It wasn't until I was in high school that I learned about the Sephardic tradition that we were the ones who were the scientists and philosophers in Spain. I really developed a sense of pride in my cultural heritage" (Glazier April 18, 1981).

Identification with Spanish language and history is so strong that the Sephardim easily refer to themselves as Spanish. A quaint parochialism in this identification sometimes takes over as in the case of a non-Jewish Spanish-speaking visitor to the Sephardic synagogue. While chatting with some of the older Ladino-speaking congregants, the visitor was asked how she managed to speak such good Spanish, although she was not Jewish! "It has been said," Rabbi Ott observes, "that if Columbus returned from the dead and wanted to converse in the Castilian Spanish he knew in life, he could more easily carry on a conversation with a little Sephardic lad in the streets of Istanbul than in Spain" (Sephardic Sisterhood Tifereth Israel, Los Angeles, 1971: vii). In a similar vein, Mr. Mordoh offered counsel to his eldest grandson and namesake about a Sephardic woman the young man admired: "Your great-grandfather used to say that once a year a small bird comes your way. When it does, grab it!" What followed was his advice to his grandson to marry "a nice Spanish girl," meaning of course a Sephardic woman (observed by Glazier at Etz Chaim Synagogue, Indianapolis, October 25, 1980).

Like other Sephardic immigrants to the United States in the years leading up to the World War I, Indianapolis Sephardim emphasized political and economic factors as primary reasons for their departure from Europe. But these changes were precipitous, interrupting, in the words of Ben Cohen, "four hundred years of success" under Ottoman rule (Glazier April 18, 1981). Economic decline and the outbreak of the Balkan Wars stimulated migration, especially when the Ottoman authority for the first time extended military conscription in 1907 to the Jews and to other minorities. The self-governing nature of Jewish communities also changed as the *beth din*, or religious court, formerly the sole venue for the settlement of disputes, was supplanted by secular public courts. Fearing the worst, Mallah Mordoh explained that he left Salonika in 1912 owing to the prospect of military service. His older brother had preceded him to the United States for the same reason (Glazier September 10, 1980).

This account of conscription challenges the legitimacy of Turkish authority to impose dangerous military obligations on the Jews, who were, after all, not Turks, either in the Turkish view or by self-definition. They were Spanish, a self-reference fully in keeping with their identity as fully observant Jews. Later, when they came to the United States, no epithet or insult leveled by Ashkenazim against the Sephardim rankled as much as the designation "Turk," which denied Jewishness and the Spanish heritage in one blow. For Mr. Mordoh, the issue was not military conscription itself but the particular political authority that imposed it. Otherwise, such a viewpoint might challenge the legitimacy of American military service and thereby equate the United States with the political system that stimulated immigration. Such a challenge never occurs in the community, for all count American citizenship as a supreme value and scorn radical criticism of the United States. Accordingly, a sharp distinction must always be drawn between America and the old country in order to legitimate immigration and to rationalize the many radical cultural changes threatening the integrity of the community. Considerable ambivalence is at play. Thus, following his account of escaping conscription into the Turkish army, Mr. Mordoh denounced those who protested registration for the American draft. They should, in his view, feel privileged to serve in the American military (Glazier September 10, 1980). The informant"s contrast between the threatening Turkish draft and the value of American military service is all the more dramatic in view of his having lost the second of his four sons, a naval ensign, in World War II. Mr. Mordoh's attitude is ratified by the Sephardic synagogue, which put up a wall plaque bearing the names of congregants, mostly World War II veterans, who served in the military.

The need to remove any doubt about the wisdom of migration, however positive the feelings may be about old-country life, was reiterated by Mrs. Mordoh in concluding her depiction about the contrasts between the urbanity and pervasively Jewish life of Salonika and the provincial town of Indianapolis in the second decade of this century. After noting that Salonika was home to sixty-two synagogues (approximately twice the actual number), she explained that its Jewish population was so large that she and Mr. Mordoh were unacquainted until they met in this country, despite their having grown up within two blocks of each other. Moreover, the city was very beautiful and up to date. Mrs. Mordoh and her sister saw the latest and most popular silent films in Salonika. Once in Indianapolis they could only lament what seemed like the ugly backwardness of a town that made them homesick for the pleasure, the beauty, and the cultural richness of Salonika:

> Mrs Mordoh: Over here, I tell you we was crying, it was so old fashioned it was unbelievable. Ya, we get along. We make money; we raised nice kids and everything—every one of us, but I tell you it was unbelievable like night and day from there to here. But thanks God. God bless America a million times! (Glazier September 10, 1980)

Reminded by Mr. Mordoh's brief interjections of what they gained in America, Mrs. Mordoh reiterated her belief that no matter how good it was there, it is very much better here. (Glazier September 10, 1980)

Some of the children of the immigrants have journeyed back to Europe to see their parents' birthplace. Several visited Salonika, stimulated by their parents' recollections of Sephardic life in Europe. The Mordohs' third son, Sol, recounted how, since childhood, he had felt the strongest desire to see the much talked about city his parents loved. Yet coming long after World War II which had decimated the Jews of Salonika and Monastir, he felt an even greater distance separated him from that once great center of Sephardic life (Glazier January 10, 1981). Such visits poignantly reinforce the knowledge that Sephardic culture in the Balkans is part of the past. Likewise, a visit to Salonika by David Profeta, another second generation member of the community, proved particularly disappointing when his search of the decimated Jewish cemetery dashed his hopes of finding familiar names on headstones or the grave sites of his grandparents (Glazier February 7, 1981).

Conclusion

While it has not been possible here to describe various public celebrations and community performances, including films, musical events, and the like, that focus attention on the Sephardic past, they function in much the same way as personal narratives and folklore in enabling the Sephardim of two generations to burnish collective memory and to declaim their identity. Such cultural mnemonics, suffused with nostalgia, serve a similar purpose before the same ever-narrowing circle of people for whom European Sephardic life and its transformation in America resonate with deeply personal meanings. But the third and fourth American generations, absent from the synagogue and from many community activities, generally find little necessity in affirming or even inventing a distinctively Sephardic identity for themselves by making sense of the European past. As they grow older it is unlikely that new imperatives may arise to prompt a reclaiming and reinvigoration of the Sephardic culture and religious practices of the immigrants from Salonika and Monastir. Likewise the formal, institutional expressions of a Sephardic revival in the United States will probably not reach deeply enough to stimulate anything resembling a cultural renaissance, either in Indianapolis or in other Sephardic communities. For the younger generations the European Sephardic past grows more distant, owing not simply to its remove in time but to its social irrelevance to people caught up in other worlds.

Works Cited

Alba, Richard D. *Ethnic Identity: The Transformation of White America.* New Haven: Yale UP, 1990.

Angel, Marc D. *The Sephardim of the United States: An Exploratory Study.* New York: Union of Sephardic Congregations, 1974.

_____. *La America: The Sephardic Experience in the United States.* Philadelphia: The Jewish Publication Society, 1982.

Barthes, Roland D. *Mythologies*. New York: Hill and Wang, 1985.

Berger, Peter L., and Luckman, Thomas. *The Social Construction of Reality.* New York: Doubleday, 1966.

Cohen, Benjamin. Letter to Jack Glazier, March 3, 1981.

Cohen, Sylvia Nahmias. *The History of the Etz Chaim Sephardic Congregation and Community of Indianapolis.* Indianapolis: Unpublished typescript, 1978.

Elazar, Daniel J. *The Other Jews: The Sephardim Today.* New York: Basic Books, 1989.

Fishman, Joshua. *Language Loyalty in the United States.* London, The Hague, and Paris: Mouton, 1966.

_____. "Mother-Tongue Claiming since the 1960's: Trends and Correlates." In Joshua Fishman, Michael H. Gertner, Esther G. Lowy, William G. Milan, eds., *The Rise and Fall of the Ethnic Revival: Perspectives on Language and Ethnicity*, 107-94. Berlin, New York, Amsterdam: Mouton, 1985.

Fishman, Joshua, Michael H. Gertner, Esther G. Lowy, William G. Milan, "Ethnicity in Action: The Community Resources of Ethnic Languages in the United States." In Joshua Fishman, Michael H. Gertner, Esther G. Lowy, and William G. Milan eds., "*The Rise and Fall of the Ethnic Revival: Perspectives on Language and Ethnicity,*" 195-282 Berlin: Mouton, 1985.

Gans, Herbert. "Symbolic Ethnicity: The Future of Ethnic Groups and Cultures in America." *Ethnic and Racial Studies*. no. (1979) 2: 1-20.

Glazier, Jack. "The Indianapolis Sephardim." *Shofar* 3 no. 3 (1985): 27-34.

_____. "Stigma, Identity and Sephardic-Ashkenazic Relations in Indianapolis." In Walter P. Zenner, ed., *Persistence and Flexibility: Anthropological Perspectives on the American Jewish Experience*, 43-62. Albany: State U of New York P, 1988.

_____. Personal Interviews in Indianapolis with Mr. Benjamin Cohen, Mr. Max Cohen, and Mrs. Gladys Cohen Nisenbaum April 18, 1981; with Mr. Mallah Mordoh and Mrs. Oro Cohen Mordoh September 10, 1980; with Mr. Sol Mordoh January 10, 1981 and February 7, 1981; and observation at Etz Chaim Sephardic Synagogue October 25, 1980.

Harris, Tracy K. "Reasons for the Decline of Judeo-Spanish." *International Journal of the Sociology of Language*, no. 37 (1982): 71-97.

Lavender, Abraham. "The Sephardic Revival in the United States: A Case of Ethnic Revival in a Minority-within-a-Minority." In Abraham Lavender, ed., *A Coat of Many Colors: Jewish Subcommunities in the United States*. 305-14. Westport, Conn.: Greenview Press, 1977.

Lewis, Bernard. *History: Remembered, Rediscovered, Invented.* Princeton: Princeton UP, 1975.

Lowenthal, David. *The Past Is a Foreign Country.* Cambridge: Cambridge UP, 1985.

Malinowski, Arlene. "Judeo-Spanish Language-Maintenance Efforts in the United States." *International Journal of the Sociology of Language*, no. 44 (1983): 137-51.

Marcus, Ivan G. "Beyond the Sephardic Mystique." *Orim*, no. 1 (1985): 35-53.

Matza, Diane. "Sephardic Jews Transmitting Culture Across Three Generations." *American Jewish History* 79, no. 3 (1990): 336-54.

Poliakov, Leon. *The History of Anti-Semitism*. Vol. 3, *From Voltaire to Wagner*. New York:Vanguard Press, 1968.

Schorsch, Ismar. "The Emergence of Historical Consciousness in Modern Judaism." *Leo Baeck Institute Yearbook.* 28, 413-37. London, Jerusalem, New York: Secker and Warburg, 1983.

Sephardic Sisterhood Tifereth Israel (Los Angeles). *Cooking the Sephardic Way*. Kansas City, Missouri: North American Press, 1971.

Steinberg, Stephen. *The Ethnic Myth.* New York: Atheneum, 1981.

Stern, Stephen. *The Sephardic Jewish Community of Los Angeles.* New York: Arno Press, 1980.

Von Treitschke, Heinrich. "Unsere Aussichten." In Detlev Claussen, ed., *Vom Judenhass zum Antisemitismus*, 110-16. Darmstadt: Luchterhand, 1879, reprint 1987.

Yerushalmi, Yosef Hayim. *Zakhor: Jewish History and Jewish Memory.* Seattle and London: U of Washington P, 1982.

Zenner, Walter P. "Chicago's Sephardim." *American Jewish History* 79, no. 2 (1990): 221-41.

◆ Afterword

Louise Mirrer

Charting Memory: Recalling Medieval Spain is an extraordinary undertaking. It seeks to understand an enigma that has baffled historians and critics of culture for many years—that is, the curious sense of belonging of contemporary peoples to a land that long ago rejected them. The essays this volume embraces find clues to the puzzle in a number of unusual locales: Spanish balconies in Morocco, crypto-Jewish ballads and prayers in the Portuguese oral tradition, a billboard in Christian Galicia advertising the "Hotel Sinagoga," the "terrified heart" of a medieval Jewish scholar, poetic longings of a modern Palestinian poet, a postcard for sale in the shops of Rabat, Judeo-Spanish onomastics, a popular Sephardic cookbook sold by the Sephardic sisterhood in Indianapolis, the devotion of young people in Tlemcen to Andalusian music, and the Buendía's (of *One Hundred Year's of Solitude* fame) keys. The essays, taken together, point to a solution that has as much to do with symbols of contemporary identity as with the artifacts of a distant past. Far removed from the conditions that initially gave rise to them in the Middle Ages, memories of medieval Spain—in literary texts, business practices, architecture, music, and so on—respond to contemporary needs for prescriptive ideologies, for symbols, and even for propaganda.

Some years ago, while on a quest to determine the relationship between a London Judeo-Spanish community and the land from which this group's ancestors had been expelled more than five hundred years earlier, I pondered some of the same issues raised by the essays in this volume. Focusing in particular on the medieval Spanish ballad tradition, which has in many respects become a hallmark of the Spanish Jews, I wondered why the group so tenaciously clung to the land that had made outcasts of them. I thought it improbable that the Jews could harbor great feelings of affection or nostalgia for this inglorious moment in Spanish history or feel rooted in its traditions. The question for me was why this community would wish to continue paying homage to medieval Spain in its songs. The conclusion I reached was that ballad singing did not serve the purpose of keeping alive for the group the Spain of its ancestors; rather it was a symbol of identity abstracted from its historic roots and maintained because it had become a clearly recognizable sign of the Judeo-Spanish character. It identified singers as Judeo-Spanish, perpetuating the official ideology of the group that this group is different and should remain different.

Several of the essays in this volume appear to confirm my conclusion. Andalusians in Morocco, for example, possess an identity based on family roots in Spain, as well as on the special set of experiences the group has had as a result of exile from the land of its ancestors. Maintaining this identity in Morocco has served the group economically, politically, and socially. Remembering the distant past is thus, for Moroccan Andalusians, a way of making clear to the group its own distinctive character. Similarly for the crypto-Jews of Portugal, the oral tradition perpetuated in folk prayers taught by mothers and grandmothers to their children and grandchildren, allowed the group to maintain a separate identity in a context that otherwise prohibited it. This identity depended on memory—not so much of the traditions of those who oppressed the group's ancestors (indeed the horrors of torture at the hands of the oppressors are often recalled in these folk prayers), but of its own, distinctive religious beliefs. In somewhat related manner, memories of Andalusia in the poetry of medieval Spain's Hebrew poets-in-exile are transformed into symbols designed to make clear the distinctive experience and character of the Jewish people. The language and imagery of these poets' works are identical to signifiers of national sovereignty; the creativity their memories spawned very much intertwined with the special identity the Jewish people held as a group whose survival defied repeated and violent separations from its homeland. Each of these examples reveals a common pragmatic imperative—namely to make plain the importance of group exclusivity.

But what of the advice of a grandfather in Indianapolis that his grandson marry "a nice Spanish girl" (meaning, of course, a woman of Judeo-Spanish ancestry)? Or the feelings of Spanish "loyalty" articulated by a historian of Algerian Sephardic origin? Or the commercial success of the "heritage industry" nourished by descendants of Al-Andalus? Clearly, there is a conflation of Spanish with contemporary signs of identity in the memory of medieval Spain described by the essays in this volume. And clearly there is a desire to preserve this *Spanish* identity; nostalgia for a distant past unexplained by the threat of religious extinction or recognition of the practical benefits of group exclusivity. Spain is, as Stacy Beckwith writes in her Introduction, both an ancient and a contemporary "home" for the peoples whose ancestors lived there; a paradise to which exiles long to return. Strangely recognizable to these groups, despite geographic, cultural, political, and linguistic remove, it continues to be the place where memory fixes, the place where the events of contemporary lives can be made meaningful. But no matter how idealized in the memories of those who fix on it, Spain necessarily eludes return. As the words of the Palestinian poet Maḥmūd Darwīsh, cited in this volume, so poignantly suggest, the exiles can return only in the imaginary:

> If I were to start all over again I'd choose what I have chosen
> Now: the roses on the fence
> I'd set out again on the road that may or not lead to
> Córdoba
> I will return, if I can, to my roses, to my steps
> But I will never go back to Córdoba.

The essays in this volume, which so thoughtfully chart memory, have caused me to rethink my earlier conclusions. Recalling medieval Spain is, I now believe, not simply a means of reiterating, for the descendants of those who called it home, the dictates and special behaviors that preserve the cultural and religious boundaries of their membership. It is instead indeed a nostalgic activity for those for whom Spain continues to be "home."

Glossary

al-Andalus. Arab kingdom(s) and territory in the Iberian Peninsula from 711 C.E. to 1492.

Almohad. A Muslim movement known in religious terms as "the Unifiers" (*al-Muwaḥḥidūn*) (Makki 1992, 70) which gained strength in Morocco and influenced the Berber tribes in the Atlas Mountains before invading the extant Almoravid Muslim state in al-Andalus, in the mid to late 1140s. The Almoravid state had emerged in the eleventh century, whence it consolidated its dominance of al-Andalus and ended previous periods of fragmentation and rule there by other Muslim dynasties. The Almohad state in al-Andalus, intermittently at war with Portugal and the kingdoms of León and Aragon, extended north to Toledo and surrounding regions at its height, ca. 1197. Following the Almohad collapse, the Naṣrid kingdom ceded Granada to the Spanish Catholic forces at the start of 1492 (84).

Ashkenazi(c)/Ashkenazim. Traditionally "Franco-German" Jews. More broadly speaking, Jews who come directly from, or whose family origins can be traced to, northern European, Slavic, and some southern European lands. Ashkenazim differ in some of their religious customs from Sephardic Jews. Yiddish, a language that is primarily a blend of Hebrew and German, Russian, and/or Polish, depending on locale or point of origin, is both a popular and literary language still variously used among Ashkenazim.

Av, Ninth of. A day in the Hebrew month of Av set aside for fasting in commemoration of three Jewish religious/national tragedies: (1) the destruction of the first divinely endowed Temple in Jerusalem and the start of the first Jewish territorial exile in Babylon, in 586 B.C.E.; (2) the Roman destruction of the second, rebuilt Temple in 70 C.E. and the Roman expulsion of the Jews from Jerusalem and Palestine. Eventually some Jews were allowed to build homes in the area of Jerusalem which afforded a view of the city, and to return to the city on the Ninth of Av to mourn the destruction of both Temples; (3) the day of the Catholic expulsion of the Jews from Spain.

Berbers. People indigenous to parts of northern Africa, especially Morocco. Conquered by the Muslims entering Morocco from the east and then variously influential in the different Muslim states ruling al-Andalus. The "Berber revolt" in al-Andalus from 1008 to1031 ended a period of sustained caliphal rule in Iberia and ushered in an era of divided control among "Petty States" (Makki 1992, 46-49). The founder of the Almohad Muslim movement was of Berber origin and the Almohad invasion of al-Andalus ca. 1145 is also justifiably termed the Berber-Almohad invasion (60-61).

***conversos*/Crypto-Jews**. Jews in Spain and Portugal who ostensibly converted to Christianity to avoid or end persecution by the Catholic Inquisition. The conversion of Jews (also identified by the Spanish slur *marranos*) into "New Christians" proceeded before, during, and after the Catholic expulsion of the Jews from Spain in 1492. Many continued to practice their Judaism underground.

dhimmis. Islamic law extending life and property protection to monotheistic minorities. In the case of the Jews these laws also recognized their status as "The People of the Book." *Dhimmis* involved setting up separate quarters in Islamic Cities for Jews (*ḥārat al-yahud*, "Jewish quarters") in which they could worship freely. From the Jewish standpoint, these laws also involved paying taxes to Islamic rulers and accepting official second-class status; a mark of ongoing national, territorial exile and loss of sovereignty.

kharja. The final mono-rhymed verse on an Arabic or Jewish *muwashshaḥ* (see below). A corpus of, now renowned, *kharjas* was found in 1948 to be composed in popular languages; amalgams of Hebrew, Arabic, and/or Spanish. The popular themes treated in these *kharjas* also tend to differ from those on which the main body of each *muwashshaḥ* focuses.

Ladino/Judeo-Spanish. The popular and literary language used by medieval Sephardim (mixing Hebrew and Spanish) that has survived in the Sephardic diaspora with various inclusions of French, Turkish, and other linguistic elements depending on the locale, often the social class, and the predisposition of its speakers to embrace influences seen as modernizing. Ladino was most often, traditionally written in a variation of Hebrew script, known as "Rashi script." When the Turkish leader Ataturk decreed in 1928 that the Turkish language would be written in Roman letters, the Sephardim in the waning Ottoman Empire variously began replacing Ladino's Rashi letters with Roman ones, as well. The journalistic press in the prominent Jewish center of Greek Salonika did not follow this trend.

Medina. Traditional Islamic City designating through its architecture, and sectioned layout, private and public spaces as well as spaces in which different monotheistic minorities were to live and could enjoy freedom of worship.

māllaḥ. Moroccan term for a Jewish quarter within a local *Medina*.

Midrash/midrashic. Both a hermeneutic process of biblical exegesis and a compilation (Book of Midrash) of individual interpretations of the Hebrew Bible.

minyan. A quorum of ten men, in Orthodox Jewish tradition, needed to perform a religious service.

moriscos. The counterpart of *conversos*; Muslims who remained in Spain after their edict of expulsion and also became "New Christians."

mudéjars. Prior to the Muslim expulsion from Spain, *mudéjars* were Muslims who lived permanently in Iberian Christian territories (Harvey 1992, 176).

muwashshaḥ/muwashshaḥāt (pl.). An Arabic poetic form distinctly Andalusian in origin and adopted by many

Andalusian Jewish poets as well. From medieval Iberian contexts it was/ has been adopted and imitated widely throughout the Arab world, although it has not entered the Arab poetic canon. The alternating rhyming pattern and final mono-rhymed verse (*kharja*) can be as much a bearer of Andalusian memory as can a *muwashshaḥ*'s content.

nagid. Hebrew title meaning "leader," given to a Jew, typically a man of letters, who rose to great political heights in the seat of Muslim power in al-Andalus, in Granada. This person would also have been a consummate "court-Jew," or intermediary for local Jewish populations.

nasi. Hebrew title meaning "prince," similarly conferred.

Nisan. Hebrew month in which the festival of Passover is celebrated.

Sepharad/Sephardic/Sephardim. The Hebrew word for Spain (Sepharad) can be traced to the biblical Book of Obadiah, where it may first have referred to an area in Asia Minor. Popular usage reoriented its application to Iberia. Sephardic, or Iberian, Jews and their descendants differ from Ashkenazic Jews in certain religious customs. Sephardim are properly medieval Spanish Jews or Jews of Spanish ancestry. In contemporary Israel the term is often conflated with "Eastern," or the more derogatory "Oriental" Jews, to include Jews of Middle Eastern origin, many of whom are of no Spanish provenance.

Talmud/Talmudic. The Talmud is the corpus of Jewish oral law. Originally an ongoing exchange of debates and *midrashim*, it was primarily organized into six Orders and recorded in writing in Palestine under Roman rule and around the time of the destruction of the second Jewish Temple in Jerusalem. The Palestinian, or Jerusalem Talmud was then introduced into rabbinic circles in Babylon, where additional layers of commentary were added to produce the fuller Babylonian Talmud.

Tishri. Hebrew month which marks the start of the new Jewish year with the festival of Rosh Hashanah, followed ten days later by the Day of Atonement, Yom Kippur.

Works Cited

Harvey, L.P. "The Mudejars." In Salma Khadra Jayyusi, ed., *The Legacy of Muslim Spain*, 176-87. Leiden: E.J. Brill, 1992.

Makki, Maḥmoud. "The Political History of al-Andalus (92/711-897/1492)." In Salma Khadra Jayyusi, ed., *The Legacy of Muslim Spain*, 3-87. Leiden: E.J. Brill, 1992.

◆ Contributors

Beebe Bahrami. She received her Ph.D. in cultural anthropology from the University of Pennsylvania in 1995, where she was a Visiting Scholar from 1997 to 1998. She is a former Fulbright scholar (Morocco, 1992-93), and has taught at the University of Pennsylvania, the Philadelphia College of Textiles and Science, and the University of Notre Dame. She specializes in memory, identity dynamics, ethnohistory, and symbolic anthropology in the Mediterranean world, focusing in particular on Spain and Morocco. She is preparing for publication a book on her historical and ethnographic research among three Andalusian communities in these two countries. She has recently published on the Spanish Muslim convert communities in Granada and has finished writing a "historical feminist adventure mystery novel" titled, *The Mystic's Talisman.*

Stacy N. Beckwith. Assistant Professor of Hebrew Language and Literature at Carleton College. She is a former Fulbright scholar (Israel, 1994-95). A comparatist, she focuses on national cartography and memory in Spanish Peninsular and Israeli literature and film. She has published on filmmaking during Spain's dictatorship, and on rabbinic Jewish folktales, and she has an article forthcoming in *Religion and Religiosity in Modern Jewish and Islamic Literatures*, edited by Glenda Abramson and Hilary Kilpatrick, in the Studies in Muslim-Jewish Relations book series. She is preparing for publication a book on national conceptualization in Israeli literature. She is also writing a book that examines ideological reasons for contemporary Spanish and Israeli authors' incorporation of medieval through twentieth century Sephardic characters, and the tenor of their representation.

Judith R. Cohen. Adjunct Graduate Faculty, York University (Canada) and Independent. She is an ethnomusicologist and performer, specializing in the Sephardic and related traditions, including her current research on the musical life of Crypto-Jewish regions along the Spanish-Portuguese border. Her publications include studies of women's roles in, and of reactions to evolving styles in, Judeo-Spanish song performance. She has released several recordings of traditional Sephardic and other music, and is currently preparing the Sephardic music entries for guides to world music and to Judaism.

Manuel da Costa Fontes. Professor of Spanish and Portuguese at Kent State University. A former NEH (1978; 1980-81) and Guggenheim (1984-85) fellow, he recorded and edited five Portuguese ballad collections (Coimbra University Press), and has published numerous articles in various journals. He is also the author of *Portuguese and Brazilian Balladry: A Thematic and Bibliographic Index* (1997), and his *Folklore and Literature: Studies in the Portuguese, Brazilian, Sephardic and Hispanic Oral Traditions* is now in press (SUNY Press). His areas of interest include medieval and Renaissance Spanish literature. He is presently working on a book about two Spanish *conversos*, Rojas and Delicado.

Libby Garshowitz. Professor in the Department of Near and Middle Eastern Studies and past Director of the Jewish Studies Program (1992-1995) at the University of Toronto. She teaches Medieval and Modern Hebrew Language and Literature and Intellectual History. Her main research and publishing interests incorporate the life and thought of Jews of medieval Spain and Jewish-Christian relations, and extend to contemporary Israeli literature. Publications include *A Study Guide for Sifron la-Student A & B*, *Shem Tov Ben Isaac Ibn Shaprut's "Even Bohan"* (Touchstone), and numerous articles on medieval Sephardic biblical scholarship.

Jack Glazier. Professor of Anthropology at Oberlin College. He has conducted ethnohistorical research among the Sephardic Jews of Indianapolis, where he examined the formation of their community, their relationship to Ashkenazi Jews, and the steady cultural convergence of both groups. His interest in immigration history led, most recently, to an investigation of how Jewish immigrants arriving in New York made their way to other parts of the country. That study, *Dispersing the Ghetto: The Relocation of Jewish Indianapolis Across America*, was published in 1998 by Cornell University Press.

Hsaïn Ilahiane. He received his Ph.D. in anthropology from the University of Arizona in 1998. He was a Weatherhead Resident Scholar at the School of American Research in 1997-98 in Santa Fe. His dissertation concerns ethnicity and agricultural production in the Ziz Valley, southeast Morocco. His reasearch interests include North African rural development, Saharan ethnohistory and political ecology, and the anthropology of colonialism.

Louise Mirrer. Vice Chancellor for Academic Affairs at the City University of New York and Professor in the Program in Hispanic and Luso-Brazilian Literatures at the CUNY Graduate School. Her most recent book is *Women, Jews, and Muslims in the Texts of Reconquest Castile*. She has published widely on medieval Spanish and Sephardic literatures, and in the areas of sociolinguistics, women's studies, and literary criticism.

Shmuel Refael. Assistant Professor of Judeo-Spanish Language and Literature in the Department of the Literature of the Jewish People, Bar-Ilan University, Israel. He specializes in Judeo-Spanish language and literature. He also focuses on Sephardic folklore and ethnography. He has published several articles on Judeo-Spanish literature, language, and folklore, including texts for elementary and advanced Judeo-Spanish language instruction.

Dwight F. Reynolds. Associate Professor of Arabic Language and Literature and Affiliate Faculty Member in Ethnomusicology at the University of California at Santa Barbara He has conducted ethnographic fieldwork in folklore and ethnomusicology in a number of Middle Eastern countries including Egypt, Morocco, Algeria, and Turkey. He has specialized in studying orally transmitted traditions that have ancient roots but are also part of modern Middle Eastern culture, such as the oral epic tradition of "Sirat Bani Hilal" and the musical traditions of medieval Islamic Spain. He performs regularly on Middle Eastern musical instruments and his publications include a study of the ethnography of performance in Arabic oral epic tradition. He has contributed to the Cambridge History of Arabic Literature and is the co-editor of the Garland Encyclopedia of World Music, 6: The Middle East (forthcoming from Garland Press).

Reuven Snir. Professor of Arabic literature at the University of Haifa Department of Arabic Language and Literature, and associate editor of *al-Karmil-Studies in Arabic Language and Literature*. He has published extensively in English, Arabic, Italian, and Hebrew on various aspects of Arabic prose, poetry, and theater, especially Palestinian literature, as well as on Arabic literature written by Jews and Hebrew-language literature written by Arabs. He is also a translator of Arabic poetry into Hebrew and Hebrew poetry into Arabic.

Sultana Wahnón. Distinguished Professor of Literary Theory at the University of Granada, Spain. She focuses on poetics, literary theory, and hermeneutics, as well as on the histories of Spanish Peninsular and Jewish thought. Her doctoral concentration on the literary aesthetics of Spanish Fascism led to studies on the critique of Spanish thought by the Generation of 1927, on the Spanish poet Miguel Fernández of the Group of 1960, and on other contemporary writers including Gabriel García Márquez, and Federico García Lorca. Her publications on literary theory include: *Introduction to the History of Literary*

Theories (1991), *Literary and Hermeneutical Knowing* (1991), and *Language and Literature* (1995). She has also published widely on contemporary theorists including Roland Barthes, Paul Ricoeur, and I. M. Lotman, and on the poetics of the medieval Sephardic author, Moses Ibn Ezra.

Index

Compiled by Stacy N. Beckwith